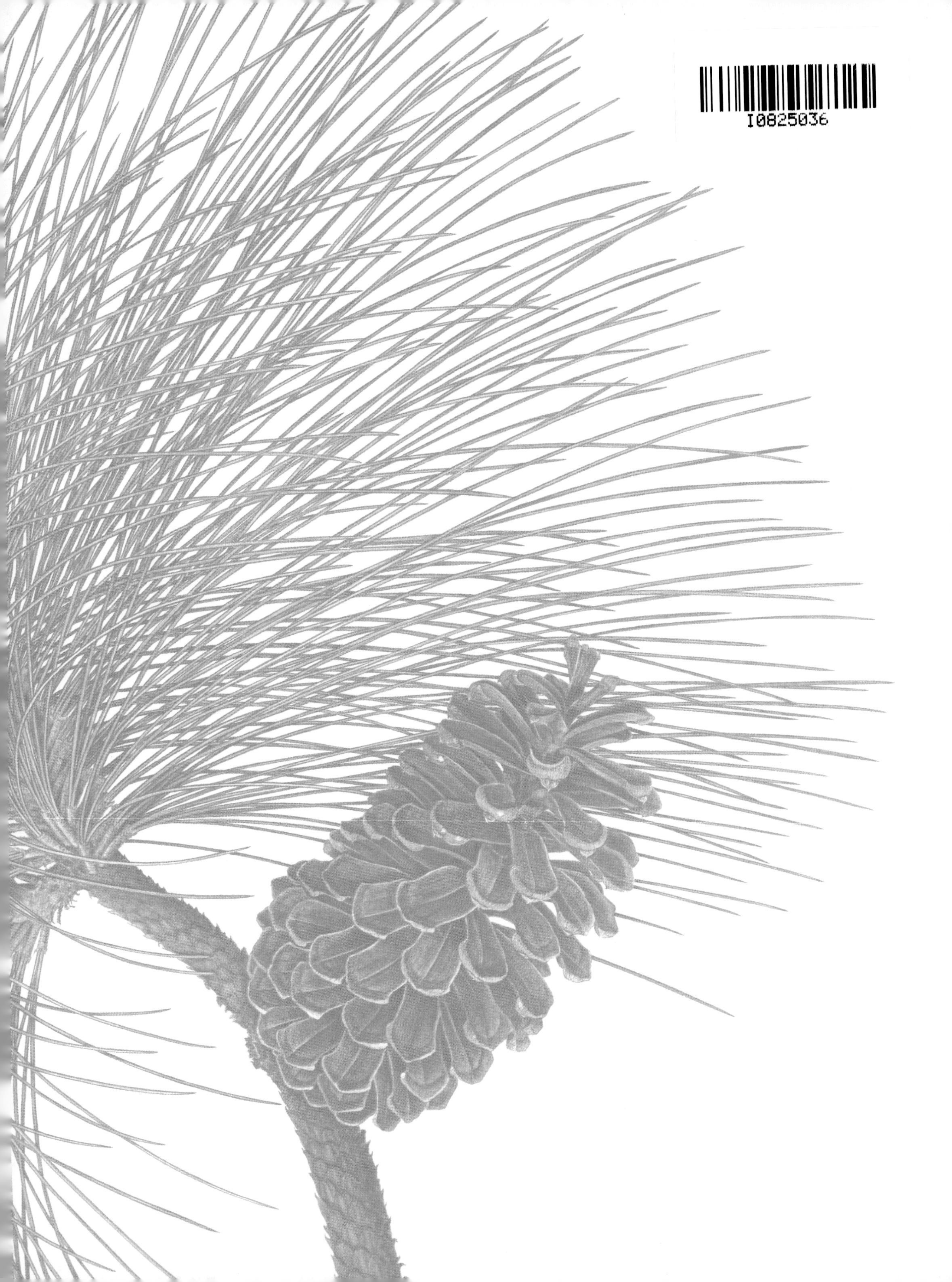
I0825036

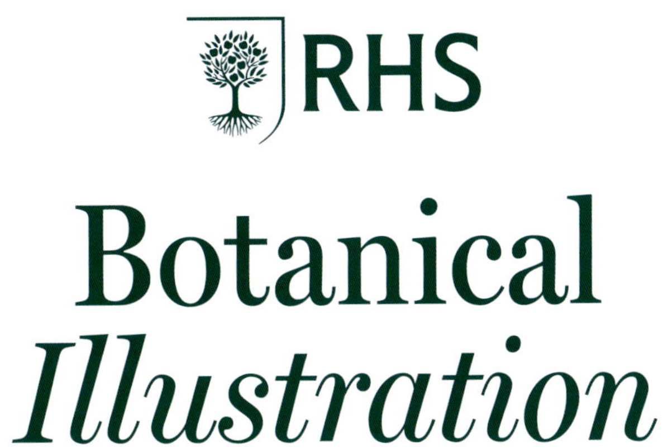

THE GOLD MEDAL WINNERS

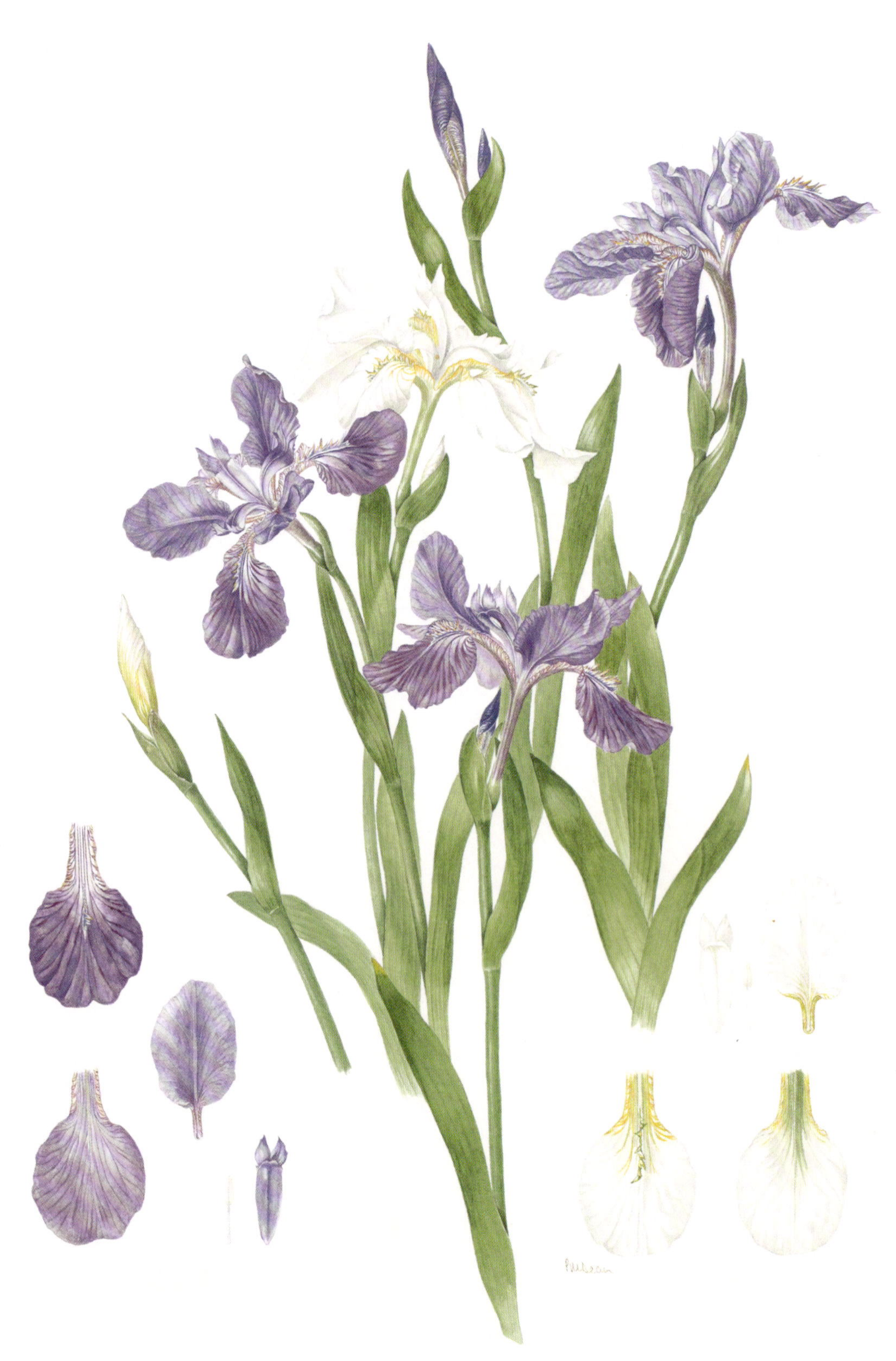

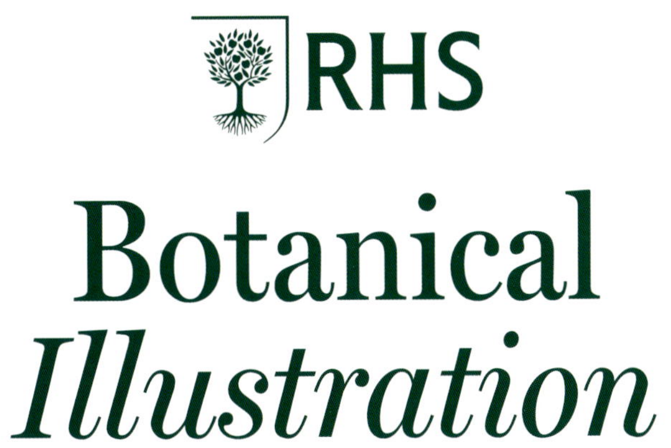

Botanical *Illustration*

THE GOLD MEDAL WINNERS

Charlotte Brooks

ACC ART BOOKS

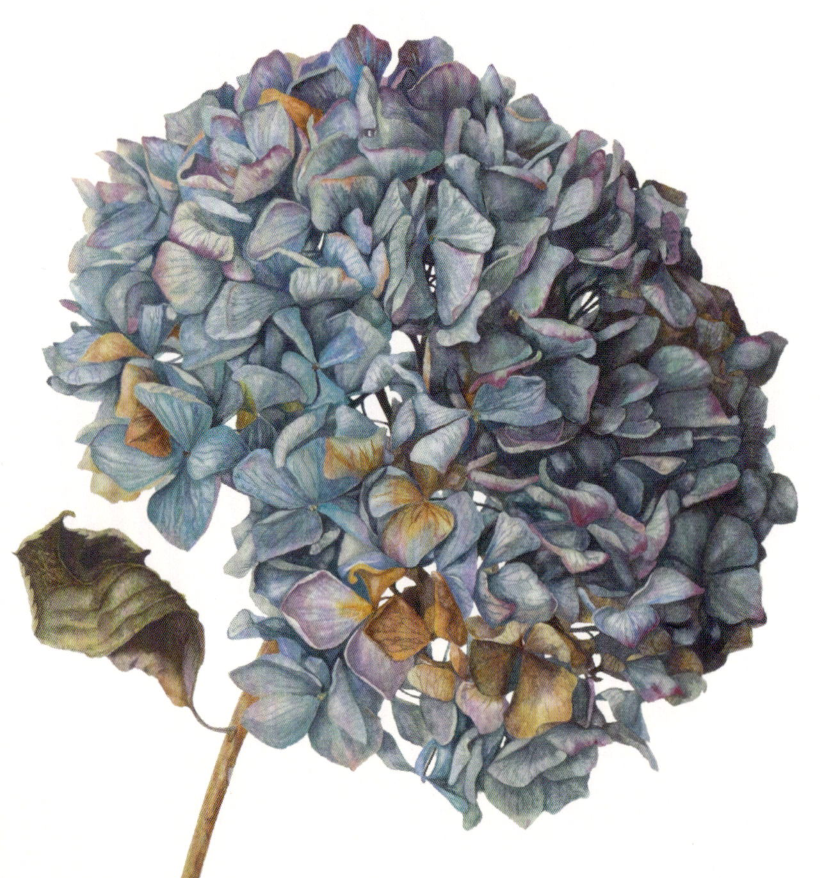

Contents

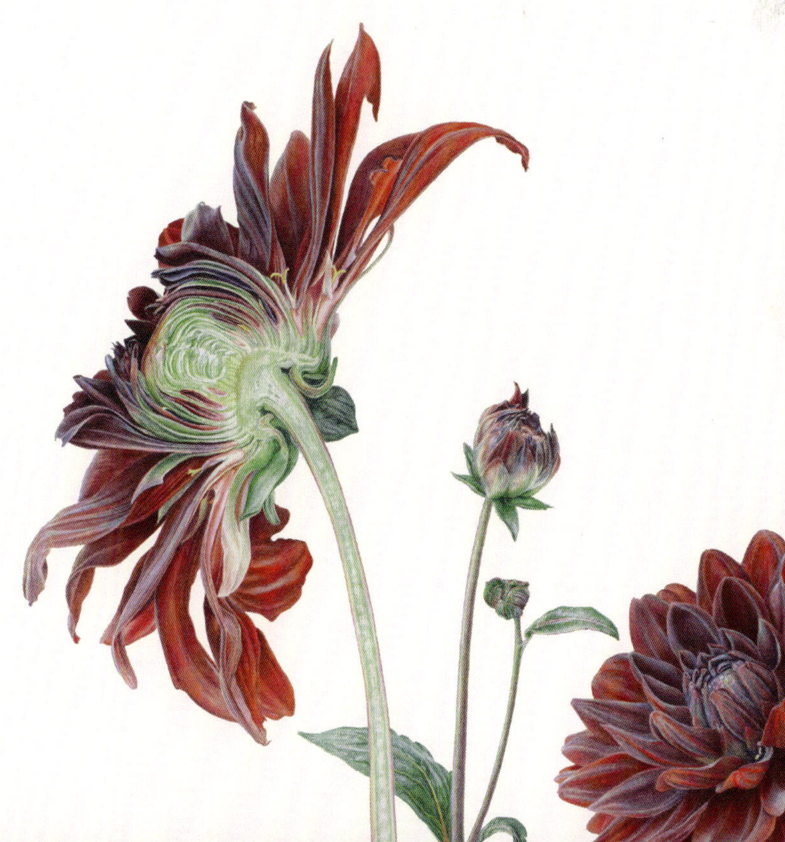

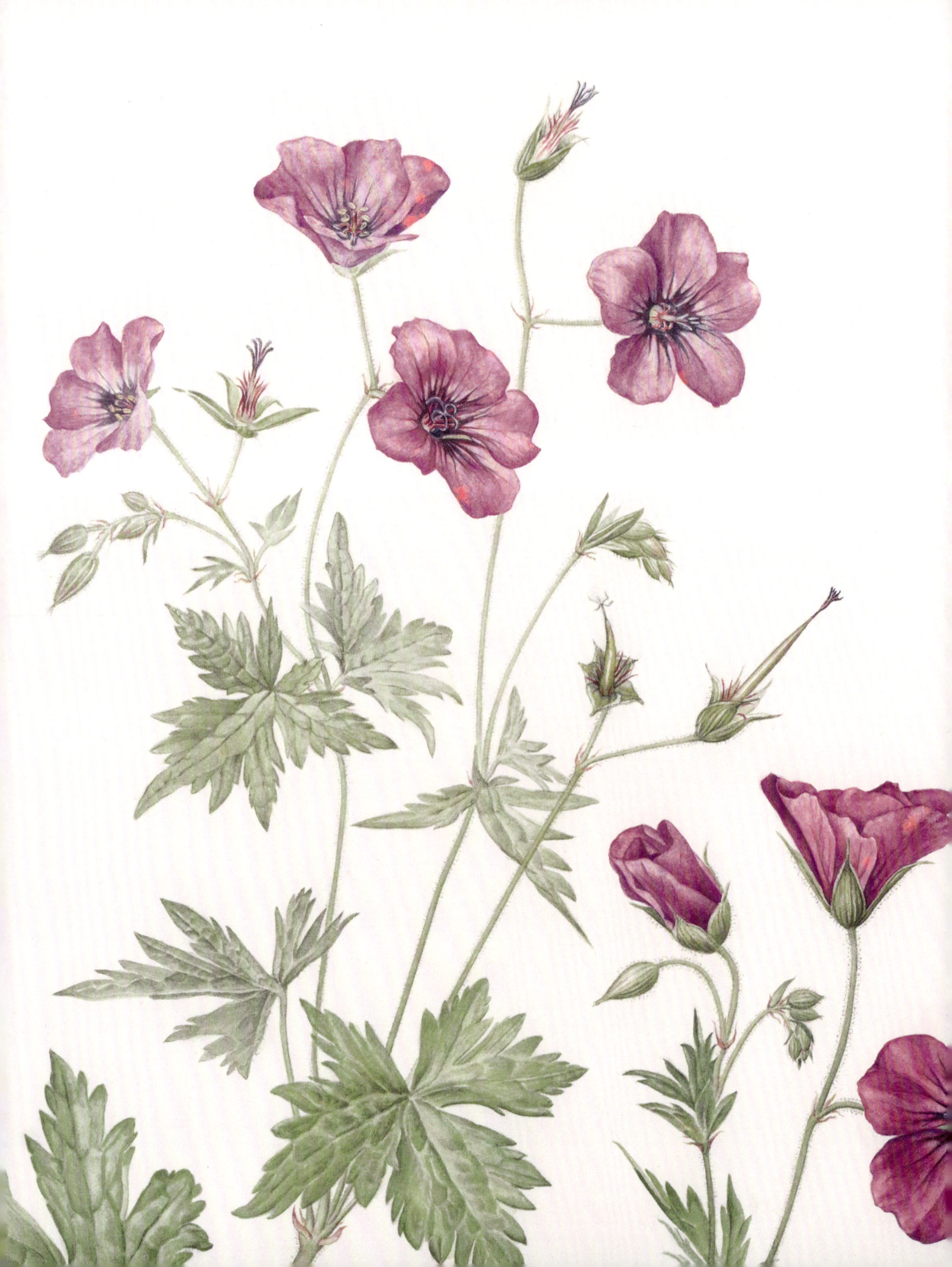

Introduction

For anyone not familiar with the Lindley Library Collections, the first question that may arise is why art is to be found with books in a library, rather than a gallery or museum? In the early days of the Royal Horticultural Society, drawings were very much used as working reference documents for plant identification and were not considered part of the library's holdings. Botanical artists supply an essential tool that enables the gathering and dissemination of knowledge. A long-established tradition exists whereby artists present the accurate portrayal of plants in a visual language that is familiar to an international audience of botanists, gardeners, collectors and growers.

The Horticultural Society of London, as the RHS was formerly known, began commissioning drawings in 1806, not long after the inaugural meeting of 1804. Paintings of specific plants were ordered and paid for by the Society's Council. Originally numbering 15 members, Council controlled all the Society's finances and the direction of its activities. Decisions were often then enacted by sub-committees of expert volunteer advisors or administrators, the number of paid staff being considerably smaller than it is now. The horticulturists who sat on Council would have been accustomed to employing illustrators and engravers. Prominent members such as Sir Joseph Banks, Richard A. Salisbury and Thomas Andrew Knight had experience of working closely with artists for research, documentation and publication, in a practice that is only slightly varied today.

The first pictures the Society undertook to commission were by William Hooker, for publication in the *Transactions of the Horticultural Society of London*, a compilation of articles by members which ran from 1805 until 1845. In the early nineteenth century, the Society was characterised by far-reaching ambitions

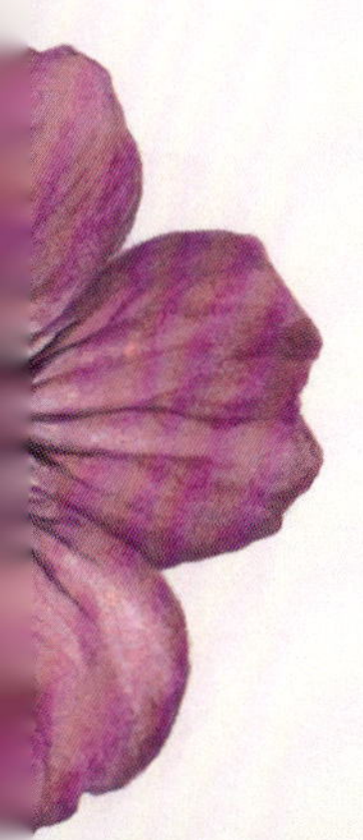
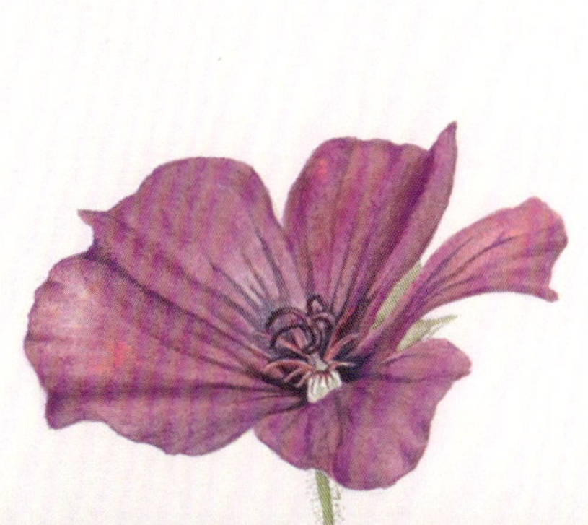
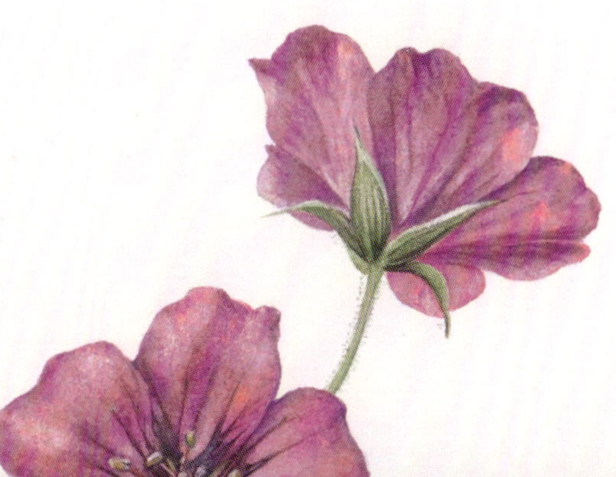

and paintings played their part in supporting the reformation of plant nomenclature, the documentation of fruit being grown privately and for trade, as well as the acquisition of new plants from far-flung places. The drawings of flowering plants and fruit created by William Hooker established a standard of botanical illustration for the Society.

In the first 50 years after the initial instruction was issued to Hooker, an impressive corpus of more than 2,000 paintings of plants, by both local artists and those overseas, had been accumulated. Yet despite the initial enthusiasm, as a collection, drawings at the RHS have had something of a turbulent history. The Society's fortunes are well documented, but an understanding of the early period helps give context to the current form of the collection. Schemes to collect and document plants both at home and abroad were time-consuming, difficult and expensive. These endeavours came at a price and in 1859, on the brink of financial ruin, the entire contents of the library and the drawings collection was sold at auction by Sotheby's, to raise funds for the Society. Through a combination of good fortune and keen judgement, many of the original paintings that had been commissioned and collected were returned to the Lindley Library throughout the twentieth century. These form the backbone of the heritage collection, which helps to inspire and inform contemporary botanical artists and researchers today.

Botanical art has seen a resurgence of popularity in the 21st century, as a wealth of talent continues to emerge around the globe. The very best botanical artists translate their close observation into an informative, scientifically accurate and beautiful picture. These works stand proud as showcases both for the plant and the artist. The Lindley Collections now number approximately 30,000 drawings, ranging in date from the early seventeenth century to the present day. Principally consisting of plant portraits, the collection also contains oils and engravings of eminent horticultural figures, and to a lesser extent, paintings of gardens and 'garden art'. The focus in recent years has been on the development of an exceptional contemporary botanical art collection.

The Society has also long held flower shows at which paintings have been judged. The medals awarded provide a standard by which the quality of an exhibit may be assessed, ranging from Bronze through to Silver, Silver-Gilt and, highest of all, a Gold medal.

An RHS Gold medal is highly prestigious and botanical artists may strive for years to develop the requisite skills to achieve it. Throughout the twentieth century, the terms 'flower painting', 'botanical art' and 'botanical illustration' became more significant and the differences between these genres better appreciated. The judging criteria employed by the Society both reflected and influenced the move towards a practice that, in turn, has seen the standard of botanical art now being created and presented for exhibition rise inexorably. The standard of artwork now seen at RHS Shows is higher than it has ever been. Although in some quarters the debate still rages over what constitutes botanical 'art' and 'illustration', in 2016 the following definition was adopted by the Society's Picture Panel, based on the understanding that a piece of outstanding botanical illustration can also be a piece of beautiful art:

"Botanical Illustration is a genre of art that endeavours faithfully to depict and represent the form, colour and detail of a plant, identifiable to species or cultivar level.

As a technical discipline, botanical illustration emphasizes the depiction of accurate information, documenting the anatomical and functional aspect of a plant throughout its life cycle.

The best botanical illustration successfully combines scientific accuracy with visual appeal. It must portray a plant with the precision and level of detail for it to be recognised and distinguished from another species."

The turn of the millennium saw the Lindley Library in London moved from the fourth floor to the newly refurbished basement. Improved research facilities and storage capacity allowed for the active development of a contemporary botanical art collection. A tentative move to acquire new paintings began in the late 1980s and was gradually built upon. So, by the time the library had moved premises, the principle had firmly been established whereby the library would aim to acquire botanical art of Gold medal standard. To date, well over 1,000 new pieces have been added to the Lindley Collections through purchase, donation and bequest. (This figure includes over 500 Orchid Award portraits commissioned by the RHS Orchid Committee, of which the library is now custodian.) Housed alongside the heritage collections, contemporary botanical art takes its place in a canon that tells the story of people, plants and art at the RHS over the past 200 years.

William Hooker (1779-1832)

Although relatively little is known about William Hooker (he shares only his name in common with the famous Hooker family of Kew and is not related to them), he was to become one of the most important artists in the Society's history, and is easily the most sought after by contemporary botanical artists and researchers visiting the library today. Hooker was already known to the Society, as he had produced the plates for and published Richard A. Salisbury's *The Paradisus Londinensis* (1806).[1] The title page to this publication describes Hooker as having been a pupil of the eminent artist, Francis Bauer. The same year, Council commissioned him to illustrate *'Polianthes tuberosa',* which was to form the start of what became loosely termed the 'Miscellaneous paintings'. These are a combination of pictures intended for publication and reference use and although they vary in style and subject matter, they were created with a common purpose. The pictures were intended to help identify plants that were either already growing in British gardens, or new plants that were thought would make interesting and valuable additions.

Also an expert on fruit, Hooker often provided advice to the Society in the consideration of new specimens, prior to the establishment of the Society's Fruit Committee (founded much later in 1858). In 1815 Council requested that he undertake an extensive project to produce a set of fruit drawings, in addition to continuing his work producing plates for the *Transactions*. The fruit paintings were intended to support a wider initiative to document and record the names and appearance of as many of the fruit varieties in cultivation in England, as was possible. This project was intimately connected with the wider work of the Society, as the members had long since recognised that there was an urgent need to support commercial fruit growers and establish more reliable naming conventions.

Following the decision made by Council, it was deemed necessary to form a working group to manage the commission of fruit paintings. The Drawings Committee met for the first time on 6 June 1815, with Joseph Sabine in the Chair. The committee agreed unanimously to the commission of 20 paintings of fruit for identification, starting with the 'Moor Park Apricot'. It became clear at the meeting of 5 January 1816, that Hooker had not been able to meet the rate of production that Council and the Drawings Committee had hoped for. Having been asked to start the project in the summer, he had already missed the spring growing season, meaning he would always be at least

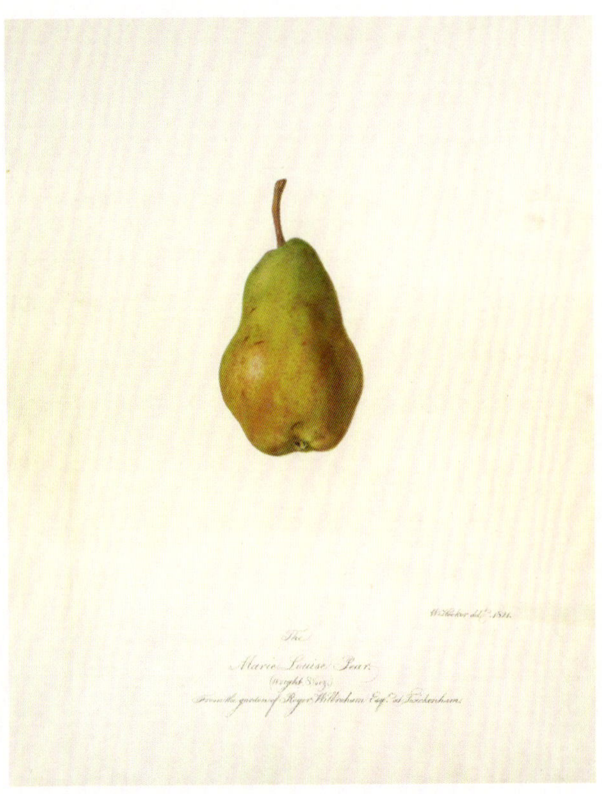

'Marie Louise Pear', one of the 'Miscellaneous' drawings
William Hooker, 1821

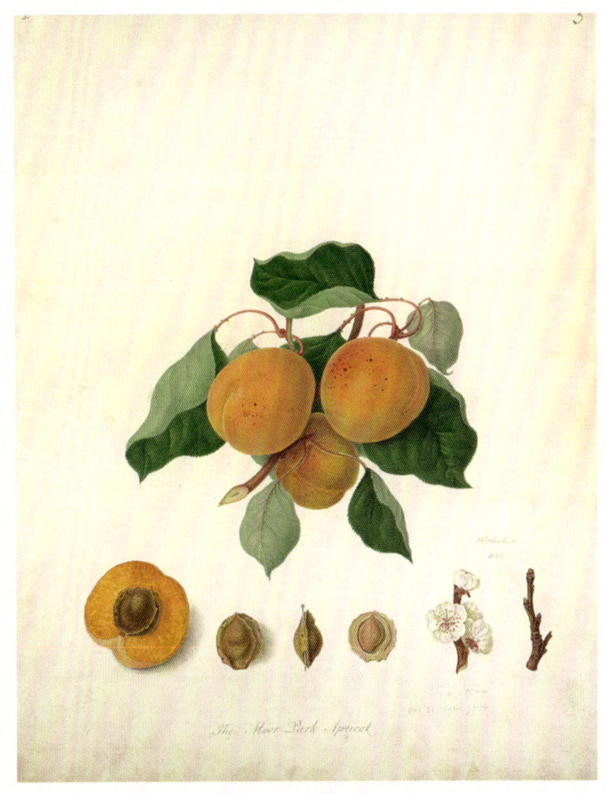

'Moor Park Apricot'
William Hooker, 1815/16

six months behind. The fruit identification pictures required complex compositions, as they had to feature the growing habit of the fruit on the branch, with bud, leaf and cut-through cross-section.

By the end of that first year, Hooker had only been able to finish seven of the 20 pictures. This was also in part due to a lack of suitable specimens, as it seems that subjects were requested without specific plants having been secured for Hooker to paint. The committee was required to meet five times during the course of 1816, to help manage the process. It is not clear who was responsible for identifying and acquiring the specimens, as members of the Society were typically encouraged to bring samples of their fruit to meetings to be recorded and observed.

The Drawings Committee accepted without question that the delay in producing the required pictures was not for lack of attention on Hooker's part, *"but the Committee find that it is not possible in the course of one single year always to obtain the various parts of the tree, its flowers, branches, leaves and fruit in proper states…."*[2] It was, therefore, agreed that a set of pictures be held as 'stock in hand' to be finished the following year, to help overcome this difficulty.

The practice was established whereby the committee would inspect finished or partially completed drawings to determine whether to accept them. It seems they may on occasion have been a little overzealous in recommending alterations. In December 1817, it is recorded that amendments should be made to two paintings of a Blue and a White Fig, respectively. However, this decision was revised at the following meeting in April 1818: *"the Committee thinking the objections were not of sufficient importance to risk the injury of the drawings."*[3] On another occasion, a figure of the 'Spring Grove Codlin' – which had been drawn for the 'Miscellaneous' collection in 1809 – was replaced in 1820 on the discovery of a better specimen; the new illustration was entered into the main fruit drawings collection. The fruit was so called as it had been found growing on the estate of Sir Joseph Banks, at Spring Grove in Isleworth. The original specimen that had been painted was not deemed typical of the fruit and, therefore, the picture was considered potentially misleading. The accuracy of the drawings was paramount and every attention to detail was paid to make these artworks a keystone to the identification work of the Society. A manuscript document in the Society's archives from 1819, describes in incredible detail the appearance of many of the apples that were presented at the Society's meetings. A typical entry, for the 'Keswick Codlin', is as follows: *"A fine handsome specimen, tall and angular with a sharp ridge generally running from the eye to the stalk, like the line left upon a wax cast at the joint of the mould."*[4] The painting reflects these elements perfectly, demonstrating the incalculable value of the immediacy of botanical illustration as a means of conveying information for identification.

Unfortunately, the committee minutes do not record where Hooker set up his easel, nor offer us any insight into how he worked. The Society had an ornamental garden in Kensington from 1818 to 1822 and an experimental garden in 1820. It was not until 1822 though, that part of the estate belonging to the Duke of Devonshire was leased and the Society's garden at Chiswick was established.

'Keswick Codlin'
William Hooker, 1819

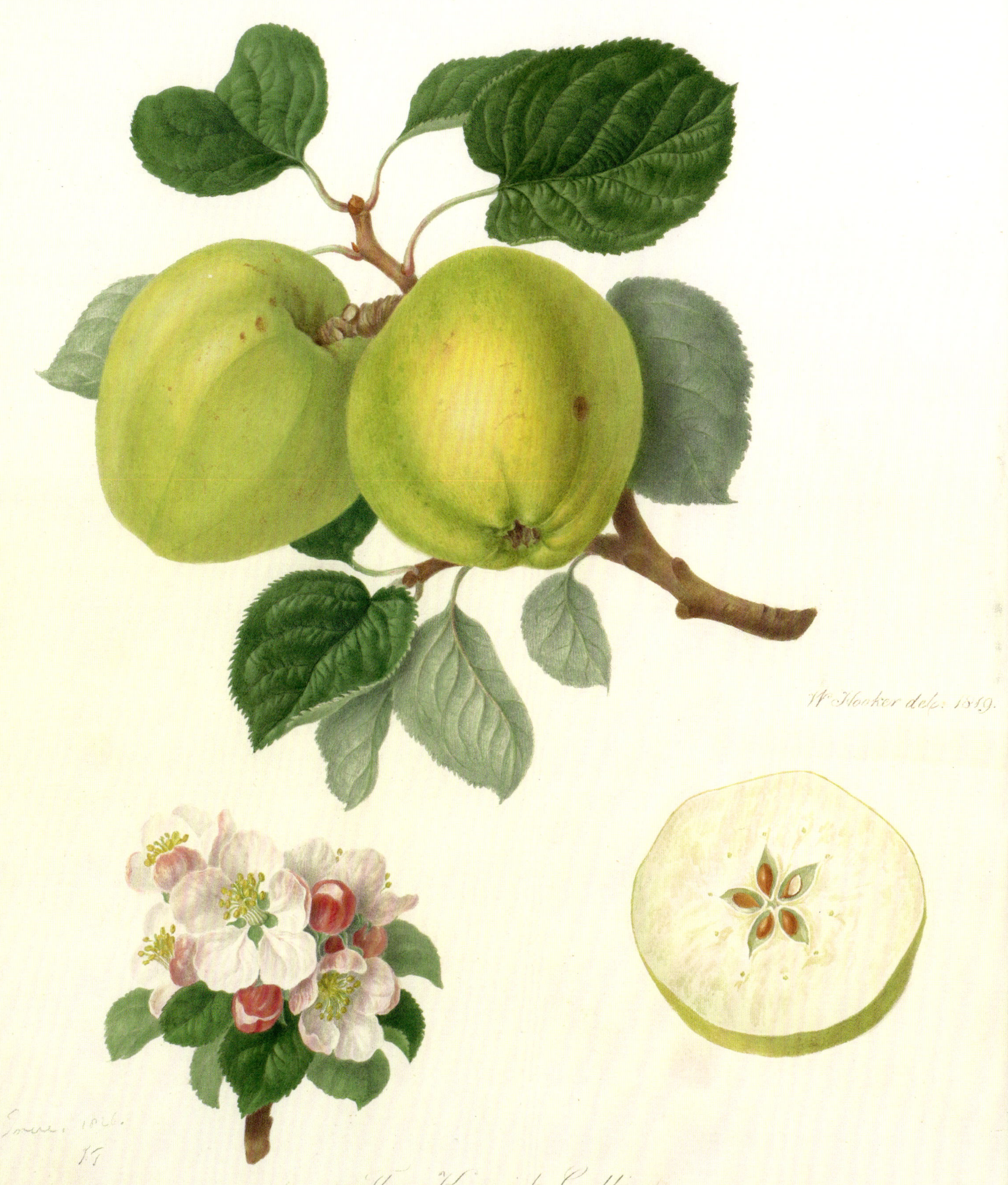

The Keswick Codlin.

A fruit garden was one of the first priorities for the garden at Chiswick, to remove the dependence of the Society on members to supply specimens for study. Over the course of the project, the minutes of the Drawings Committee reveal that there were regular updates and alterations to the list of pictures being 'ordered', depending on the availability of specimens and Hooker's workload.

It does seem that Council thought William Hooker had endless capacity, as not only was he producing the fruit identification paintings, plates for publication in the *Transactions* and still more 'Miscellaneous pictures', he was also called upon to produce illustrations for less scientific purposes. The 'Royal Signatures Collection' of decorative signed borders, for example, celebrates the royal connections and patronage enjoyed by the Society. The first of these, dated 1816, was created in honour of HM George III's wife, Queen Charlotte – née Princess of Mecklenburg-Strelitz – and features her namesake, the *Strelitzia.* Hooker was to continue to paint these surrounds until 1820. When the signatory was not associated with a particular plant, Hooker was able to incorporate his fruit studies in the compositions, as with the designs for both Prince Leopold (1817) and King George IV (1820).

Hooker was therefore exceptionally busy with work for the Society, and the task of completing all the commissioned works must have seemed overwhelming. Unfortunately, he never did manage to keep pace with the demanding schedule set out by the Society. Although in 1820 a new artist, Charles John Robertson of Soho Square, had been asked to help, by 1822 Hooker was suffering such poor health that he could not continue. A number of drawings remain unfinished and unsigned, although they are identifiable as Hooker's by the distinctive soft stipple application of paint. In addition to Mr Robertson, Miss Barbara Cotton, Mrs Augusta Withers and Miss Sarah Ann Drake were all employed to produce fruit and flower paintings. The fruit identification project largely came to an end in 1830, the final picture being of the 'Musch Musch Apricot' by Augusta Withers. Paintings of flowers continued to be added sporadically, with the final two paintings coming much later, in 1844. The Royal Signatures Collection was to gain in significance following financial difficulties in the late nineteenth century, when Prince Albert was elected as President and arranged a new charter that established the patronage for the re-named *Royal Horticultural Society.*

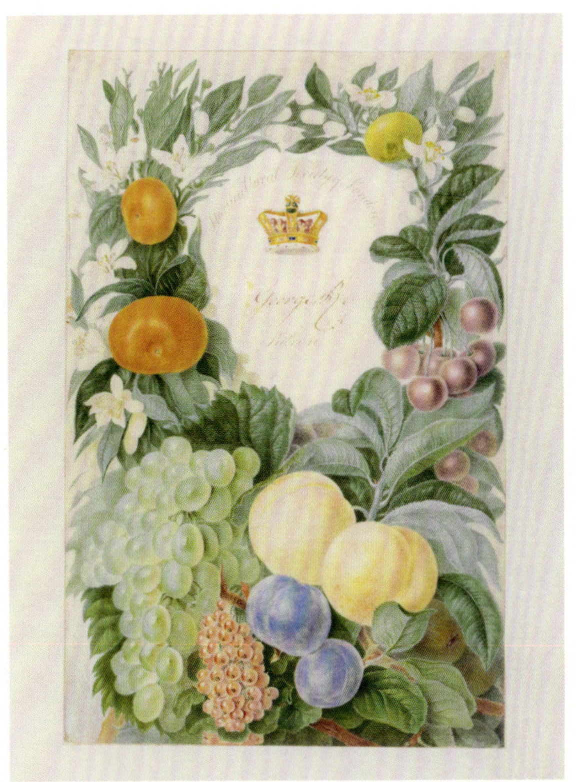

HM George IV, Royal Signatures Collection
William Hooker, 1820

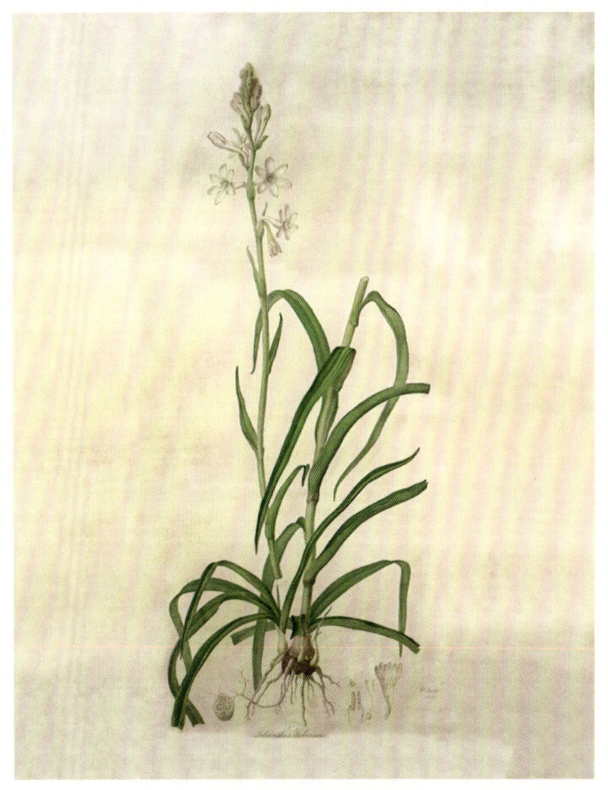

Polianthes tuberosa
William Hooker, 1806

As the initial commissioning process had been so challenging, it is often difficult to disentangle those paintings by Hooker that were originally part of the 'Miscellaneous' set and those that were intended for the fruit identification project. For simplicity's sake, the 244 watercolours housed in ten green-marbled albums, known collectively as *Hooker's Drawings of Fruits*, are in large part the fruit identification paintings. The principal exception to this is Volume 10, which does not contain any fruit illustrations or works by Hooker and largely consists of paintings of rose cultivars by Edwin D. Smith and John Lindley, painted between 1820 and 1833. Despite this, it bears the same title and is considered part of the main 'Fruit' collection. The original set of

'Miscellaneous' pictures, which was started 1806 with the *Polianthes tuberosa*, was added to over time to include new cultivars, such as Narcissus, Amaryllis and Chrysanthemums by a number of other artists. In what would appear to be a departure from the usual commissioning procedure, copies of other pictures were also added to the collection in 1820: *"Mr Sabine reported that he had sent two East Indian Drawings to have copies made of them by the Misses Francillon for the inspection and approval of the next Committee."* By 1821, works by Ferdinand Bauer (younger brother of Francis) and Clara Maria Pope also appeared, as well as an album of nineteenth-century drawings of American Apples previously owned by William Coxe. The 1859 sale catalogue from Sotheby's lists 27 separate lots of *"Magnificent botanical drawings"*. Of these, four of the lots are described as 'Miscellaneous' drawings, including works by Bauer, Hooker, Lindley *et al.*, which add up to nearly 600 watercolours.[5] Whilst some of the 'Miscellaneous' paintings have returned to the collection, there are many that have since found their way either into private hands or public collections elsewhere.

The two copies of East India Company drawings referred to previously, made by Sarah Ann Francillon and Elizabeth Francillon, hint at a much larger preoccupation. During this period, the Society was not content with acquiring paintings of plants growing in England, but also sought an understanding of those growing overseas. In tandem with the work on fruit, they engaged with what was to become an undertaking of immense significance, when in 1817 they appointed Mr John Reeves as a corresponding member. A tea inspector for the East India Company, he was based in Canton (Guangzhou) and Macau, and perfectly placed to support the Society.

Reeves Collection

John Reeves was to spend the next 13 years sending plants, seeds, herbarium specimens and paintings of plants from China to the Society in London. These included ornamental varieties as well as wild flowers, fruit, vegetables and plants of economic importance. Painted by local Chinese artists, under Reeves's supervision, this collection numbers over 900 individual paintings. Letters and articles from the period, some written by Joseph Sabine and published in the Society's *Transactions*, record the use made of the Chinese pictures as a means of identifying new specimens. Although it is now known that at least four

Chrysanthemum indicum ('Toze Fung Ny' or 'Purple Pheasants Tail')
RHS Reeves Collection, *c.*1817–1831

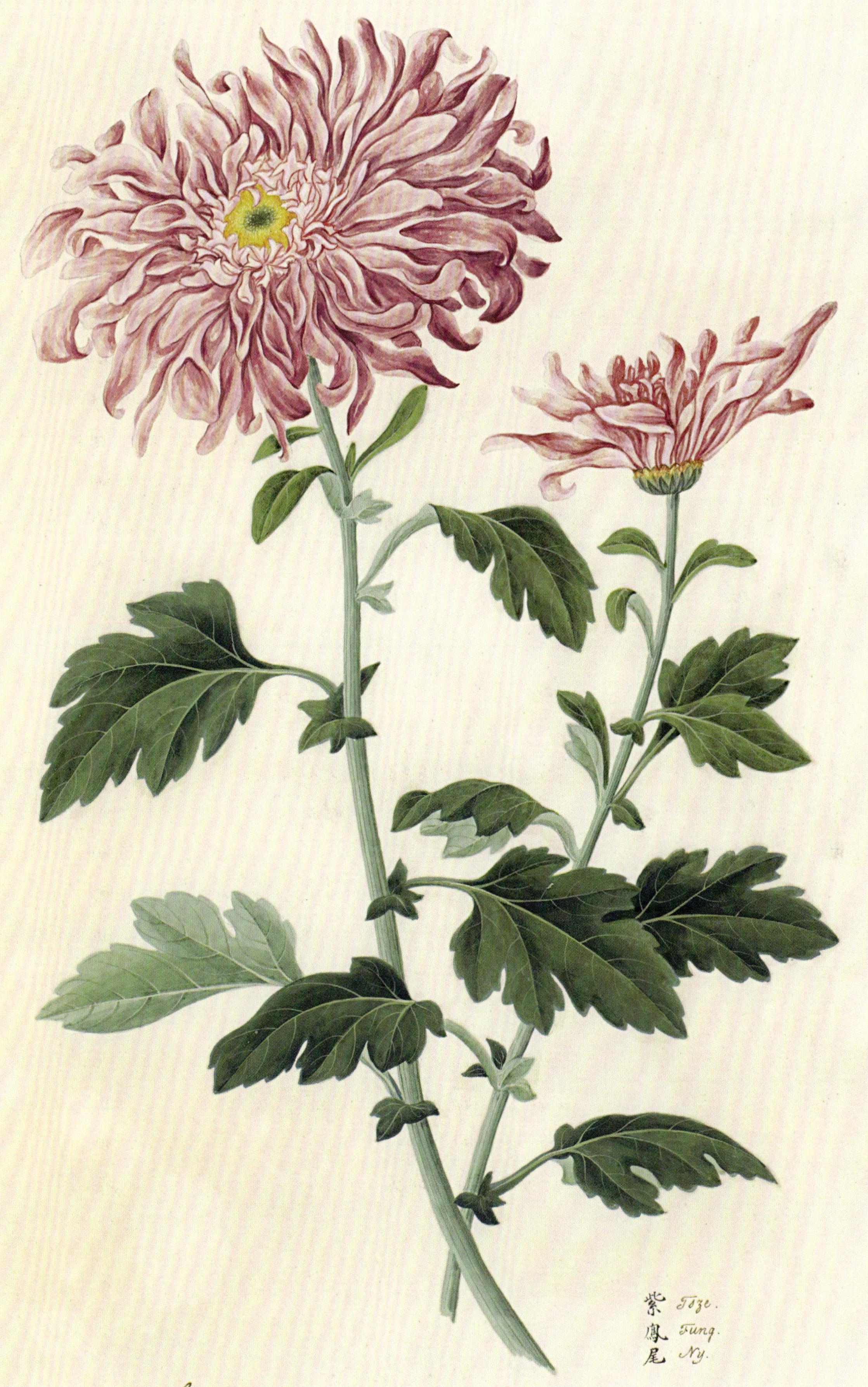

Chrysanthemum Indicum. Var. Purple Pheasants Tail.

artists were working with Reeves in China, at the time he was credited with having employed *"one of the best native artists"*.[6] The paintings he had sent back were originally accumulated in batches of loose sheets, to be bound into albums at a later date. Just as the Drawings Committee had overseen and approved the works painted by William Hooker, they were also responsible for approving the drawings sent from China. It has become apparent that Reeves had more than one copy of each picture made by his artists and, whilst some of these were kept for his own reference purposes, on occasion duplicates were sent to the Society and also possibly elsewhere. Reeves had enjoyed the support of Sir Joseph Banks until his benefactor's death in 1820. Through Banks, he had made and maintained a network of plant enthusiasts with whom he exchanged plants, drawings and correspondence, facilitated through the East India Company connection. Joseph Sabine and John Lindley provided the principal points of contact between Reeves and the horticultural world in London.

Following his return to England in 1831, Reeves continued to work closely with the Society. At some point, probably around 1837, the drawings were re-bound and re-ordered according to genus and plant family; it is likely Reeves was involved with this process. When the Society's financial stability was first questioned, instructions were given for duplicate paintings to be sold. However, in the end, all of the paintings from China unfortunately met the same fate as the rest of the collections and the albums were sold in 1859. It was not until the twentieth century that the paintings started to make their way back to the Society.

The re-acquisition of some of the key works in the twentieth century, as well as the permanent loss of others, has helped shape our thinking about the purpose and value of the art collection. Many of the early principles for commissioning and composing studies of plants that were established by the Society in the nineteenth century, are still in practice today. Most importantly, these endeavours cemented the relationship between scientific practice and art. An important lesson was also learned and the Lindley Library Collections are now held in a separate Trust, meaning they cannot be sold or disposed of again.

Collecting in the Early Twentieth Century

Following the dramatic turn of events in 1859, the early twentieth century saw a somewhat fallow period of art collecting for the RHS. A 'Special Library Committee' had been appointed in 1910 to facilitate a closer working relationship between the Lindley Library and the RHS. This committee met fortnightly and was to advise Council on recommendations for the acquisition of new or old rare books; however, little mention is made in the Library Committee Minutes of the acquisition of drawings.[7] An explanation is offered by E.A. Bunyard in his report to Council in 1925: *"It has not been the policy of the Council in the past to purchase drawings, as it would be extremely difficult to assign a limit to such practice."* However, exceptions were made and one notable deviation from this policy was the Society's Collection of Orchid Award Paintings. Nelly Roberts, under the auspices of the President Sir Trevor Lawrence, became the first 'Orchid Artist' in 1897. Commissioned on behalf of the RHS Orchid Committee, her portraits are still used for reference and comparison. Nelly Roberts held the post for 56 years and is still the longest-serving artist for the RHS. In 1900, on the recommendation of the Committee, Council awarded Roberts a Gold medal for the 400 or so orchid portraits completed to date. By the time she retired in 1953, she had far exceeded that number, having painted over 4,500 orchid portraits, constituting more than half the current collection. Recent research has resulted in greater recognition of Nelly Roberts's work and revealed a long-standing error in the spelling of her name in RHS records.[8] Now rectified, where possible corrections are being made. Work is ongoing, with new portraits painted by the current Orchid Artist, Deborah Lambkin. This makes the Orchid Award Paintings the longest continuously commissioned collection of paintings at the RHS. However, until quite recently, the orchid portraits were not counted as part of the library's holdings and were housed separately in the Orchid Committee room.

Another exception came in the form of a further 100 Chinese watercolours of plants (with little provenance information), which were purchased in 1912. This was the same year some of the 'Miscellaneous' paintings by William Hooker came on the market. A further opportunity for the re-acquisition of the ten albums of *Hooker's Drawings of Fruits* presented itself in 1926 and allowed Council to re-recognise the merits of botanical art: *"the HOOKER drawings... form a standard which all present and future artists may profitably consult."* [9]

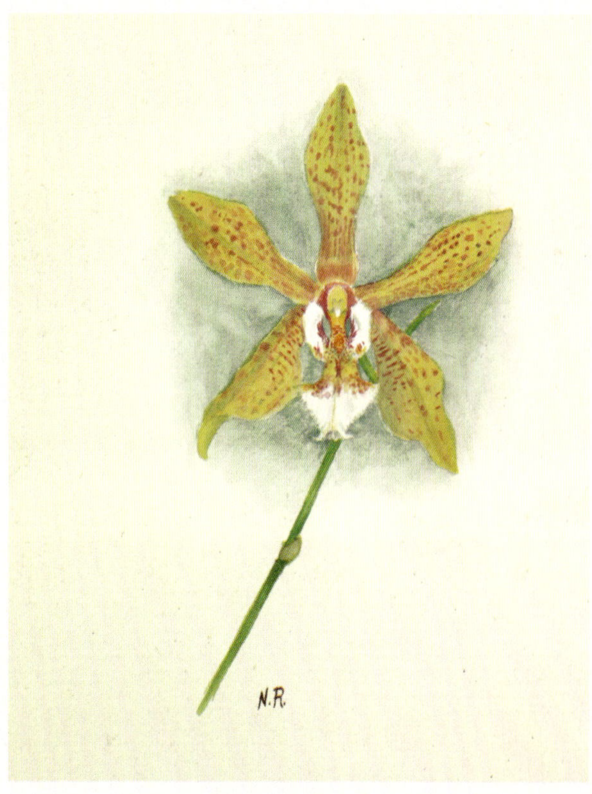

Phalaenopsis 'Mrs James H. Veitch'
Nelly Roberts, 1899

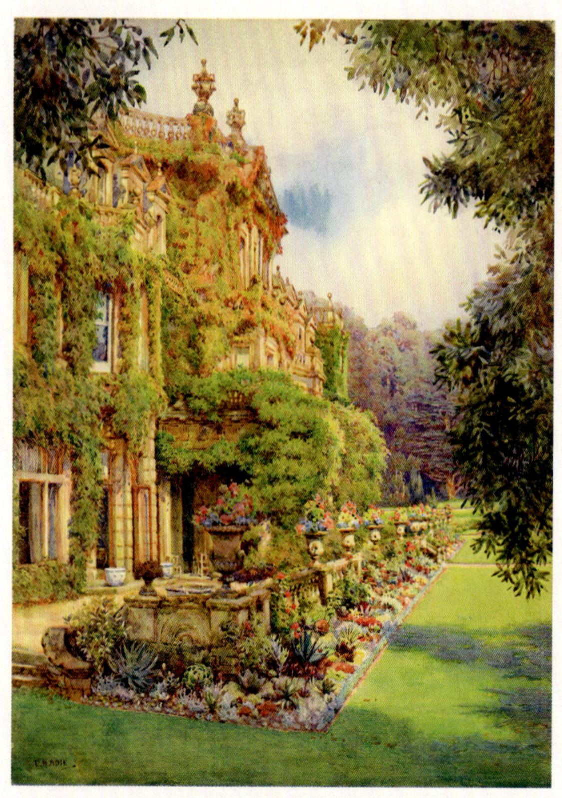

Dyffryn House and garden
Edith H. Adie, 1923

Then, in 1936, an exceedingly generous bequest by Reginald Cory changed the shape of the art collection, expanding it beyond anything the RHS would have been able or willing to achieve by its own means. Cory came from a family made wealthy through shipping and coal exports, who resided at Dyffryn House in South Wales. A dedicated horticulturist, he was an active member of the Society and contributed to a number of committees, including the Library Committee, as well as being a member of Council. Cory had an excellent eye and acquired several thousand original botanical artworks and horticultural books, including five albums of the previously sold Reeves collection. Cory purchased the five 'small' Reeves albums from the booksellers Henry Sotheran & Co. in 1908 and they were subsequently included in his bequest to

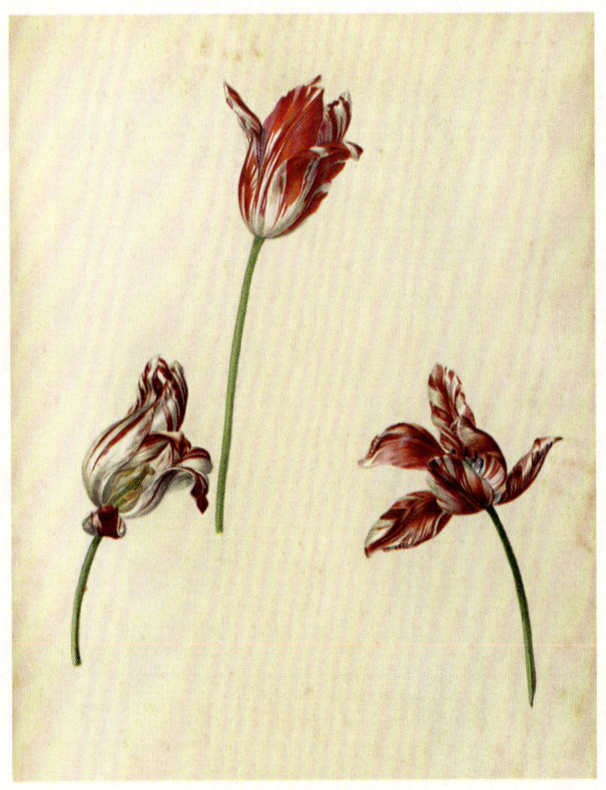

Tulipa 'Semper Augustus'
Pieter van Kouwenhoorn, 1630s

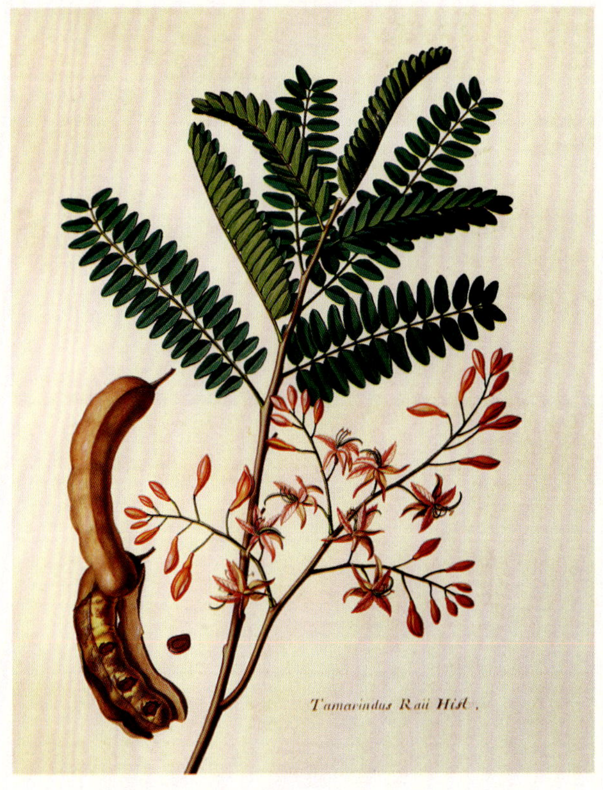

Tamarind
Claude Aubriet *c.*1700

the library. The remaining three 'large' volumes were purchased by the Society in 1953 from the antiquarian booksellers Heywood Hill.

Drawings by Pieter van Kouwenhoorn, the famous Bauer brothers, Georg D. Ehret, Claude Aubriet, P.J.F. Turpin and Margaret Meen to name but a few, were also received as part of the Cory Bequest. Cory was reportedly such an avid collector that in some instances works were transferred straight from the auction house to his basement unopened, to remain there until his death. One cannot but assume that it was something of a personal crusade for him to provide the Society with a ready-made botanical art collection. Prior to his death, Cory requested that all of his papers be destroyed, making it impossible to know for sure. In any case, his gift was really the start of what can be called the 'art collection' at the RHS.

As it now stands, botanical art in the Lindley Collections represents a broad geographic range in terms of both the plants that are represented and the artists who painted them. Illustrations from the seventeenth century onwards feature newly propagated exotics, showy ornamentals and plants of economic significance. The existence of such pictures reveals not just the appearance of the plants, but also which of them were highly prized by wealthy collectors and horticulturists. Kouwenhoorn's album of drawings from the Netherlands illustrates many of the popular ornamentals that gained great attention in 1630s. Amongst them are fabulous varieties of tulips, including the renowned 'Semper Augustus'. Garden writer Anna Pavord observes that, *"by the 1640s, when tulipomania was officially over, there were thought to be only twelve bulbs of 'Semper Augustus' still in existence."* [10]

As, over time, varieties have ceased to exist in cultivation, these illustrations become even more important as a source for historical research. Claude Aubriet, who travelled with the botanist Tournefort from France to the Levant in the early eighteenth century, recorded his observations in over 600 pen-and-ink wash drawings. His full-colour paintings on vellum, painted in the French court style, include edible 'exotics' such as pomegranate, vanilla and tamarind. These help describe the fascination with tropical plants that offered, among other things, flavours not commercially available in France at this time.

Though Cory's bequest had installed an historic collection of botanical art at the RHS, the library paid relatively little attention to contemporary artists at that time. Intermittent donations and bequests of personal artworks were received, but there was no real focus on developing the collection further. At this point, our attention can turn to other committees within the Society, and the exhibition and judging of pictures at RHS shows.

Edward Augustus Bowles was a key figure in the Society for the first half of the twentieth century and was well acquainted with Cory. A keen plant collector, horticulturist and accomplished botanical artist, he was appointed to the Scientific Committee in 1901 and subsequently had a role within the newly formed Library Committee. He sat on a total of 19 committees, as well as serving on Council over a period of 40 years. The Drawings Committee that had overseen William Hooker's commissions had long since ceased to meet, following the sale of the library collections. It was principally via the Scientific Committee, or exhibition at shows, that the RHS had the opportunity to engage with artists.

One such occasion came in 1912 when the Scientific Committee met, with Bowles in the Chair, to consider the work of Miss Massee. She presented *"excellent coloured drawings of various types of plants, faithfully coloured and showing dissections of the essential parts."* [11] (Drawings of insects and pests by George Massee and his daughter Ivy were gifted to the RHS in 1999, and it is most likely she is the same artist who first came to the attention of the Scientific Committee.) The following year, 1913, saw an array of floral paintings and garden art exhibited under canvas at the 'Chelsea Show'. In 1914 The Bromsgrove Guild was awarded a silver-gilt cup for 'Pictures and Statuary'. For the 1915 Chelsea Show, a committee of judges made up of E.A. Bowles, Reverend Wilks and Alfred Parsons was appointed for 'Paintings and Statuary'. They awarded five medals: a silver Flora to Mrs Fisher; and four silver Banksian medals to Miss Lamont, Miss Pilkington, Mrs Townsend and Miss Warrington, respectively. Although off to a promising start, exhibits of judged paintings at the Chelsea Show came to an abrupt halt with the outbreak of the Great War. Following the introduction of compulsory conscription in 1916, which included many of the nurserymen, the Society felt moved to cancel the Chelsea Show until after the war had ended.

A new medal was instituted in 1919 to commemorate Lord Grenfell, a former Field Marshall, on his retirement as President of the RHS. The 'Grenfell' was to rank between a Flora and Banksian medal, and in the first instance was issued for a variety of categories of exhibit, but not for paintings.

It was several years later, in 1926 (the same year that the albums of Hooker's Fruit were re-purchased), that the Committee was again asked to judge picture exhibits at the Chelsea Flower Show. At the suggestion of HM Queen Mary, an additional piece of land was also acquired:

"A special Art Tent for pictures of plants and gardens was provided, the Commissioners of the Royal Hospital having very kindly allowed the Society to rent an

additional piece of land in the Ranelagh Gardens. This innovation, which arose out of a suggestion made by HM The Queen, proved popular with both exhibitors and visitors."[12]

Records show that four artists were awarded the first medals in the Grenfell range: Miss W.M.A. Brooke received a Silver-Gilt; and Mrs N. Blacklock, Miss E. Savory and Miss J.N. Williams were all recipients of the Silver Grenfell.

Throughout the late 1920s and early '30s, a great range of paintings of flowers and gardens was exhibited alongside photographs, at the Chelsea Show and at the Society's fortnightly shows. The judges listed in attendance at Chelsea were numerous, totalling 46 in some years. Notable amongst them were Bowles and Cory, as well as artists Charles Curtis and Frank Galsworthy. Galsworthy was in fact the first artist to be awarded a Gold medal in 1930, for his display of 'floral paintings'. The works exhibited varied from specific studies of a given genus, to more general 'floral' or 'flower' paintings. Paintings of gardens were also seen and regularly won awards. The name of one artist stands out, not for her award, but because prior to having won a Bronze Grenfell medal, Edith Helena Adie's paintings had caught the eye of Reginald Cory. Adie spent the summer of 1923 at Cory's house, Dyffryn in South Wales, painting scenes of his garden. The resulting watercolours, now in the Lindley Collections, offer the most complete representation of his gardens before they fell into disrepair. Adie's pictures have been critical in restoring the garden to its former glory and Dyffryn is now a National Trust property.

Amongst the numerous vague descriptions of the pictures on display, the term 'botanical' crept into the records in 1928. Miss Matilda Smith was posthumously awarded a Silver Veitch Memorial Medal in 1926 for 'botanical draughtsmanship'. Matilda Smith created many of the original drawings that were then reproduced as lithographic plates by John Nugent Fitch for *Curtis's Botanical Magazine*. The term was not used again until 1933 when Mrs V.G. Jeffery was awarded a Grenfell medal for her exhibit of 'Botanical Paintings'. Two pictures thought to be by this same artist, one dated 1931, are now held in the library. Although unfortunately their provenance is unknown, Mrs Jeffery is credited as a contributing artist for *Amateur Gardening* magazine during this period.

Rhododendron neriiflorum

Original drawing by Matilda Smith, lithograph by J.N. Fitch

reproduced in *Curtis's Botanical Magazine,* 1917, Vol 143, plate 8727

8727

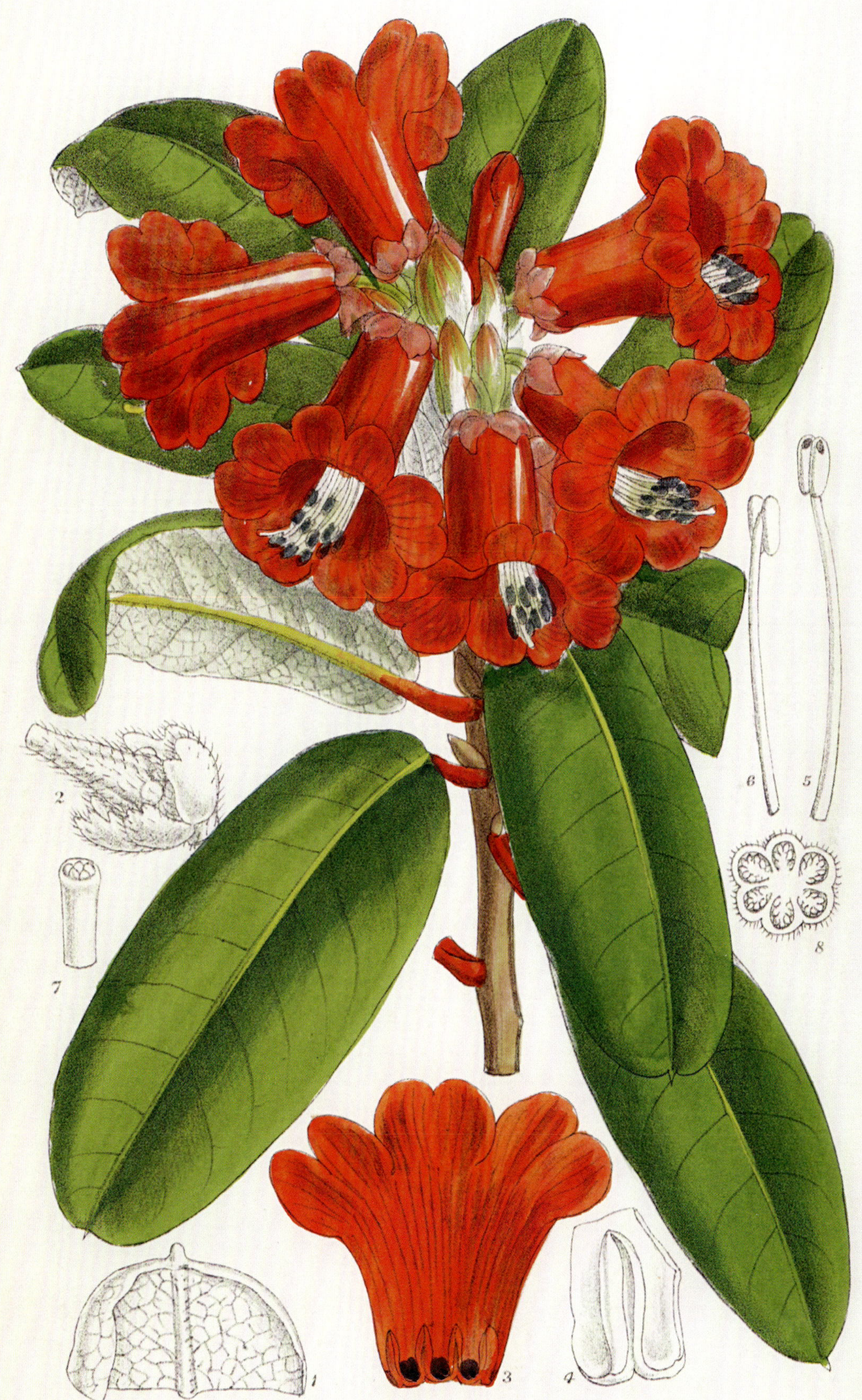

M.S. del. J.N. Fitch lith.

Vincent Brooks, Day & Son Lt[d] imp

L. Reeve & C[o] London.

In 1934, in a 'Notice to Fellows', the arrangements for judging were formalised and space allocated at the Fortnightly Shows at the Westminster Halls, *"for pictures and photographs of plants, flowers, gardens"*.[13] This was the last year that exhibits of judged botanical art were to feature at Chelsea. 1935 saw a number of significant changes to reflect the high regard in which botanical art was being held, and a large display of 29 artists' works was shown at the 'Exhibition of Paintings and Drawings' in October. This exhibition set the precedent for paintings to appear during the winter shows at the Society's Westminster Halls, to help fill the gaps when there were fewer plants to display. Specific guidelines were issued stating the abiding principle that works must be of 'horticultural or botanical interest':

"Pictures and photographs of plants, flowers, and gardens, and plans and models of gardens, may be exhibited at the Society's fortnightly shows during November, December, January and February. Only works which are definitely of horticultural or botanical interest are invited. Paintings of flowers should be at least life-size; miniatures are unsuitable for the Society's exhibitions. Pictures executed in needlework or modelled in paper, and all fanciful or fancy-work objects, pictures, calendars, Christmas cards and similar articles are also unsuitable and may not be shown."[14]

It was also decided that the Grenfell medal should be reserved explicitly for exhibits of pictures, photographs and similar objects of horticultural interest; it was struck in Bronze, Silver and Silver-Gilt.[15] The Paintings Committee, as it had become known, was well established for judging displays of paintings and photographs. Like Bowles, Galsworthy had also been approached to paint the decorative detail for a Royal Signature painting, for HM George V. The Gold medal had originally been instituted in 1898. It was re-designed in 1929 as an award for exhibits of 'special excellence', thus sitting outside the Grenfell medal range. Yet, despite its revival, the Gold was hard to achieve; only five were issued between 1930 and 1963, four of which to Galsworthy.

E.A. Bowles was no doubt hugely influential in the development of botanical art practices during the mid-twentieth century period. In 1929 he completed the decorative border for Queen Mary's signature, and was also awarded his first medal, a Silver Grenfell, for 'flower paintings'. Bowles counted a number of artists amongst his horticultural friends, including Frank

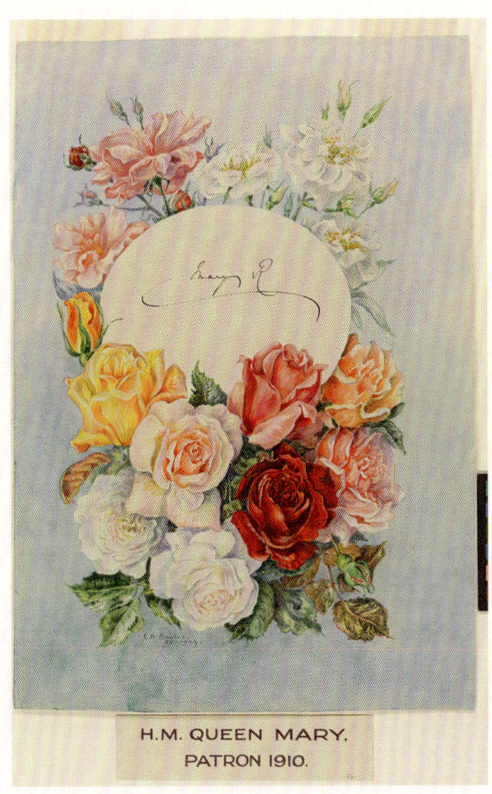

Royal Signatures Collection: HM Queen Mary
E.A .Bowles, 1929

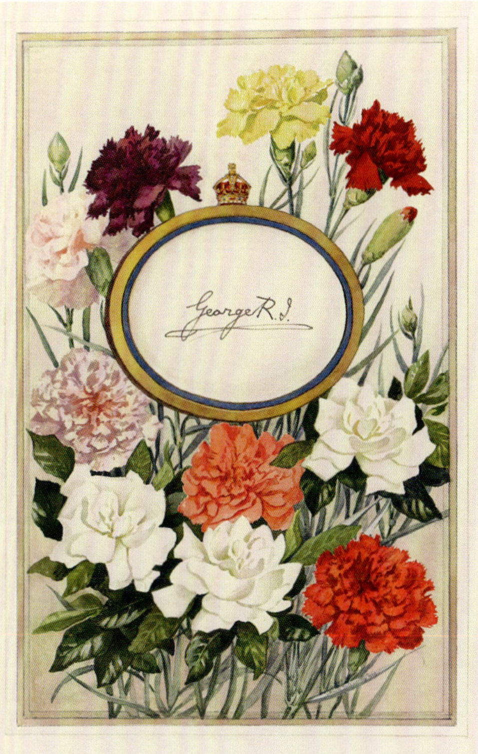

Royal Signatures Collection: HM King George V
Frank Galsworthy, 1929

Galsworthy, Lady Beatrix Stanley, Reginald Farrer and Alice Bickham. He sought to encourage and offer advice where possible, and is known to have corresponded with Lady Beatrix about her watercolours, whilst she was in India.[16] Bowles and Galsworthy had met at the RHS, and maintained a long friendship. They would paint together, and pick flowers from Bowles' garden at Myddleton House, arranging them in his antique vases for pleasing compositions.[17] Thus, in an informal manner, Bowles initiated what has become an exceptionally valuable part of the exhibiting experience, by offering feedback and encouragement to artists exhibiting with the RHS.

Having been one of the original members of the Paintings and Statuary Panel from 1915, Bowles served on judging panels at the Chelsea Show and joined the Picture Committee in 1938, for which he would act as Chair for the next 16 years. Although his style was often somewhat looser and more painterly than we would expect to see of a botanical artist today, he was a skilled draughtsman. His personal drawings were bequeathed to the Lindley Collections in 1954 and number over 400 watercolours and pencil sketches of different plants. Renowned for his interest in bulbs and alpines, nearly half of his artworks are of the genus *Galanthus*. Bowles might be counted amongst a group of 'artist-plant enthusiasts' that prevailed throughout the mid-twentieth century. They thought of themselves as plant people first; painting was a means of expressing their passion and to document their collections.

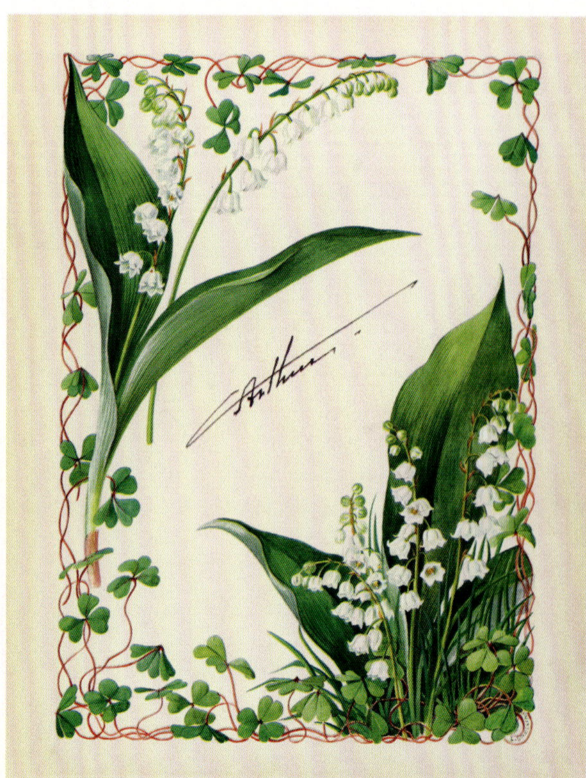

Royal Signatures Collection: HRH Duke of Connaught
Lilian Snelling, *c.*1924

War Years

For the second time in a century the world found itself at war, and the last exhibit of paintings at an RHS Show during this period was recorded in 1941. Medals of recognition were issued to Lilian Snelling and Nelly Roberts for their extensive services to botanical illustration. Lilian Snelling received the Silver Veitch medal (plus £25) in 1924 and the Society's highest accolade, the Victoria Medal of Honour in 1947. Nelly Roberts was awarded the Silver Veitch Memorial medal in 1953.

Both Lilian Snelling and Nelly Roberts had long and illustrious careers. Snelling's earliest studies of flowers found in and around her home town of St Mary Cray, reveal a keen interest in the natural world. The

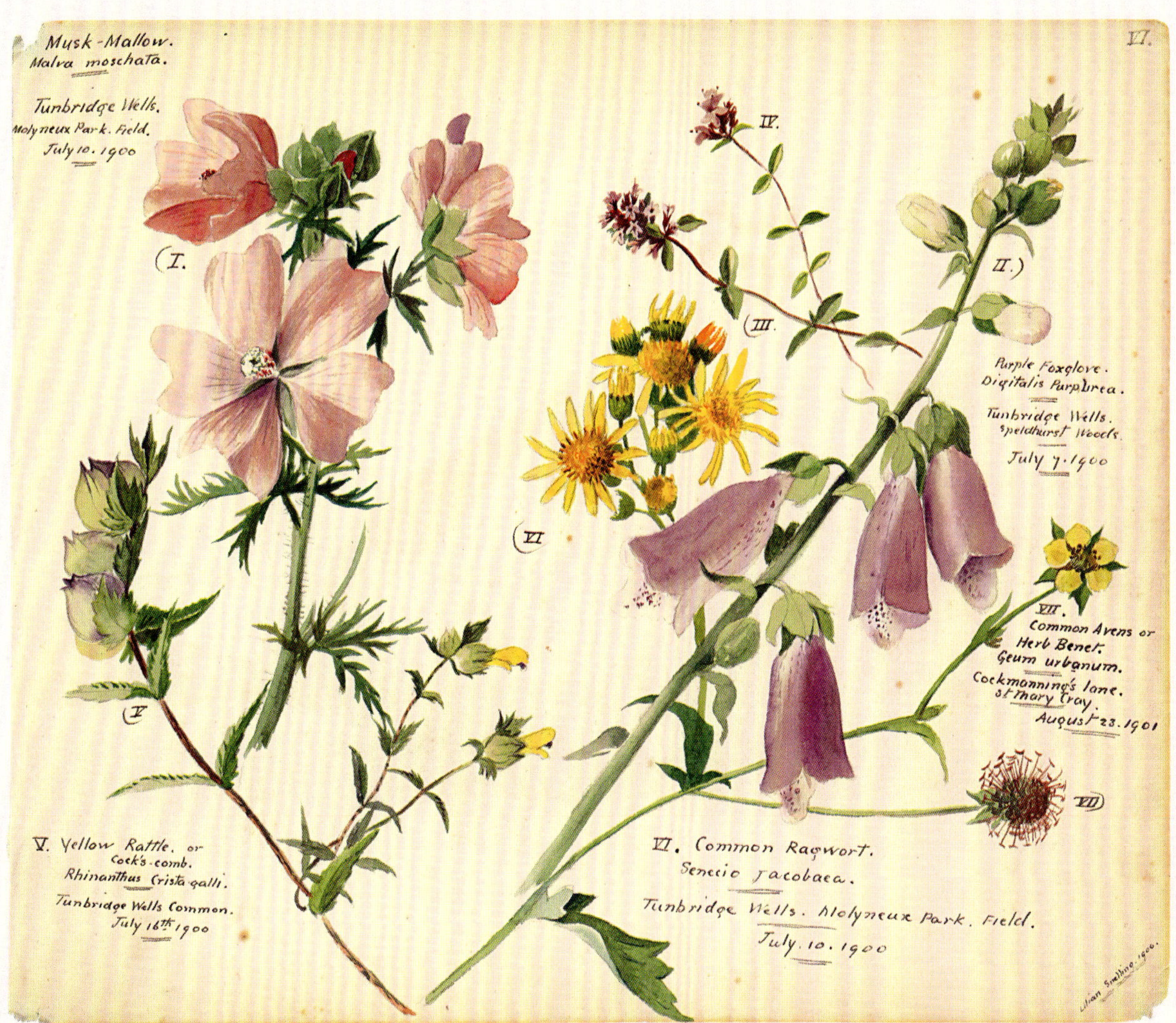

'Wild flowers'
Lilian Snelling, 1900–1901

impressionistic groupings of hedgerow plants, from the early 1900s, are accompanied by Latin name, common name, date and location – indicating she had understood the value of such paintings as a means of documentation. Her appointment at the Edinburgh Botanic Garden as a botanical artist in residence in 1916 confirmed her talent, following which she became the principal artist for *Curtis's Botanical Magazine* between 1922 and 1952 (during which period it was published by the RHS). In accordance with what had become a tradition for RHS artists, Snelling was invited to paint a decorative border for a new Royal

Signature, this time the Duke of Connaught. She was also awarded a Silver Grenfell at the 1935 exhibition, for commissioned paintings of the genus *Paeonia,* included in the monograph by F.C. Stern.

But it seems that after the war and without Bowles to champion the cause, the Society's interest in exhibiting and collecting botanical art began to wane. Wilfrid Blunt, in his lecture on the history of botanical illustration of 1951, feared that *"the great age of flower-painting certainly lies behind us. The photographer can do in a few seconds what an artist takes many hours to perform...."*[18] And yet here Blunt inadvertently identified exactly why botanical art cannot be replaced by photography. The time, study, understanding and skill that all go into creating a painting cannot be replicated in the click of a button. The preoccupation with photography and concern over its potential to replace botanical art was exacerbated because, up until the 1960s, it was not uncommon for photographs to be exhibited alongside illustrations. The rules were revised in the 1960s and a Photographic Committee was formed in its own right. Little was Blunt to realise though, that a great resurgence was on the horizon that would lead to a renewed interest in botanical art exhibitions and bring a talented new generation of artists to the fore.

Plant Collecting and Painting

In the meantime, two artists exhibited in 1960, both with paintings of plants seen in challenging environments. John Paul Wellington Furse undertook expeditions to the Middle East, Turkey, Iran, Iraq, Russia and Afghanistan, plant collecting, painting and photographing plants in their natural habitat. He had first exhibited with the RHS during the 1930s whilst serving in the Navy. Furse was awarded a total of 32 medals between 1934 and 1968, including four Golds and the Victoria Medal of Honour in 1966, for *"plant collecting in foreign parts and enriching our folios with exquisite paintings of these plants as he saw them and our literature with exciting accounts of these journeys."*

Patrick Synge's obituary of Furse states that his travels *"resulted in the most extensive collection of choice bulbs from Afghanistan, Iran and Turkey at Wisley that has ever been accumulated. Many of the bulbs had to be collected blind out of flower, so that in the next spring season [John] Paul and Polly would drive over to Wisley and he would paint and record each one as it flowered. So each form and variant was recorded in a mass of drawings, and notes on which future students can draw since he gave most of them to the library of the RHS."*[19]

Allium mirum

Admiral J.P.W. Furse, 1965

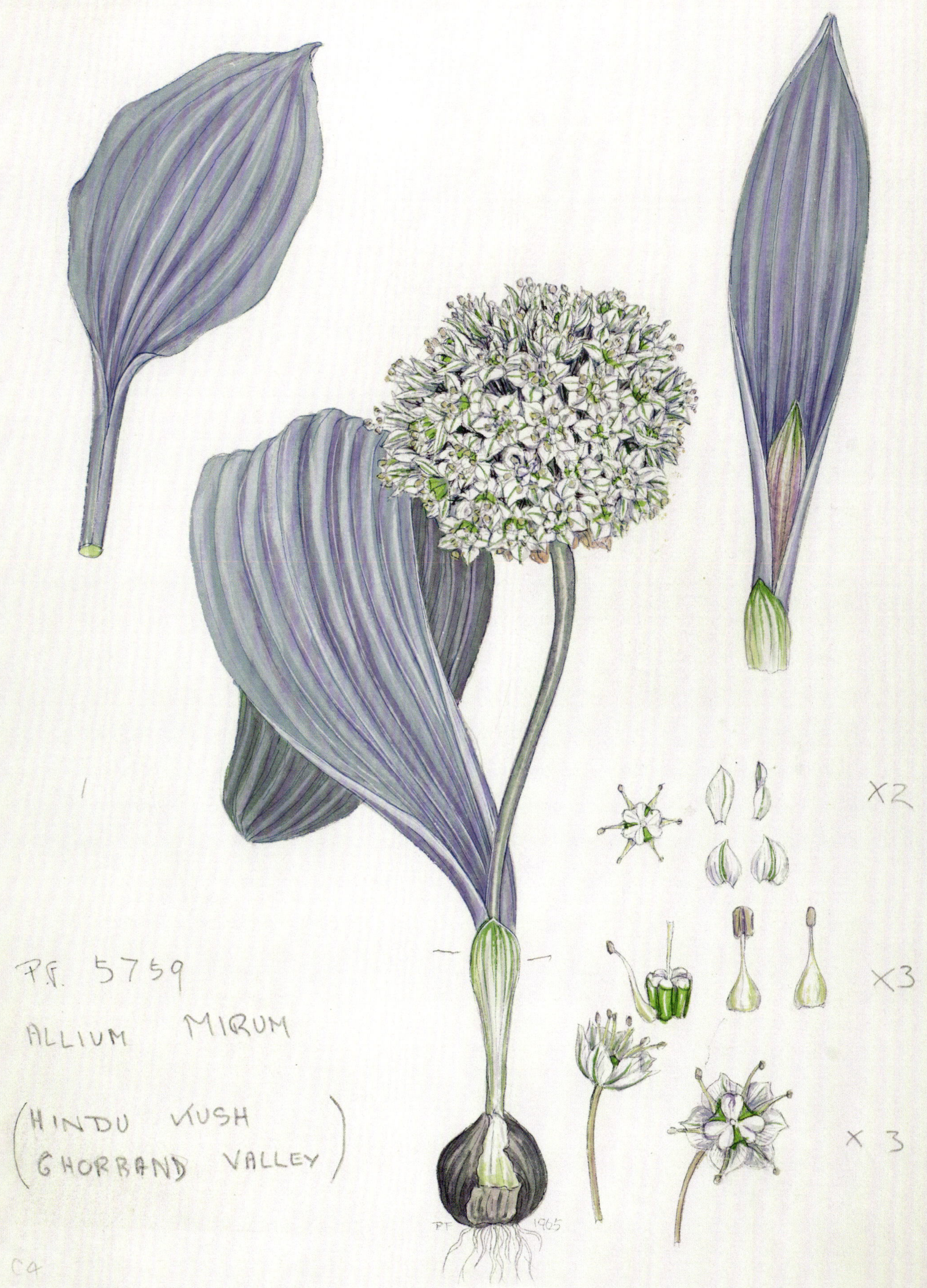

X2
X3
X 3
P.F. 5759
ALLIUM MIRUM
(HINDU KUSH
GHORBAND VALLEY)
PF 1965
C4

Furse had a lifelong passion for fritillaries and had drawn nearly every known species of lily. There are over 800 watercolours by him held in the Lindley Collections and those pictures, notes and photographs not held at the RHS are at RBG Kew. Margaret Mee was the other well-travelled artist to exhibit alongside Furse in 1960, with her paintings of plants from the Amazon, for which she was awarded a Silver-gilt medal. Blunt wrote of Mee: *"her paintings, scrupulously accurate botanically, are so well composed and so sensitive to form and textures that they stand as beautiful pictures in their own right."*[20]

Whilst Furse was to dominate many of the exhibitions throughout the 1960s, another artist of supreme talent was also to step forward and achieve great acclaim. Mary Grierson was awarded her first Gold medal in 1966 and went on to receive a further four gold medals and a Gold Veitch Memorial Medal between 1969 and 1990. The President's address from 1985 reads as follows: *"Horticulture owes a great debt to the artists, of whom you are one, who record meticulously plants in a manner in which they can be enjoyed by future generations. It therefore gives us great pleasure to recognise your consummate skill with this Gold Veitch Memorial Medal."*[21]

A New Phase in Collecting

In a meeting of the Picture Committee held in 1990, it was acknowledged that very little in the way of botanical art had been acquired for the library collections between 1950 and 1987.[22] Four years previously, Elizabeth Banks had outlined her concerns and frustrations regarding the state of the contemporary collection in a letter to the then Chair, Lady Loder. The opening statement is revealing: *"I understand that you have managed to persuade the RHS to buy some modern botanical drawings to augment the Lindley Library Collection. Well done!"*[23] One of the first works purchased in this new phase was *Pinus wallichiana* by Annie Farrer, purchased in 1987.

In the same letter, Elizabeth Banks reiterated that if the Lindley Library wished to hold a representative collection, it was necessary to choose botanical pictures from those artists who had already been recognised, and who had been awarded a Gold medal. Not an unreasonable assumption, but it needed repeating on more than one occasion. With new collecting aims, the emphasis was placed on the artist and the quality of their work, rather than solely on the subject matter depicted, which served as a departure from previous years. However, throughout the 1980s the library had been managing on a very limited budget and as such the desire to develop a contemporary art collection was at odds with the demands on the library's book purchasing, preservation and maintenance budget as well as space and facility for storage. There was also the challenge of adopting a suitable procedure, as the Library Committee and Picture Committee did not meet at the same time or share the same priorities, and on more than one occasion a member felt moved to resign over picture expenditure.

It was not until 1989–90 that a special budget was agreed for the library to be able to re-house and catalogue its existing drawings, acquire contemporary artworks and administer the Orchid Award paintings.[24] The Picture Committee Minutes of the following year record that the budget for the acquisition of contemporary artworks had been revised and responsibility given to the Librarian to purchase paintings, with advice from the Picture Committee.[25] As part of this initiative, the Picture Committee agreed that it was important to have Mary Grierson's work represented in the collection, resulting in the acquisition of the illustration of *Eccremocarpus scaber*. At the same time, Grierson was invited to join the Society's Picture Committee in her capacity as a practising artist; she served as a judge between 1991 and 1997. During this period, Grierson was also called upon to help boost the collections, by providing a list of artists whose work should be included by means of donation, bequest or purchase. And so for the first time, the value of a relationship between the library collections and research facilities, Gold medal winning artists and Shows started to be recognised. Shirley Sherwood, renowned collector and supporter of botanical art, also leant her support to the initiative; she was invited to join the Picture Panel as a judge in 1995 and continues to attend meetings today.

Medals and Awards

The Veitch Memorial Medal (VMM) and the Victoria Medal of Honour (VMH) are the highest awards of recognition offered by the RHS, outside the arena of judged exhibits. Awarded to British horticulturists in honour of the special contribution they have made, the VMH was instituted in 1897. It is only ever held by 63 recipients at a time, in commemoration of Queen Victoria's reign, which lasted for 63 years. Four botanical artists have held the VMH: Lilian Snelling, J.P.W. Furse, Mary Grierson and Vera Higgins.

The VMM is awarded to persons of any nationality who have made an outstanding contribution to the advancements and practice of horticulture. This award has been conferred on Wilfrid Blunt, Anne-Marie Evans (a highly influential botanical art teacher, who inspired a generation of artists), the botanical art patron Shirley Sherwood, and eight botanical artists: Matilda Smith, Worthington G. Smith, Lilian Snelling, Nelly Roberts, Margaret Stones (VMM Silver and Gold), Mary Grierson, Stella Ross-Craig and, most recently, Gillian Barlow.

Gillian Barlow has been incredibly valuable as a member of the Society's Picture Panel since 2005; she has held the position of Chair for over ten years. During this time, she has witnessed the advance of botanical art exhibits from occupying a small corner at the Society's winter flower shows, to becoming a presence that commands an entire Hall in its own right. In 2016, the new London Botanical Art Show witnessed the highest number of artists to date, as well as the most Gold medals: 33 artists representing 11 countries, with 13 gold medals awarded. The standard of art on display has been increasing year on year, and the presentation and staging has been updated to reflect the seriousness of the event: the hall is now akin to a gallery space, with fixed white walls. In 2018, another record was broken, as over 40 artists signed up to exhibit in the highly anticipated 'London Plant & Art Fair' in the summer.

Barlow writes on the experience of being both an exhibiting artist and a judge:

"Showing work to one's peers and to the general public at RHS Shows raises an artist's profile, enables fruitful exchanges with other exhibitors and visitors, and often inspires an artist to develop their ideas and improve their technique. As artists often work in isolation, exhibiting can enhance the feeling of being part of a wider creative community. In the past ten years, this sense of community has, for many artists, been hugely broadened by the use of social media, blogs, online groups, website galleries, offering a virtual acquaintance with artists and their work. This has been a game-changer in this field of endeavour as much as in most other areas. The award of a medal, particularly of a Gold medal, raises an artist's standing and reputation among peers, buyers, and students worldwide, and is considered a guarantee of excellence, within RHS criteria.

When feedback is offered to the exhibiting artists, the Panel's comments are generally welcomed, especially if the artist has gained a lower medal than was hoped.

Feedback has helped to raise standards year on year, but has not led to a narrower offer by exhibitors merely anxious to fulfil judges' perceived criteria. On the contrary, the diversity and range of work has increased, with greater care in choosing an interesting project or coherent theme. Much higher quality of execution is now aided by an initial screening of potential exhibitors at an annual Selection Meeting, whose work needs to reach at least Silver medal standard before the artist is accepted to exhibit. In the past ten years we have sought to improve the consistency of the judging by providing clearer guidelines for artists and more concise criteria for judges. Gold medals are only given for exhibits of outstanding quality, whatever their diversity of approach, or visual impact."[26]

As the standard of botanical art seen at the Society's shows has increased and the capacity of the library to collect examples of such excellence has improved, so have the opportunities to help support new generations of artists. In being able to share the best in contemporary botanical art, the Lindley Library seeks to foster a wider community of enthusiasts, who can come together through their passion for plants and art.

In 2019, the last exhibits of judged botanical art were staged at the RHS Lindley Hall. The July show coincided with one of the hottest summers to date (hitting 38 degrees Celsius) meaning visitors and exhibitors struggled with London heat and melted train tracks. After such success in 2018, the difficult conditions for 2019 somewhat took the shine off the visitor experience of the show.

The following year, as spring approached, the Botanical Art and Photography Show was scheduled to open in April 2020. Hopes for a more clement experience diminished as news started to spread around the world of a fast-moving virus that was to put a halt to all ordinary activity, specifically any social gathering. As events were put on hold, flights cancelled and border controls tightened, increasingly anxious messages from artists filtered through regarding the show. In line with UK government advice, the RHS took the decision in March to cancel all its forthcoming events, prior to what became an unprecedented period of social isolation, known as lockdown.

When the world began to emerge from the Covid-19 restrictions months later, it was to an altered social landscape. Visits to indoor venues were initiated cautiously and still the following year there was much hesitancy over travelling, visiting galleries and meeting others indoors. This coincided with a decision taken by the RHS to pause hosting RHS shows at the Lindley Hall and focus more on special-interest flower shows at the gardens. Revenue from commercial letting of the hall was now too important to ignore after such a long period of closure.

However, some creative thinking and fortuitous conversations led to a new opportunity for the Botanical Art and Photography Show. A high-profile art gallery just off the King's Road in Chelsea, was keen to forge a partnership with the Society. Saatchi Gallery offered generous space in its galleries to showcase contemporary botanical art and photography. A new era had arrived, albeit tentatively, for the show to fulfil its earlier promise and inhabit the expansive white walls at what had once been the Duke of York's Headquarters. An arrangement was fostered whereby the Saatchi Gallery presents a contemporary art installation at the Chelsea Flower Show.

In a rapid turnaround, a two-day botanical art show, staged according to each exhibitor's own design, became a unified, gallery-worthy exhibition, open for three weeks. All the exhibitors who had been waiting to bring their work to the RHS in 2020, were advised of the new arrangements, and 15 artists agreed they were ready to participate. All the artists eligible to exhibit with the RHS were automatically allocated an additional year in which to prepare their works.

One of the significant differences between a 'show' and an 'exhibition', is the presence of the exhibitors. Artists were used to the idea that they would choose their mounts and frames, install their own display, present their own text, and sit alongside their pictures for two days, speaking to other exhibitors and members of the public. Of course, with many restrictions still in place, depending on the country and region, this was no longer possible or desirable. But it was also counter to the expectations of an art gallery, which may hold special events for artists and public to meet but had no expectation that artists would be on hand throughout the exhibition.

The shift to a gallery presentation also meant that artists could no longer just arrive and hang their own works – these are now sent in advance and framed according to agreed specifications. For the first time, the display is curated and promoted with professional interpretation, and a preview and awards event is held to honour each exhibitor's achievements. The teams at the RHS and

Saatchi Gallery work closely together to bring the show to fruition.

The core elements of the show remain the same. Exhibits are presented on a theme, judged according to strict criteria by a panel of botanical art experts; artists may receive an RHS medal and one of the additional awards of recognition. Over the past few years, the partnership with Saatchi Gallery has helped to raise the profile of botanical art within contemporary art. In 2024, the exhibition was extended to a six-week run, the longest duration yet. Schoolchildren, community groups and the wider gallery-visiting public now join dedicated fans of botanical art, to appreciate the best in contemporary practice.

In the meantime, a new gallery opened at RHS Garden Wisley, programmed with exhibits curated by the library team, featuring botanical art from the library collections. In 2024 there was also the much-anticipated launch of the RHS Digital Collections platform, featuring images from the RHS Libraries and Herbarium. Looking to the future, even more of the art collections will be made available as a digital resource online, to support the research and study needs of this international community.

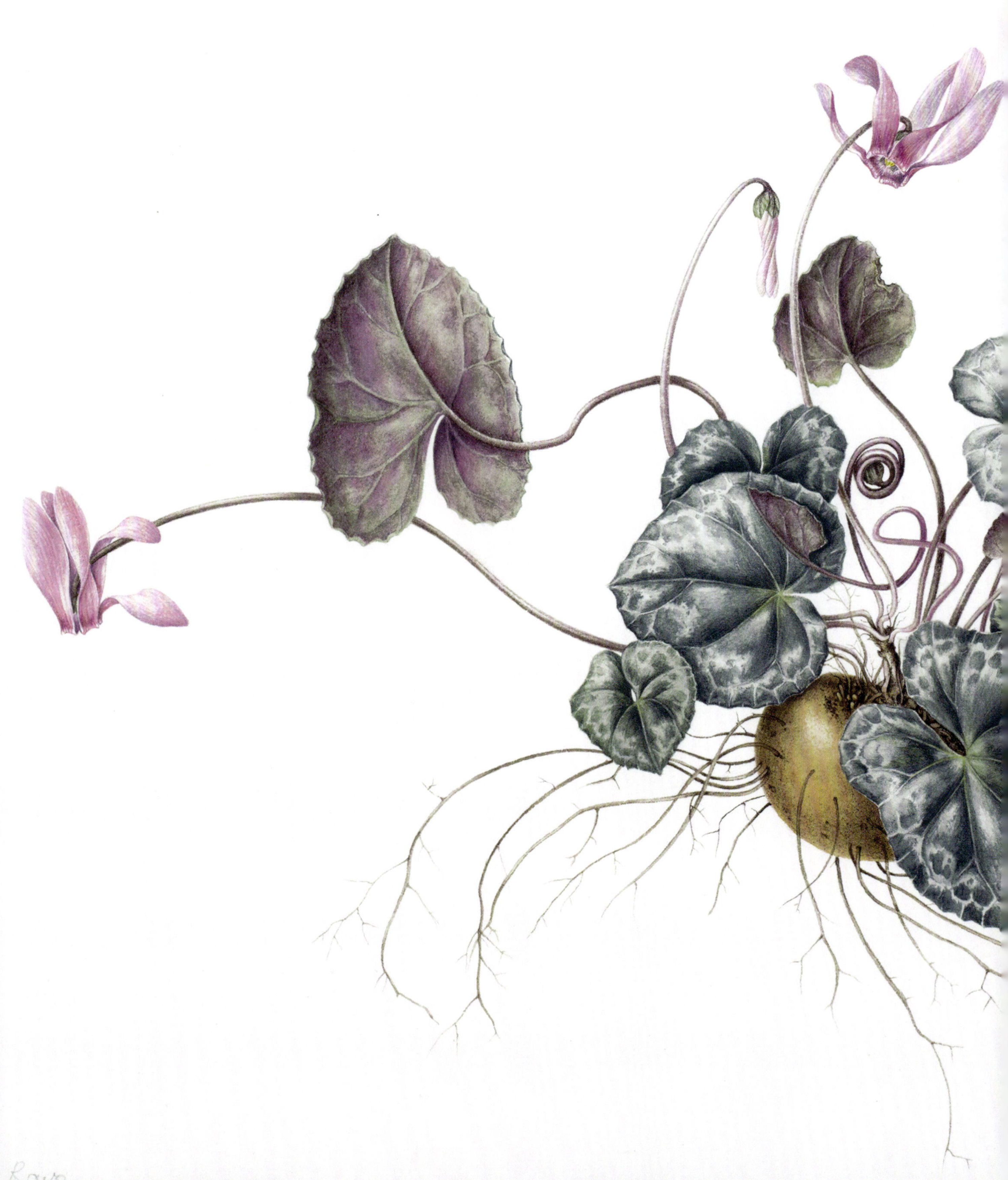

The *Artists*

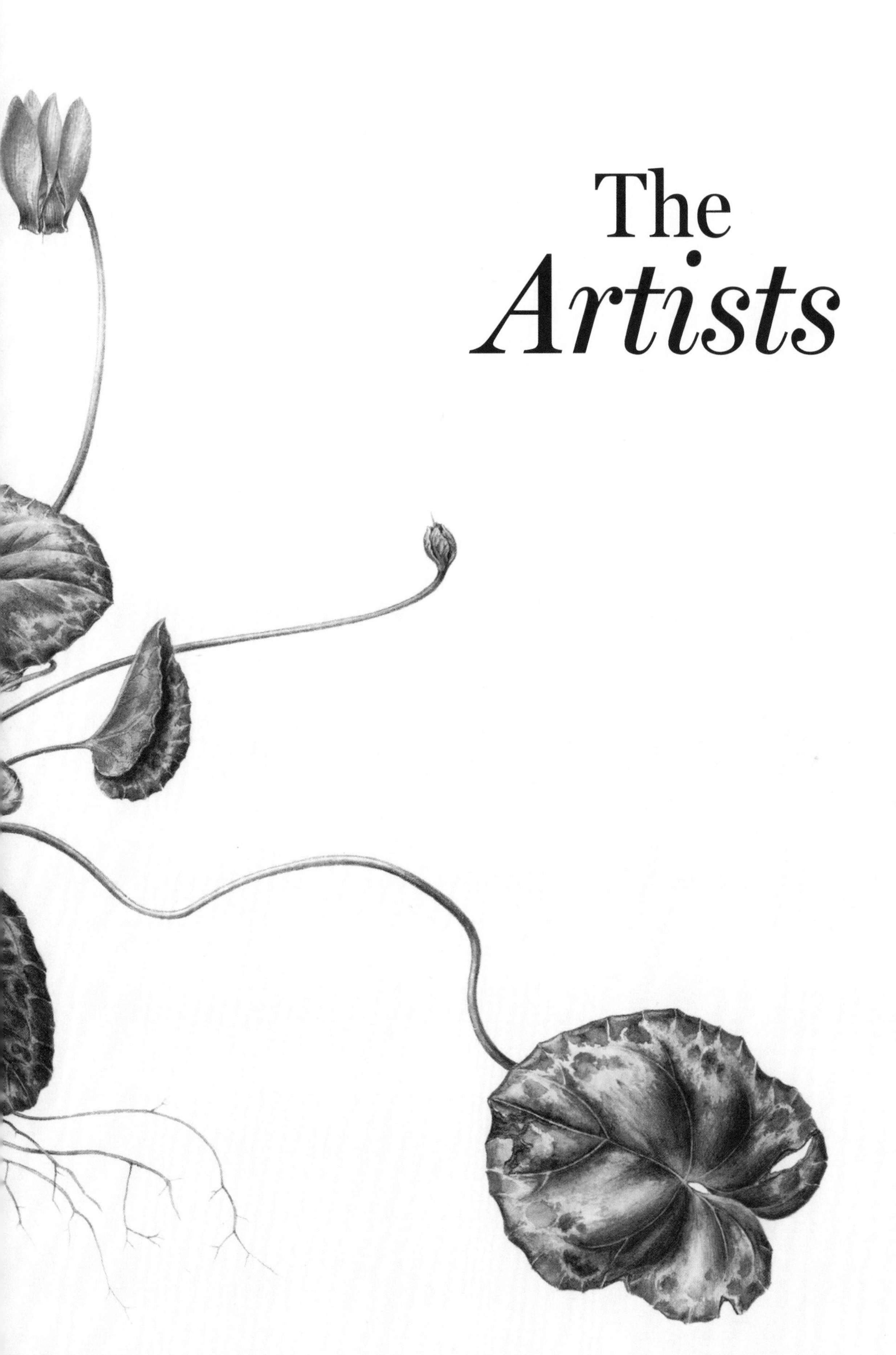

Mariko Aikawa

RHS medal history

Gold medals: 2016 (and Best Botanical Art Exhibit), 2021

Mariko Aikawa took up botanical painting in 2004, following a career as a translator and interpreter in Tokyo. She became a member of the UK-based Society of Botanical Artists in 2009 and has exhibited with them on a number of occasions. In 2016, she was awarded a Gold medal and Best Botanical Art Exhibit with the RHS for her series of paintings of *Tillandsia*.

The genus *Tillandsia* is a favourite of Aikawa's; she grows them at home or sources specimens from a local nursery. Having turned to botanical art after her family had grown up, she is now dedicated to painting. These incredible air plants offer the perfect opportunity to study the specimen from bloom to root. Heavily scented, they flower extensively over several weeks. *Tillandsia straminea* is renowned for being one of the most impressive and prolific of all air plants, increasing in size with each subsequent generation. This particular painting is one of the largest watercolours in the library collection, painted at life-size on paper measuring 100cm x 64cm.

Tillandsia straminea, 2014

Watercolour on paper

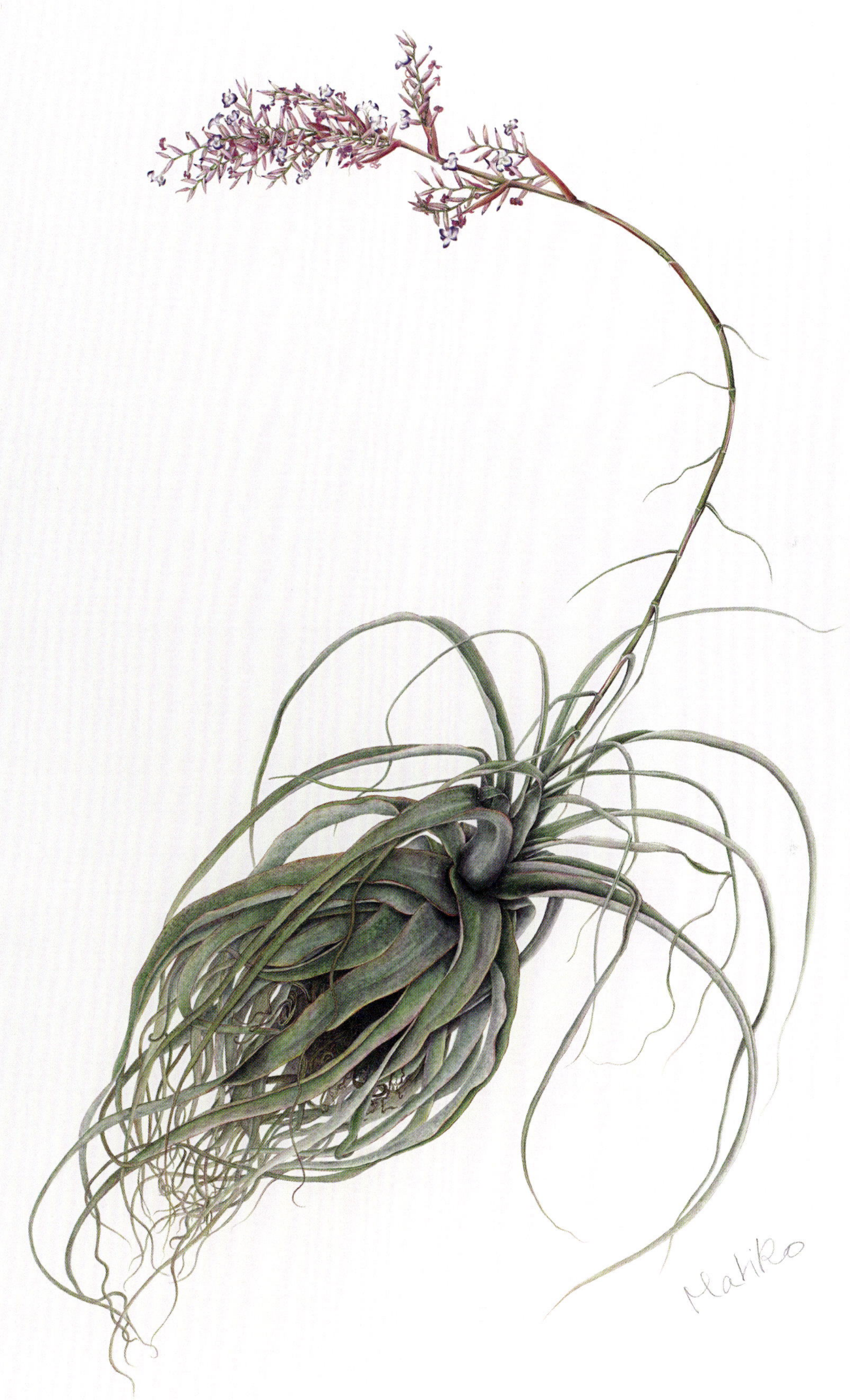
Makiko

Gillian Barlow

RHS medal history

Gold medals: 1994, 1997

Joint Gold medal with Ann Swan and Pauline Dean: March 1999

Silver-Gilt medal: 1991

Gold Veitch Memorial medal: 2015

Gillian Barlow studied at the Slade School of Fine Art and later gained an MA in Art History at the University of Sussex. Following her passion for plants, she has focused on botanical illustration for the past 30 years. Exhibitions in the UK, USA and India, contributions to publications such as *The New Plantsman* and *Curtis's Botanical Magazine*, and many teaching commitments have confirmed her position in the botanical art world. Barlow also undertook the role of assistant artist for the RHS Orchid Committee for several years, before becoming a member of the RHS Picture Committee. Barlow continues to serve as Chair of the Picture Panel, judging exhibitions of botanical art at RHS shows and offering invaluable feedback. She was awarded a Gold Veitch Memorial Medal in 2015, in recognition of her outstanding contribution to the advancement of the science and practice of horticulture, through botanical art.

Drimys winteri, 2007

Watercolour on paper

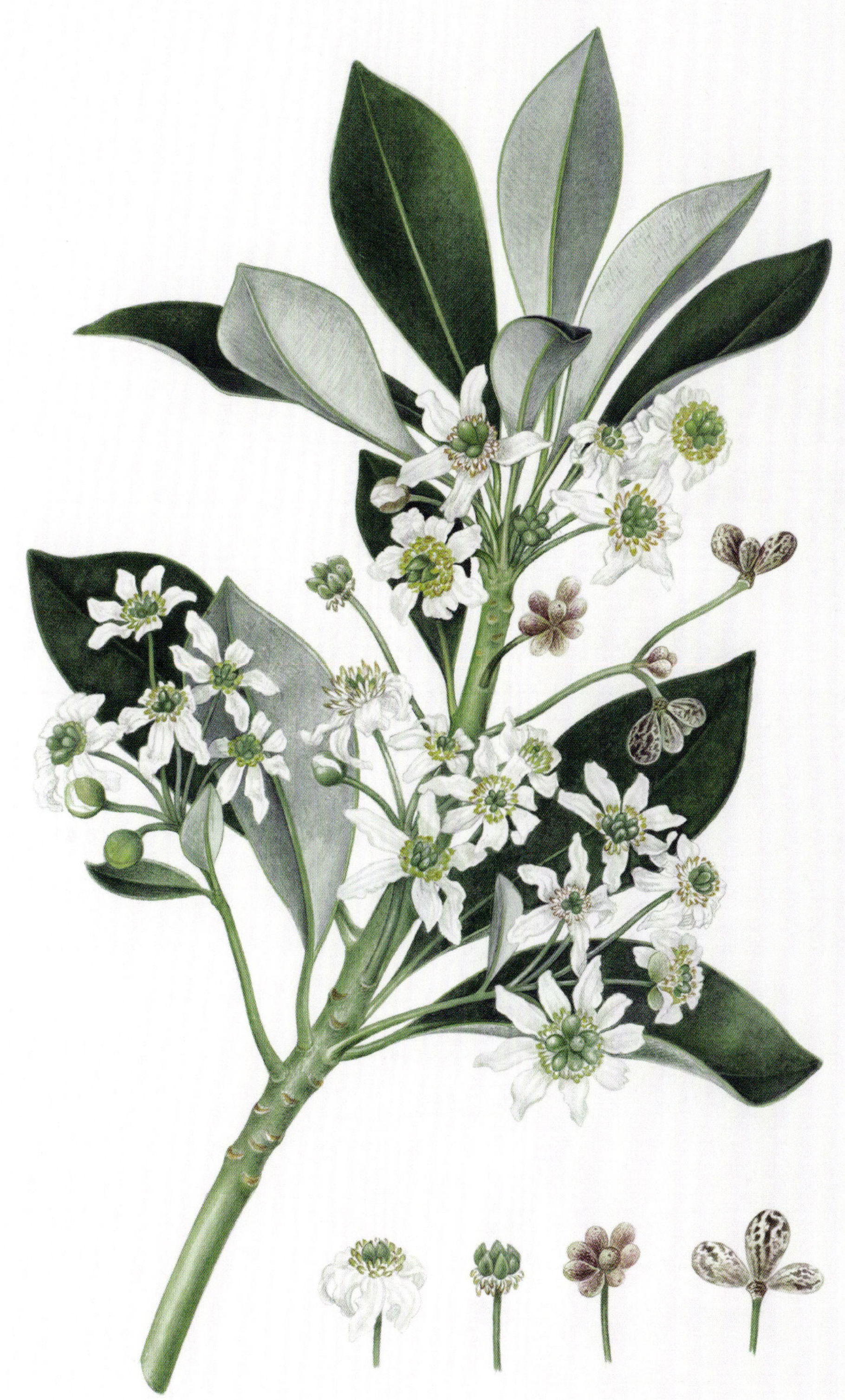

GB 2007 *Drimys winteri*

"This bushy plant, Paeonia potaninii, *required considerable editing of the masses of leaves, removing many stems to reveal an underlying structure without losing the sense of there being lots of foliage relative to the number of rather small flowers. Positions of removed leaf stalks are suggested. The flower colour was an unusual pinkish bronze, difficult to match without making it dull. Exploratory drawings and colour notes go into the sketchbook, then some rough layouts. Pieces of plant may be drawn on tracing paper, and coloured cut-out sketches of flowers at various stages can be placed on the layouts (in positions appropriate to growth pattern!) as aids to laying out a complex subject, and to establish some sort of composition before drawing the plant directly onto the painting paper. I draw freehand, rather than using tracings or a light-box, as this keeps a sense of risk and liveliness often lost when tracings are used. The plant is lightly drawn, with no details, as guidance for placing the subject on the paper. I block in various areas with light or dark colour to suggest 3-D form, going straight for the correct colours, not using thin washes first. I do not build up colour gradually, but go for it directly. Most of the work is done with a dry brush on top of the blocked in areas. Sometimes whole areas can be washed out if the tonal balance gets muddled. The finished painting must be clearly in my mind before I start using colour. If it is not in my mind, I do more preparatory sketches and layouts until I can visualise the end product. Of course, the painting also takes its own direction as I go, but the overall conception remains."*

Paeonia potaninii, 2009

Watercolour on paper

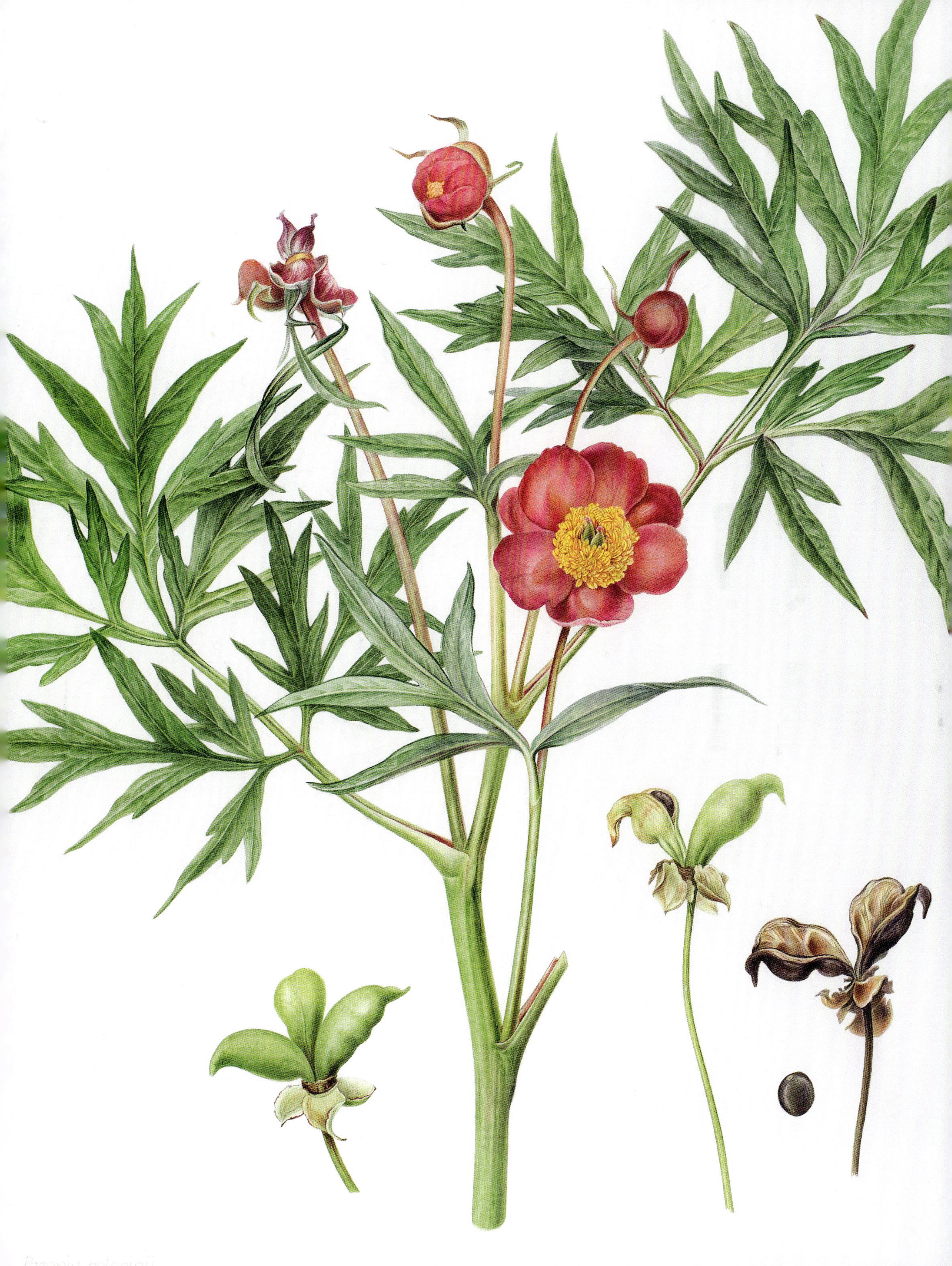

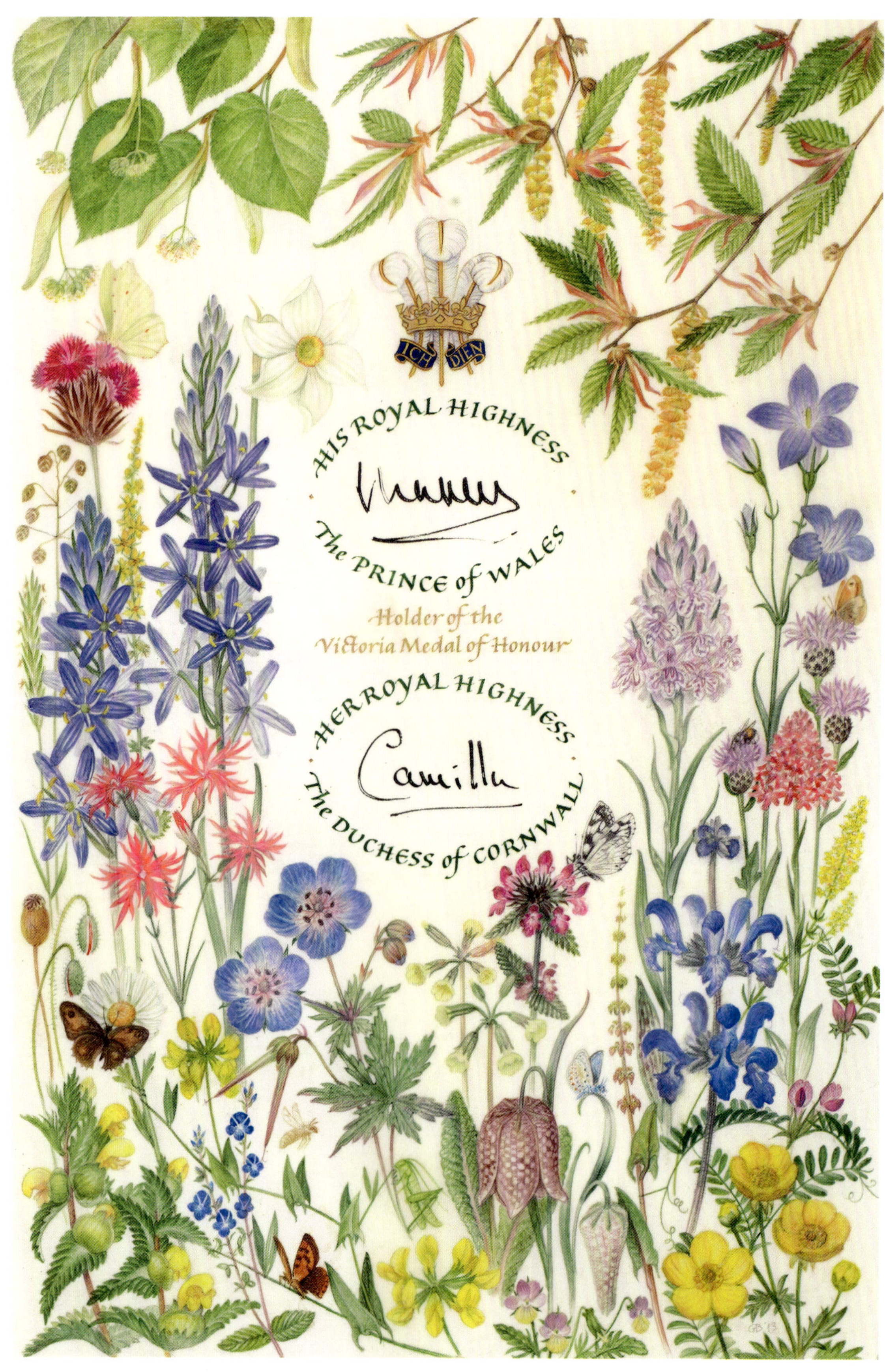

HRH Prince Charles and HRH The Duchess of Cornwall, 2013

Watercolour on vellum

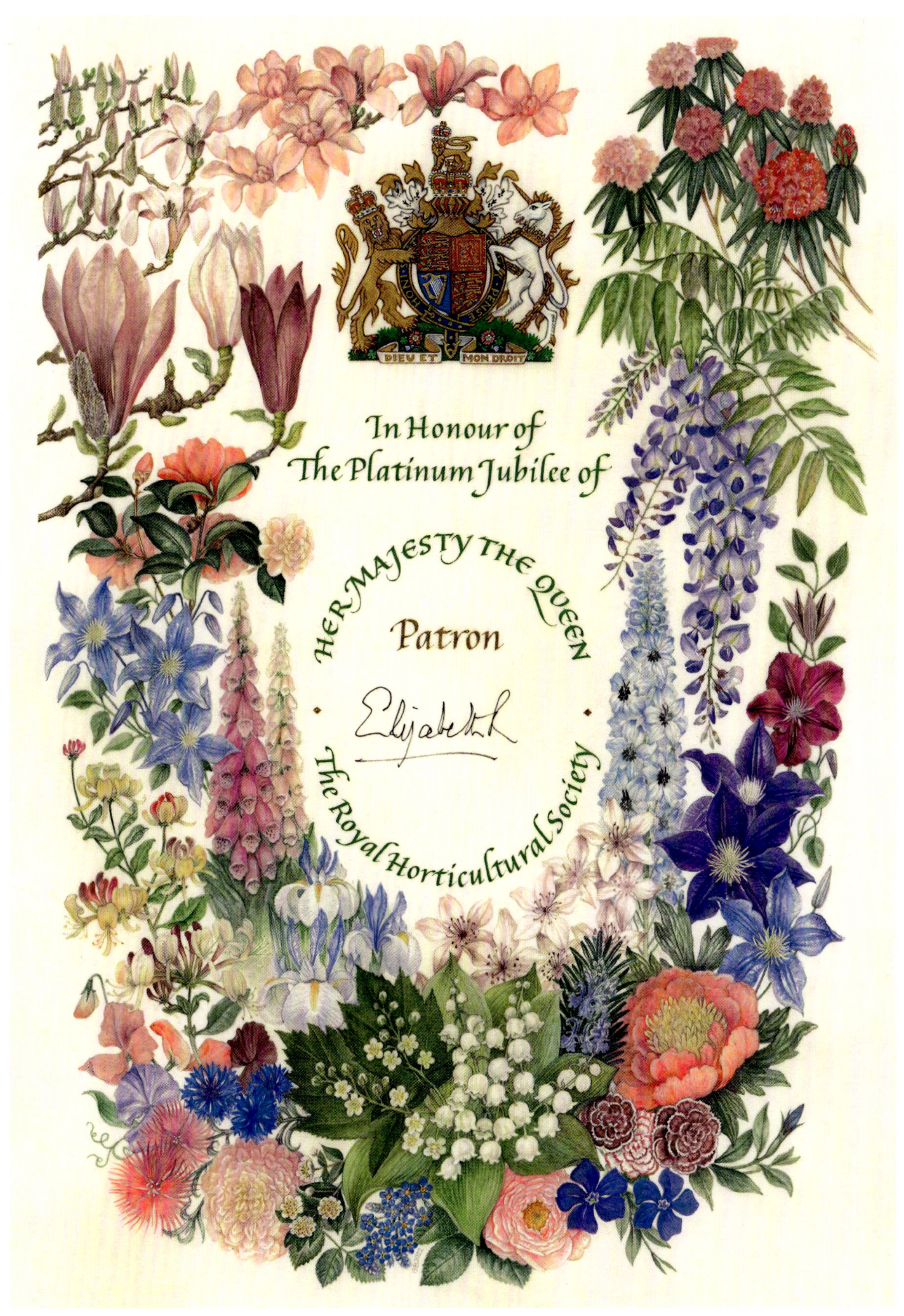

HM Queen Elizabeth II, Platinum Jubilee, 2022

Watercolour on vellum

Bernard F. Carter

RHS medal history

Gold medals: 2012, 2017 (and Best Botanical Art Exhibit)

Silver-Gilt medals: 2010, 2013, 2021

Silver medals: 2004, 2019

Bernard Carter first exhibited in 2004 at the BBC's *Gardeners' World* live show at the NEC in Birmingham, and was awarded a Silver medal. He went on to exhibit at the RHS Malvern Spring Festival in 2010, 2012, 2013, and then again in 2017.

This painting was exhibited as part of a group of paintings entitled 'Seed Heads', at RHS Malvern Spring Festival in 2017. Having chosen seed heads as a subject to paint in 2016, because of the way the light plays through them in late autumn, the challenge was then to find and complete the series in time for exhibition in May 2017.

"I would paint as much as possible in one day, take photographs, press a leaf, and do paint colour coding, which enabled me to pick up the painting at any time in the future. I began the sessions in a gazebo tent by the river in my garden, something I found very conducive, surrounded, as I was, by the sounds of nature and flowing water; and finished them the following spring in my temporary studio. 'Meadowsweet' is one of my favourite flowers, with its scented frothy heads the colour of champagne. Vast clumps of them grow in an abandoned quarry, now a nature reserve, on the hillside above my cottage."

Filipendula ulmaria, September 2016–March 2017

Watercolour on paper

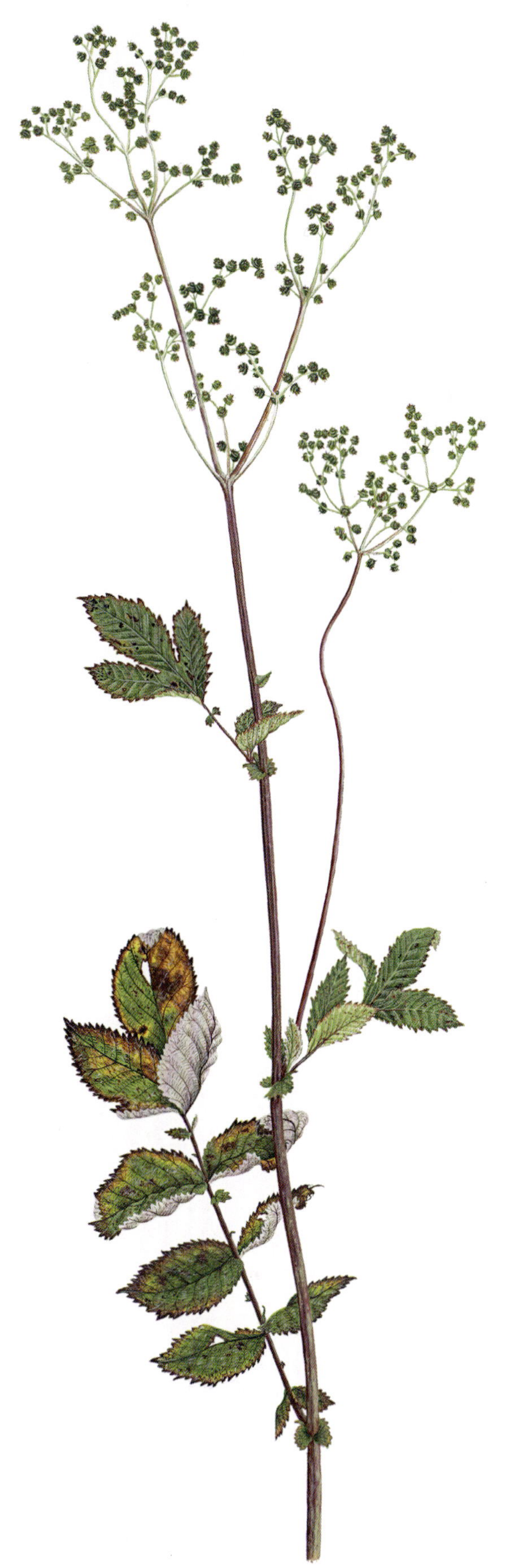

Hyunjin Cho

RHS medal history

Gold medal: 2024

Silver medal: 2022

Hyunjin Cho graduated as a Master of Craft Design Education in 2004, from Kyung Hee University Graduate School of Education, in Seoul, South Korea. Following a move to the United States, Cho undertook the Filoli botanical art certificate course in California, between 2019 and 2021. Her work has been regularly exhibited in South Korea, the USA, UK and online. Cho has gained numerous awards including Highly Commended and Artist's Choice for the Margaret Flockton Award and her drawing was selected for the University of California Botanical Garden Florilegium, all in 2022. In 2024, she was awarded a Gold medal by the RHS for her pen and ink drawings of 'Succulents studied in Stippling'.

"I've been captivated by drawing old succulents lately, marvelling at their resilience and unique shapes. Opting for black ink, I aimed to emphasise form over colour, using stippled drawing to build texture and depth. Maintaining an orderly pattern within their complexity proved challenging yet rewarding. Despite the time-consuming process, it brought a sense of peace and tranquillity. My hope is that viewers will appreciate the magnificence of these plants while finding comfort in the artwork's serene portrayal."

Tillandsia xerographica, 2024

Pen-and-ink stipple drawing on paper

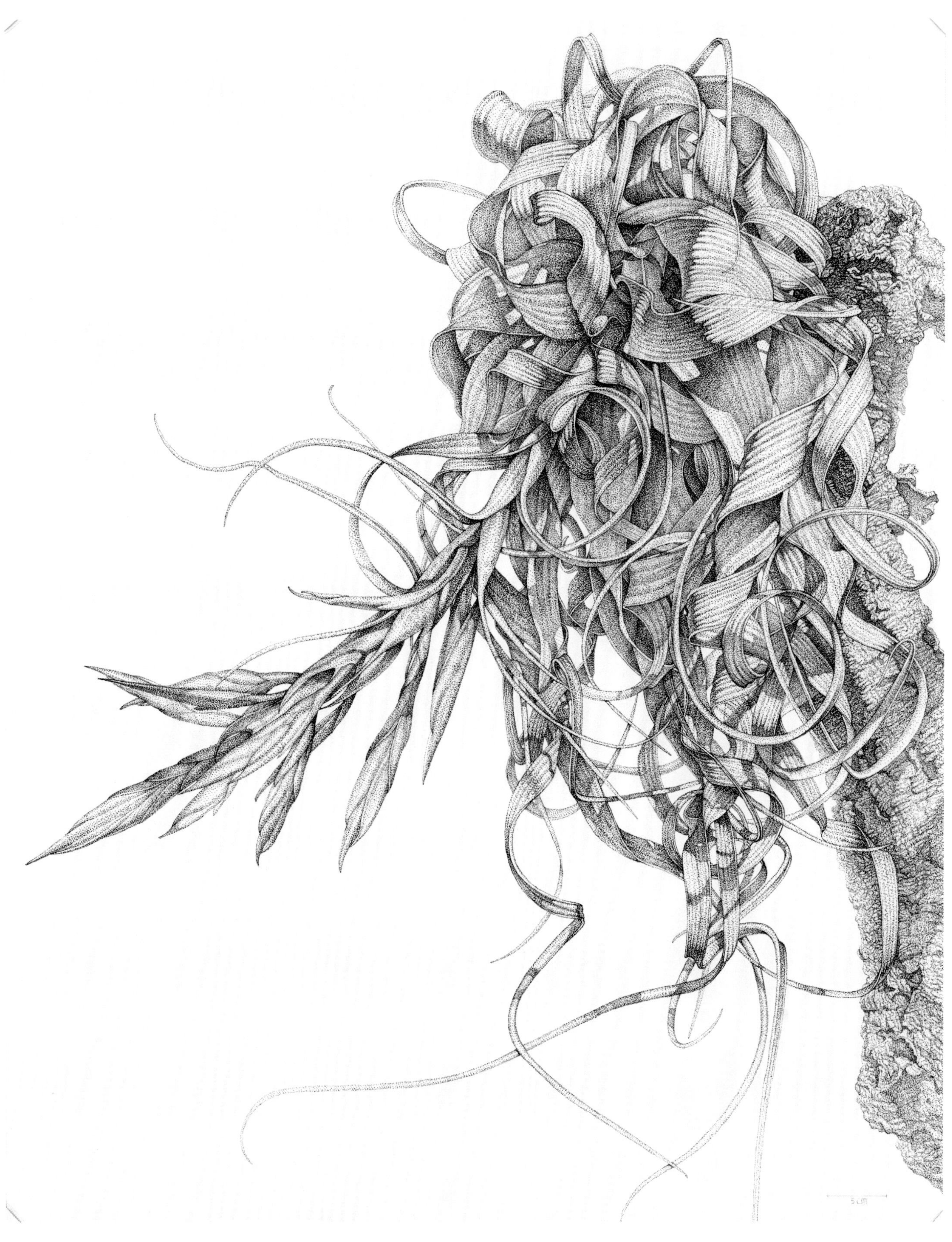
5 cm

Susan Christopher-Coulson

RHS medal history

Gold medals: 1999, 2001

Susan Christopher-Coulson first exhibited with the RHS in 1999, for which she was awarded a Gold medal; another followed two years later. She prefers to work in coloured pencil and was an early proponent of it for botanical art. This versatile medium has gained in popularity amongst botanical artists since Miss Cox first exhibited in coloured pencil at the RHS in 1986.

The fruits depicted in this piece were all grown in the artist's garden in Lancashire; she often finds inspiration from plants she has nurtured herself or found in the local countryside. This piece is typical of Christopher-Coulson's graphic composition, in which specimens are placed alongside one another as though just picked from the garden, to allow for a comparison of size, texture and shape. Each piece of fruit, or cluster, is grounded by shadow, to help accentuate the form and prevent them from appearing to 'float free'.

Christopher-Coulson is an experienced botanical art tutor, who has contributed to the Distance Learning Diploma Course for the Society of Botanical Artists. Committed to supporting the SBA, she became Vice President in 2010 and won a number of prestigious awards. Christopher-Coulson also teaches workshops at various venues, including RHS Garden Wisley, and has recently attended the RHS London Botanical Art Shows demonstrating her technique.

'In Celebration of Summer Garden Fruits', *c.*2011

Coloured pencil on paper

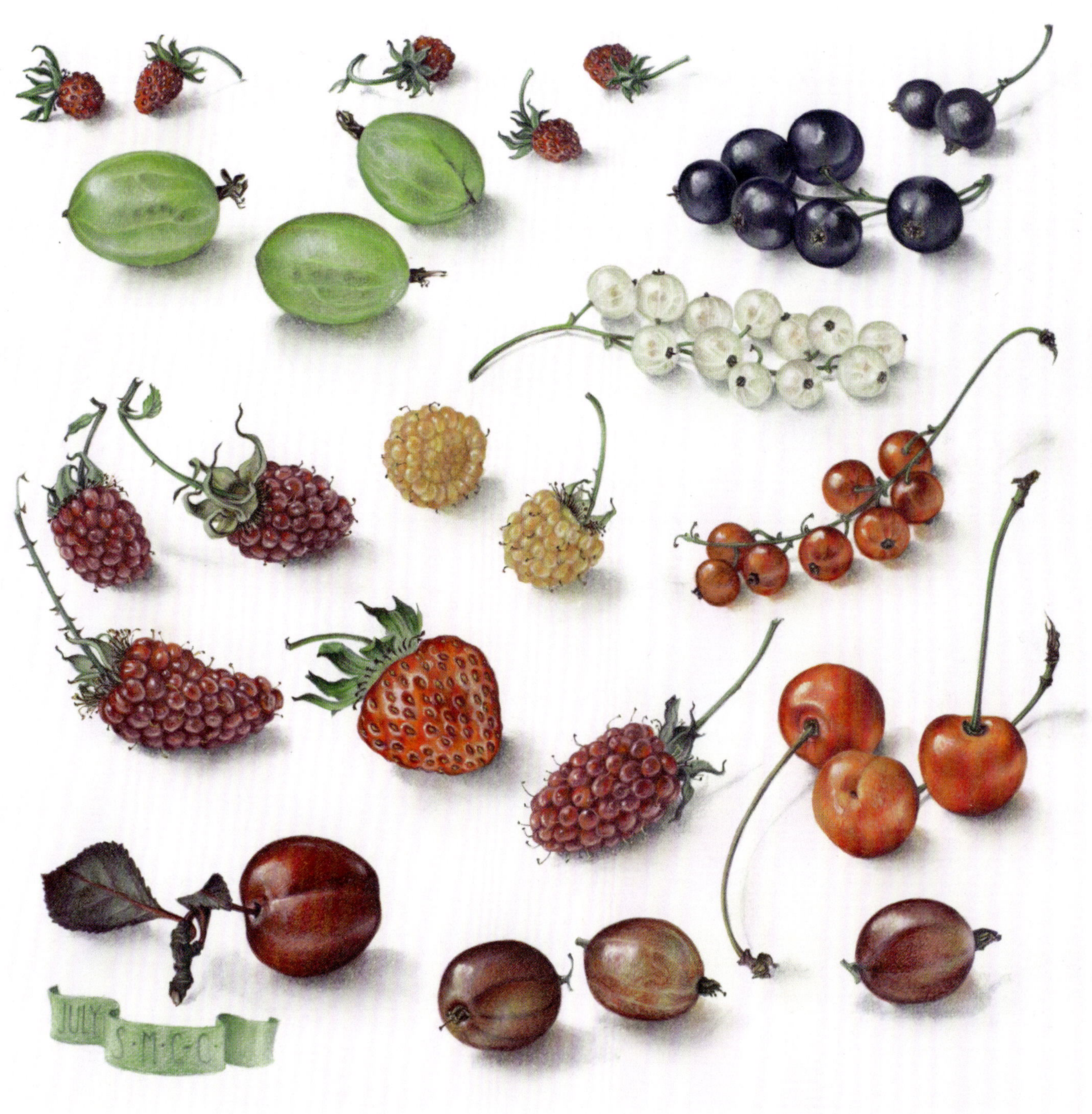
JULY
S·M·C·C·

Samantha Cook

RHS medal history

Gold medal: 2006

Samantha Cook exhibited her botanical art works for the first time at the RHS in 2006, with a display of 'Exotic Fruits in Watercolour'. Having previously followed a career in textile design, she adapted her drawing technique to complete the Botanical Illustration Diploma Course at The English Gardening School, where she was tutored by Anne-Marie Evans.

This distinctive composition features both graphite and a limited colour palette of watercolour, which enabled her to highlight the texture and structure of the dragon fruit. Cook has incorporated many of the traditional elements of botanical illustration, with cross-sections and magnifications, in a strikingly contemporary design. The placement of different observational angles of the fruit around the central cross-section, allows for a detailed analysis of its form. The absence of foliage or branches is a deliberate choice to create a clean, stark image.

Selenicereus megalanthus, 2002

Graphite and water colour on paper

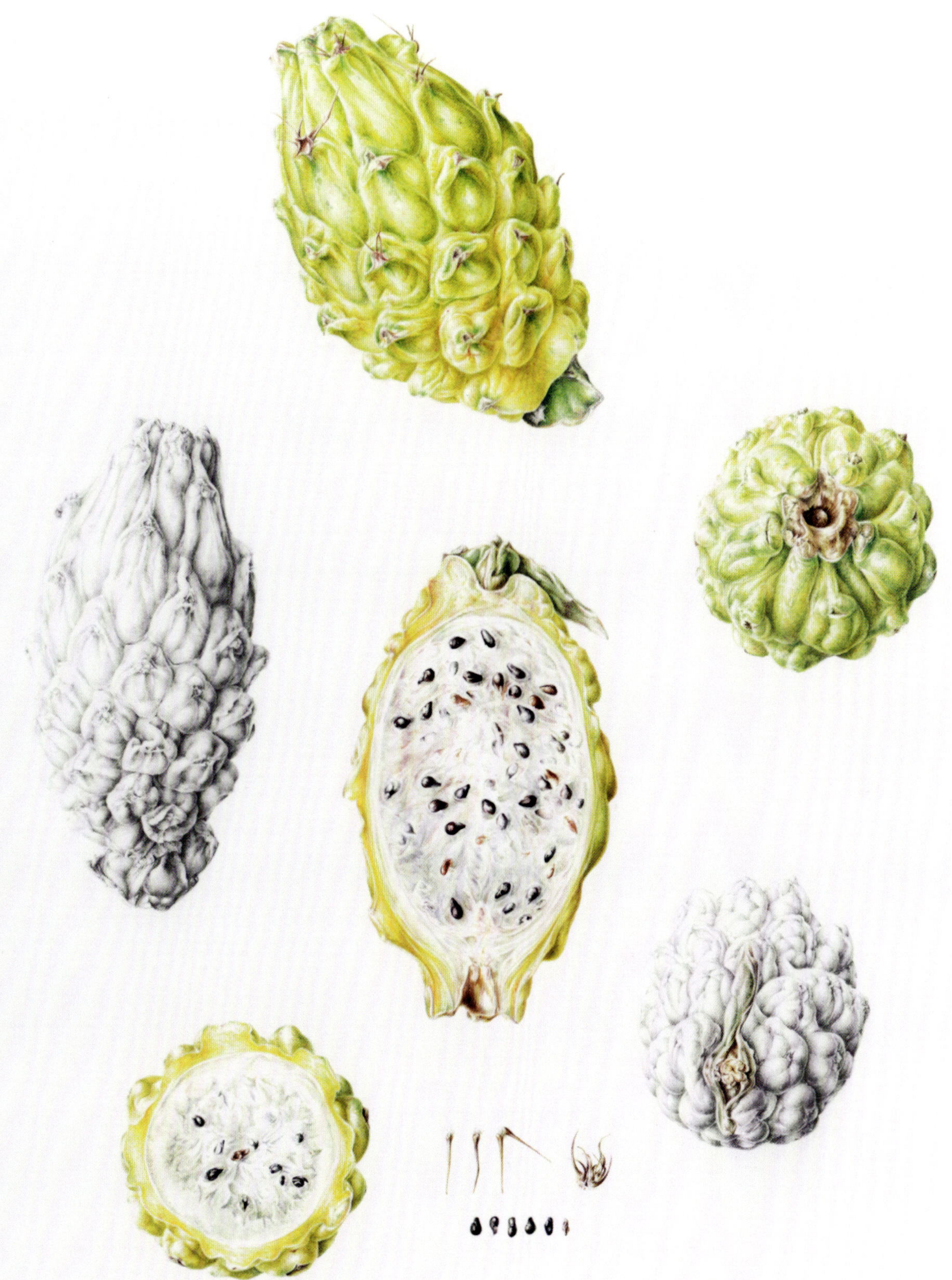

Sally Crosthwaite
(1944–2017)

RHS medal history

Gold medal: 2001

Silver medals: 1998, 2008

Sally Crosthwaite was one of the founding members of The Chelsea Physic Garden Florilegium Society, formed in 1995. Having studied under Anne-Marie Evans, she then gained a distinction for the Diploma Course of Botanical Illustration from the English Gardening School. Crosthwaite was first awarded a Silver medal by the RHS in 1998; she went on to win a Gold medal in 2001 for 'Watercolour paintings of *Iridaceae*'. Two of the paintings from this display were subsequently purchased for the Lindley Collections and are featured here.

With the painting of *Gladiolus murielae,* Crosthwaite adopted an established technique for illustrating white flowers on a white background, by setting them against dark green foliage. By arranging the composition in such a way, the artist minimises the amount of pigment that is required, using the white of the paper to provide the base colour for the flower, then adding a colour wash and specific detail as required.

Crosthwaite's work was exhibited all over the world, and she also enjoyed commercial success with images of her paintings being reproduced on decorative homeware, fine china and a range of greeting cards.

Gladiolus murielae (syn: *Gladiolus callianthus*), 2001

Watercolour on paper

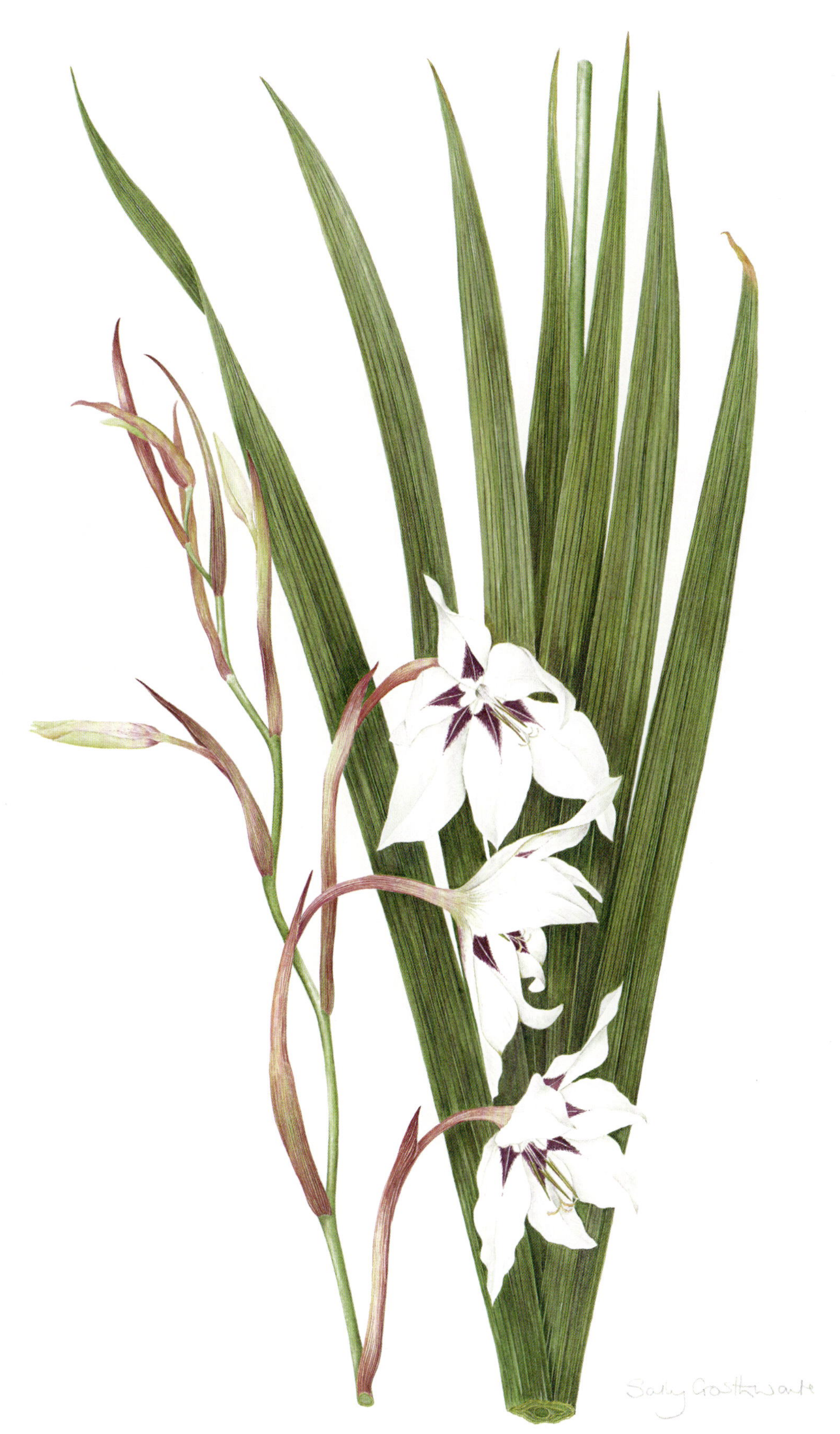
Sally Crosthwaite

Gladiolus communis subsp. *byzantinus*, 2001

Watercolour on paper

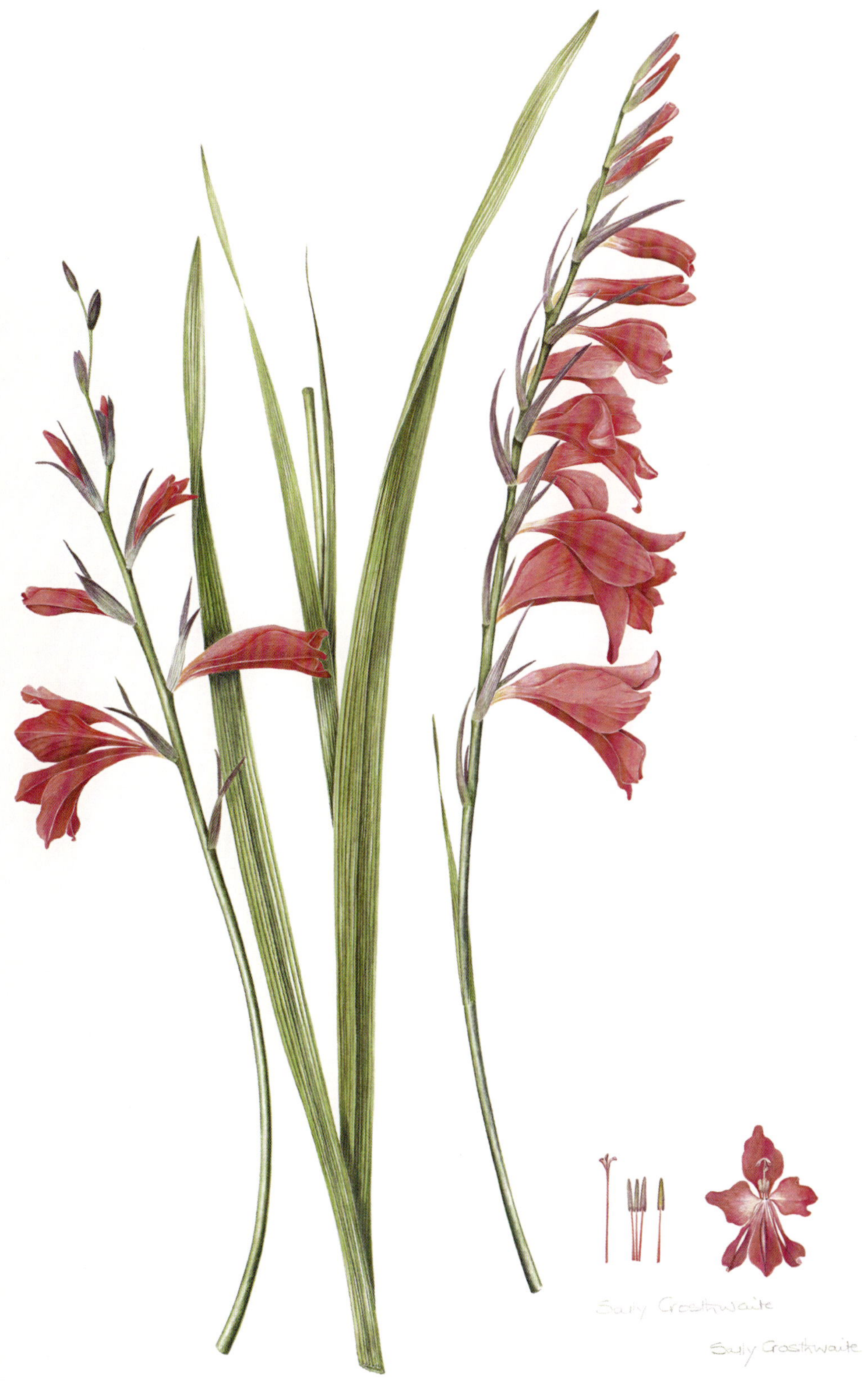

Iradaceae - gladiolus communis
subsp byzantinus

Brigitte Daniel

RHS medal history

Gold medals: 1998, 1999, 2001, 2003, 2005, 2007, 2010, 2012 (and Best Exhibit)

Silver-Gilt medal: 2000

Silver medal: 1997

Brigitte Daniel exhibited with the RHS on ten occasions between 1998 and 2012. During this period she was awarded a total of eight Gold medals, in addition to being judged the Best Exhibit at the RHS Malvern Spring Festival in 2012. Daniel has a long-held fascination for *Primula auriculas* and she has returned to them as a favourite subject to paint over many years. Three of the illustrations featured here were produced as part of a group of ten 'show auriculas' that Daniel exhibited at the RHS in 2007. She described them as the *"latest chapter painted from my collection of these fascinating plants."*

The works held in the Lindley Collections demonstrate Daniel's versatility as an artist, tackling single specimens as well as complex group compositions. With exceptional control, Daniel has depicted the finest markings on the auriculas. The pale grey fringe contrasts with the deep colour to the centre of the flower and is just visible against the white background. By comparison, the restricted colour palette of the *Solanaceae* emphasises the form and structure of the dried plants, in a far more architectural composition. *"I am very fond of that painting as it was seed pods that first caught my attention and 'botanised' me."*

Primula auricula 'Silverway', 2006

Watercolour on paper

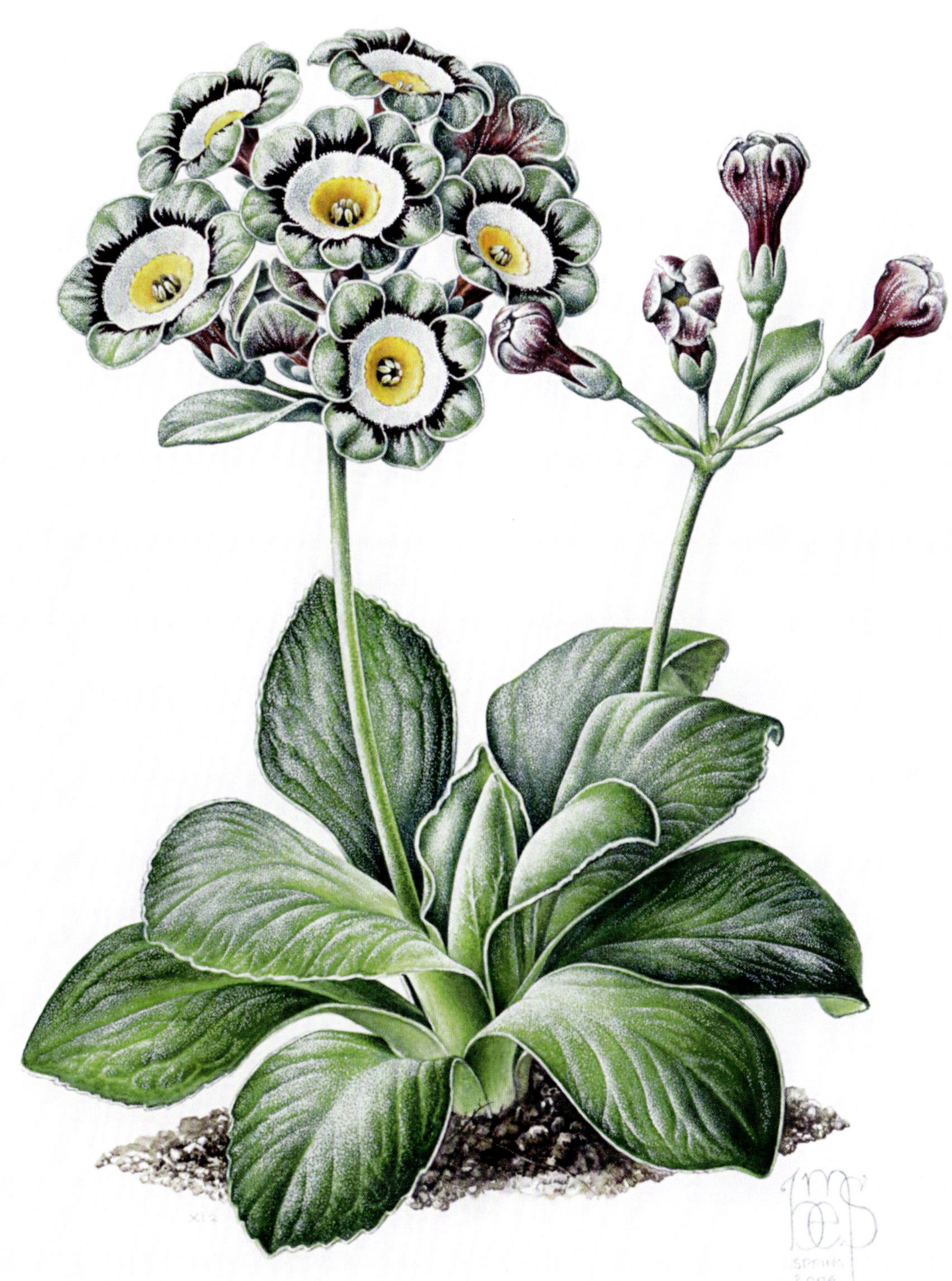

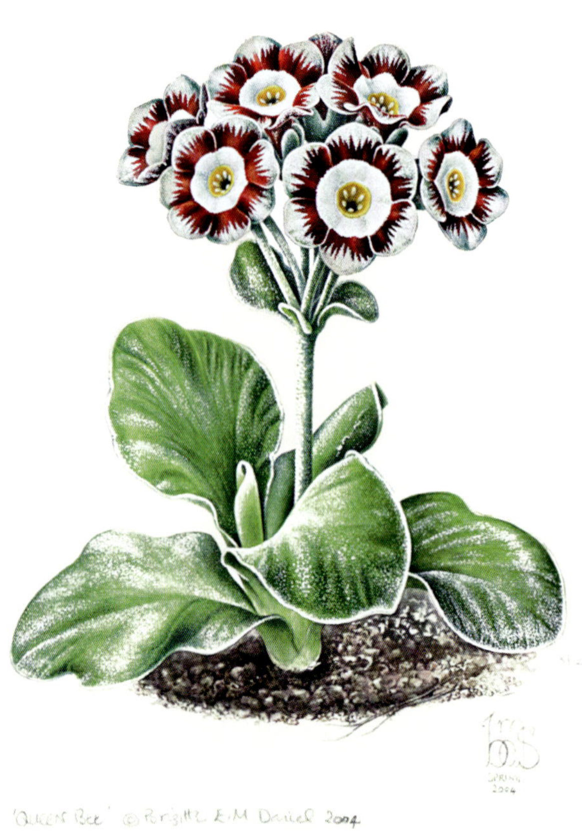

Primula auricula 'Queen Bee', 2004
Watercolour on paper

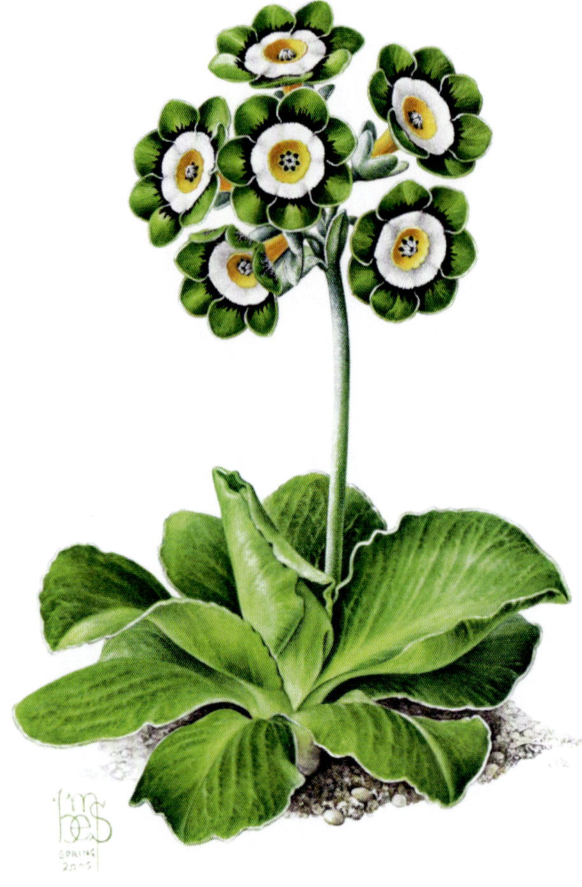

Primula auricula 'Prague', 2005
Watercolour on paper

Daniel grew up surrounded by woodlands and developed an early fascination with the natural world. Ill health led her away from an academic career in botany to develop her skill as an artist. Amongst her many accolades, Daniel was one of the first tutors on the Society of Botanical Artists' Distance Learning Course.

'*Solanaceae* from a Winter Garden: Thorn Apple, Henbane and Nicandra', 2003
Watercolour on paper

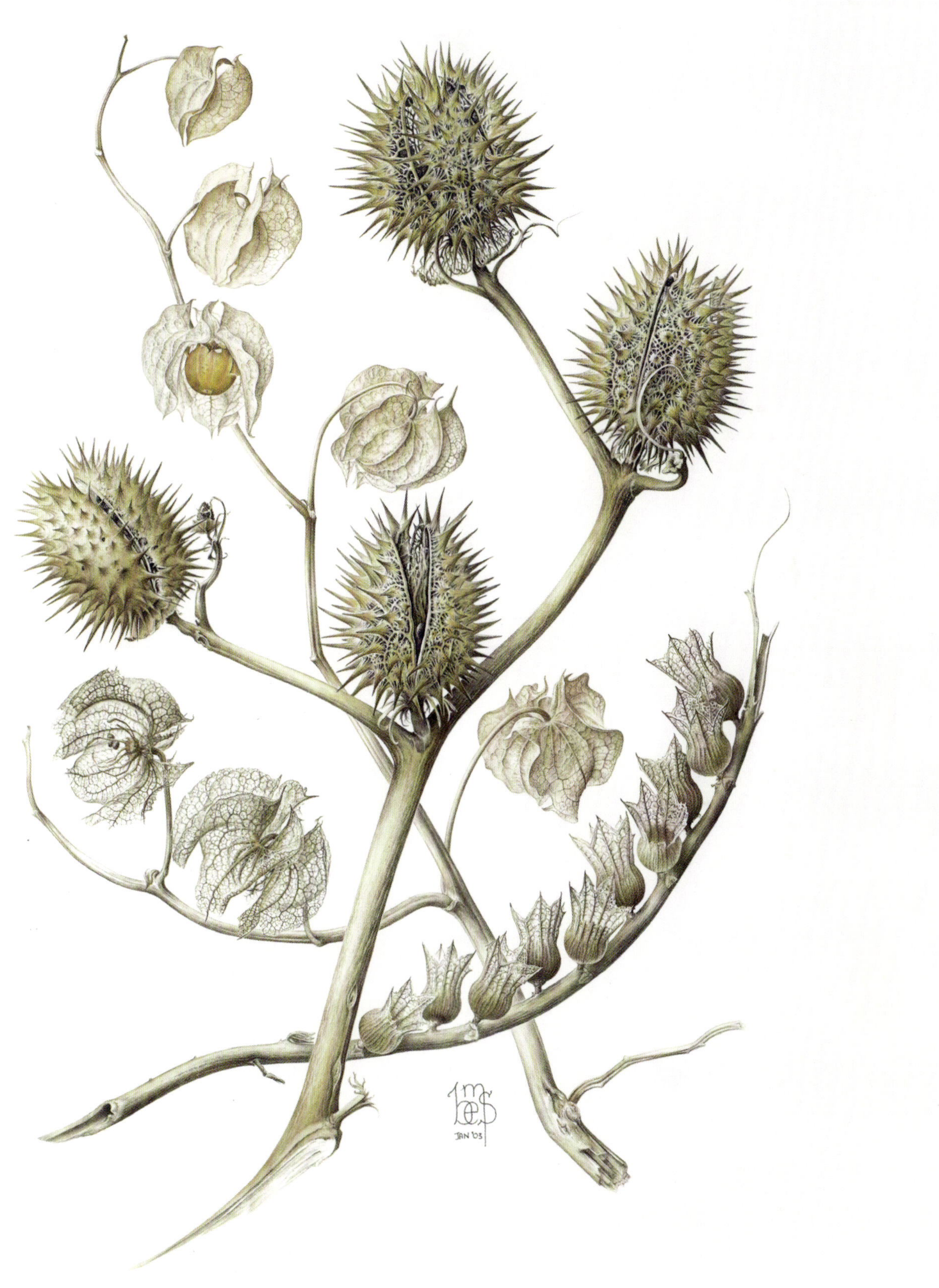

 (ADDED JAN'06 Nicandra & Henbane 2006) Thorn apple - *Datura stramonium* seed pods

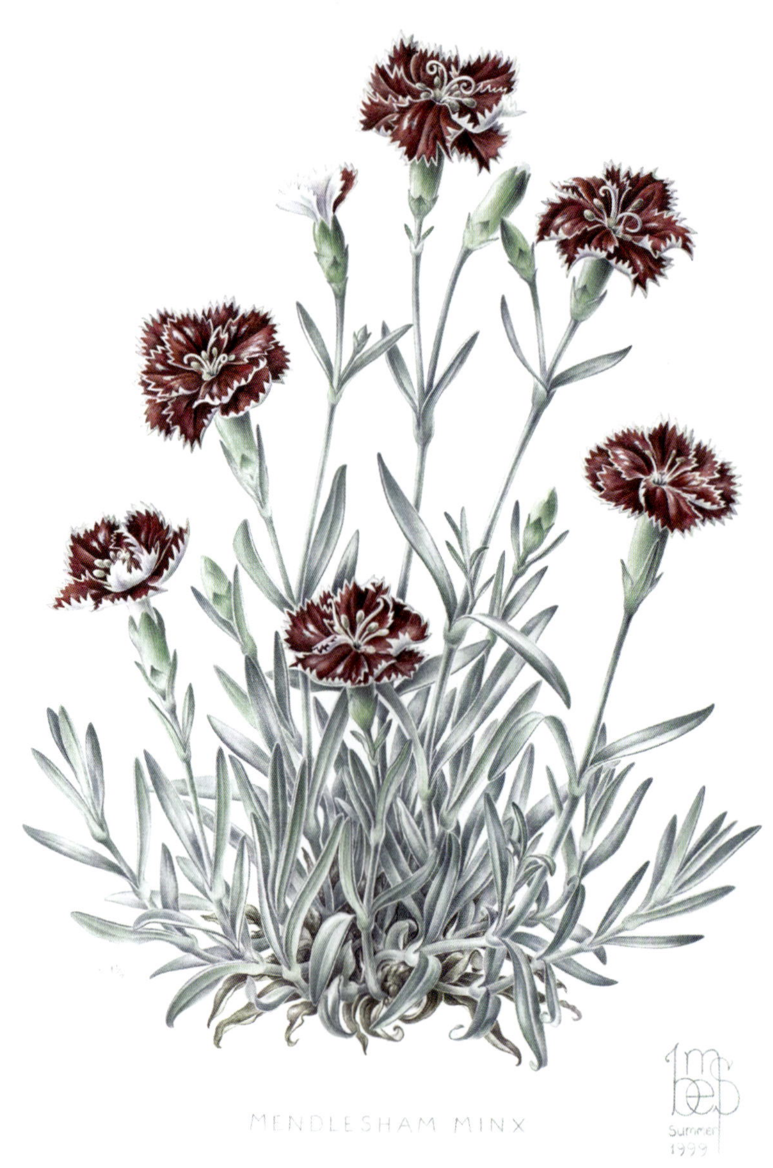

Dianthus 'Mendlesham Minx' = 'Russmin' (syn: Mendlesham Minx, pink), 1999
Watercolour on paper

Geranium wallichianum 'Buxton's Variety', 2004
Watercolour on paper

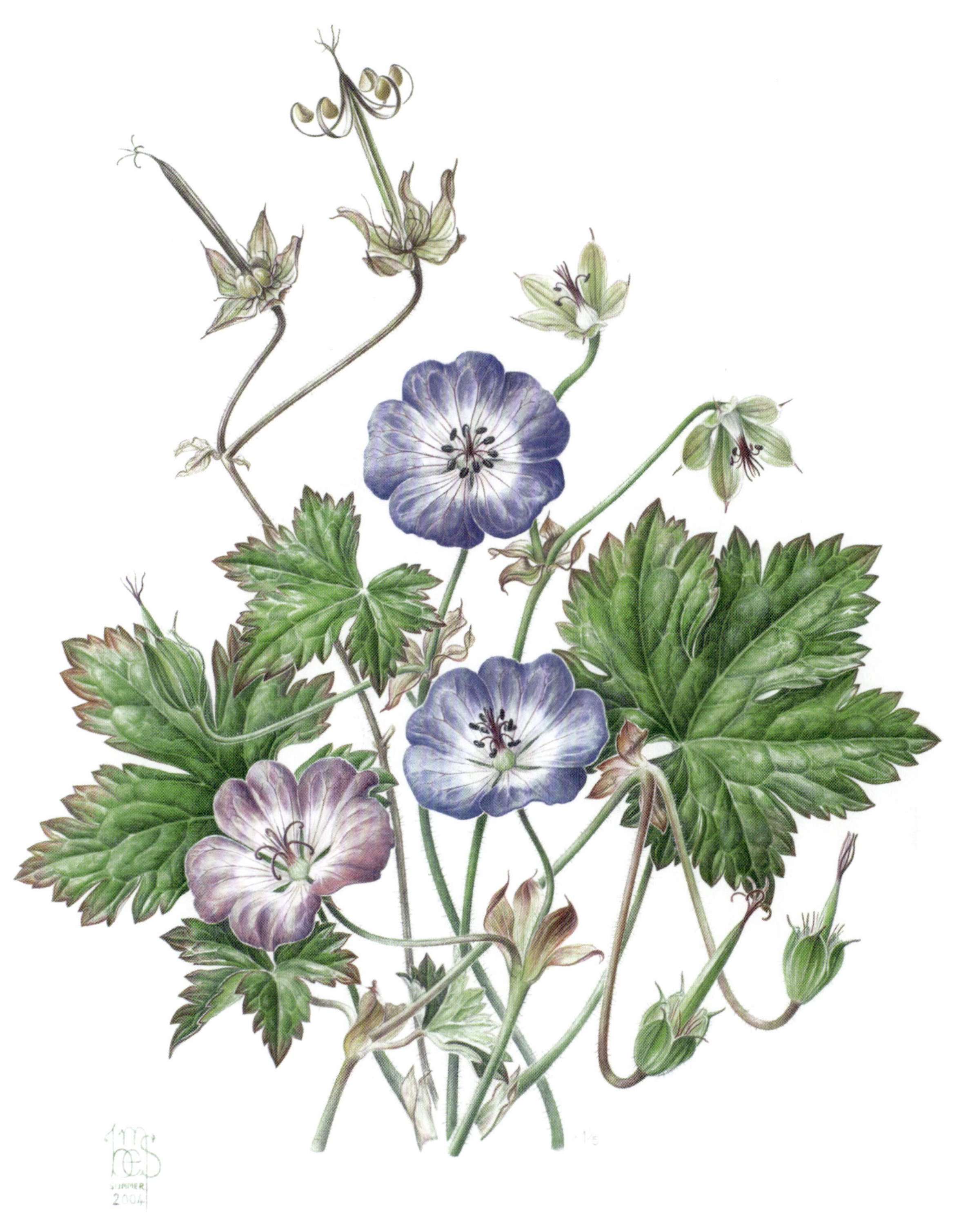
SUMMER 2004
205 x 2
Geranium wallichianum 'Buxton's variety'
© Brigitte E.M. Daniel 2004

Pauline Dean
(1943-2007)

RHS medal history

Gold medals: November 1989, February and November 1991, 1993, 1995, December 1999, 2001, 2002

Joint Gold medal with Gillian Barlow and Ann Swan: March 1999

Silver-Gilt medals: January and November 1988, 1996

Silver medal: July 1989

Pauline Dean exhibited with the RHS a total of 13 times over the course of 14 years, first winning a Silver-Gilt medal in 1988, which made her determined to try for a Gold medal. With this in mind, Dean started working on a series of Iris paintings. She was awarded a Gold medal sooner than she had expected when the following year her illustrations of fungi caught the judges' eye.[1]

She continued amassing paintings of irises. She allowed herself two years to research, study and paint, working with closely with Ray Jeffs of the British Iris Society. The resulting exhibition at the London show in 1991 was approximately eight metres long and contained 24 paintings; Dean was awarded her second Gold medal. (Artists today are limited to 5.5 metres.)

Helleborus foetidus, 1996

Watercolour on paper

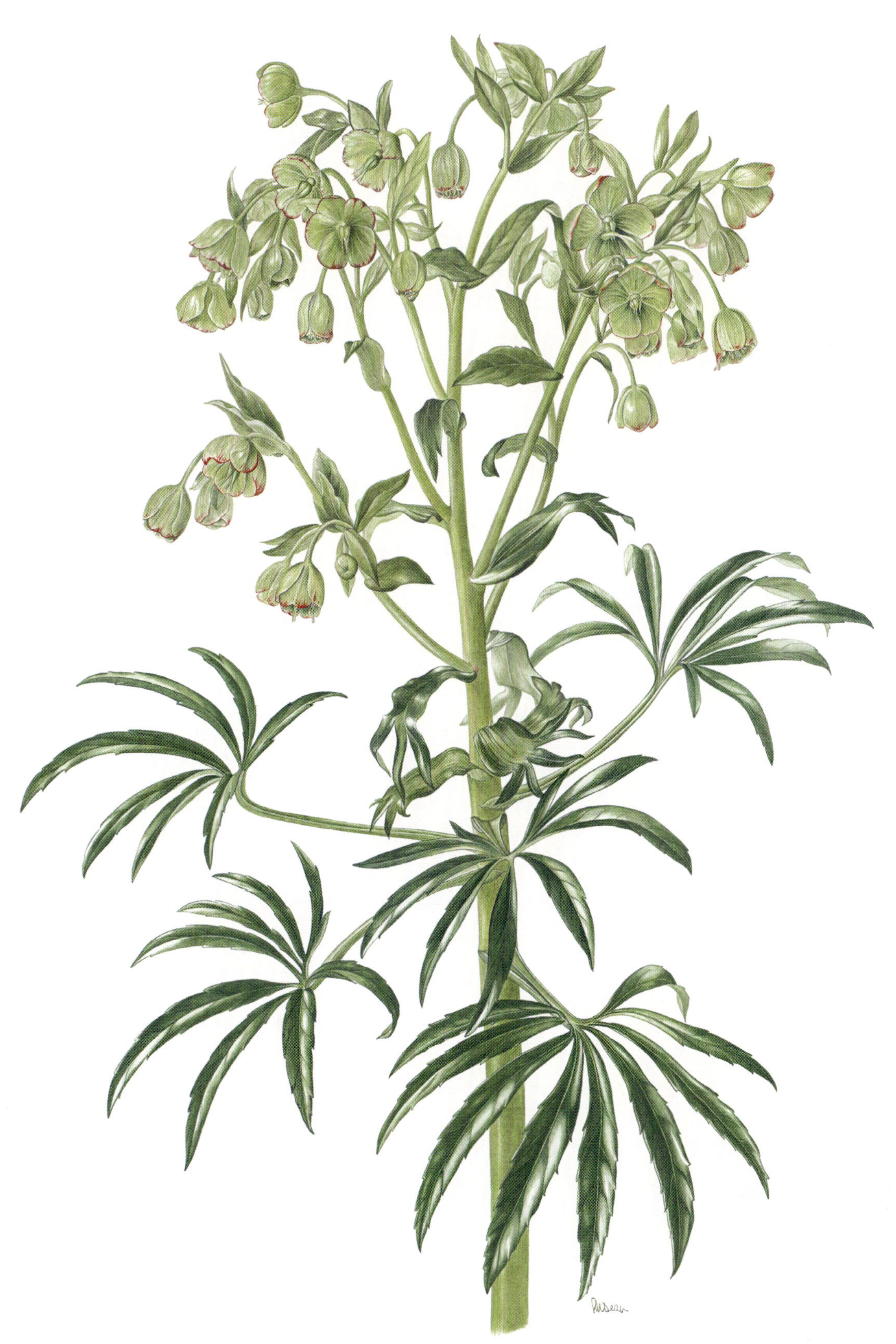

The painting of *Iris tectorum* Burma form featured here is from that impressive display. At the point of acquisition, Brent Elliott, former RHS Librarian, recalls that the artist apologised that the roots were not included, as the owner of the plant refused to let her dig it up to study them. Elliott observed that alongside the standard portrayal of the flower, with the petals twisted in their usual Iris fashion, Dean had placed some specimens of individual petals that she had ironed flat to show their scalloped shape, which is very different from how they appear in their normal habit.

Following her early success exhibiting at the London Shows, Dean was commissioned to provide illustrations for *The New Plantsman*, as well as decorative floral designs for plates by Royal Worcester. Her line drawings feature in the *RHS Dictionary of Gardening* and she was highly regarded as the botanical painting course tutor at RHS Garden Wisley for 11 years.

Iris tectorum Burma form, 1991

Watercolour on paper

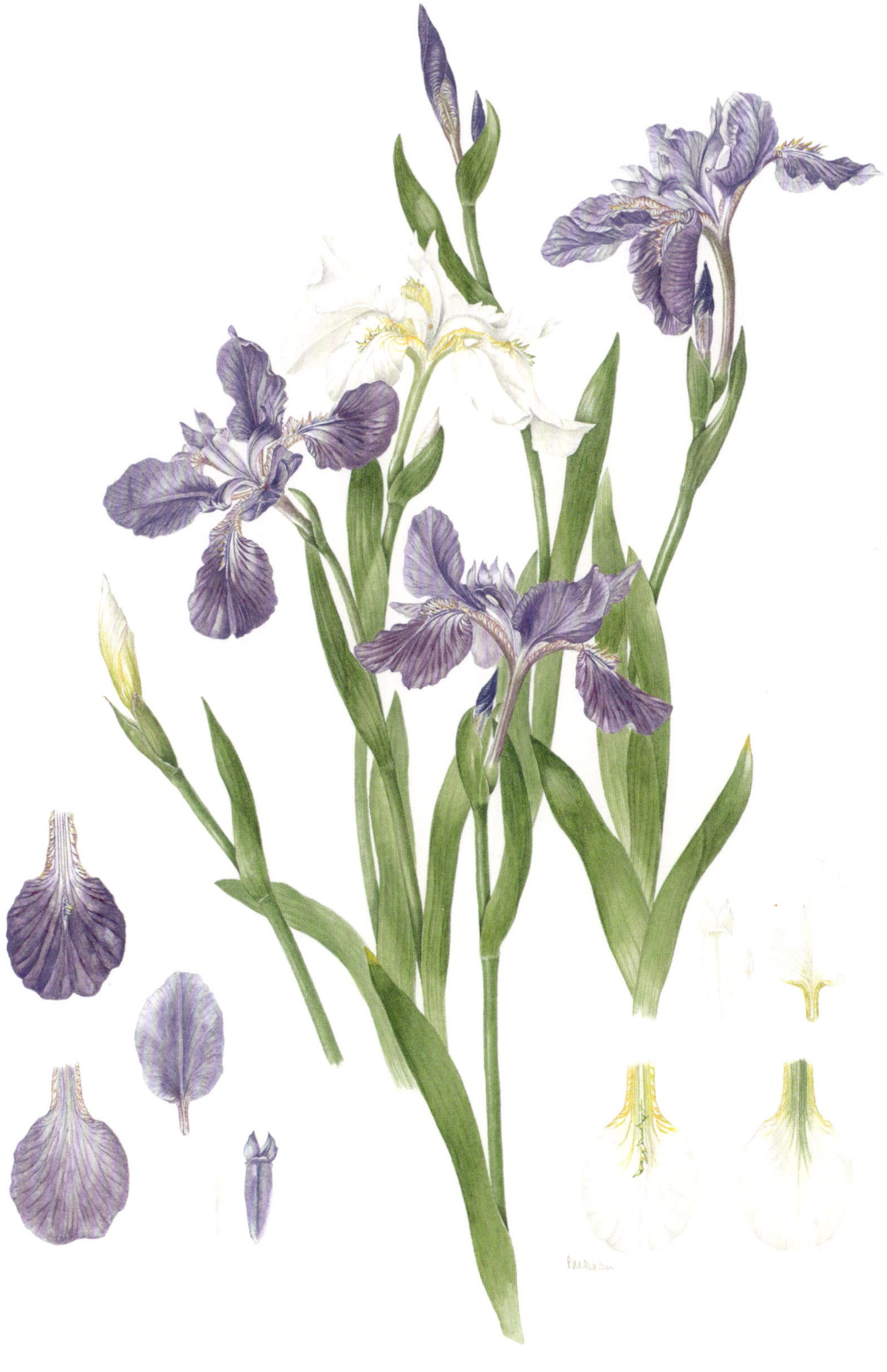

Sansanee Deekrajang

RHS medal history

Gold medal: 2016

Silver-Gilt medal: 2014

Silver medal: 2013

Sansanee Deekrajang was born in Bangkok, Thailand. She has a degree in art and early on specialised in fine art printmaking. Having a fascination for plants, Deekrajang taught herself botanical illustration and first exhibited with the RHS in 2013, for which she was awarded a Silver medal. In 2015, Deekrajang prepared her set of six pictures for exhibition; unfortunately, one of the paintings was damaged in transit. As a minimum of six paintings is required, her exhibit could not be judged. Undaunted, Deekrajang returned the following year, when she was awarded a Gold medal for her display of 'Tropical Climate plants'; one of which was the painting of *Alpinia galanga* featured here.

When asked about her painting process, Deekrajang says she does not make preparatory drawings or sketches, but thinks through her composition, planning it all in her mind before starting work. This is all the more impressive as her composition is awe-inspiringly complicated, incorporating all the traditional elements of botanical art in a sophisticated arrangement. The colour change of the leaves reveals crucial information about the health of the plant, showing what it looks when suffering from a lack of nutrients.

Alpinia galanga (Thai ginger), 2015

Watercolour on paper

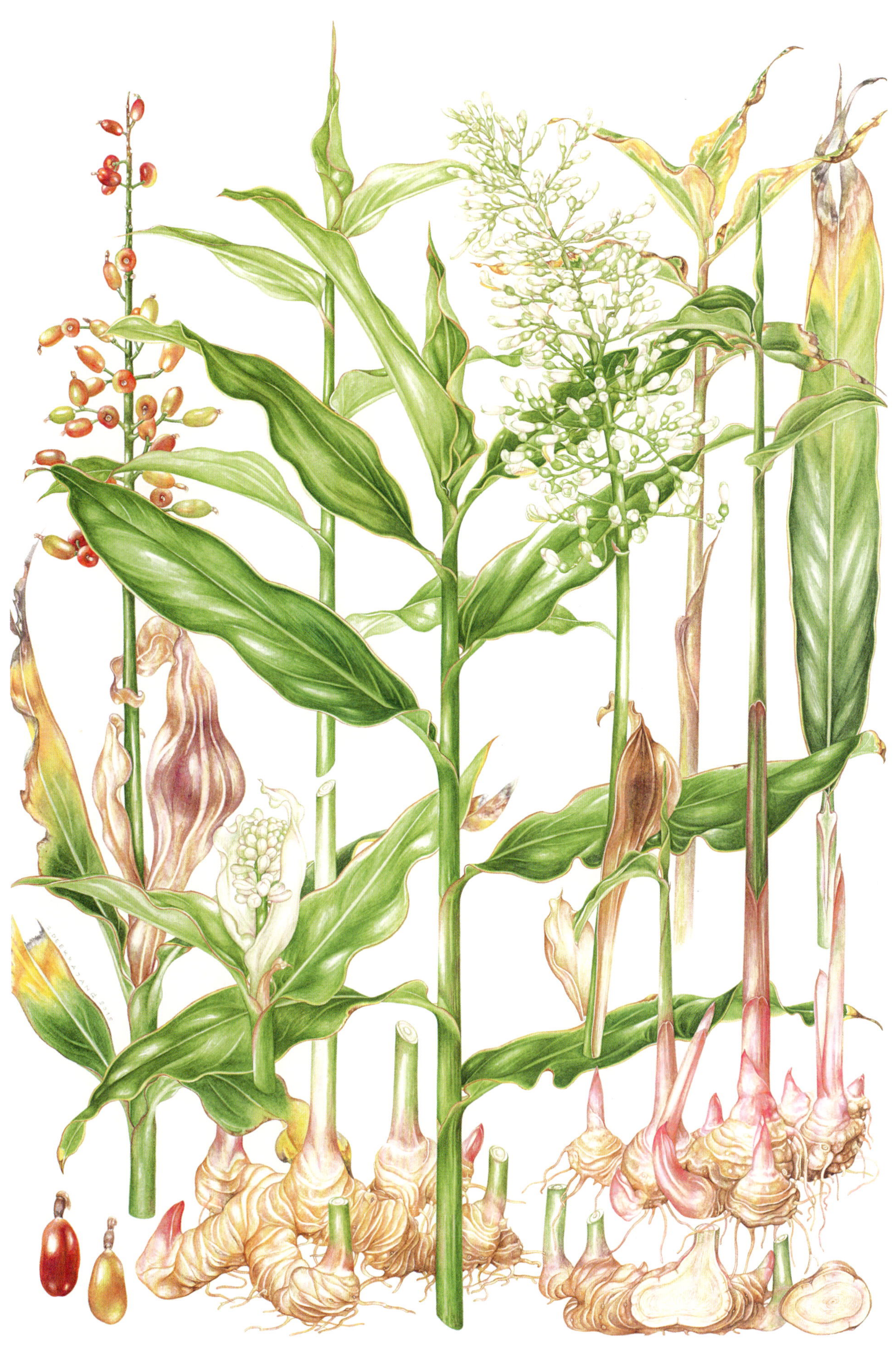

Elisabeth Dowle

RHS medal history

Gold medals: 1986, February and October 1989, 1992, 1994, 1997, 1998

Silver-Gilt medals: 1983, 1984

Bronze medal: 1982

From 1986 to 1998, Elisabeth Dowle was awarded seven RHS Gold medals. Specialising in edible plants, and in particular fruit, Dowle has produced numerous illustrations of apples, pears and edible herbs for publication.

Dowle always works from specimens, under natural light. She will return to a piece over a period of many weeks, to incorporate the different growing stages and cross sections of fruit. She has developed a compositional style that in part echoes William Hooker's nineteenth-century paintings of apples.

The painting featured here, of Apple 'Blenheim Orange', was specifically identified by the Picture Committee as a painting that would be of great benefit to the Lindley Collections; it was recommended for purchase in 1989. Intended for identification, the painting includes the apple on the branch, as seen growing from various angles and changes in colouration, accompanied by the blossom and a cut section of fruit. The painting was reproduced in *The New Book of Apples* (2002) by Joan Morgan and Alison Richards.

Apple 'Blenheim Orange', 1986

Watercolour on paper

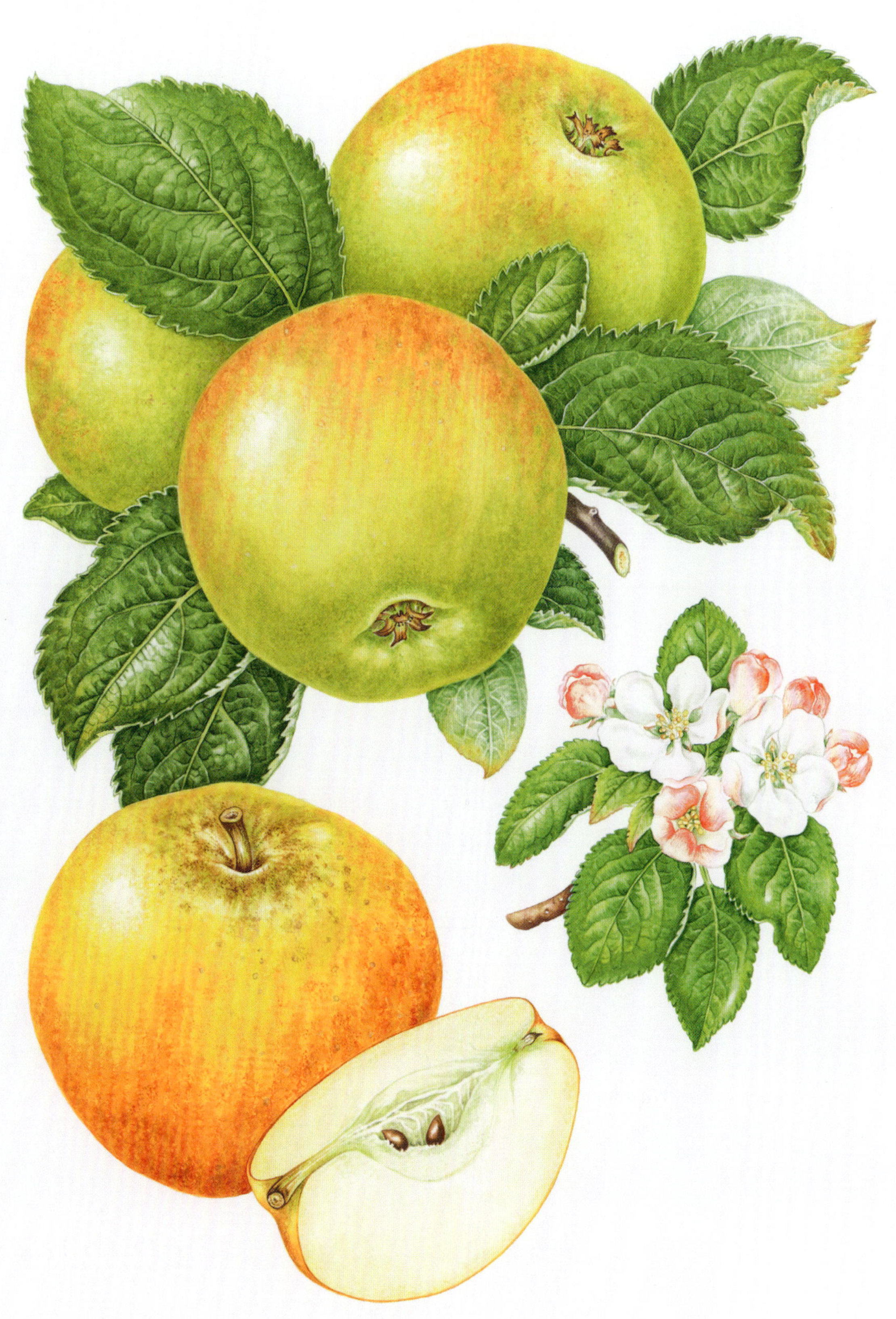

Janet Dyer

RHS medal history

Gold medal: 2013 (and Best Botanical Painting)

Silver-Gilt medal: 2014

Janet Dyer first exhibited with the RHS at the Malvern Spring Festival in 2013, where she won a Gold medal for her exhibit of 'Non-native plant invaders'. In addition, she was the recipient of the Best Botanical Painting Award for the full watercolour version of *Heracleum mantegazzianum,* featured here. Having not long finished the Diploma of Botanical Illustration at the RBG Edinburgh on the same subject, Dyer had undertaken extensive preparatory work that included a pen and ink drawing, colour matching and pencil sketches.

"Portraying this plant was the most difficult painting I had ever done! Giant Hogweed had never been illustrated botanically before, probably because of its size and toxicity. (Chemicals in the sap of the Giant Hogweed can cause the skin to become very sensitive to sunlight, which can result in severe burns.) It presented a huge challenge, and certainly collecting, handling and drawing, in spite of precautions, resulted in a damaging reaction that lasted some time! This spectacular plant from the Caucasus was introduced into Britain in 1817 and recommended by John Loudon, in The Gardener's Magazine *in 1836. Gertrude Jekyll also enthusiastically planned it into her garden designs between 1890 and 1912. However, because it was so successful, the plant spread speedily into the wild and today is a huge problem throughout Britain and Europe, where all sales and cultivation are now banned."*

Heracleum mantegazzianum, 2010

Watercolour on paper; pen and ink on paper; colour study

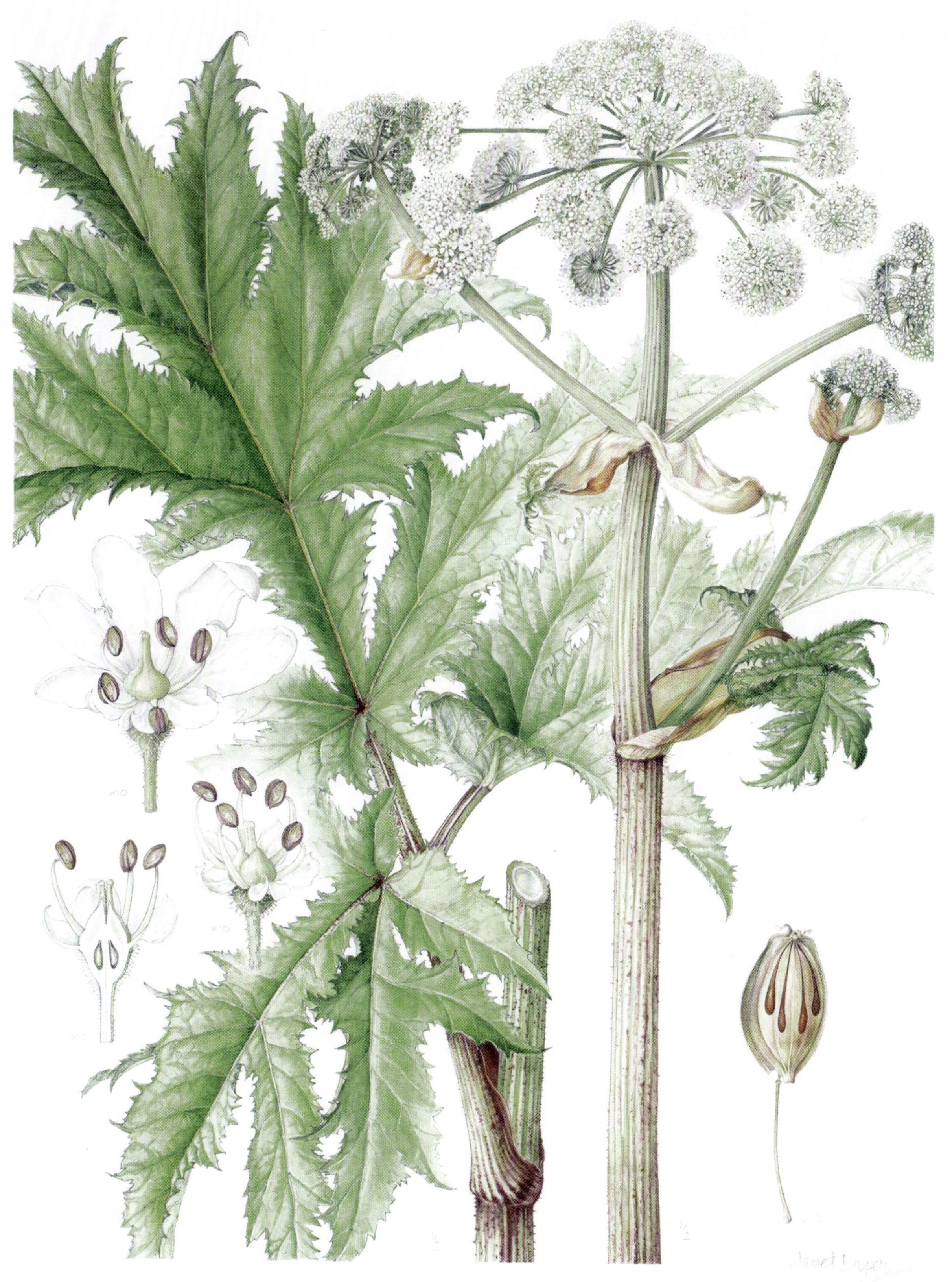
Giant Hogweed Heracleum mantegazzianum Somm. & Lev.
Janet Dyer

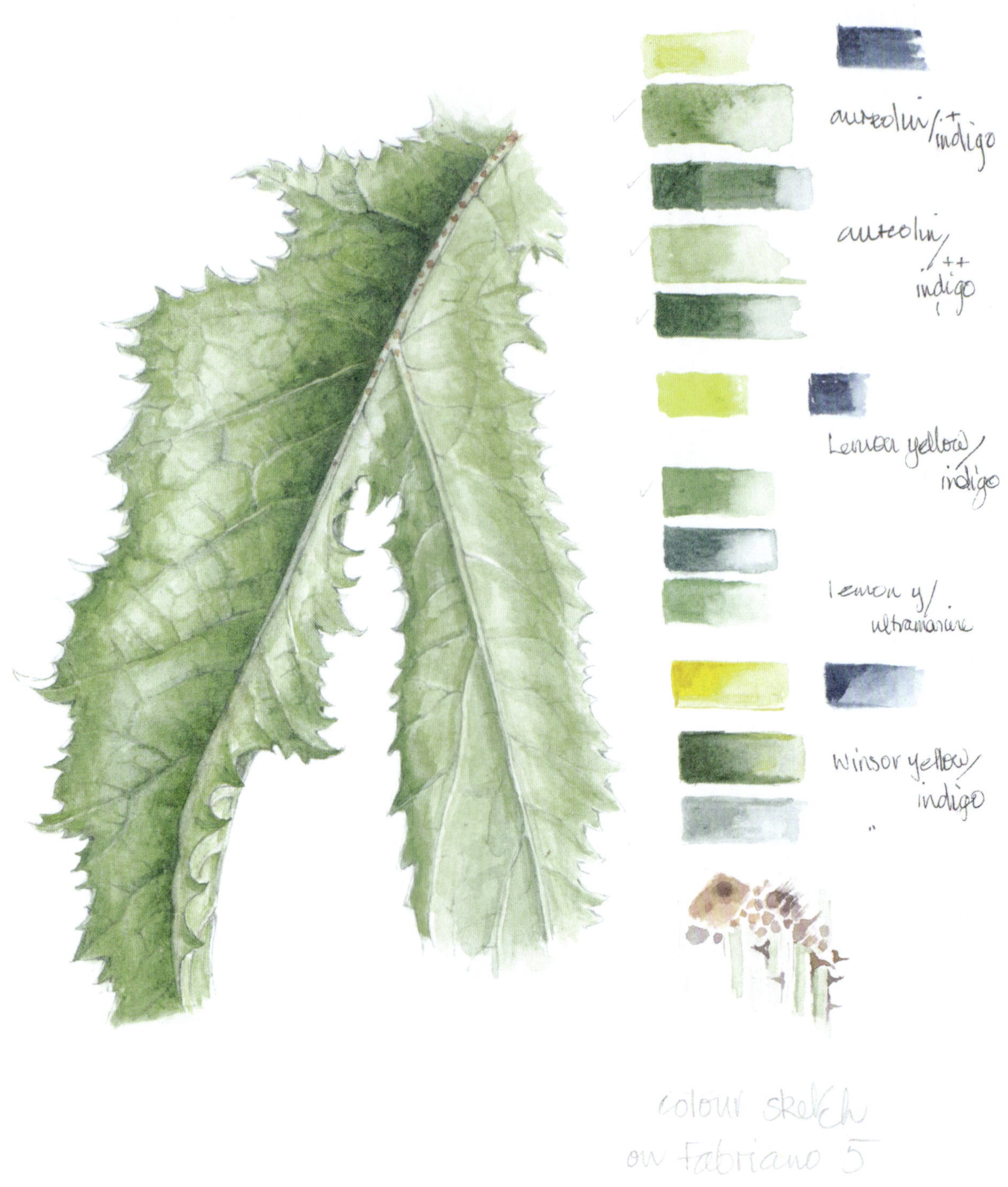

Dyer originally trained in botanical illustration at the Forest Botany Herbarium at Oxford University, following which, she studied under Stella Ross-Craig and Margaret Stones at RBG Kew.

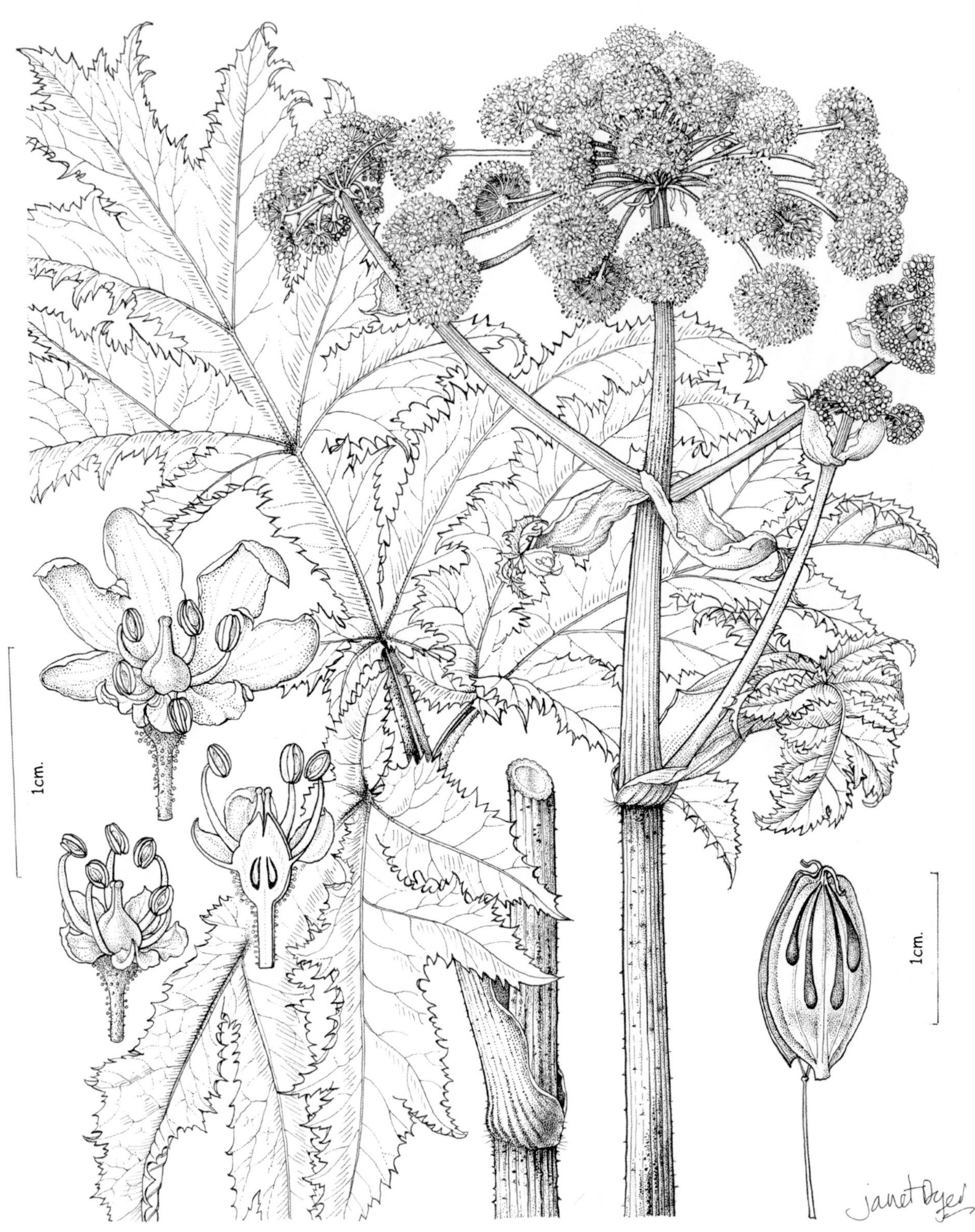
1cm.
1cm.
Janet Dyer

Jean Emmons

RHS medal history

Gold medals: 2005, 2011 (and Best Botanical Painting)

The four *Iris* cultivars depicted here formed part of Jean Emmons' Gold medal-winning display of 'Pacific Coast Irises', exhibited at the BBC's *Gardeners' World* live show at the NEC in Birmingham, 2005. Emmons followed this with another Gold medal display in 2011 of 'Mushrooms of the Pacific Northwest', for which she was also awarded Best Botanical Painting.

As she is a keen gardener, Emmons prefers to paint specimens she has grown herself on Vashon Island. The irises proved to be a particular challenge, as an unexpected storm damaged the flowers, meaning the paintings had to be completed over two growing seasons. All four of these varieties are Californian hybrids, bred by notable iris grower, Joseph Ghio.

Emmons has varied her approach to the composition of specimens, creating the impression of plants growing in situ. She has captured the intensity and beautiful range of colours associated with the Pacific Coast Irises. The striking differences in the colouring and pattern found on the petals of these varieties is particularly easy to appreciate when the paintings are viewed alongside one another.

Iris 'Wildest Imagining', 2005

Watercolour on paper

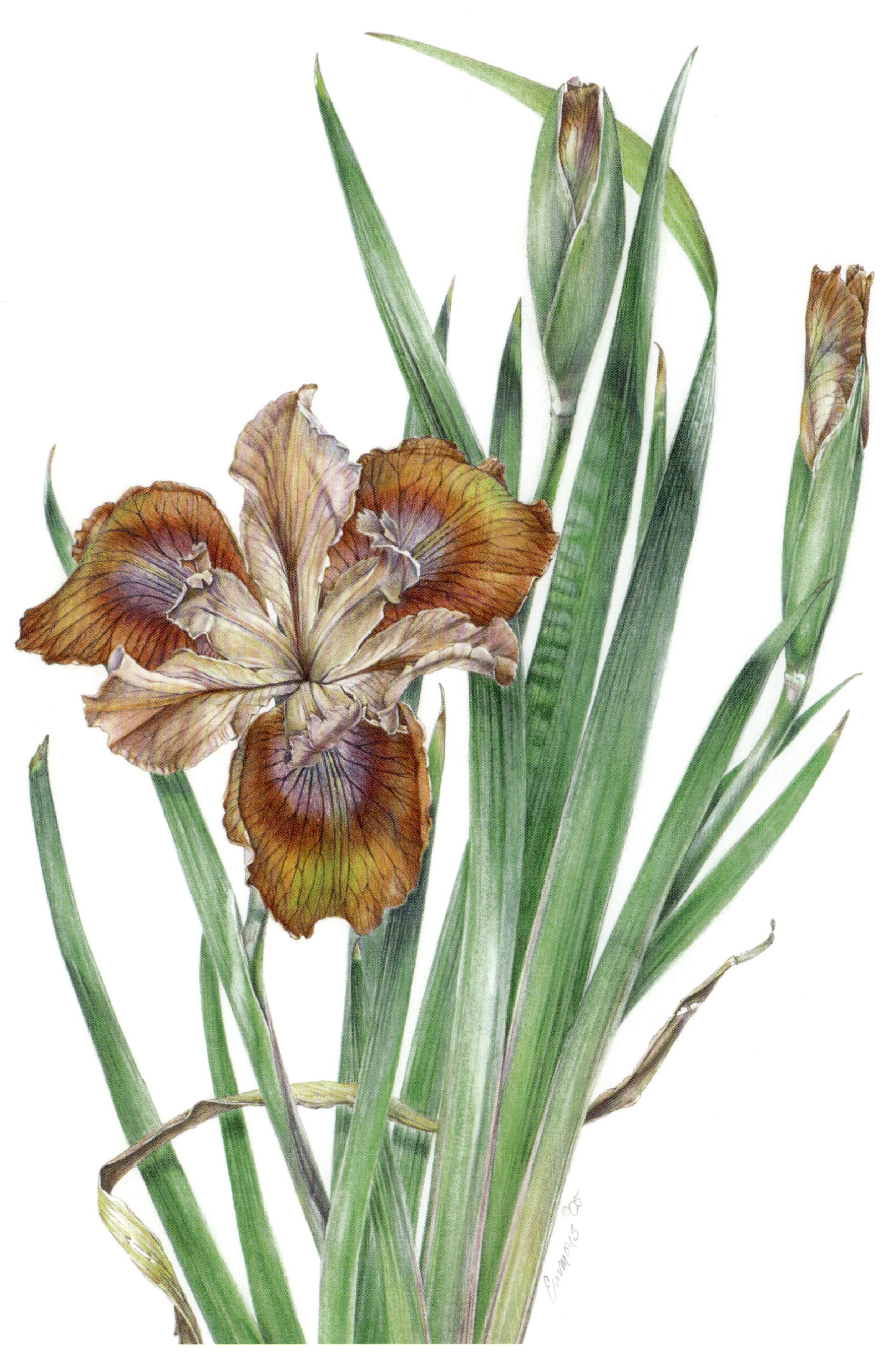

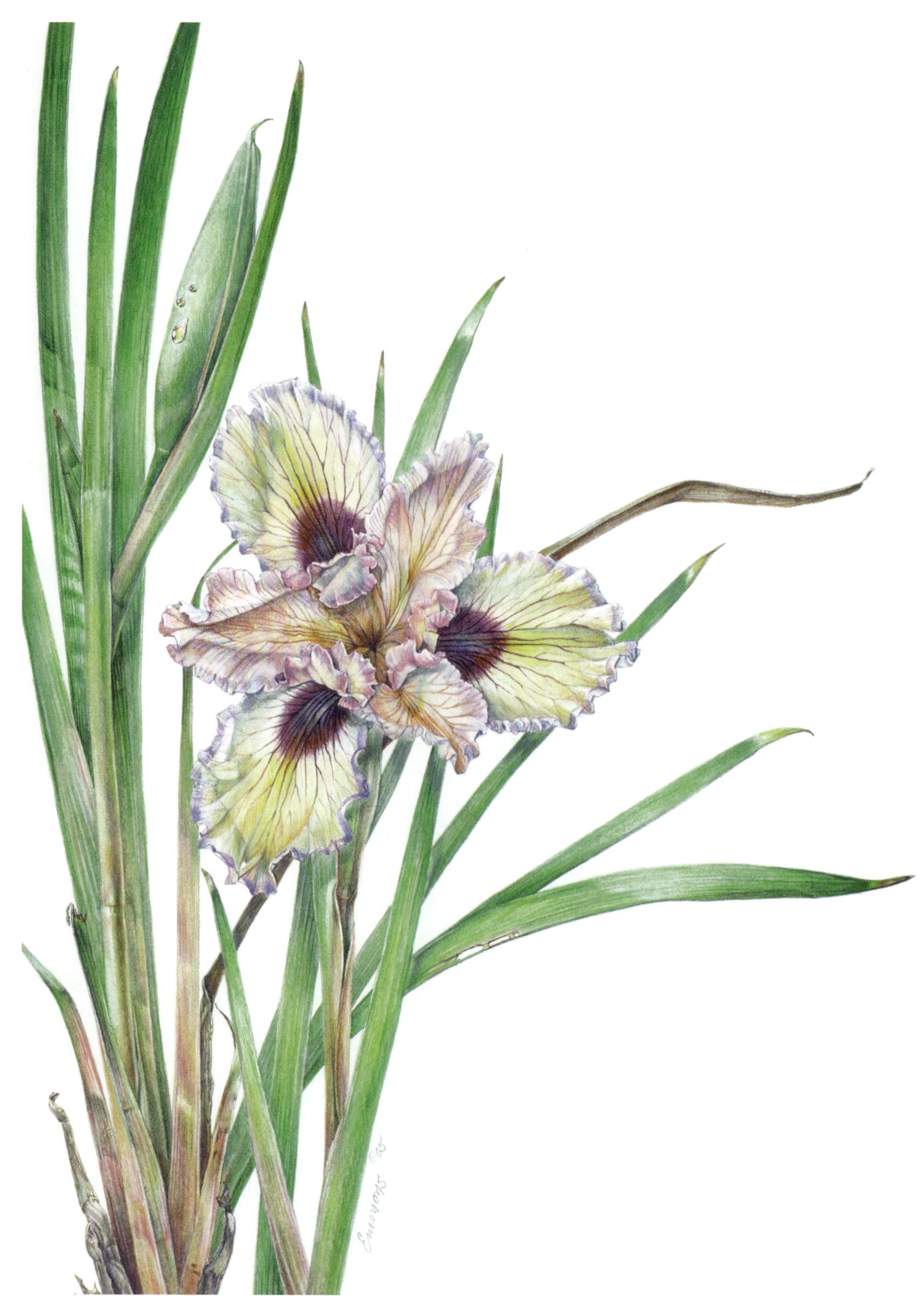

Iris 'With This Ring', 2005

Watercolour on paper

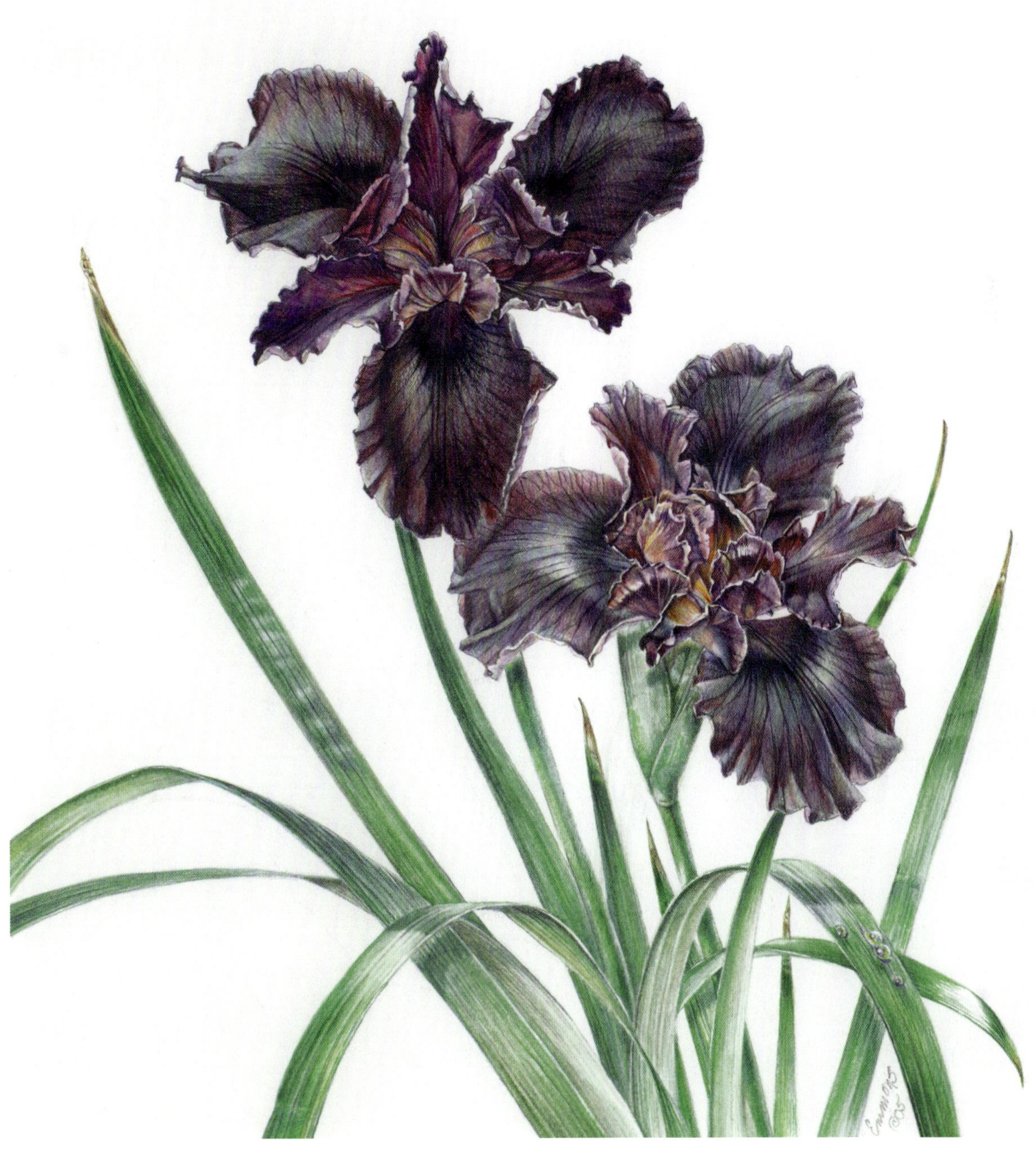

Iris 'Night Gown', 2005

Watercolour on paper

Iris 'Tulum', 2005

Watercolour on paper

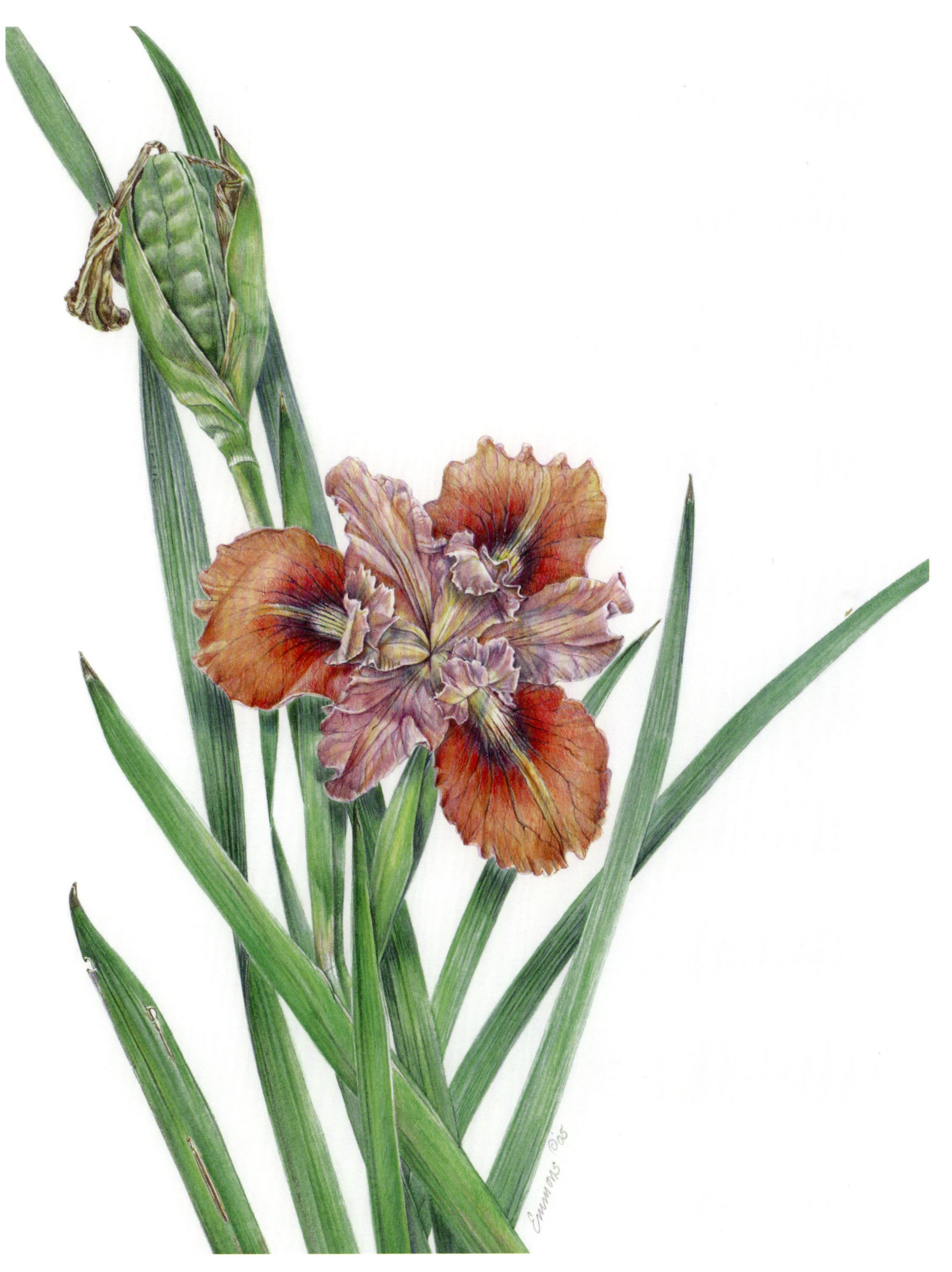
Emmons ©05

Ann Farrer

RHS medal history

Gold medals: 1982, 1984, 1985, 1987, 1988, 1990

Ann Farrer exhibited with the RHS on six occasions and was awarded a Gold medal each time. Her exhibit staged in 1991 was deemed worthy of a Gold medal, but it could not be formally judged as there were too few paintings on display. Farrer also served as a judge on the Picture Panel from 2004 to 2011.

Farrer has always been renowned for her meticulous attention to detail and her paintings take hours of painstaking work. The illustration of *Pinus wallichiana* is an incredible case study, where the branch and needles to the fore are echoed by those in a paler pigment behind. The concentration of fine needles is contrasted with the solidity and texture she has captured in the pine cone. This was one of the first paintings purchased for the Lindley Library's contemporary botanical art collections in 1987.

Farrer studied English and Art History at Manchester University, following which she began her painting career at the British Museum (Natural History), with a piece she produced for their Herbarium. This led to over 30 years spent as a botanical illustrator and teacher at RBG Kew. Having started with black and white line drawings, Farrer's first coloured plates for *Curtis's*

Ilex colchica, 1993

Mixed media on board

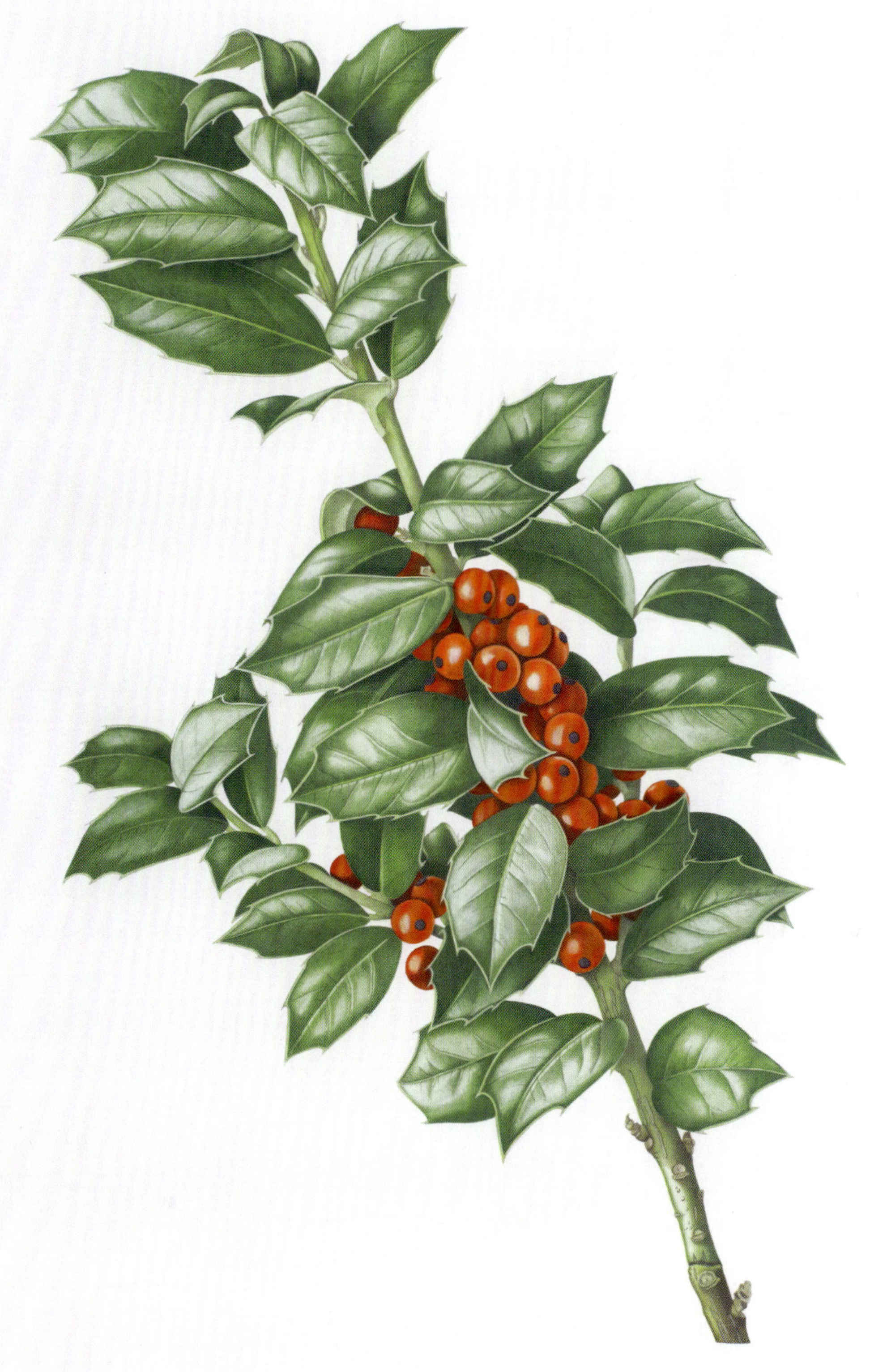

Ilex colchica.
Ann Farrer 1993.

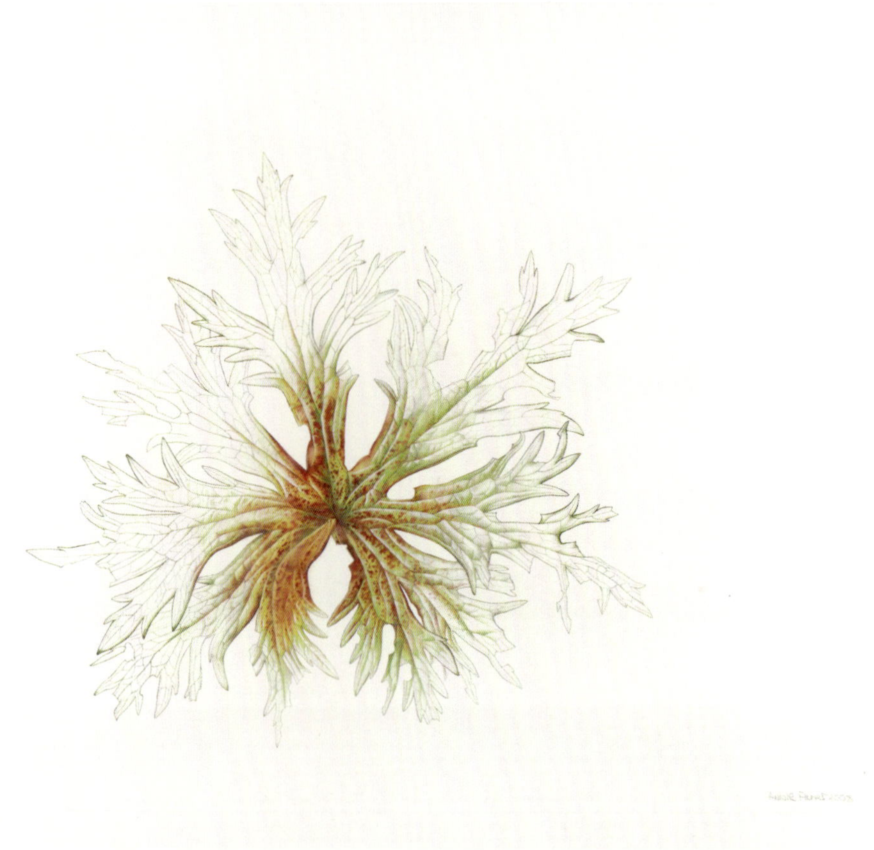

Geranium pratense leaf, 2008
Watercolour and graphite on paper

Botanical Magazine appeared in 1987. Alongside these works she also produced illustrations for a number of plant monographs.

In more recent years, Farrer has moved her focus from 'classical' botanical illustration to art works inspired by the form, shape and texture of the natural world. The *Geranium pratense* leaf is almost abstract, with the outer edges fading imperceptibly to a simple graphite outline. The intensity of the pigment at the centre of the leaf reveals the colour change in the Geranium as the flowers fade in the autumn, with the foliage turning from green to bronze.

Pinus wallichiana, 1987
Painted from material grown at Wakehurst Place, Sussex

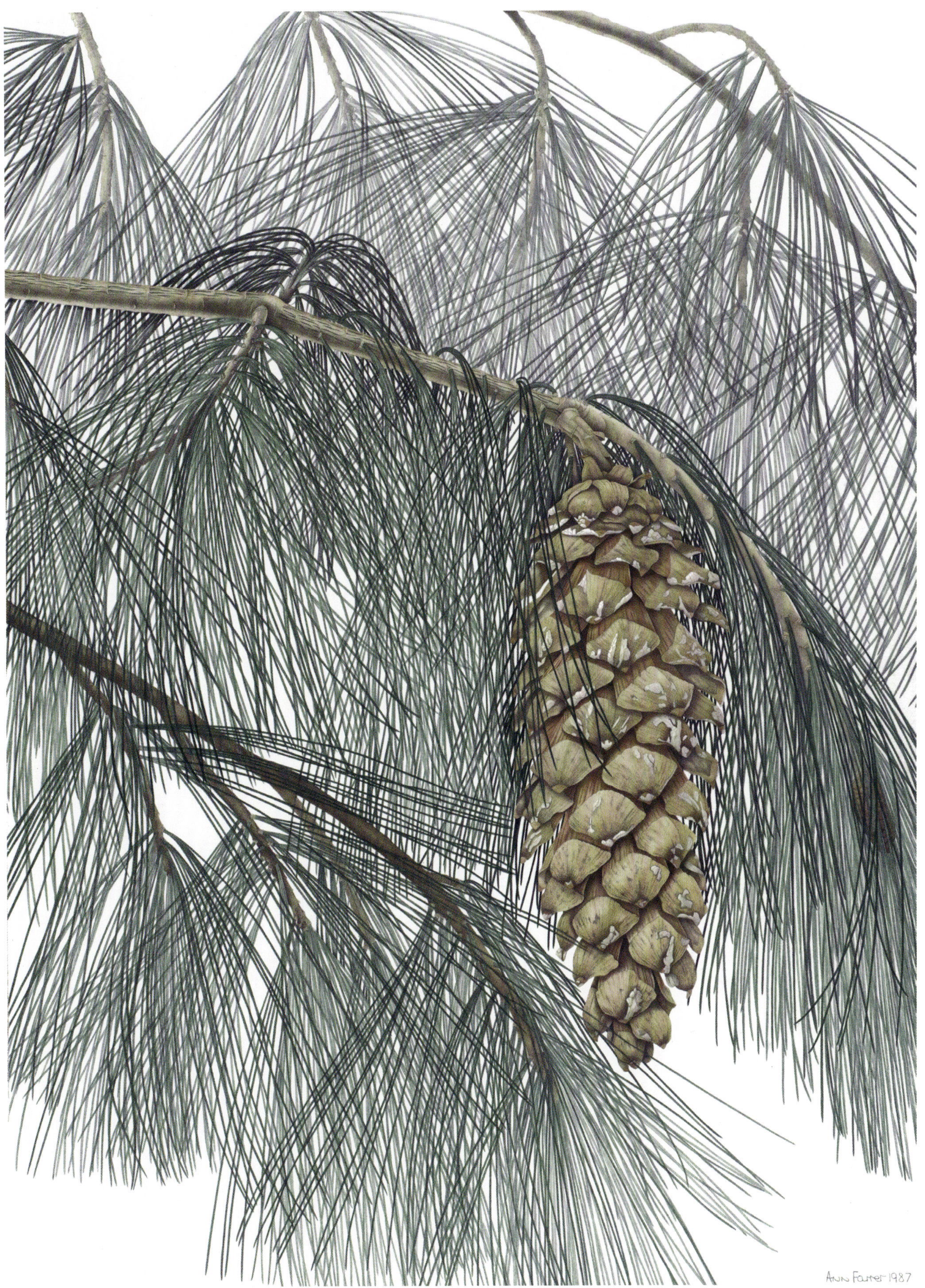
Ann Farrer 1987

Ros Franklin

RHS medal history

Gold medal: 2015

Silver-Gilt medal: 2021

This illustration of *Arisaema speciosum* var. *mirabile* is one of a series of seven paintings exhibited under the title 'Arisaemas for the sheltered garden or greenhouse', for which Ros Franklin was awarded a Gold medal at the RHS Malvern Spring Festival in 2015. The series was painted over three growing seasons between 2013 and 2015, to allow her to study the botany of the genus and develop her compositional style.

Franklin documented her progress throughout the long painting process, making sketches and taking photographs of both her painting and of the plant, as well as making colour swatches to match the pigments accurately. The variety 'mirabile' is renowned for its extended spadix and required careful attention. The specimen was arranged with scaffolding to support it, in order to maintain its position throughout the period. Franklin has used the spadix in the composition to link the detail of the 'male' flowers to the main specimen.

Following a career as a Geophysicist, Franklin re-trained as a Garden Designer. A place on the Board of Trustees at RBG Kew led her to becoming a founder and lifelong member of The Eden Project in Cornwall. Having gained a Diploma in Botanical Painting and Illustration from The English Gardening School, thirteen of her paintings are held by the Eden Project Florilegium Society.

Arisaema speciosum var. *mirabile*, 2013–2015

Watercolour on paper

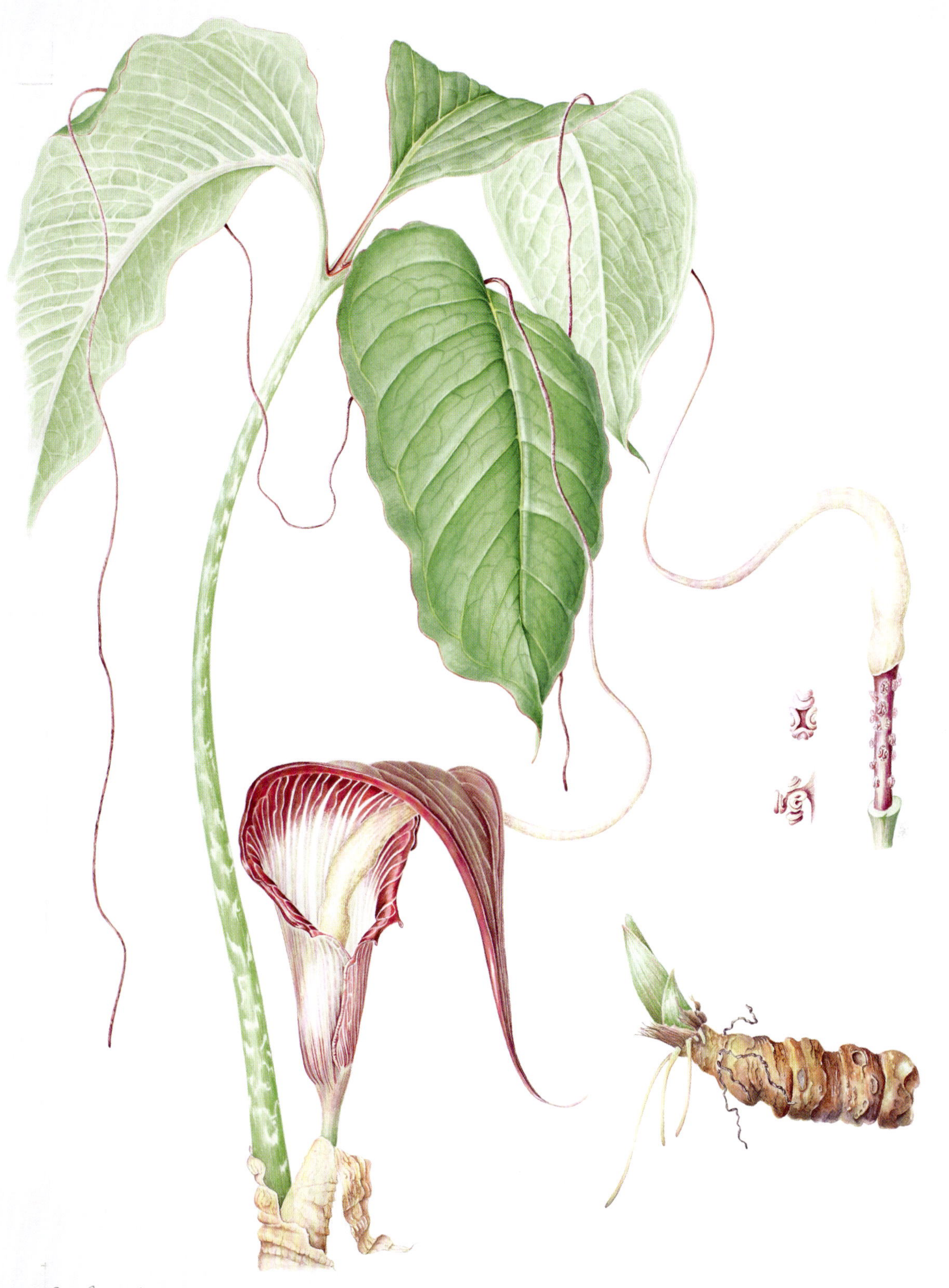

Ros Franklin © 2015
FLS. FEPFS
Exhibited at The RHS Botanical Art Show (2015) – Malvern
Arisaema speciosum
var. mirabile

Bridget Gillespie

RHS medal history

Gold medals: 2002, 2008, 2017 (and Best Botanical Painting), 2018

Bridget Gillespie has been a botanical artist for over 20 years and says she has been drawing for as long as she can remember. She originally trained as a graphic designer, but gradually started to specialise in botanical art. Gillespie was awarded her first Gold medal with the RHS in 2002, for her display of 'Watercolour paintings of plums', two of which are featured here. Following this success, Gillespie was awarded another Gold medal in 2008 for 'Watercolour of Pears'. A third Gold medal was accompanied by the Best Botanical Painting award for her study of *Beta vulgaris* in 2017, and most recently, a fourth Gold medal was achieved in 2018 for a series of paintings depicting 'A year in the Yorkshire Hedgerow'.

Painted with an immediacy that brings the fruit to life, Gillespie has beautifully captured the character of the *Prunus domestica.* The grouping of the plums shown growing on the branch are compelling as their weight forces the branch to bow; the delicate changes in colour as the fruit ripens, is balanced against the twist of the leaves.

Gillespie runs practical botanical art classes and also lectures on the subject. A number of her classes have been held in The Orchid House at Helmsley Walled Garden in North Yorkshire. She also contributed paintings of 50 varieties of fruit to the book *The Northern Pomona – Apples for Cool Climates* (2007) the profits from which help to support Helmsley Walled Garden.

Prunus domestica 'Purple Pershore', 2001

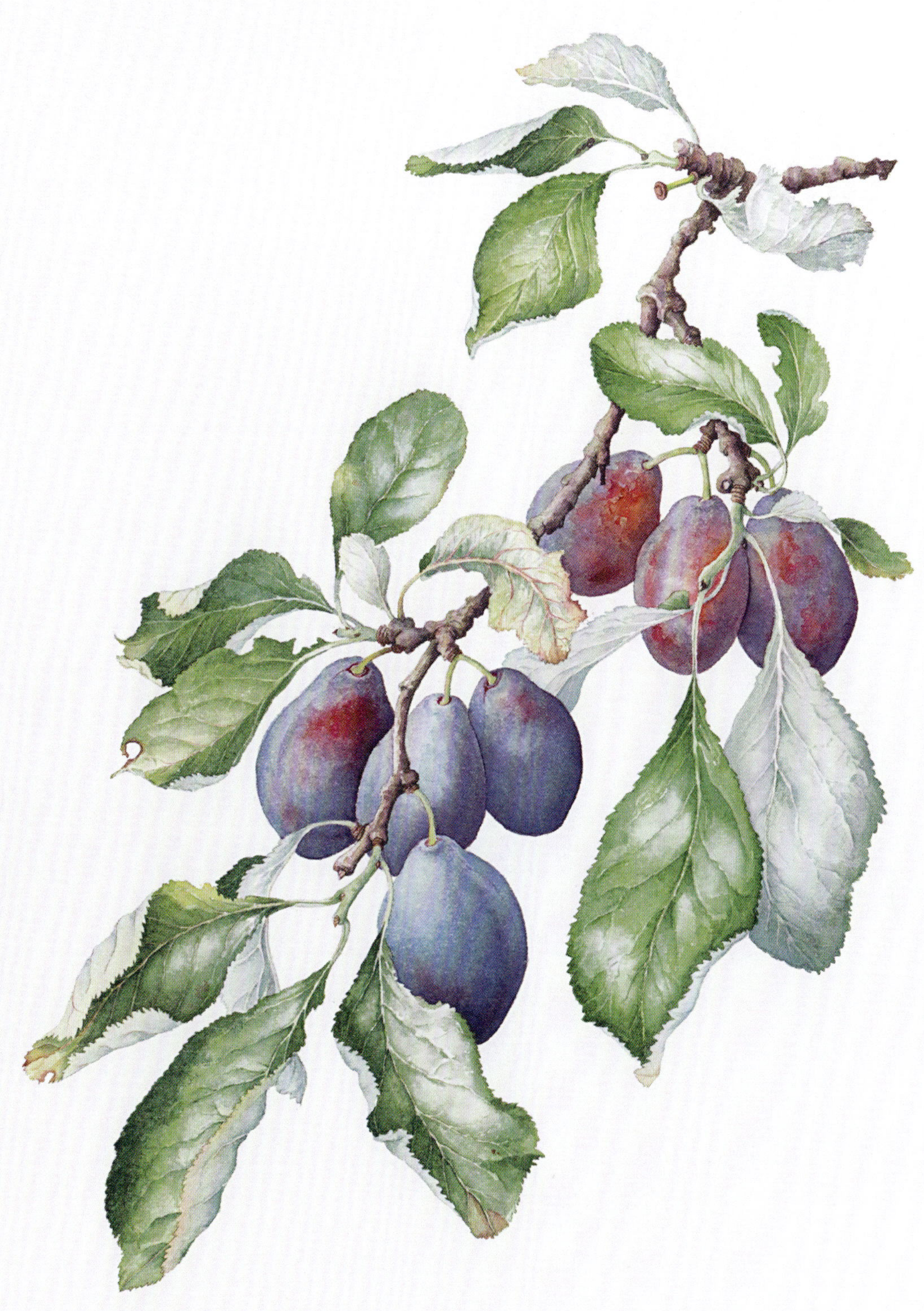

Prunus domestica 'Purple Pershore'
BRIDGET GILLESPIE 2001

Prunus domestica 'Giant Prune', 2002

Watercolour on paper

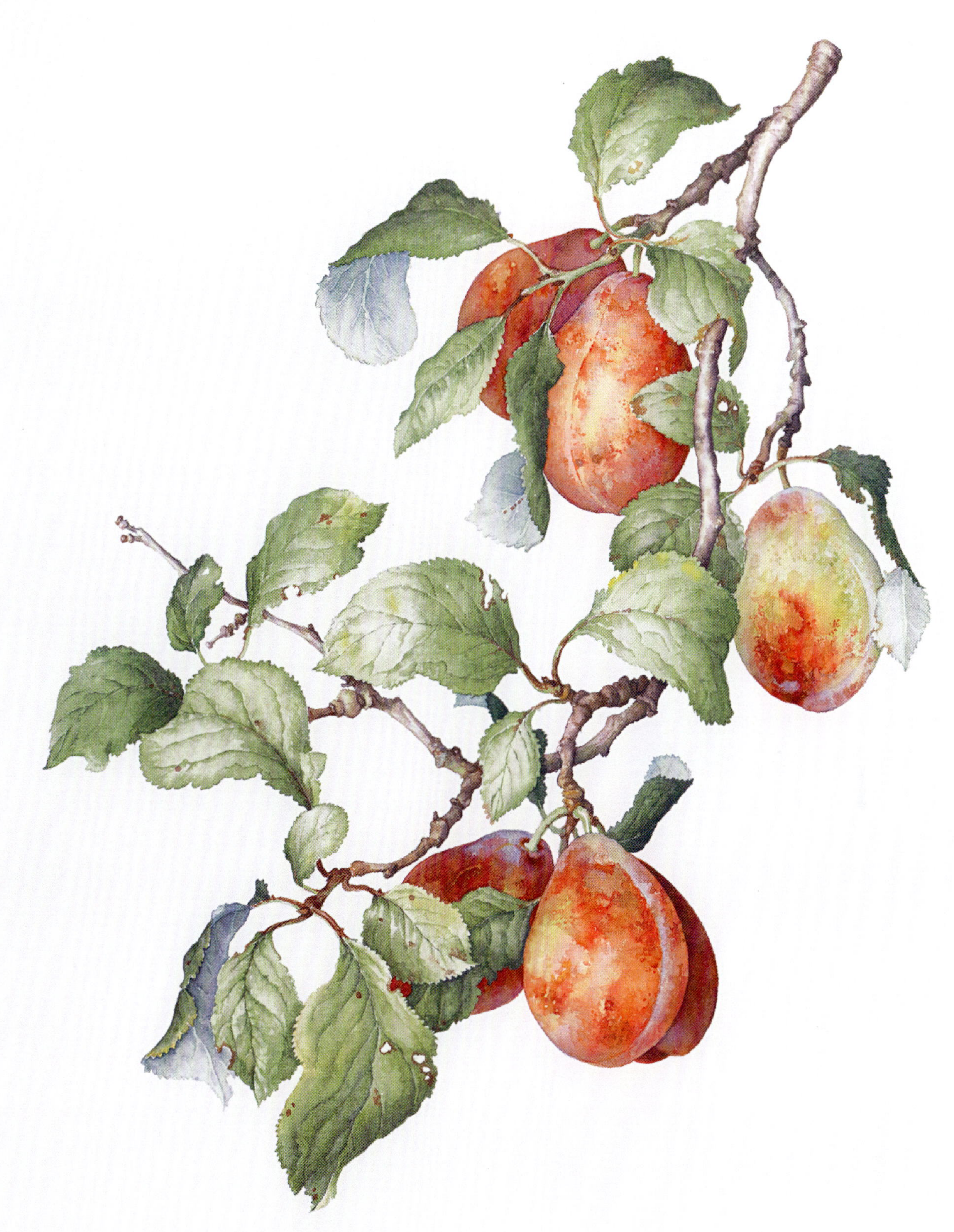

Prunus domestica 'Giant Prune' B.GILLESPIE

Norma Gregory

RHS medal history

Gold medals: 2006, February 2008, 2011

Silver-Gilt medals: December 2008, 2016

Silver medal: 2005

Norma Gregory exhibited with the RHS on a number of occasions between 2005 and 2016, winning first a Silver medal, then both Silver-Gilt and Gold medals. The paintings featured here of *Allium ampeloprasum* were exhibited in her February 2008 display 'Aspects of Garlic'. The *Rheum* formed part of the 2011 exhibit 'A Rooted Fascination'.

Having taught herself to draw and paint, Gregory has always had an interest in the creative arts. She began painting still life studies and gradually became more interested in botanical studies. She always works in watercolour, with graphite pencil. Gregory originally trained as a teacher, she then gained a qualification in Adult Education and transferred to working for HM Prison service organising training courses. She currently teaches botanical art to local groups in Northamptonshire.

For her painting of the *Rheum* (rhubarb) from 'A Rooted Fascination', Gregory delved beneath the surface to look at the structure of the roots. An approach not usually taken by botanical artists, this project was an impressive endeavour as the paintings provide valuable information about how these plants store their energy.

Rheum, 2010

Watercolour on paper

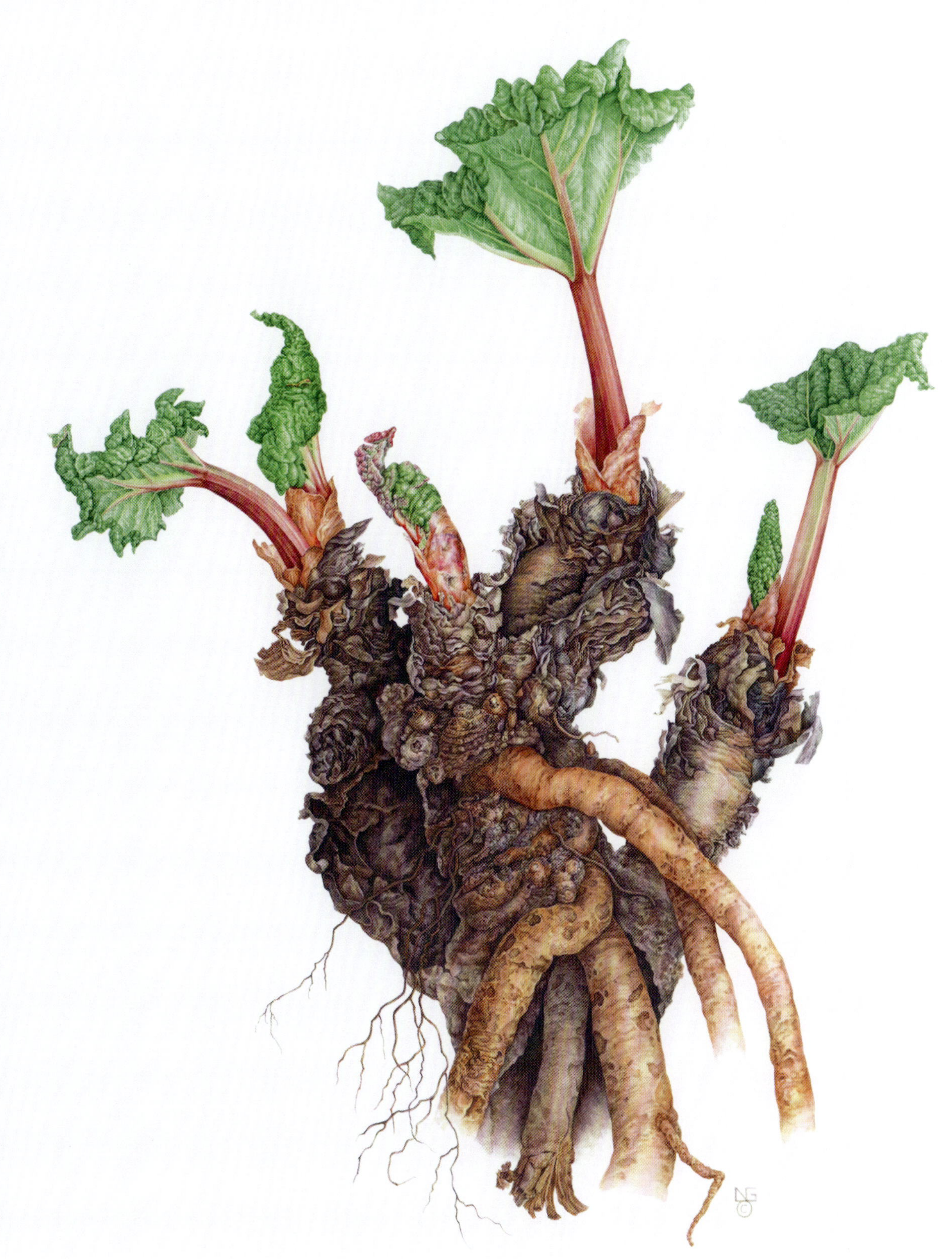

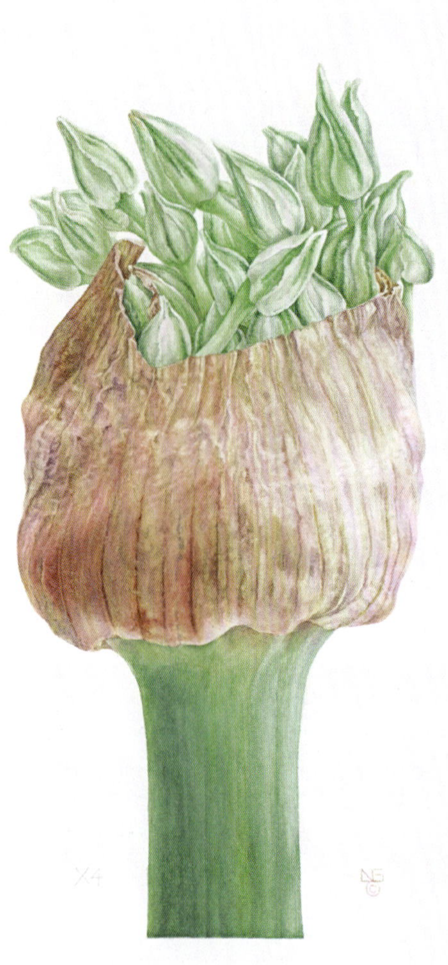

"Every early spring, for a number of years, my attention was drawn by the emergence of the first vivid scarlet and magenta 'limos' that suddenly appeared amid a mound of dead rhubarb leaves. I just had to paint it! From then, my thoughts were how was I going to present it as a finished painting?

I needed a very mature crown, as being from the 'Rhubarb Triangle', I knew they produced massive roots! My very elderly neighbour had a large very old bed of it and between us, we dug up quite a few until I found one where the root system and emerging leaves would make an interesting and well balanced painting. Using a large bowl and a block of florists' oasis, I sat the Rheum on top,

Allium ampeloprasum flower scape, 2007
Watercolour on paper

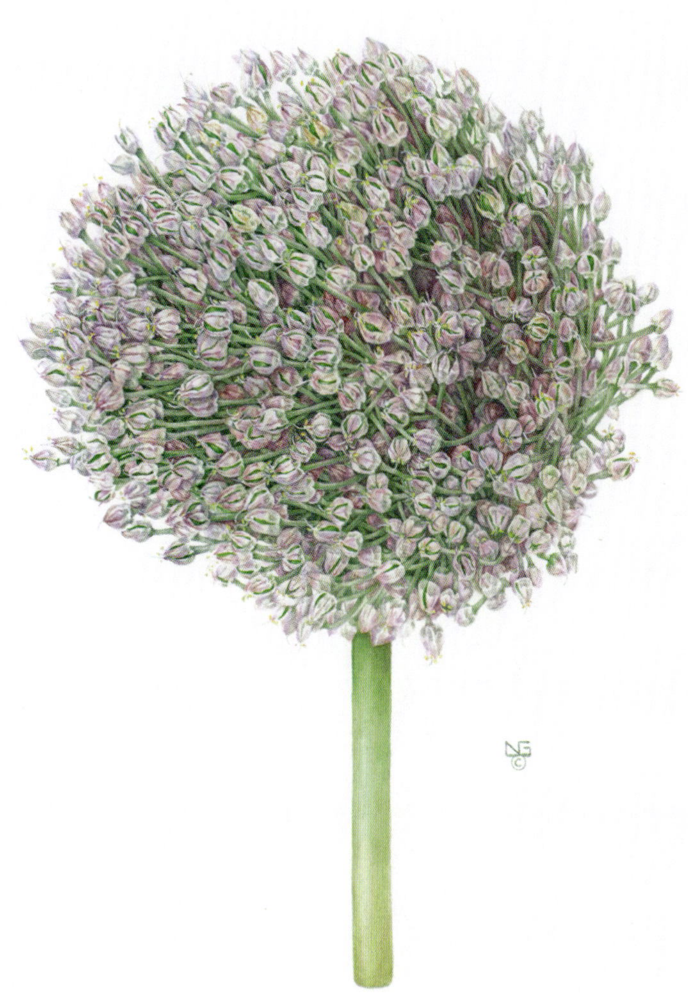

pinning it in place with the roots in the water. I recorded the development of the emerging leaves at various stages, to give me more interesting shapes and colours. I spent a long time mixing these and matching them to the plant.

My main method of working is 'wet into wet', applying light washes of colour, concentrating on getting a three-dimensional effect. When I am satisfied with this, I then paint the various parts using 'wet into dry', always thinking of the form of it and the tonal changes needed to enhance it more. I may do many layers of paint, especially in building up the dark areas. The very last step is to paint the fine details and check my outlines to ensure they are as clean as I am capable of getting them!"

Allium ampeloprasum flower head, 2008
Watercolour on paper

Mary Grierson
(1912–2012)

RHS medal history

Gold medals: 1966, 1969, 1973, 1978, 1990

RHS Victoria medal of Honour: 1997

RHS Gold Veitch Memorial medal: 1985

Mary Grierson is one of only two botanical artists to have been awarded both a Gold Veitch Memorial medal and the RHS Victoria medal of Honour, for her services to botanical art and contribution to horticulture. (Lilian Snelling was the other artist to receive both awards.)

Grierson was encouraged in her art – her mother being an artist – and she developed a fondness for working in watercolour from a young age. Her early career as a cartographer during WWII meant she had to demonstrate her ability to observe and draw accurately. After the war she was inspired to undertake the botanical illustration course at Flatford Mill, Suffolk, which had been set up and taught by John Nash. Grierson started to develop her skill and continued to attend the course over the following ten years. Her second career as a botanical illustrator for the Herbarium at RBG Kew spanned 12 years from 1960 to 1972. In 1966, the same year she was awarded her first Gold medal with the RHS, Grierson took over running the botanical illustration course at Flatford Mill from John Nash. She exhibited with the Society on a further four occasions, each time being awarded a Gold medal. After her retirement, Grierson continued to produce illustrations for publications such as *Curtis's Botanical Magazine,* as well as for private commissions.

Lilium, 1965

Watercolour and ink on paper

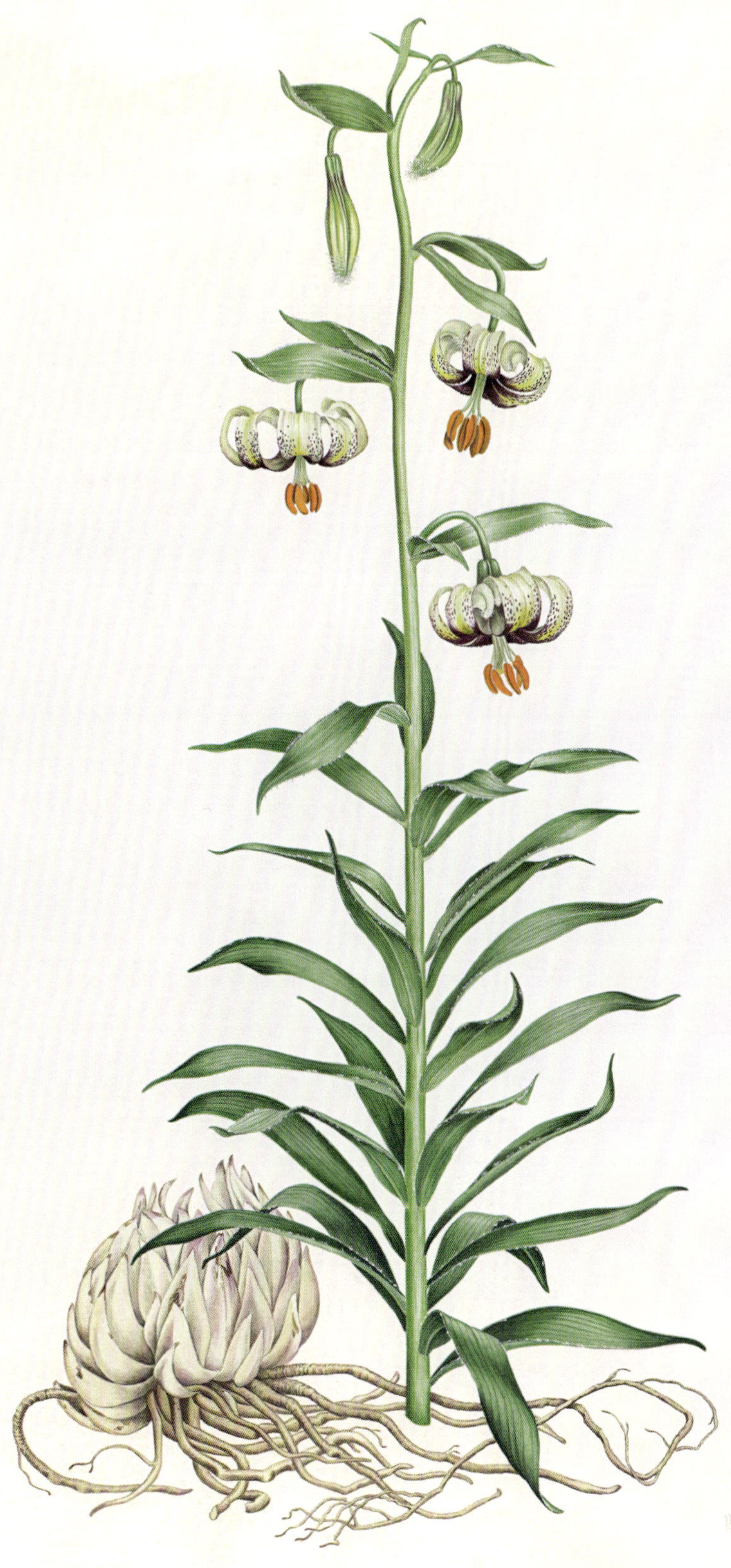

L. ciliatum

Mary Grierson

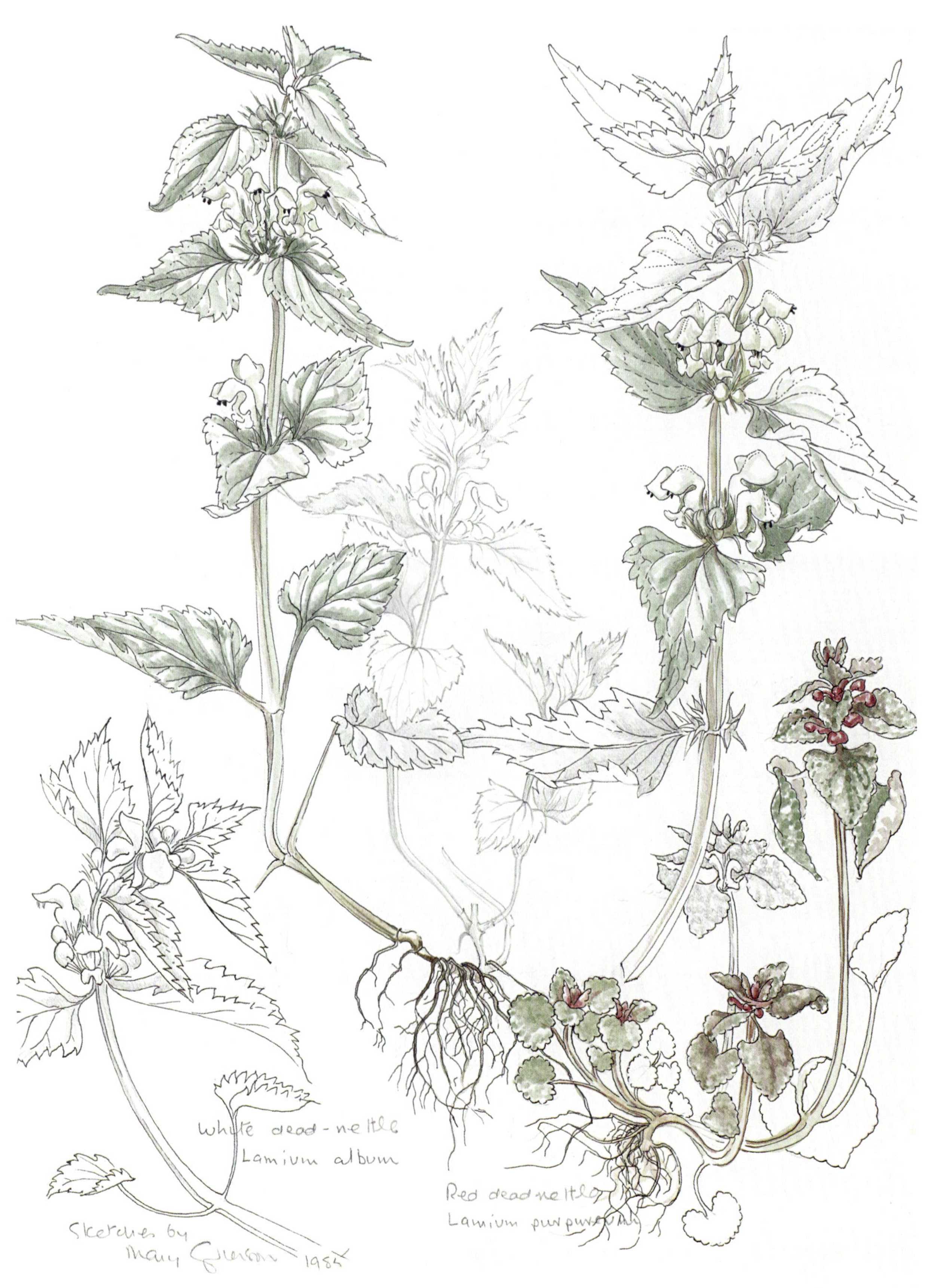

Lamium album and *Lamium purpureum*, 1985

Pencil, pen and ink and watercolour on paper

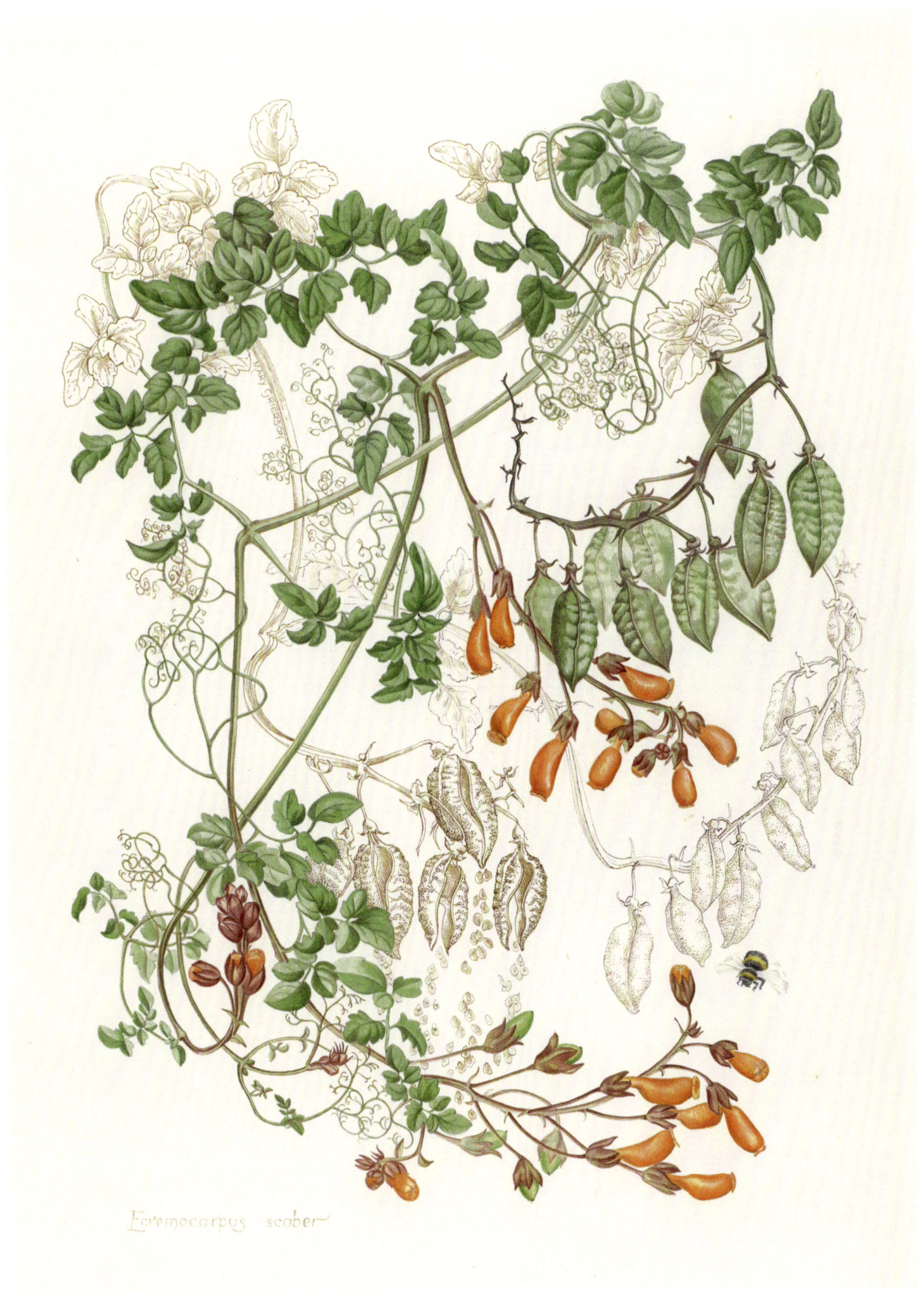

Eccremocarpus scaber, *c.*1985

Watercolour and ink on paper

Coral Guest
(1955-2021)

RHS medal history

Gold medals: 1984; 1986

Silver-Gilt medal: 1983

Coral Guest studied at Harrow School of Art in the 1970s, before training in fine art and art history at Chelsea College of Arts. Thereafter, she trained in the practice of large-brush calligraphic painting at Seitai-ji Soto Zen Temple, Yamanashi Prefecture, Japan. In 1991, RBG Kew took the unprecedented step of inviting her, a fine art painter, to become Flower Painting Tutor.

Guest was one of the first contemporary artists commissioned for the Lindley Collections. She chose to paint this study of *Lilium regale,* as it has a personal connection. The accompanying studies were not part of the original commission but formed an important part of Guest's own exploration. The studies demonstrate something of the challenge faced by botanical artists when matching pigments for accurate colour rendering. Guest worked in a white studio in natural light, and as such she was very aware of the play of light and shadow on the living specimen and how this translates to the painting.

"I work from live plant specimens, and this often involves growing the plants that I paint and draw. At the time of this commission, I was occupied with the accurate depiction of white flowers

Lilium regale, 2000

Watercolour on paper

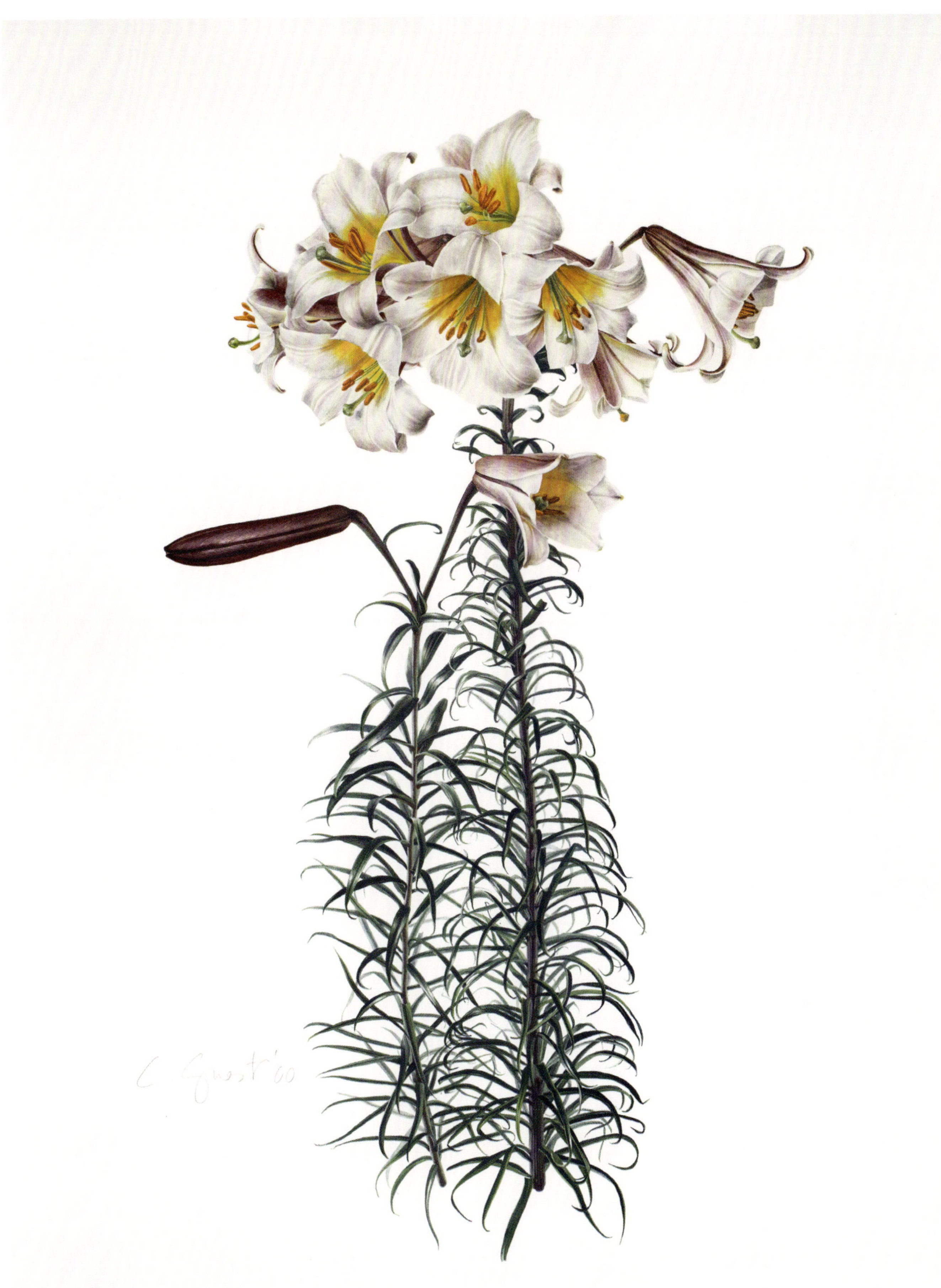

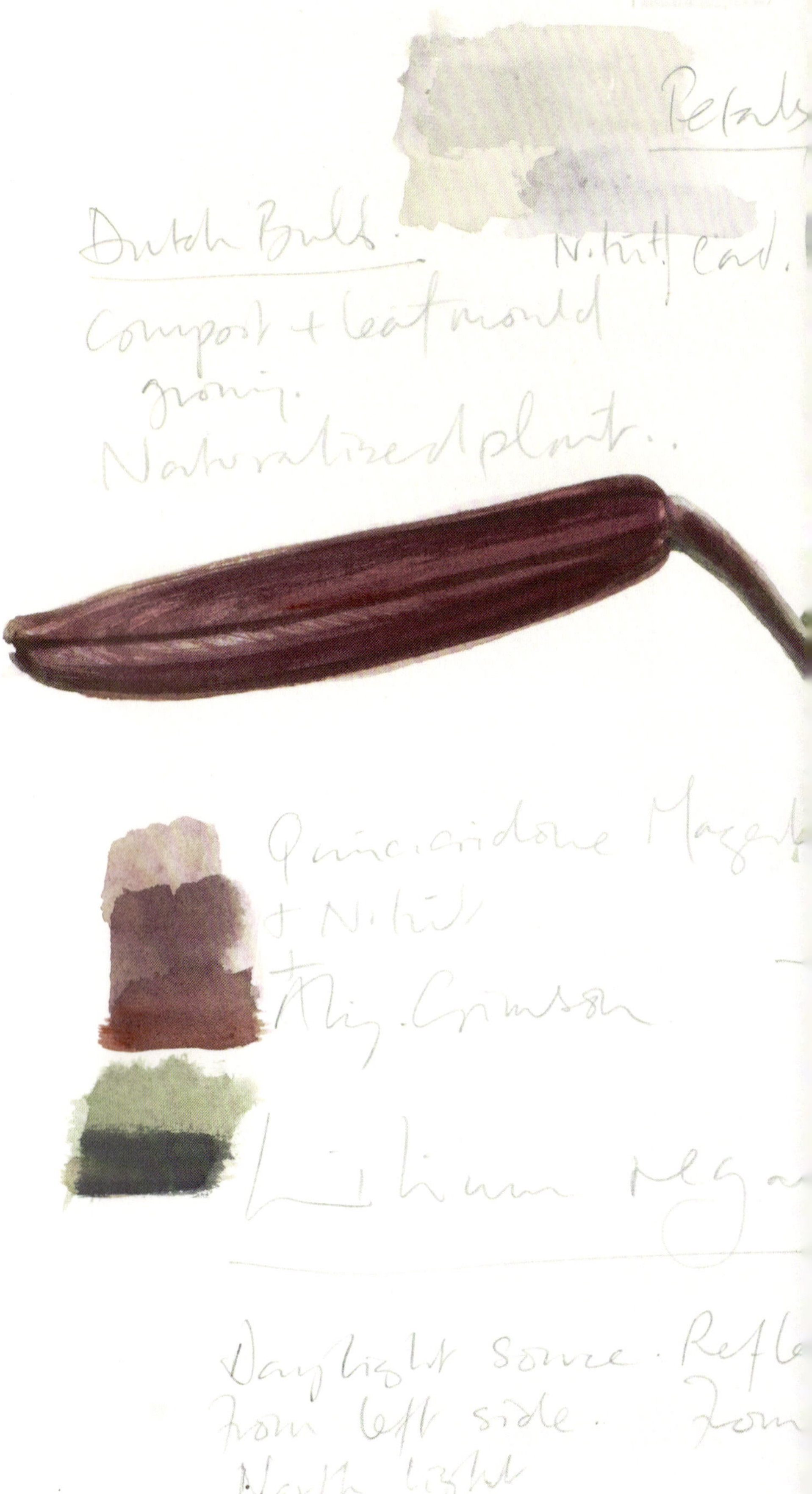

Petals

Dutch Bulb.

Nitri[illegible] cad.

compost + leaf mould
growing.
Naturalized plant..

Quinacridone Magenta
+ Nitril
+
Aliz. Crimson

Lilium Megan[illegible]

Daylight source. Refle[illegible]
from left side. from
North light

Pals

N. tint

Flower stem in graining pigment

/ ceruleanB.

North light →

N. Tint
+ Quin Magenta
+ Aliz Crimson

Anthers:

Cad. lemon
Cad. red
N. tint

Leaves & Stem

cad lemon
cerulean
F. Ultra + N. tint

Style:
leaves:
stems:
+ Flower Stalks

Stem from main flower bulb

light
sht.

C Grierson 2000

on white paper, using the purist method of watercolour painting wherein the brightest highlights are left unpainted and no actual white paint is used. In the Lilium regale *work, I set out to balance the whiteness of the blooms with the whiteness of the space that the paper represents.*

The Lilium regale *painting demanded colour study work to enable enough information to be gathered for a finished artwork. The colour studies were completed by depicting the chosen view of the blooms with their colouring. This was achieved by rapid work over several hours. The Colour Studies differ from the conventional preliminary sketches as they are created out of a sense of urgency and an immediate response to the plant.*

I wanted to paint a study of the lily bulb because of the strange dichotomy between the floriferous light-filled flowers and the gross impression of the swollen storage unit in the darkness of the earth. I felt it would be a beautiful idea to include the soil in the Colour Study, particularly as the work was for the RHS and nature of the soil is relevant to the gardener.

When the precision painting was complete I then attempted to remove a section of the pot in order to view the bulb in situ, proceeding gently to chip away at the pot using a mallet and a small chisel. Eventually, a series of cracks appeared, and a triangular section of the pot fell away. The lily bulb managed to stay in position for the Colour Study painting, being sprayed gently with water for the duration of the work. The bulb was then removed from the pot and replanted, and the offset and bulblets were extracted and re-potted too. One of these bulblets grew into the 2007 lily painting now in the Shirley Sherwood Collection."

Preliminary sketches for flower head and bulb, 2000

Watercolour and graphite on paper

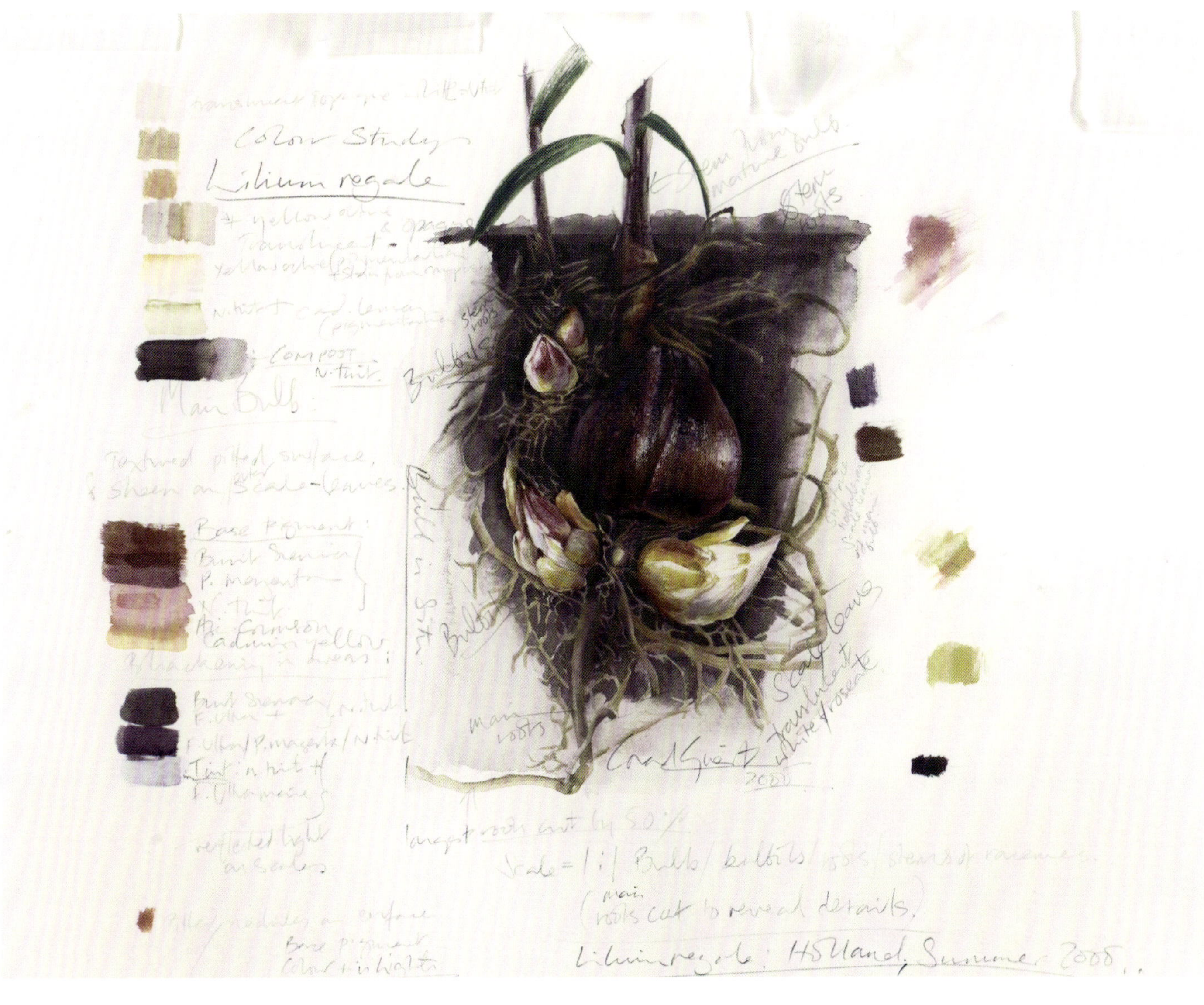
Colour Study
Lilium regale
COMPOST
Main Bulb
Textured pitted surface,
Base Pigment:
Stem
Bulblets
Bulb in Situ
Scale leaves
main roots
Scale = 1:1 Bulb / bulblets
(main roots cut to reveal details)
Lilium regale: Holland, Summer 2005

Regine Hagedorn

RHS medal history

Gold medals: 1999, 2000, 2005

Silver-Gilt medal: 1998

Regine Hagedorn exhibited with the RHS four times between 1998 and 2005, first gaining a Silver-Gilt medal, followed by three Gold medals.

Her study of *Rosa pimpinellifolia* 'Single Cherry', featured here, was part of her 2005 exhibit 'Watercolour paintings of fruits & seeds'. As the title of the series indicates, the artist's emphasis is on the fruit and seeds rather than a more typical view of the bloom. Hagedorn studied design and jewellery at the *Ecole des Art Decoratifs* in Geneva and went on to develop a career as a designer and artist. Her formative training is visible in this perfectly balanced composition, with the skilful placement of each botanical element. This piece offers a contemporary rendering of the traditional life-cycle stages commonly included in botanical art.

With incredibly fine brush work, Hagedorn has captured the detail and deep colour of the rose hip as it appears on the branch and in magnified cross-section, set opposite the spent flower-head from which it was formed. The transient colours of the leaves as they change, is captured in multiple renditions and indicates the seasonal change throughout the autumn.

Rosa pimpinellifolia 'Single Cherry', 2004

Watercolour on paper

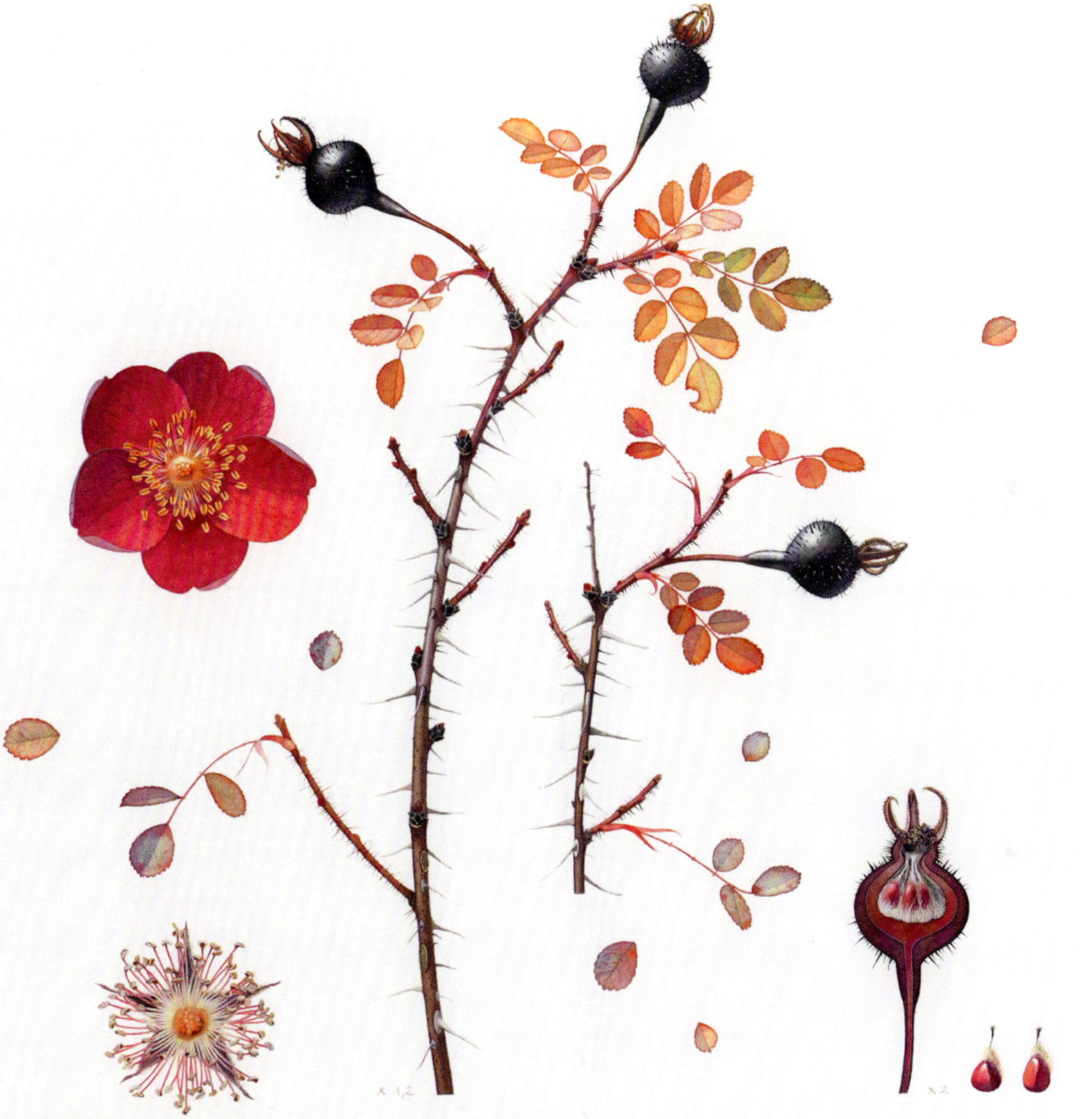

x 1,2

x 2

ROSA PIMPINELLIFOLIA

'SINGLE SHERRY'

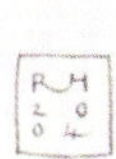

Eiko Hamada

RHS medal history

Gold medal: 2008

Silver-Gilt medal: 2004

Eiko Hamada first exhibited with the RHS in 2004 with 'Vegetables in watercolour & pencil', for which she was awarded a Silver-Gilt medal. She returned to exhibit again in 2008 and was awarded a Gold medal for 'Conifers in watercolour & pencil'.

The *Pinus thunbergii* (Japanese Black Pine), featured here, was one of the pictures she showed in 2008. Completed in January 2007, it was painted in Shizouka Prefecture. *Pinus thunbergii* is native to coastal areas of Japan. This piece is a painstaking study that took many months to complete.

Hamada's talent has been recognised with many prestigious awards and her paintings have featured in exhibitions in the UK, USA and Japan.

Pinus thunbergii, 2007–2008

Watercolour on paper

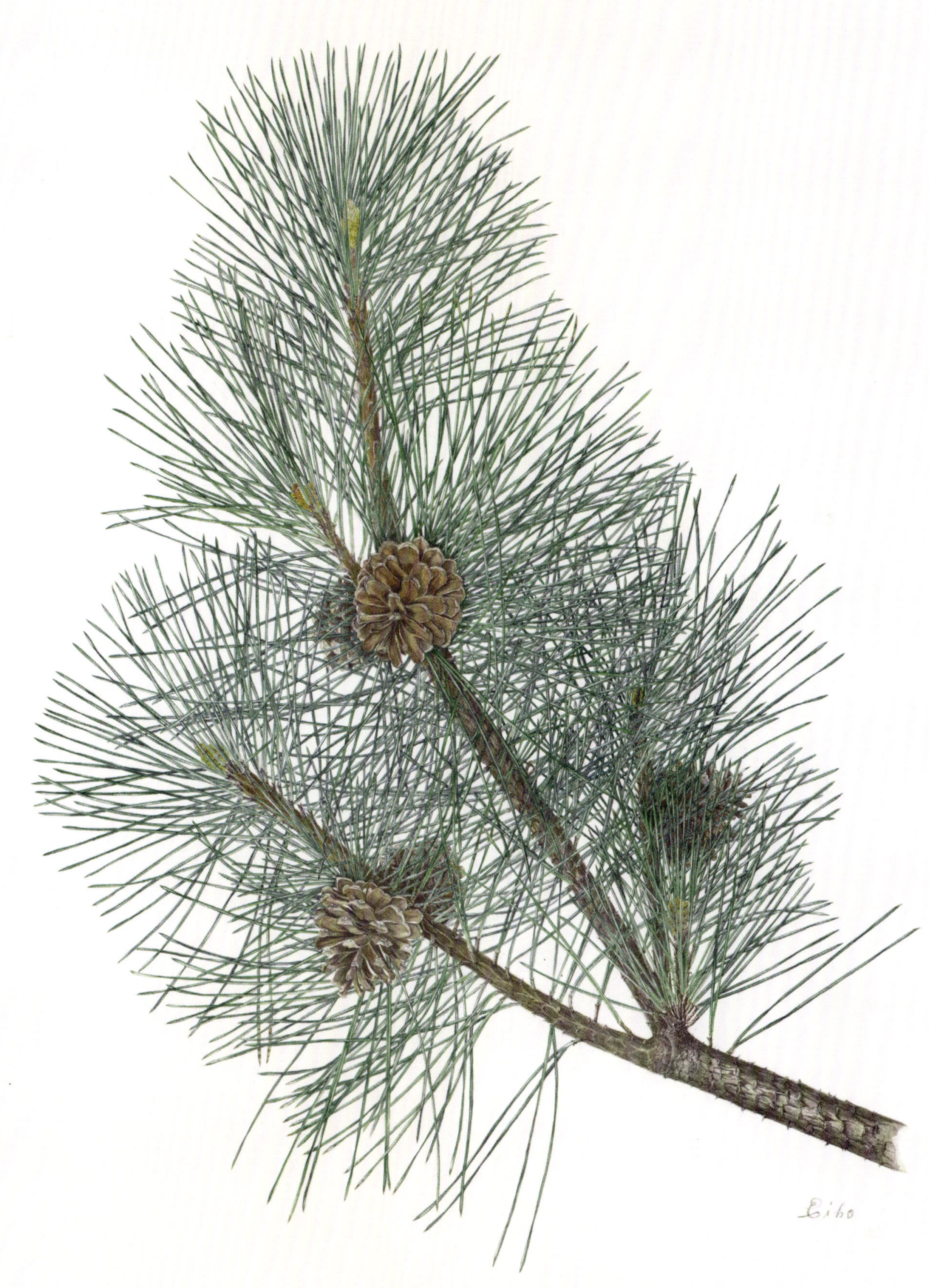
Eiko

Yoko Harada

RHS medal history

Gold medal: 2022 (and Best Botanical Artwork)

Yoko Harada started her botanical art journey in 2010. Her first botanical painting tutor was UK-based artist, Elaine Searle. In 2018, Harada went on to graduate from the Royal Botanic Garden Edinburgh (RBGE) Diploma in Botanical Illustration, with a distinction and an award for coming top of her class. She now studies under Mieko Ishikawa in Tokyo. Her work has been exhibited with the American Society of Botanical Artists (ASBA) and with the RBG Edinburgh.

In 2022, Harada gained a Gold medal and award for Best Botanical Artwork, with the RHS, for her exhibit of 'The Genus *Arisaema* in Japan'. Since then, Harada's *Arisaema* paintings have received further recognition. She was awarded Best in Show at the ASBA 26th Annual International Exhibition in 2023 and one of her paintings is also now held in the Hunt Institute in Pittsburgh. Harada has been selected for an artist's residency at Oak Spring Garden Foundation in Virgina, USA in 2025.

Harada first encountered the genus *Arisaema* in a Tokyo botanical garden. She was immediately fascinated by its huge, snake-like flowers. Dr Jin Murata, former director of the Koishikawa Botanical Garden, University of Tokyo, agreed to help her by checking the paintings for botanical accuracy.

"Painting the plants in their natural habitat, at different stages of growth, required multiple trips to four Japanese prefectures between 2019 and 2021 – a great challenge, given the Covid-19 pandemic. Arisaema *are dioecious, with flowers that switch between male and female, so I needed to obtain at least three samples of each species: one main sample plus one of each sex. Each painting took at least a full year, and two to three years where I had to wait for new specimens."*

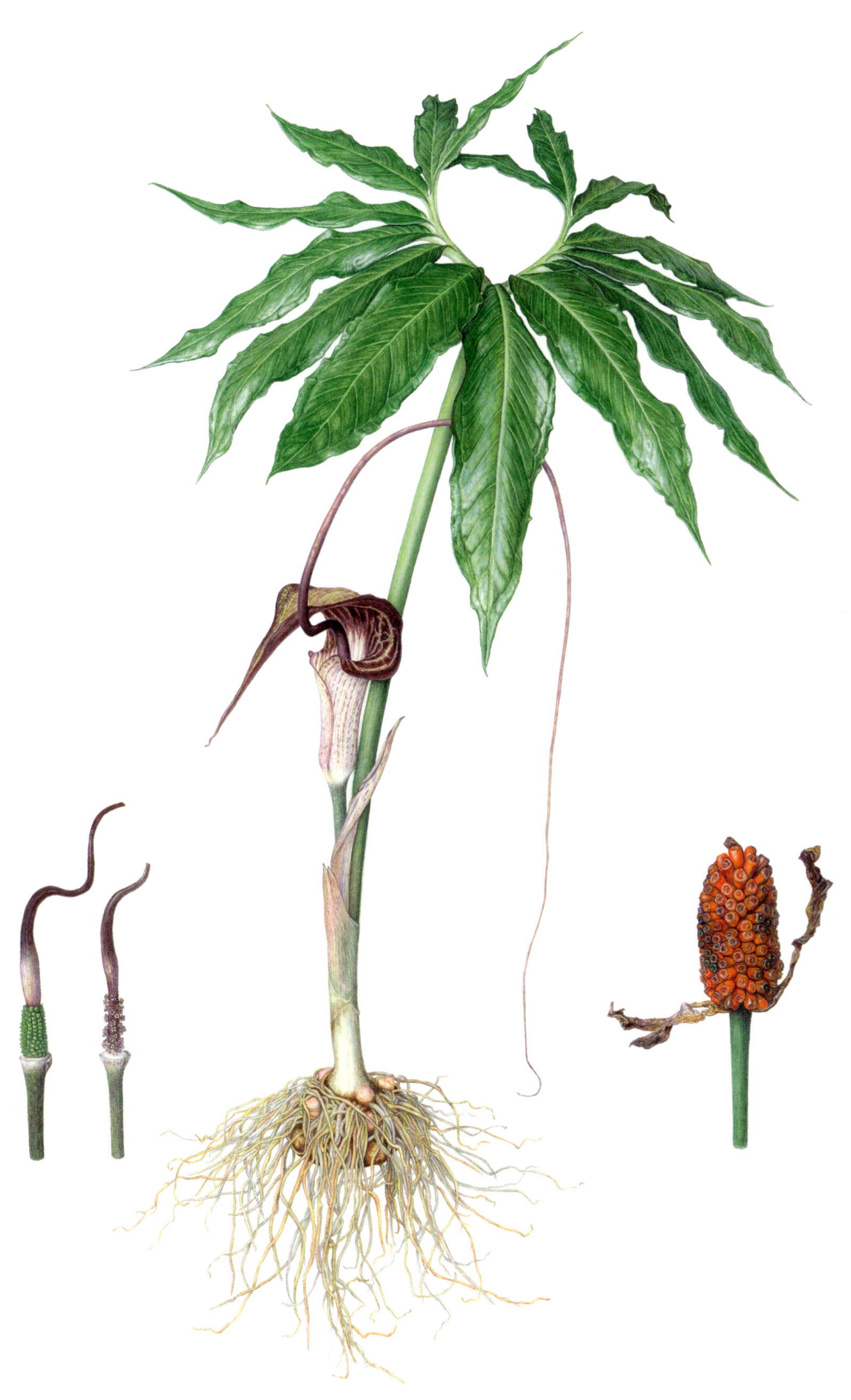

Arisaema thunbergii subsp. *urashima*, 2019–2021

Watercolour on paper

Celia Hegedüs

RHS medal history

Gold medals: 1995, 1996, 1998, 2000, 2001, 2004

Silver-Gilt medals: 1993, 1997, 1999

Celia Hegedüs exhibited nine times with the RHS, winning six Gold medals between 1995 and 2004.

Having been encouraged to paint from childhood by her mother, Hegedüs continued her training at the Hammersmith School of Art and with City and Guilds. She exhibited at the Royal Academy's summer exhibition in 1993 and 1995. She is renowned for her work on vellum and has extensive experience of managing this challenging medium, which is extremely sensitive to changes in environmental humidity levels. Hegedüs prefers to stretch and mount her own vellum, in order to manage the correct tension.

The painting featured here of *Iris pseudacorus* was purchased from the artist in early 2000, as part of the library's newly established programme of purchasing the work of outstanding Gold medal-winning artists. It originally formed part of Hegedüs's display from 2000.

Iris pseudacorus, summer 1999

Watercolour on vellum mounted onto board

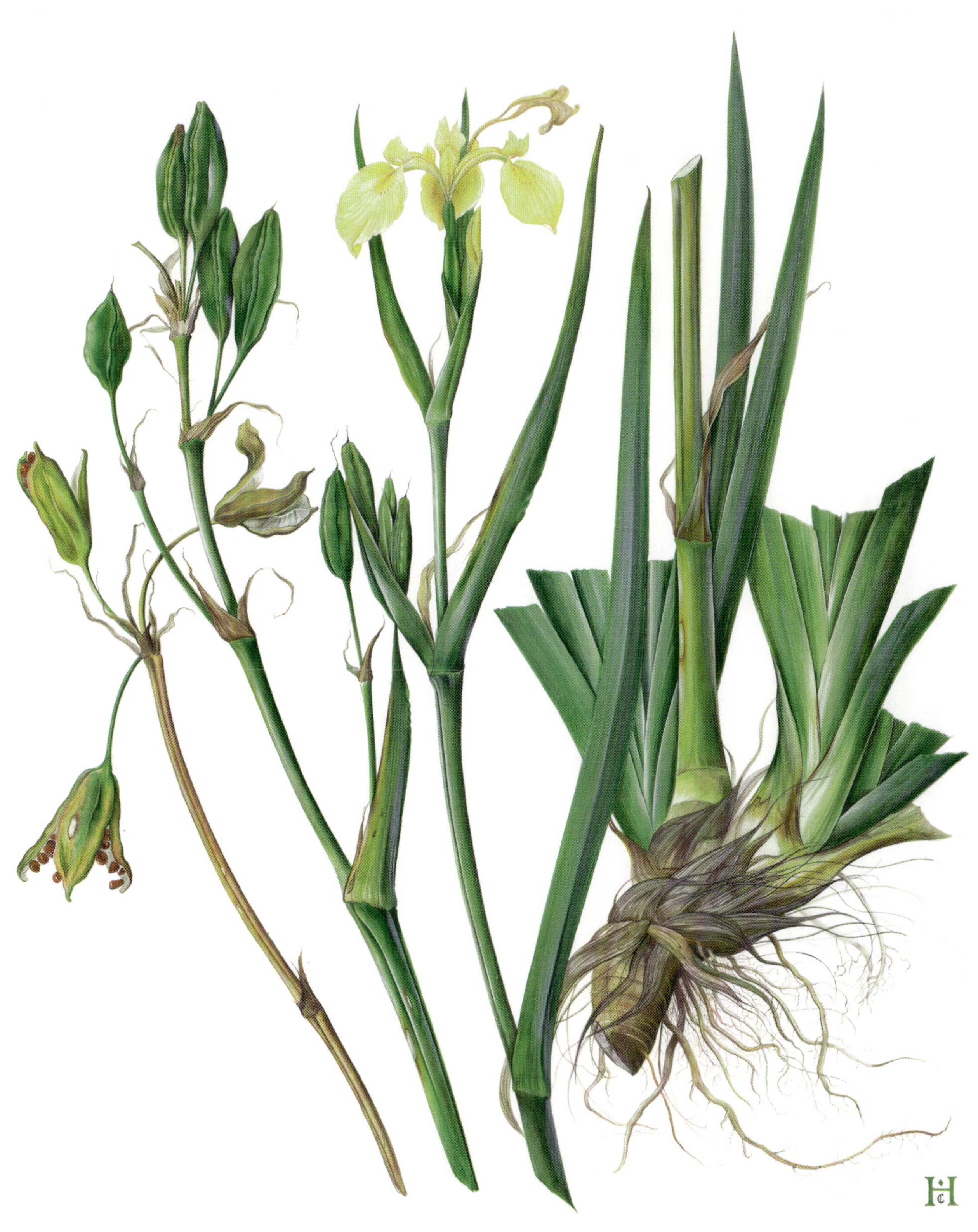

"It was painted from life from a specimen I had growing in a pot. The flowering stem was painted first. I then painted the roots and leaves and then the green pods. The dried seed pods were composed from previous studies and the painting took approximately three weeks.

The appeal of this particular Iris dates back many years to when I first saw a painting of it by Pieter van Kouwenhoorn reproduced in The Art of Botanical Illustration *by Blunt and Stearn. The painting was a major inspiration for me when I began to paint botanical studies and remains my favourite."*

Inspiration: *Iris pseudacorus* by Pieter van Kouwenhoorn (*c.*1630s)
from the RHS Lindley Collections

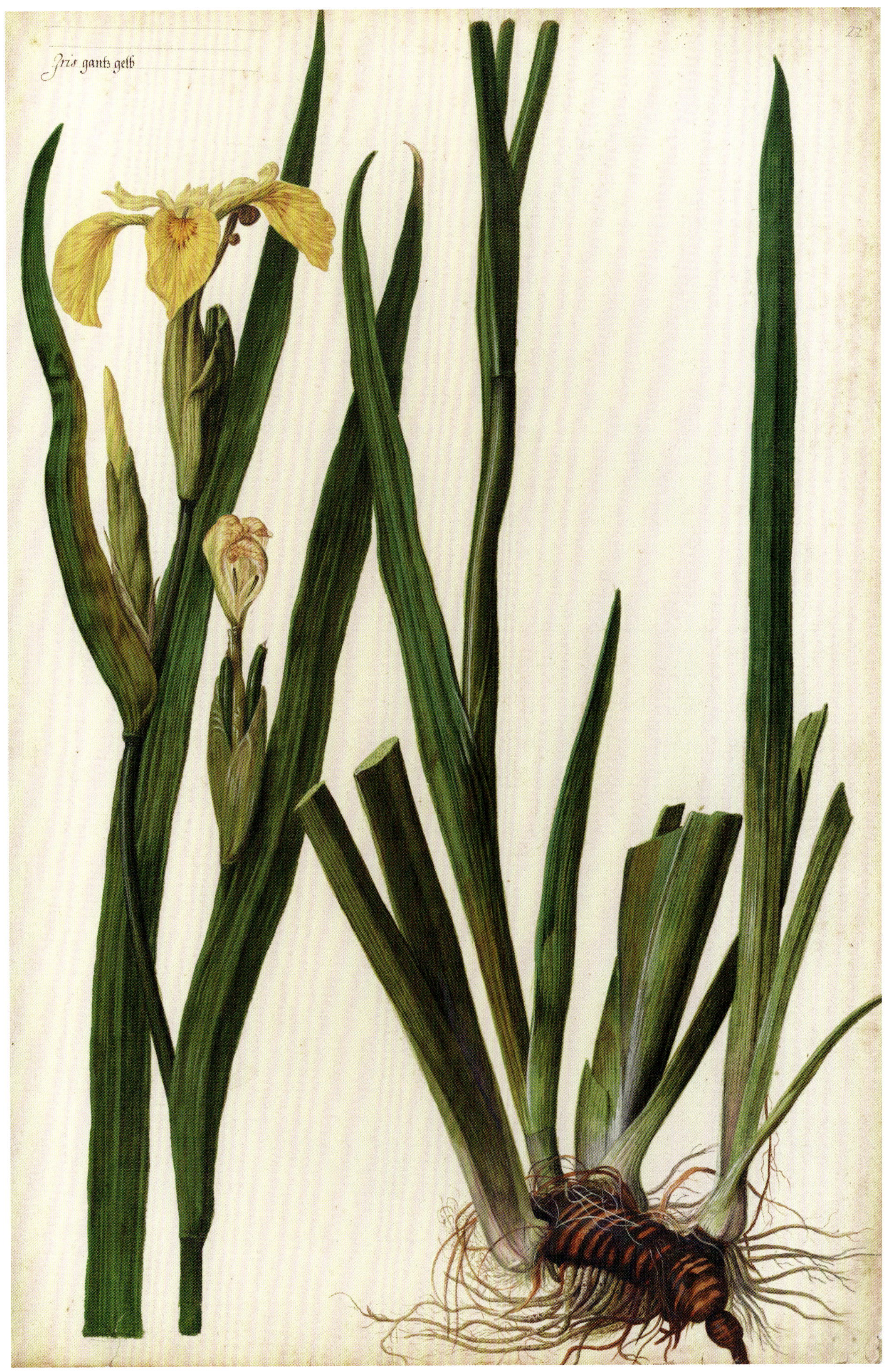
Iris gantz gelb
22

Asuka Hishiki

RHS medal history

Gold medal: 2023

Asuka Hishiki was born in Japan, where she continues to live and work. With a focus on oil painting, she gained a Master of Fine Arts degree from Kyoto City University of Arts, Japan. She has a long-held fascination for the natural world. Her career in botanical art took off with a first-place award in 2010 at the Mills Pond Gallery in New York, USA. This led to numerous exhibitions, plus teaching workshops and residencies.

In 2023, Hishiki exhibited with the RHS for the first time, where she gained a Gold medal for her series 'Pomona: Fruit on a Tree'. She explained that when preparing to undertake a new series, the most important step for her, was to fall in love with her subject. Whilst preparing for her RHS display, she struggled to find a suitable theme, but then gazing out of the window:

"I saw a persimmon tree in our backyard and an image of a beautiful goddess looking over the fruit trees appeared in front of me, and she handed me a branch with fruit on it. A theme popped up to my mind, POMONA! It was like being in heaven working with the fruit. The Buddha's hand had such a soothing scent. I really felt like I was a part of a myth in Ancient Rome, with fruits around my table."

Citrus medica var. *sarcodactylis* (Buddha's hand), 2022

Watercolour on paper

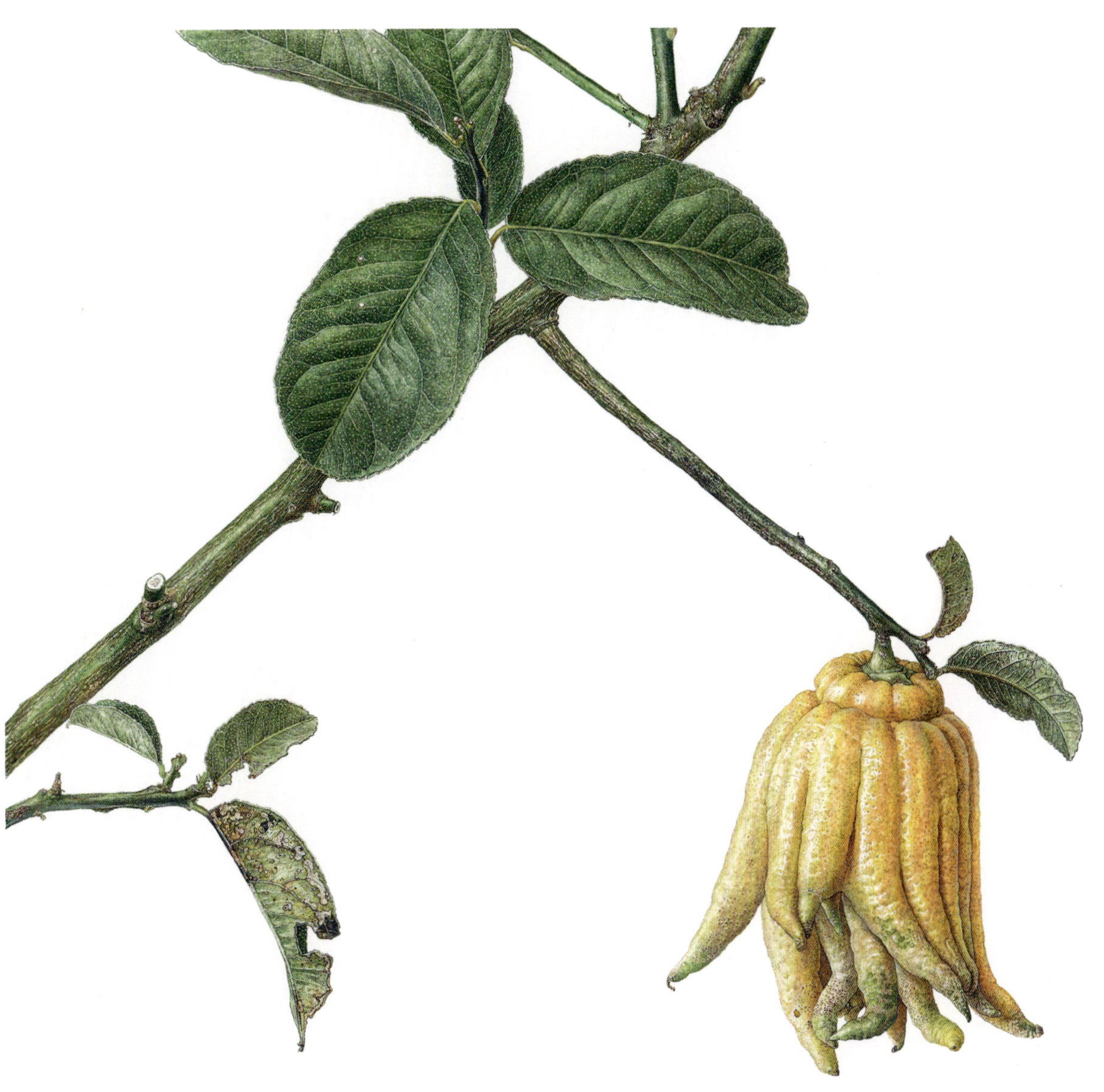

Hideo Horikoshi

RHS medal history

Gold medals: 2015 (and Best Botanical Painting), 2018

Horikoshi has exhibited twice with the RHS and both times he has been awarded a Gold medal.

This illustration of *Solanum tuberosum* 'Danshaku', was exhibited at the RHS in 2015 as part of a series entitled 'Traditional Root and Tuber Crops in Japan'. Hideo Horikoshi was awarded a Gold medal and Best Botanical Painting, for another of the paintings in the set, *Daucus carota* 'Kintokininjin'.

Horikoshi lives in Tokyo, where he grows over 70 different varieties of vegetables on his allotment. This Irish Cobbler potato was painted over a period of 5 months and was based on observations made over two growing seasons.

Now considered a national favourite in Japan, the Irish Cobbler was first imported in 1907 by Baron Ryokichi Kawada; in Japan it was renamed the 'Danshaku', which means 'Baron' in Japanese, in his honour. It has become the most popular variety of potato in Japan and is used in a number of national dishes. Sadly, this variety is no longer in cultivation in Ireland.

Solanum tuberosum 'Danshaku', 2015

Watercolour on paper

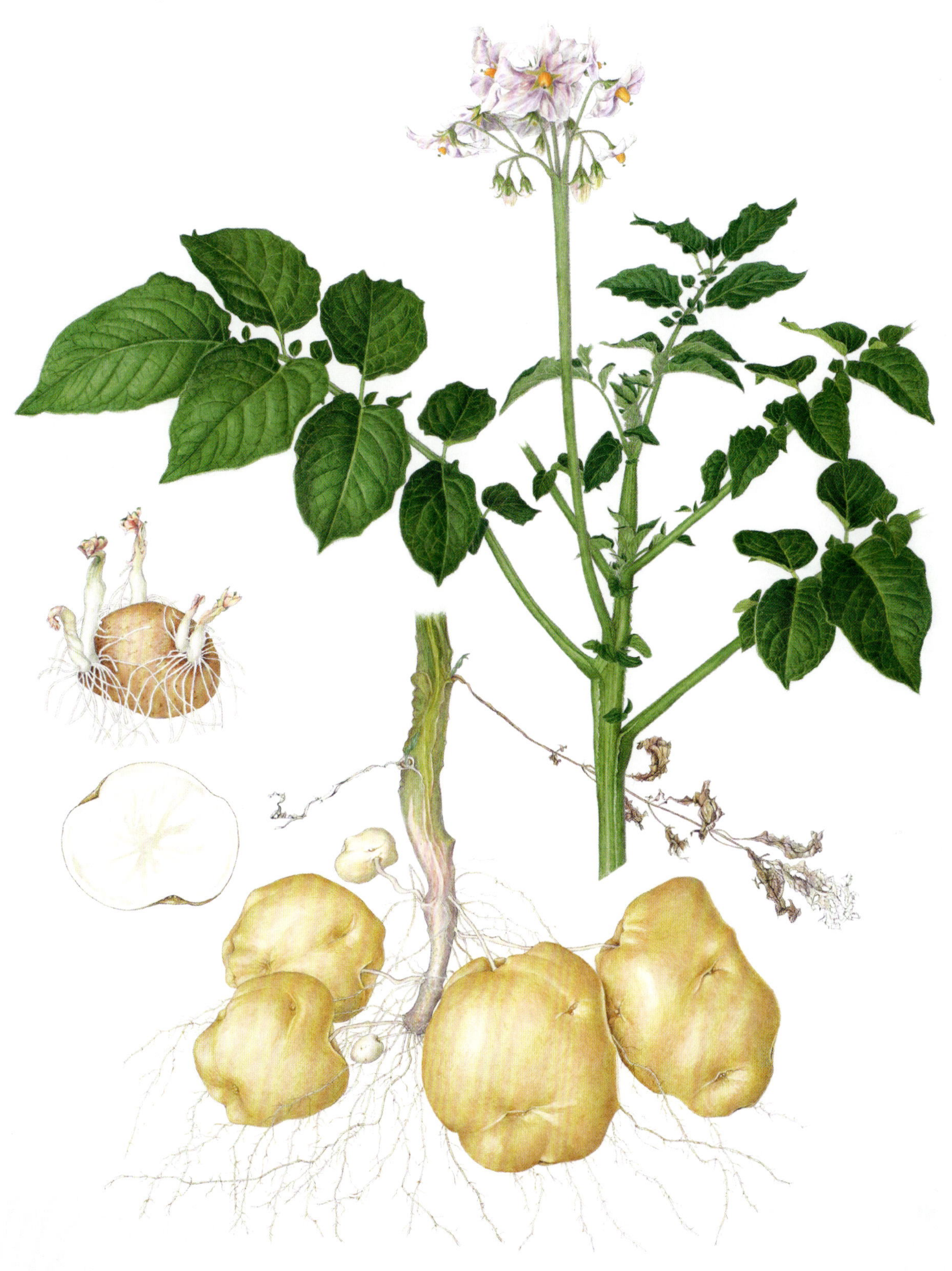

Horikoshi's early training in Agriculture and Technology was subsequently followed by a passion for botanical art. For his display of watercolours of classical Japanese chrysanthemums in 2018, Horikoshi spent the season of 2015 studying and sketching his specimens at the National Museum of Japanese History and Shinjuku Gyoen National Garden in Japan. He started painting during the flowering season in November 2016 and finally finished the following November. These rare *Edo-giku* chrysanthemums only grow in these locations, so required a lot of time spent observing them in situ. His tutor and mentor is Mieko Ishikawa, also a recipient of an RHS Gold medal.

Chrysanthemum × *morifolium* 'Edo', 2016–2017

Watercolour on paper

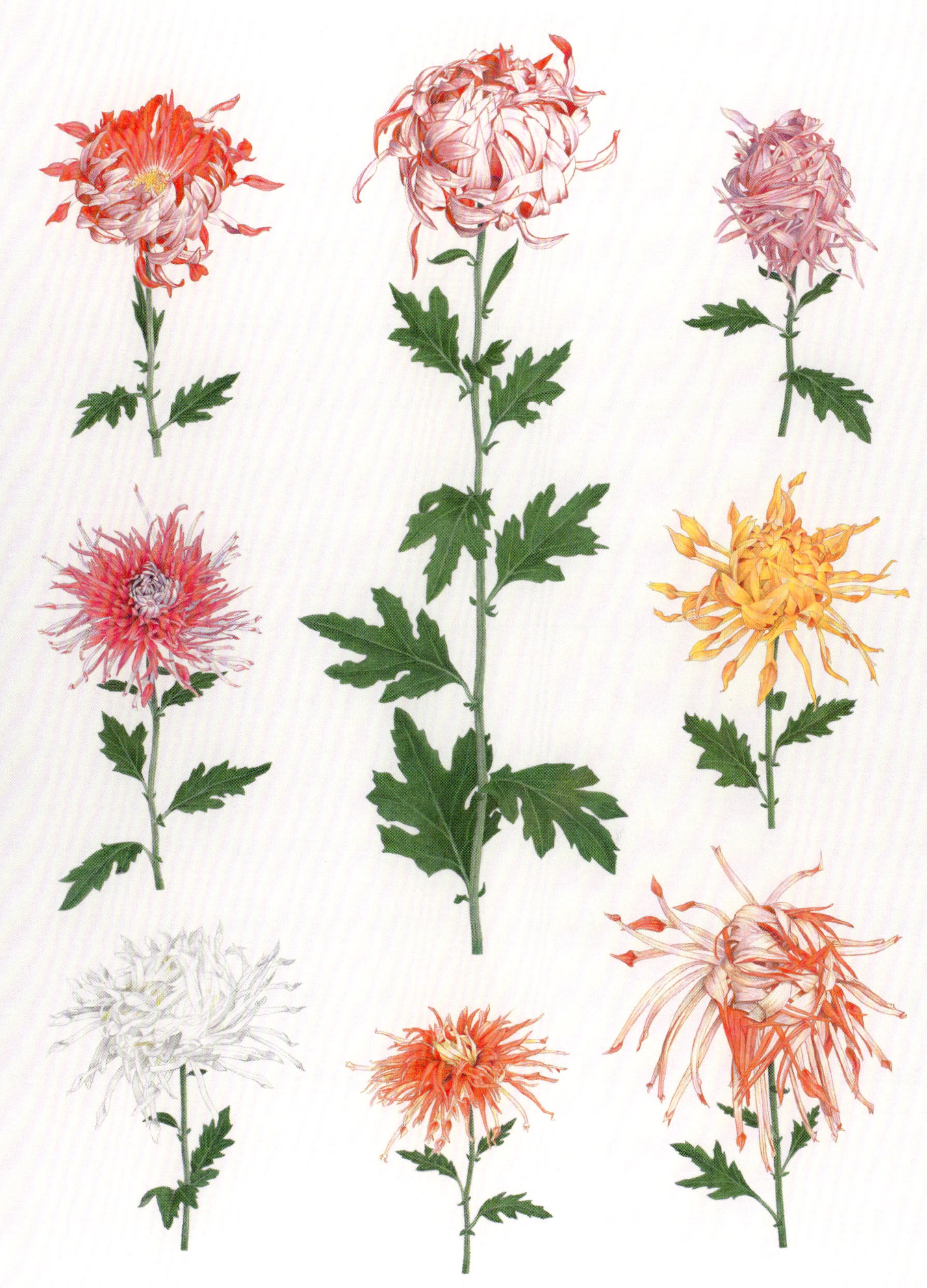

Annie Hughes

RHS medal history

Gold medals: 2011, 2012 (and Best Botanical Painting), 2013, 2017

Annie Hughes has won a total of four Gold medals for exhibits of botanical art between 2011 and 2017. For the painting featured here of *Astrophytum ornatum,* exhibited in 2012, Hughes was also awarded Best Botanical Painting. The same year, Hughes painted '*Citrus* no. 3 (with lime)', which was part of her Gold medal-winning display in 2013.

Hughes' approach to each of these paintings was very different:

"I work in the wet-on-wet method. This is something that was learnt many years ago in my work as a Textile Designer. This can be a very free-and-easy way of painting, on the other hand it also demands the tightness and precision needed for a Paisley design or a Plaid, two very opposite techniques not dissimilar to Botanical Art.

My 'Citrus' painting was very straightforward: colouring each element in turn, washing in the colour and finishing with dry brush. Until the cross-section of the fruit – this had to be worked segment by segment and each vesicle painted separately to capture the translucency and moisture of the fruit, as well as the oil glands on the skin.

Citrus no.3 (with lime), 2012

Watercolour on paper

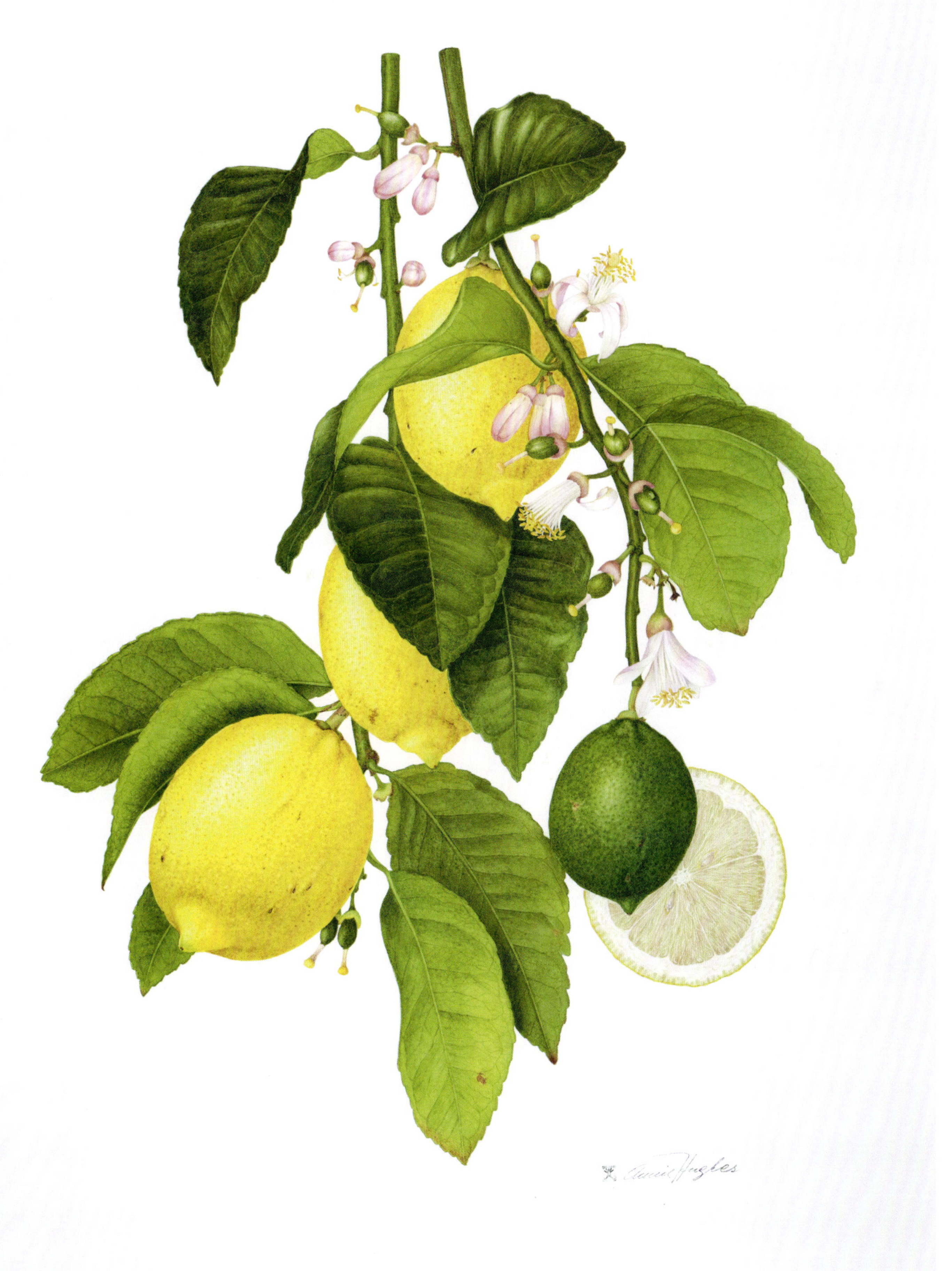

The Astrophytum ornatum *cactus, incidentally, had to be painted twice, as the first one was rejected by the grower I went to for advice. The problem was the spots, or 'flocking'. They were not in the correct pattern indicative of this particular species, so it had to be painted again.*

I tackled the cactus painting in a very methodical way. Each section of the plant was worked separately: first the spines had to be masked with a dip pen, next the body colour was applied with all the tonalities required. In turn, all sections were worked in the same fashion. As soon as the body was painted satisfactorily, the masking had to be removed quickly as to not damage the paper. The next step was to paint the spines with all their own details, then those troublesome spots in the correct pattern and, lastly, the flower and the pebbles.

I took the painting to the grower for his critique and he gave his approval.

As with all my work I try to combine the looseness of a flawless wash, which is very important to me as I do not like to see brush marks; this gives me the platform on to which all the detail is then added. This, combined with a very sound design, should make for a very pleasing artwork."

Astrophytum ornatum, 2012

Watercolour on paper

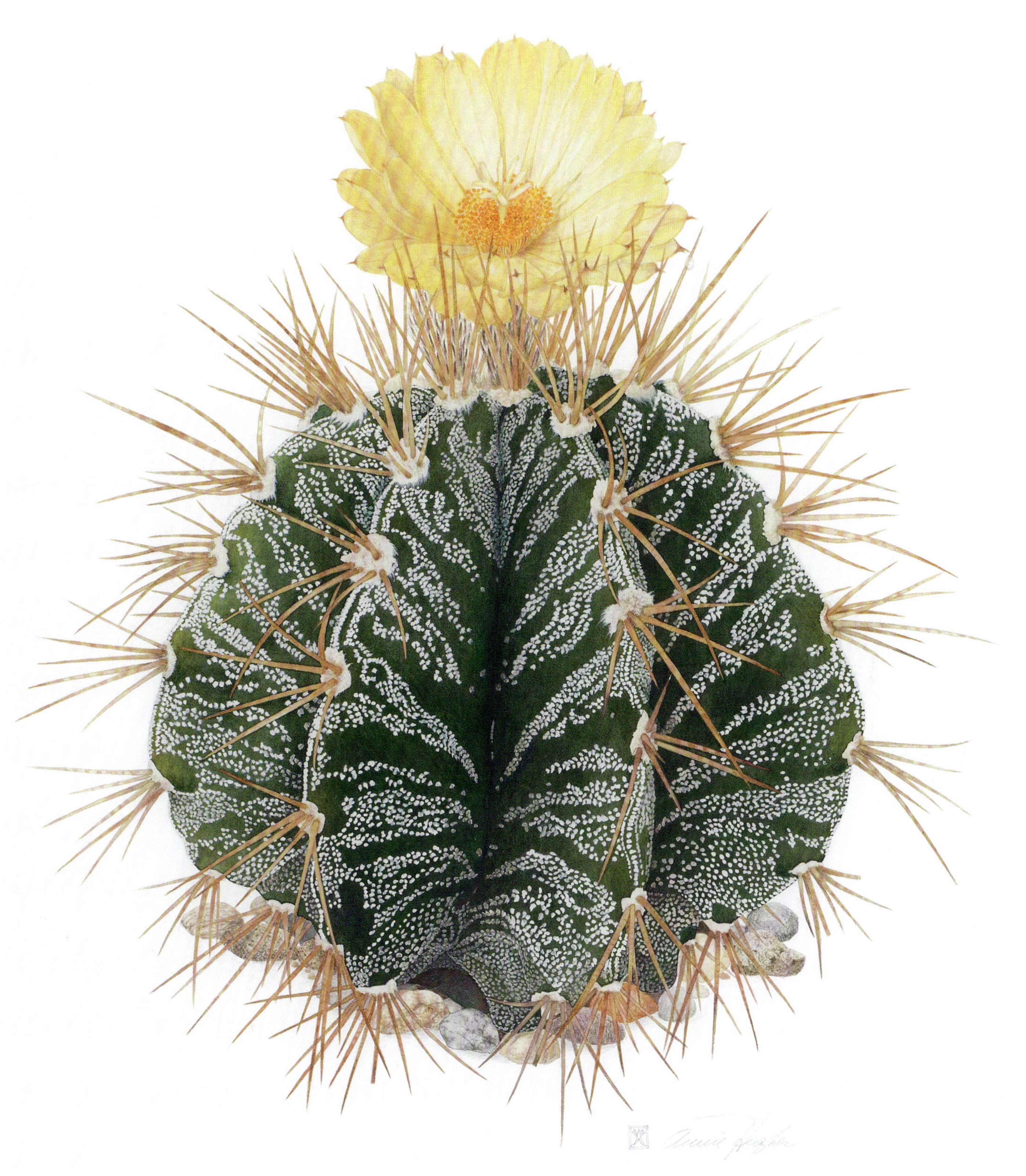

Mariko Ikeda

RHS medal history

Gold medals: 2017 (and Best Botanical Art Exhibit), 2019

Mariko Ikeda's *Pandanus* paintings, exhibited at the RHS in 2017, saw her awarded a Gold medal as well as Best Exhibit. This picture of *Pandanus dubius,* executed in her home town of Tochigi in Japan, she describes as the *"hardest picture I have ever painted"*. All of the pieces exhibited were of specimens seen growing in their natural habitats. The fruit featured here weighed over 12 kg and was collected from the coastal forest of Guam Island in the Pacific.

The painting itself took two months to complete, but between Ikeda's research and waiting to receive permission to work on the island, the project took five months in all. Yet, she described the wonderful experience of seeing this habitat and the excitement of being there, which helped her to overcome the difficulty of painting this challenging fruit.

Pandanus dubius, 2016

Watercolour on vellum, stretched

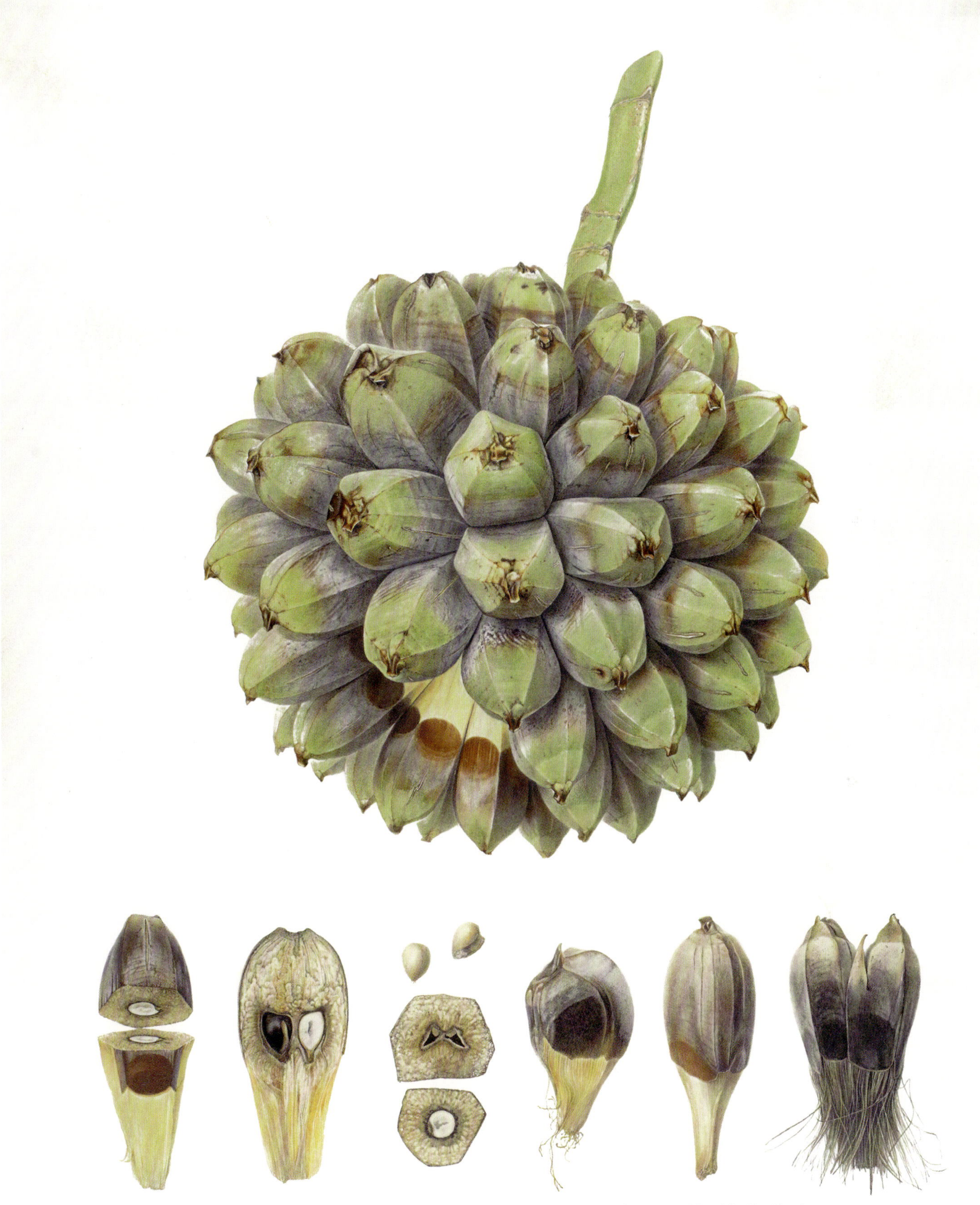
Pandanus dubius Sprengler
20th June 2016 Mariko Ikeda

Jackie Isard

RHS medal history

Gold medal: 2022

Jackie Isard had a long career as a graphic designer based in South West England, having graduated with a degree in graphic design from Ravensbourne University, London in 1989. A garden design course ignited her passion for plants, and in 2015 she decided to try botanical art. She exhibited with the Society of Botanical Artists for the first time in 2016. Now a Fellow, she teaches regular classes and specialist workshops in person and online.

Jackie's passion for wild flowers informed her series of paintings for the RHS titled 'Wet meadow wildflowers – their pollinators and as food plants', for which she was awarded a Gold medal. Extensive research over a five-year period, meant she came to understand and appreciate the delicate ecosystem of water meadows, and the interaction between the plant habitats and their pollinating insects and bees.

"For my exhibition theme I selected wet meadow wildflowers because they are under threat due to intensive farming methods and the draining of floodplains.

Before I drew each plant, it was important to me to understand their botany and life cycle. I studied the plants throughout the seasons, made botany notes, matched the colour to live specimens and studied details under a microscope."

Geum rivale (water avens) with *Bombus pascuorum* (bee), 2020

Watercolour on paper

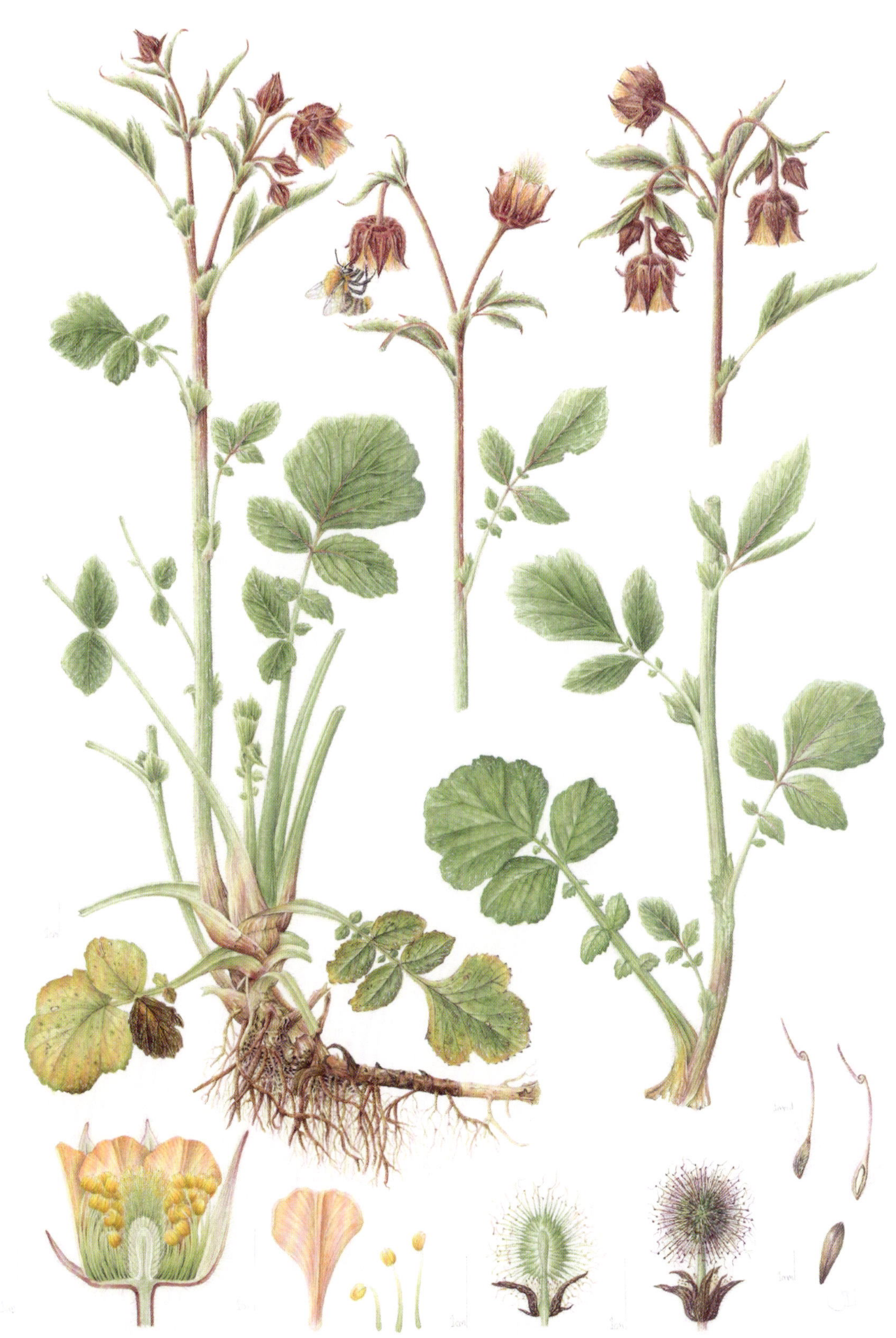

Mieko Ishikawa

RHS medal history

Gold medal: 2006

Mieko Ishikawa was awarded a Gold medal in 2006 for her exhibit of 'Sakura: flowering cherries of Japan in watercolour', which included this painting of *Prunus pendula* 'Pendula Plena Rosea'. This series of ten paintings took Ishikawa five years to complete; she estimates it took 60 hours of work, carried out over many months, to complete each piece.

Ishikawa also takes a particular interest in plants found in the tropical rainforests of Borneo. She has travelled there several times in order to paint plants in their native habitat and seeks to capture them at life size, where possible.

Ishikawa graduated in Visual Communication and Design from Musashino Art University in Tokyo. She later studied under artist Junzo Fujishima, before becoming established as a freelance botanical illustrator. Ishikawa has taught extensively throughout Japan and six of her students have been awarded RHS Gold medals, including Hideo Horikoshi, Mariko Ikeda and Yoko Harada.

Prunus pendula 'Pendula Rosea' (drooping rosebud cherry), 2006

Watercolour and graphite on paper

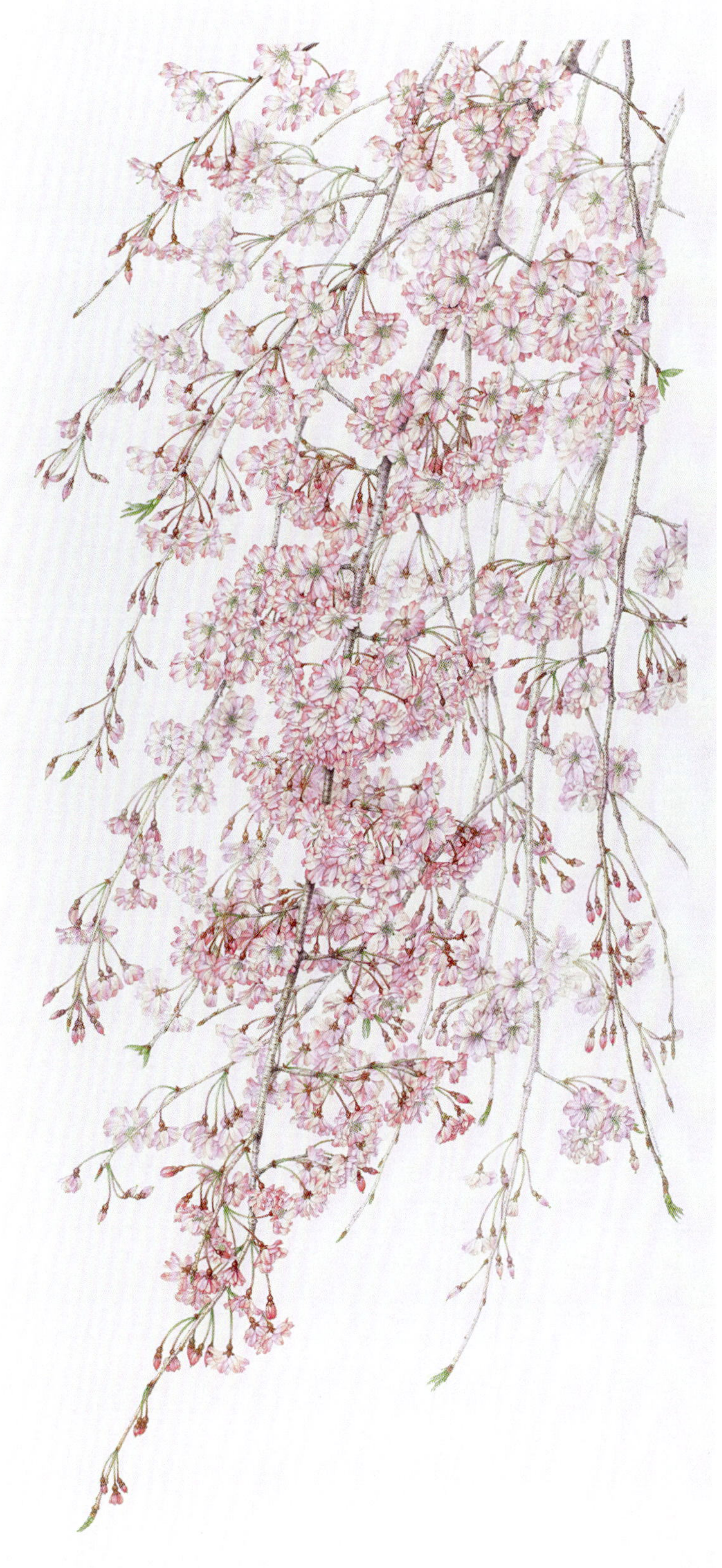

Caroline Jackson-Houlston

RHS medal history

Gold medal: 2018 (and Best Botanical Art Exhibit)

Silver-Gilt medal: 2019

Silver medals: 2000, 2001

Following early exhibitions in 2000 and 2001, which resulted in Silver medals, Caroline Jackson-Houlston continued to paint botanical and other wildlife subjects. Her display in 2018 of '*Passiflora*' resulted in the sought-after Gold medal and award for Best Botanical Art Exhibit.

Jackson-Houlston considers watercolour the best medium for botanical painting, though she would not call herself a watercolourist. Her typical method is to lay the specimen on paper to gain a rough working layout, and then to set up the design with lightly pencilled geometric forms to indicate the main masses of the painting. The parts of the plant are then measured using a ruler and/or dividers, and key divisions or shapes – such as centres of flowers, main lines of petals or leaf junctions on stems – are very lightly pencilled in. The specimen is then drawn directly and in detail on to hot-pressed 300gsm paper, as the artist finds that copying reduces spontaneity and accuracy. Although she retains photographic references as a back-up, all colour-matching, sizing and drawing is done direct from the plant. Jackson-Houlston describes herself as a very slow painter. She uses colour washes for large areas of leaf or petal, but most of the detail is dry-brush work. Tiny colour samples are dabbed onto the edge of the paper and matched directly against the specimen. White gouache may be used, especially for hairs against blocks of darker colour.

Passiflora × *violacea*

Watercolour on paper (completed January 2018)

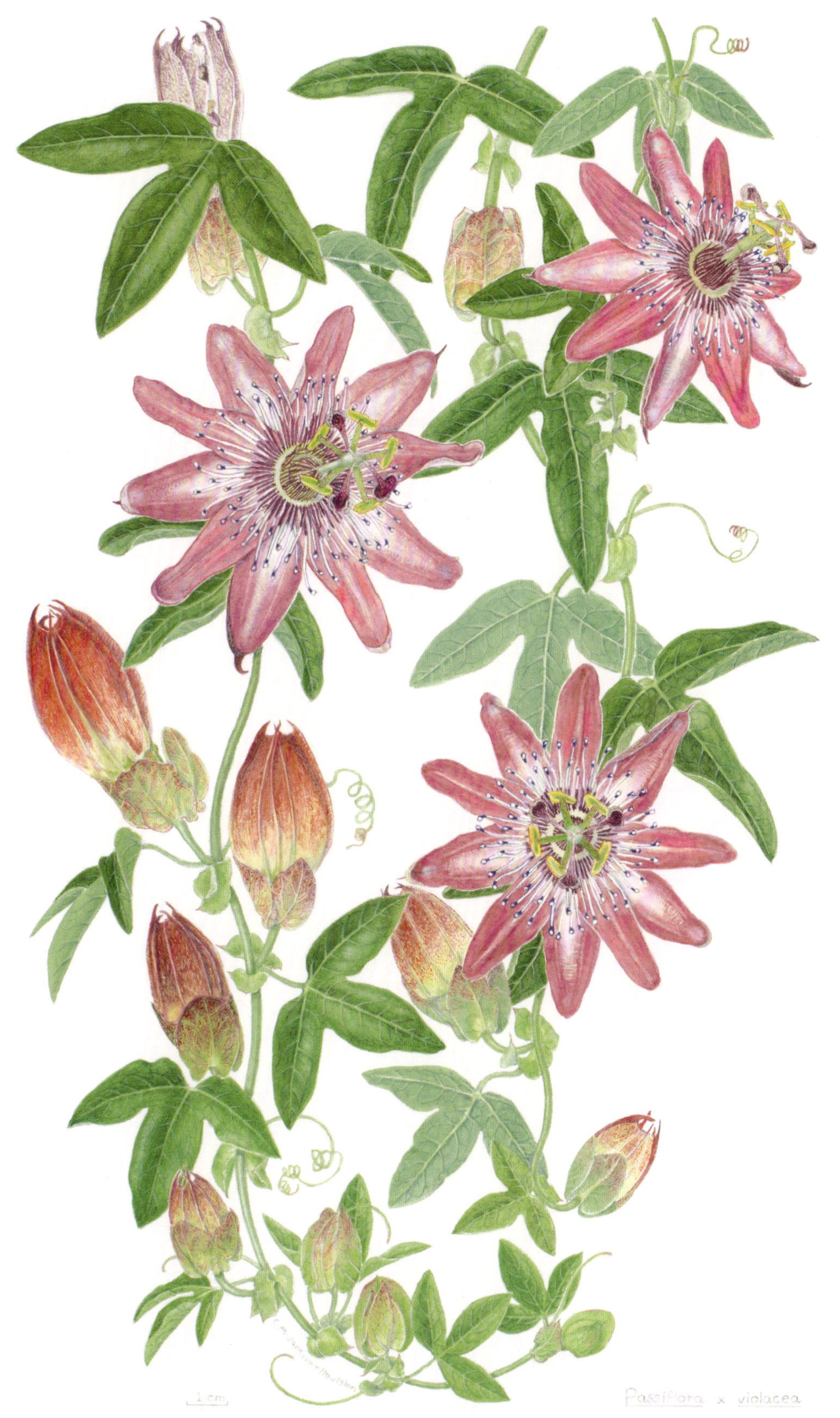
C.M. Jackson-Houlston
1 cm
Passiflora x violacea

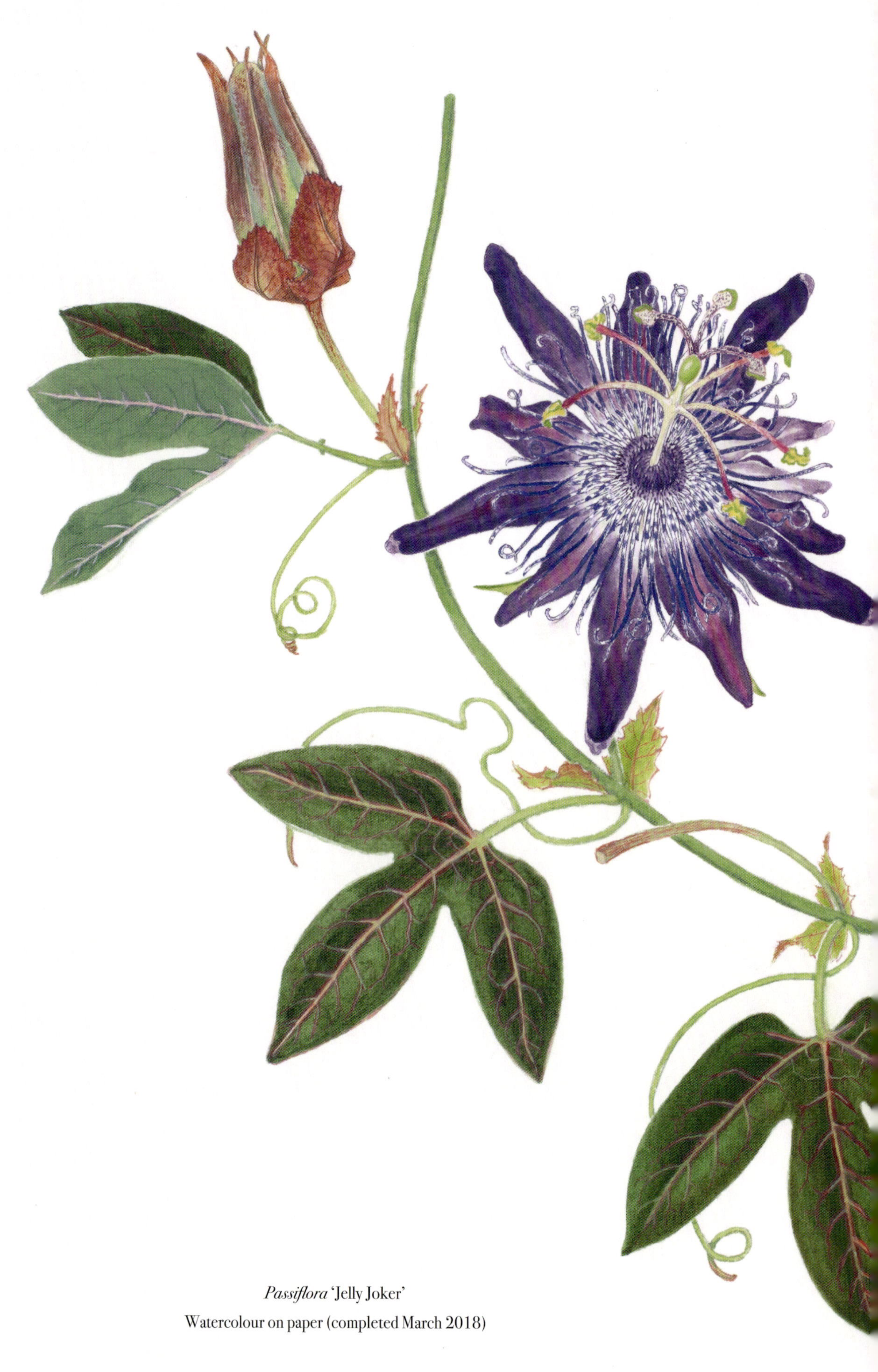

Passiflora 'Jelly Joker'

Watercolour on paper (completed March 2018)

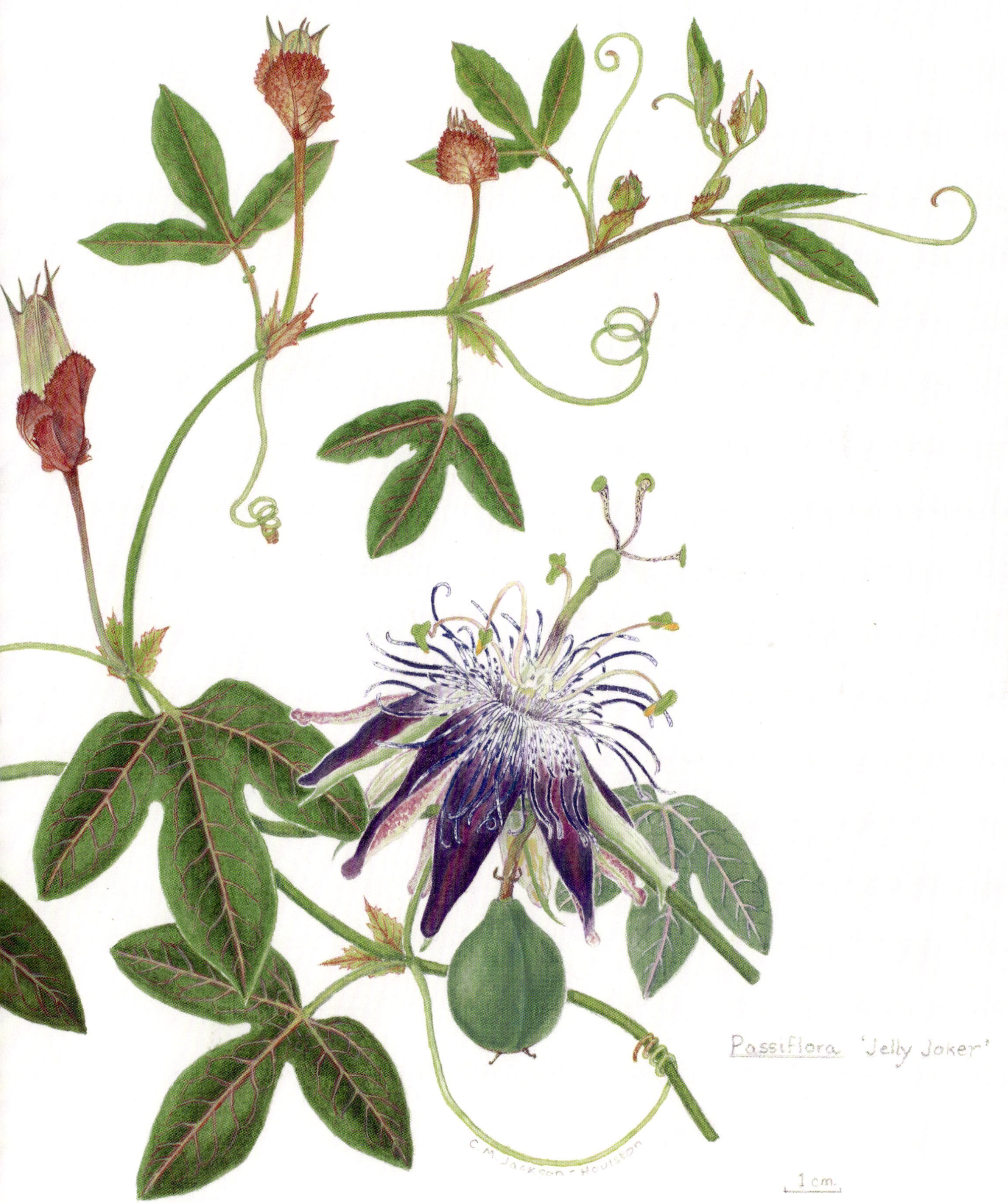
Passiflora 'Jelly Joker'
C.M. Jackson-Houlston
1 cm.

Carolyn Jenkins

RHS medal history

Gold medal: 2011 (and Best Exhibit)

Silver medal: 2016

Carolyn Jenkins first exhibited with the RHS in 2011, winning a Gold medal and Best Exhibit for 'The Anatomy of Flowers', which included the picture of *Helleborus* × *hybridus* featured here.

Jenkins had been a gardener and illustrator for over 20 years before studying for her Diploma in Botanical Painting at the English Gardening School, in 2009.

She has a fascination for the internal structures of plants, having been drawn to the work of late nineteenth-century botanical illustrator, Arthur Harry Church. Originally developed as botanical teaching aids, Church's 'mechanical' drawings sought to describe the development of the flower and the way in which it is pollinated.

Helleborus × *hybridus*, 2010

Watercolour on paper

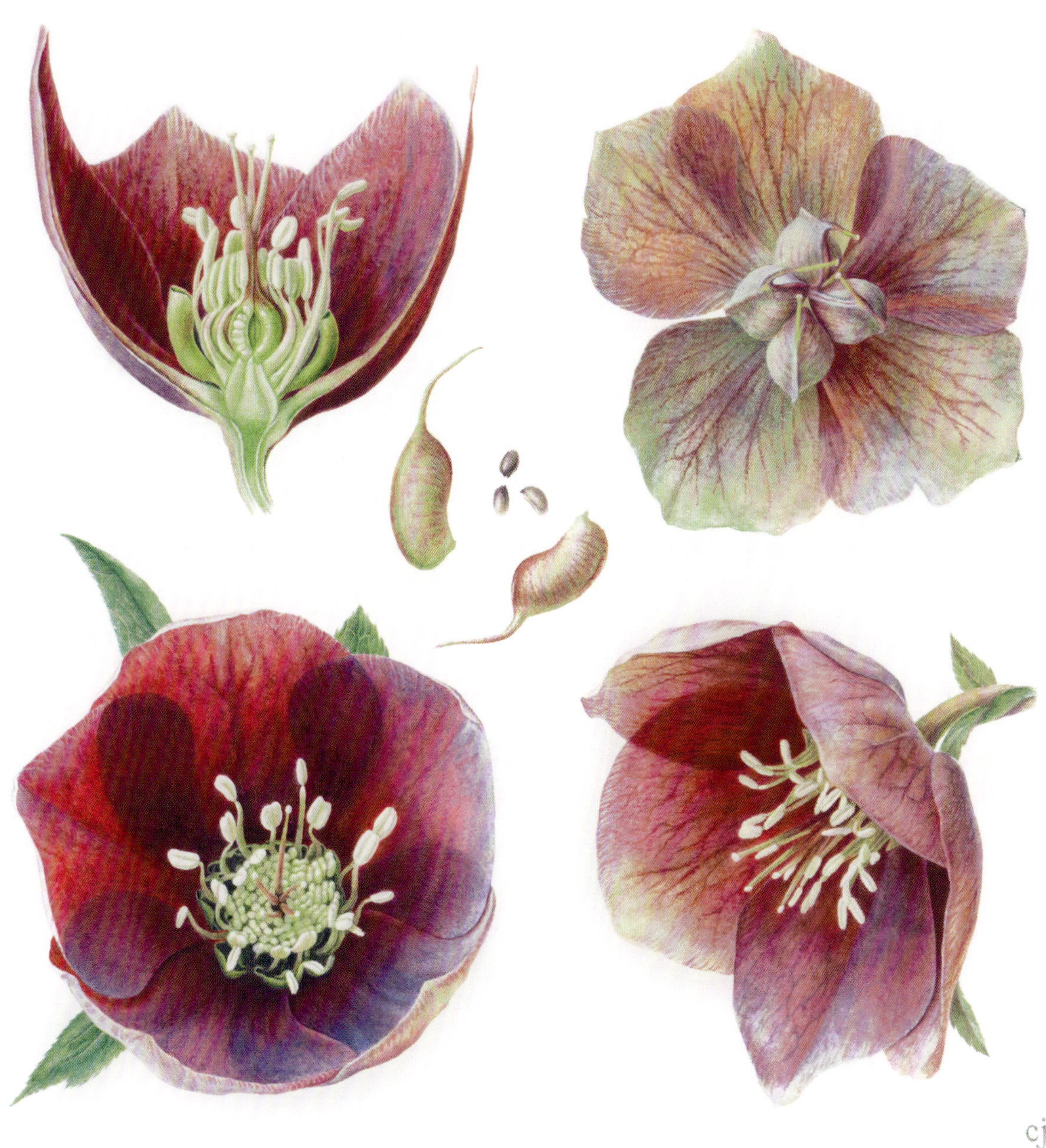
cj

Jenkins takes inspiration from Church's striking compositions, updating this approach to create pictures that are both technical and beautiful. The illustration of *Helleborus* × *hybridus* is constructed to show the difference in appearance between the unpollinated flower and the fertilised flower following pollination, where the nectary ring and anthers have fallen away leaving just the inflated seed follicles (or pods) and sepals. The seed follicles and their seeds also sit at the centre of the composition and help provide a point of focus to the painting.

Jenkins further develops the theme with her painting of *Dahlia* 'Arabian Night'. It is in contrast to a more classical approach to botanical illustration, where the full bloom of the flower head is complemented with a cross-section or magnified detail to the side. Conversely, in this picture Jenkins has sought to present the anatomical structure of the flower as the central image. In microscopic detail she reveals the way in which the flower head (or 'capitulum') of the dahlia is made up of a prolific number of colourful florets in concentric rings.

Dahlia 'Arabian Night', 2011

Watercolour on paper

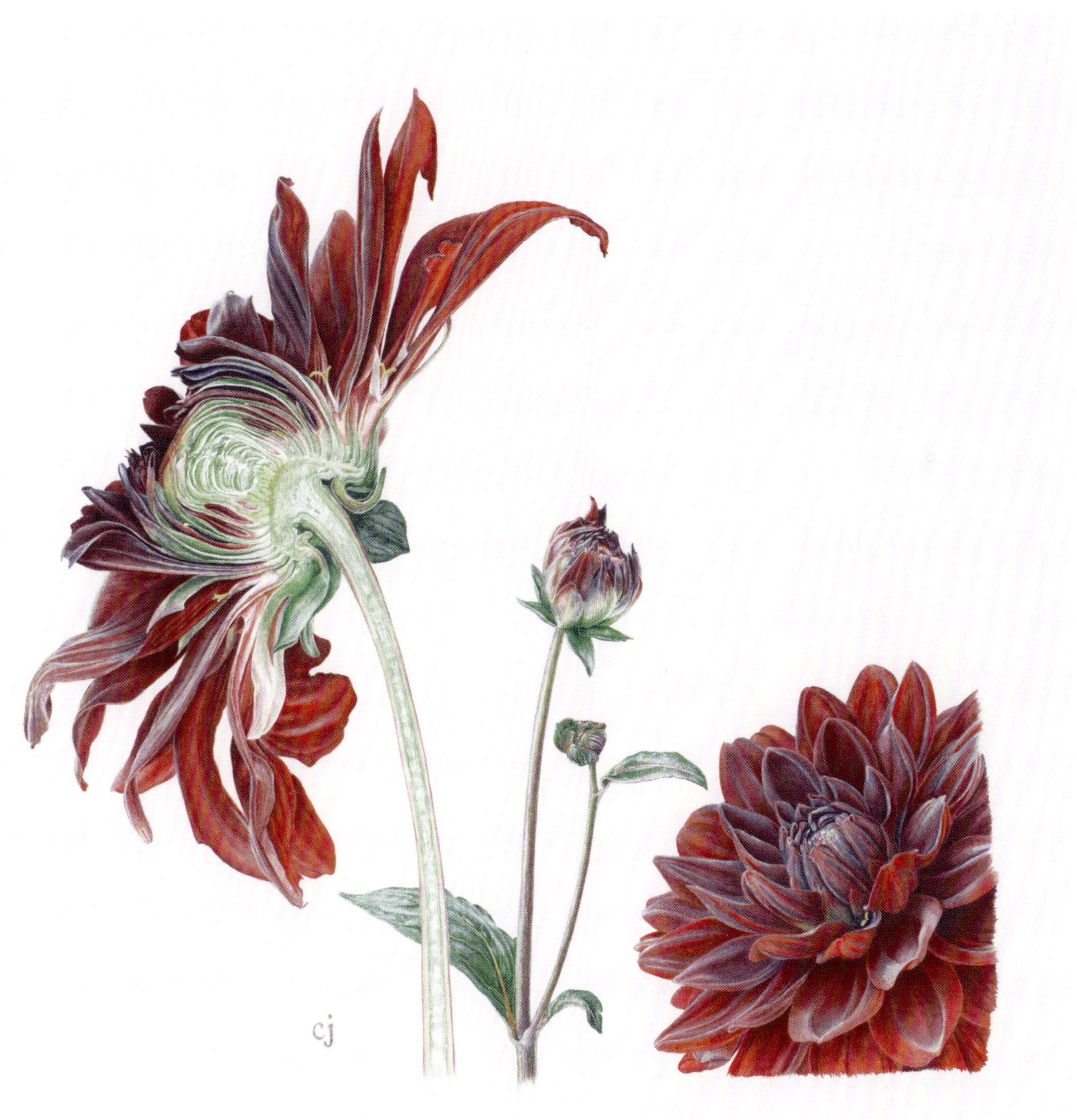
cj

Jenny Jowett
(1936-2019)

RHS medal history

Gold medals: 1988, February 1989, 1996, 2006

Silver-Gilt medals: 1986, July 1989, 1991

Silver medals: 1975, 1979

Jenny Jowett was awarded a total of nine medals, including four Gold medals, for exhibits of botanical art at RHS Shows between 1975 and 2006.

Jowett enjoyed a career as a botanical artist, teacher and landscape painter over many years. She completed over 1,051 paintings for inclusion in public and private collections, as well as for publication. She painted and taught in her garden studio, at home in Berkshire, with much of her inspiration coming from the rare and unusual plants she grew at home or from other local gardens and nurseries.

Helleborus × *sternii* 'Blackthorn Strain' was painted from a specimen bred by Robin White of Blackthorn Nurseries. Completed in March 1988, it was displayed as part of a series of 'Hellebores' that won a Gold medal the following February.

Helleborus × *sternii* Blackthorn Group (syn: *Helleborus* × *sternii* 'Blackthorn Strain'), 1988

Watercolour on paper

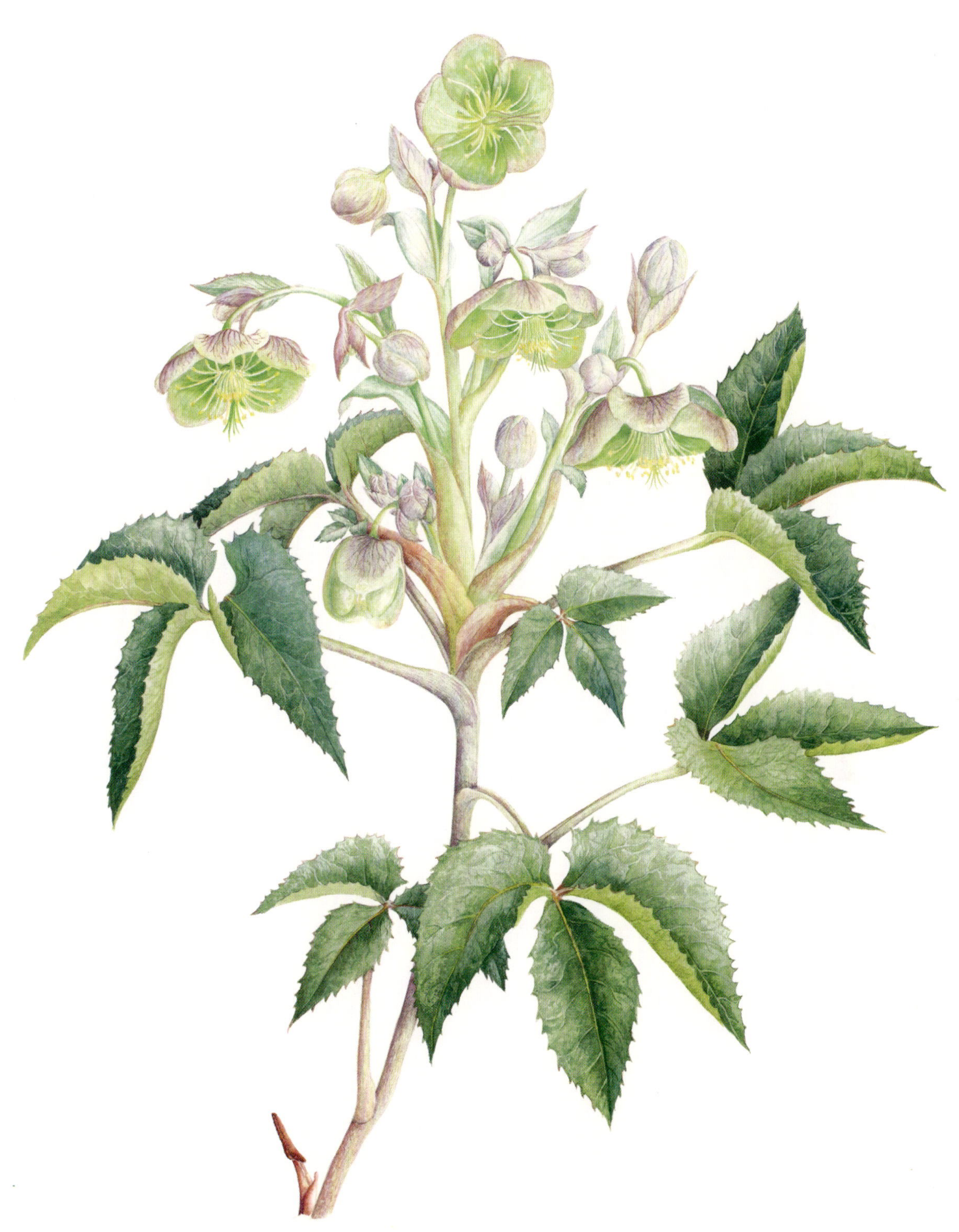
Helleborus × sternii Blackthorn strain

Cornus 'Eddie's White Wonder' was one of a number of paintings Jowett exhibited at Oxford Botanic Gardens in 2009. She had been able to take the specimen from a large local garden with an extensive collection of ericaceous plants including Rhododendrons, Cornus and Camellias.

Until her death in 2019, Jowett ran the botanical painting course at Flatford Mill in Suffolk, having been persuaded to take it over in 1985 by Mary Grierson, who had succeeded John Nash.

Cornus 'Eddie's White Wonder', 2009

Watercolour on paper

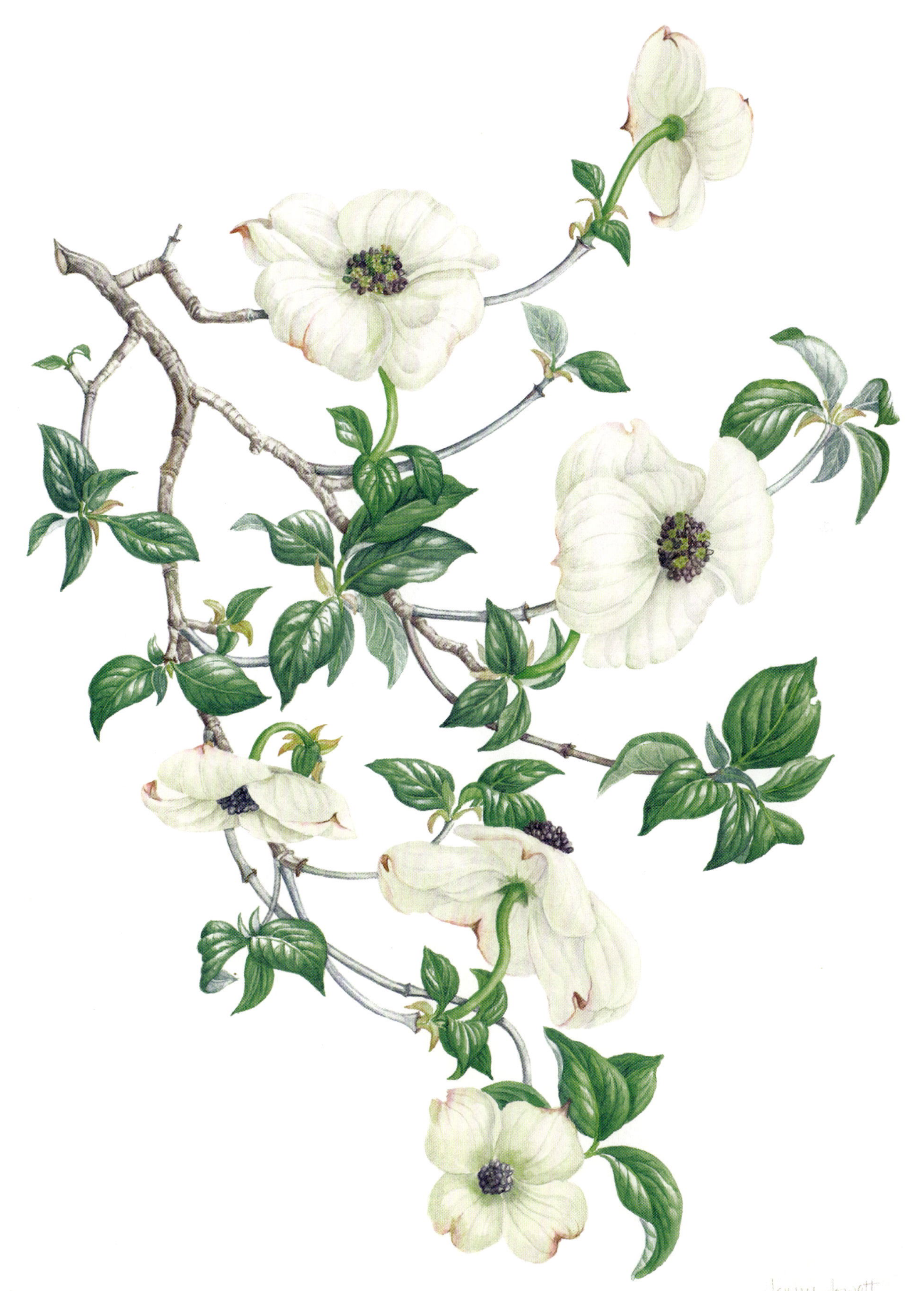
Jenny Jowett

Mitsuko Kurashina

RHS medal history

Gold medal: 2022 (and Judges' Special Award)

Mitsuko Kurashina lives and works in Japan. Originally from Aomori Prefecture, she is now based in Tokyo. Her early career as a graphic designer was followed by a period working at Yuzen Kimono studio. During this time, Kurashina also studied botanical art, culminating in a course in plant ecology. She has been painting as a freelance botanical artist since 2010.

Absorbed by the process of renewal, Kurashina has focused for many years on the plants that emerged after the Great East Japan Earthquake and Tsunami of 2011. The natural disaster resulted in terrible loss of life and extensive environmental damage. However, Kurashina came to see signs of new life as signs of hope. Her exhibit for the RHS in 2022, was presented under the title 'tsunami plants", deliberately written in lowercase letters, to soften the impact. Kurashina was awarded a Gold medal and the Judges' Special Award for these artworks.

"My paintings show coastal plant colonies thriving in inland areas. They show endangered plants flourishing. They show the germination of seeds from soil banks. I visited the sites to study the plants closely in the field. A withered stem told me how the plant looked the previous year. Grains of sand surrounding the plant allowed me to feel the history of the place. You can see in my paintings that little grasses were already beginning to sprout while we human beings were still recovering from great hardship."

Lysimachia maritima (sea milkwort), 'Certain Place in Miyagi', 2021
Watercolour on paper

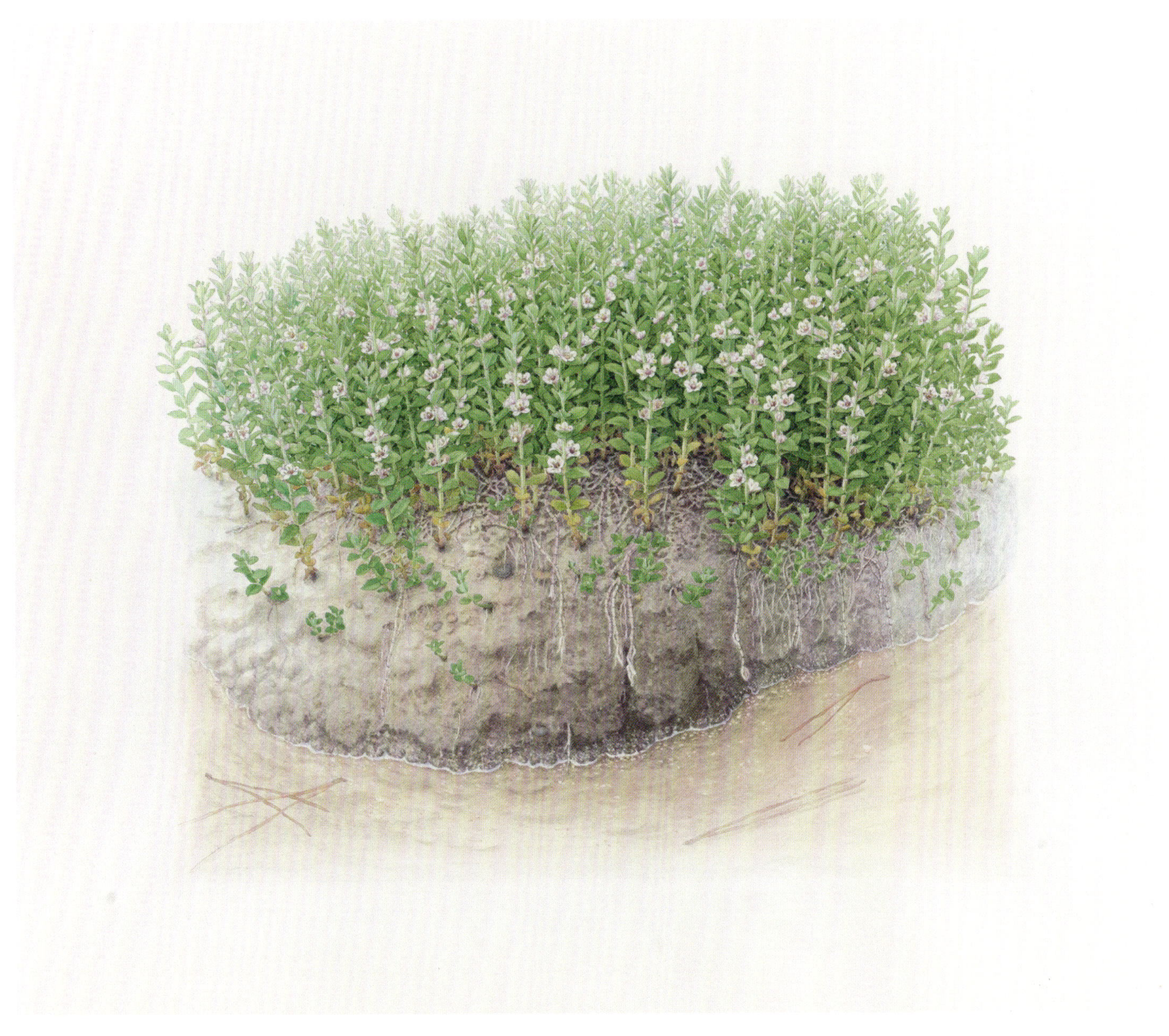

Deborah Lambkin

RHS medal history

Gold medal: 1999

Silver medals: 1997, 1998

Deborah Lambkin, who trained at the National College of Art and Design in Dublin, has been awarded three medals by the RHS, including a Gold medal in 1999. She has been the official Orchid Award Artist for the RHS since 2005. As such, Lambkin is commissioned by the RHS Orchid Committee to paint the award-winning orchid plants, numbering up to 25 paintings per year. Thus far, she has painted well over 500 specimens that have been presented by breeders from across the world.

Lambkin's work continues a tradition that started in 1897, when Nelly Roberts was appointed as the first Orchid Artist. The paintings are used for reference by the committee when new awards are being made. The style and composition of the pictures is dictated by the committee and includes detail of the form, colour and pattern found on the inflorescence.

"At the RHS Orchid Meeting I discuss with the members which aspects of a flower or plant are the identifying characteristics that must be displayed in my painting. Then at my desk I examine the specimen in magnified detail noting the structure, textures and colours. I then plan the composition for my painting.

Anguloa clifonii 'Saint Helier', 2005

Watercolour and graphite on board

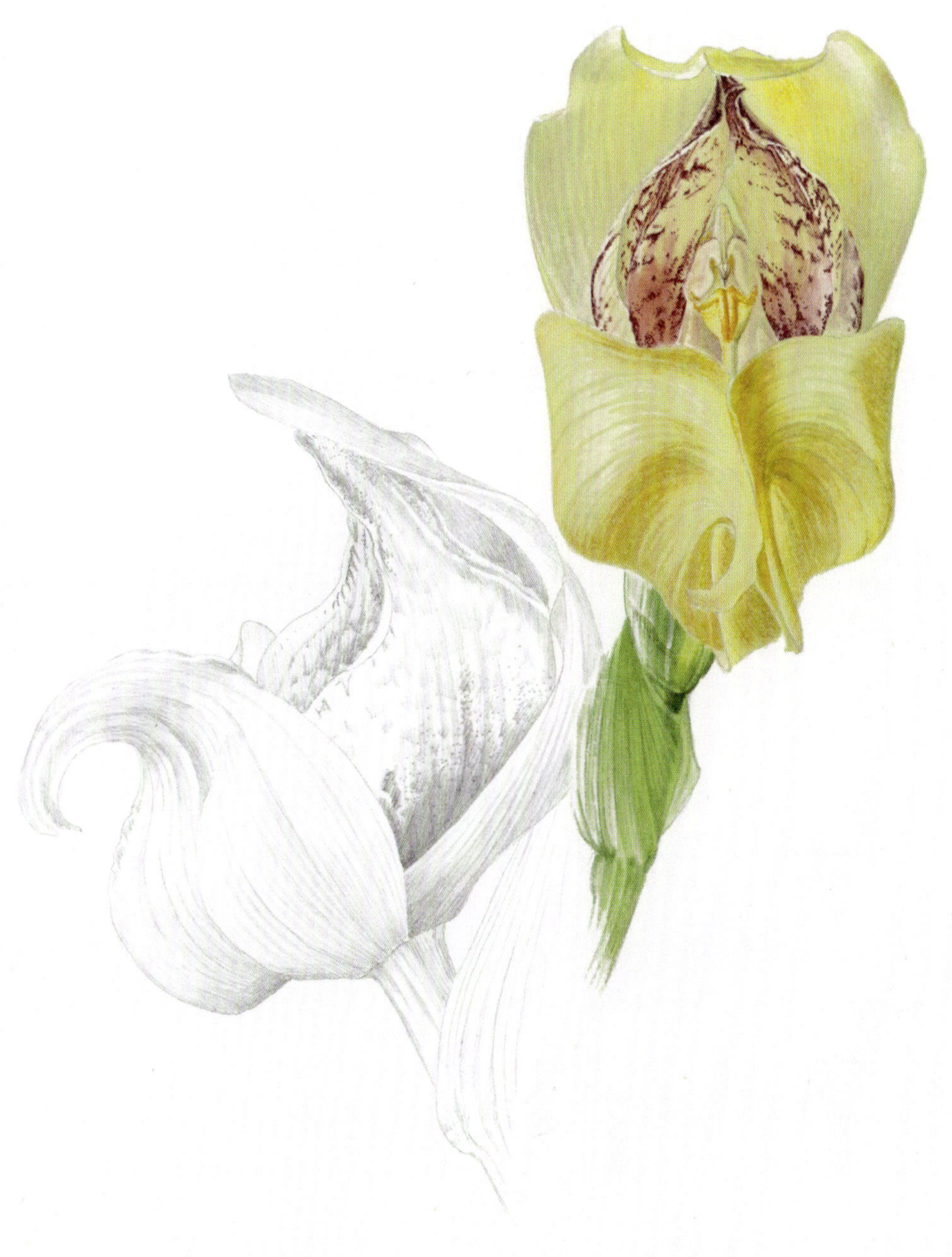
Deborah Lambkin

Using a fine propelling pencil with an 'H' lead and a dividing tool, I measure back and forth, cross checking my measurements carefully to ensure that my painting is the exact size of the actual flower. I also take perspective and foreshortening into consideration to make the orchid look natural. If the pencil marks are too strong I often rub them down with an eraser to soften them before painting, especially on pale flowers.

I then paint in layers in watercolour starting with the paler colours and gradually bringing in stronger colours and building in more detail. I always start painting the parts of the flower that are the furthest away from me and working forward towards the front, ie. dorsal sepal, lateral sepals, petals and finally lip. I also tend to add any strong markings and patterns last. Every so often I return to the pencil drawing and measuring stage to double check my measurements and to sharpen up any details that may get obscured while painting. Seeing the orchid begin to appear solid and true to life on the page is very satisfying.

It is very important to work from live plant material for continual reference and comparison of my painting in progress. My aim is to achieve the highest level of scientific accuracy and the closest, if not the actual, colour match possible. Because these paintings are for an archive collection, I use archive-quality materials. I choose paint colours that are fully permanent, which means they should not fade with time. The paper I use is Fabriano hot pressed 600gsm, which is chlorine- and acid-free and 100% cotton. It is a very heavy paper and does not need to be stretched."

Paphiopedilum Le Pulec 'La Collette Tower', 2016

Watercolour and graphite on board

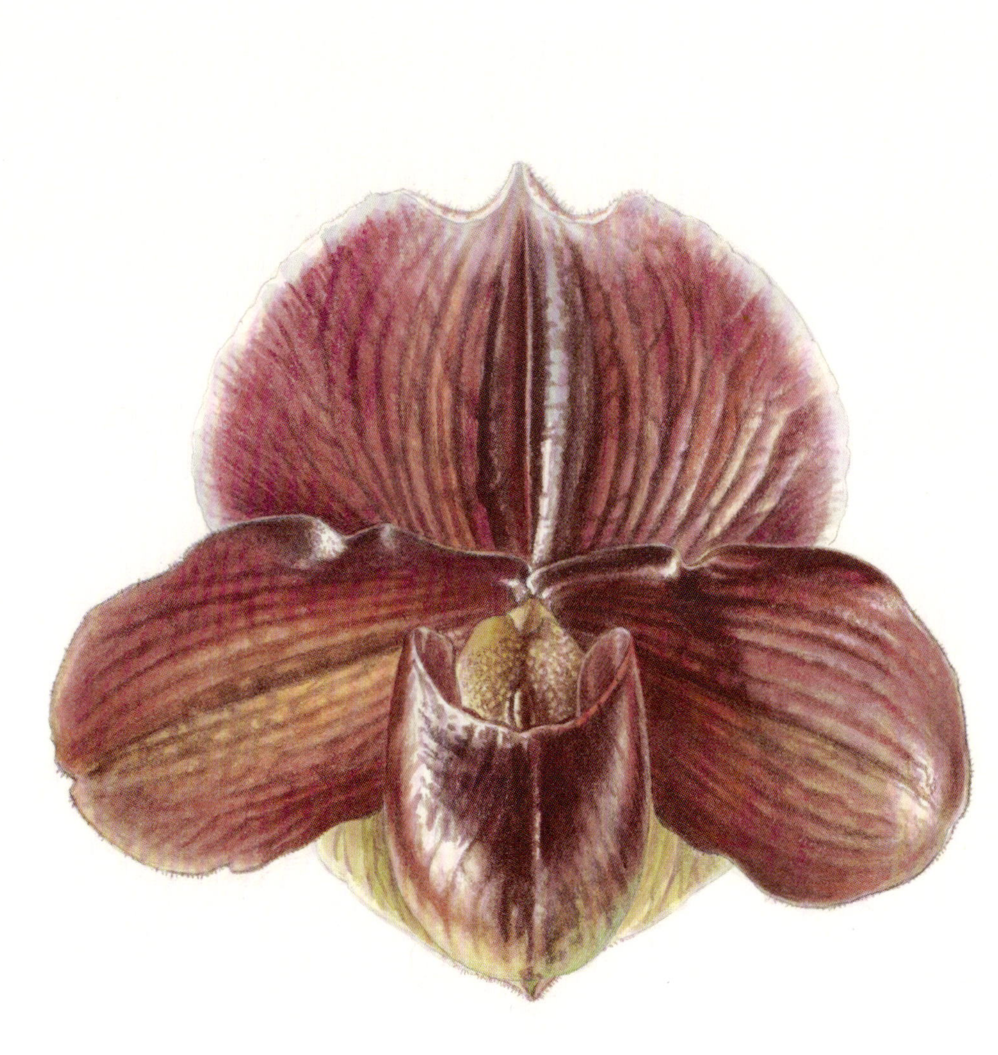

Louise Lane

RHS medal history

Gold medals: 2012 (and Best Botanical Art Exhibit), 2014, 2019

Louise Lane first exhibited with the RHS in 2012, showing her graphite pencil drawings 'Native Ferns of the Peak District'. She was awarded a Gold medal and Best Exhibit for her works, two of which were subsequently purchased for the Lindley Collections. Lane then went on to demonstrate her versatility as an artist, when she won a Gold medal in 2014 for her display of watercolour paintings of '*Ophrys* of Menorca'.

Lane spent many months researching the native ferns that grow in the Peak District. *Asplenium scolopendrium* (or Hart's Tongue Fern) can be found growing in the White Peak of the Peak District. It favours both woodland areas and rocky crags. *Pteridium aquilinum* (or Bracken) is the most dominant fern in the upland areas. Lane's composition offers a sense of how these ferns grow, with the fronds unfurling as they develop.

Having undertaken formal art training in Graphic Design & Illustration at Leeds Polytechnic, Lane went on to work as an illustrator of children's books. She has worked as a primary school teacher and lectured on the Botanical Art Certificate course at Sheffield Hallam University. Most recently, Lane inspired audiences with her watercolour demonstrations at the RHS Botanical Seminar Day in 2018.

Pteridium aquilinum, 2012

Graphite on paper

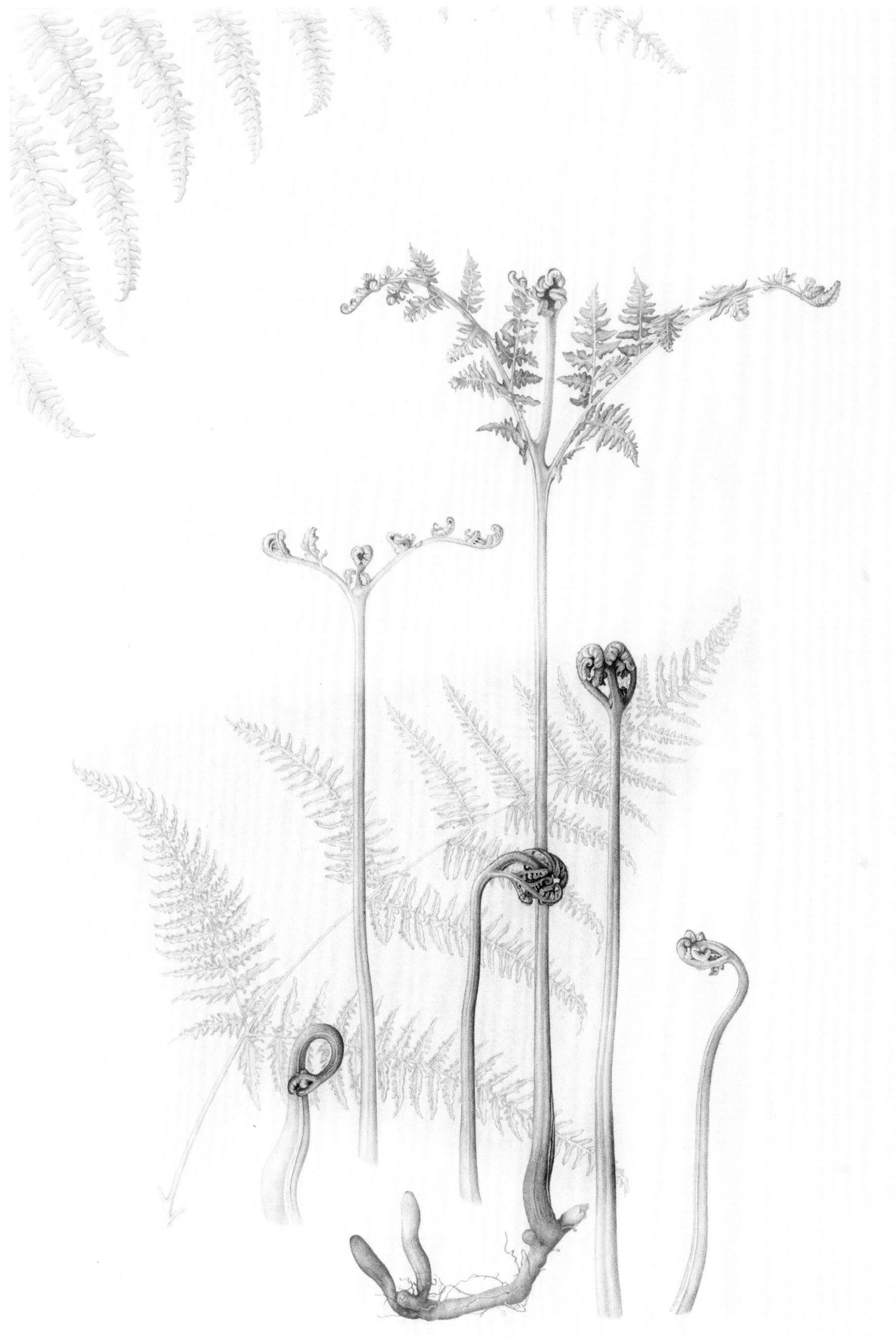

Asplenium scolopendrium, 2012

Graphite on paper

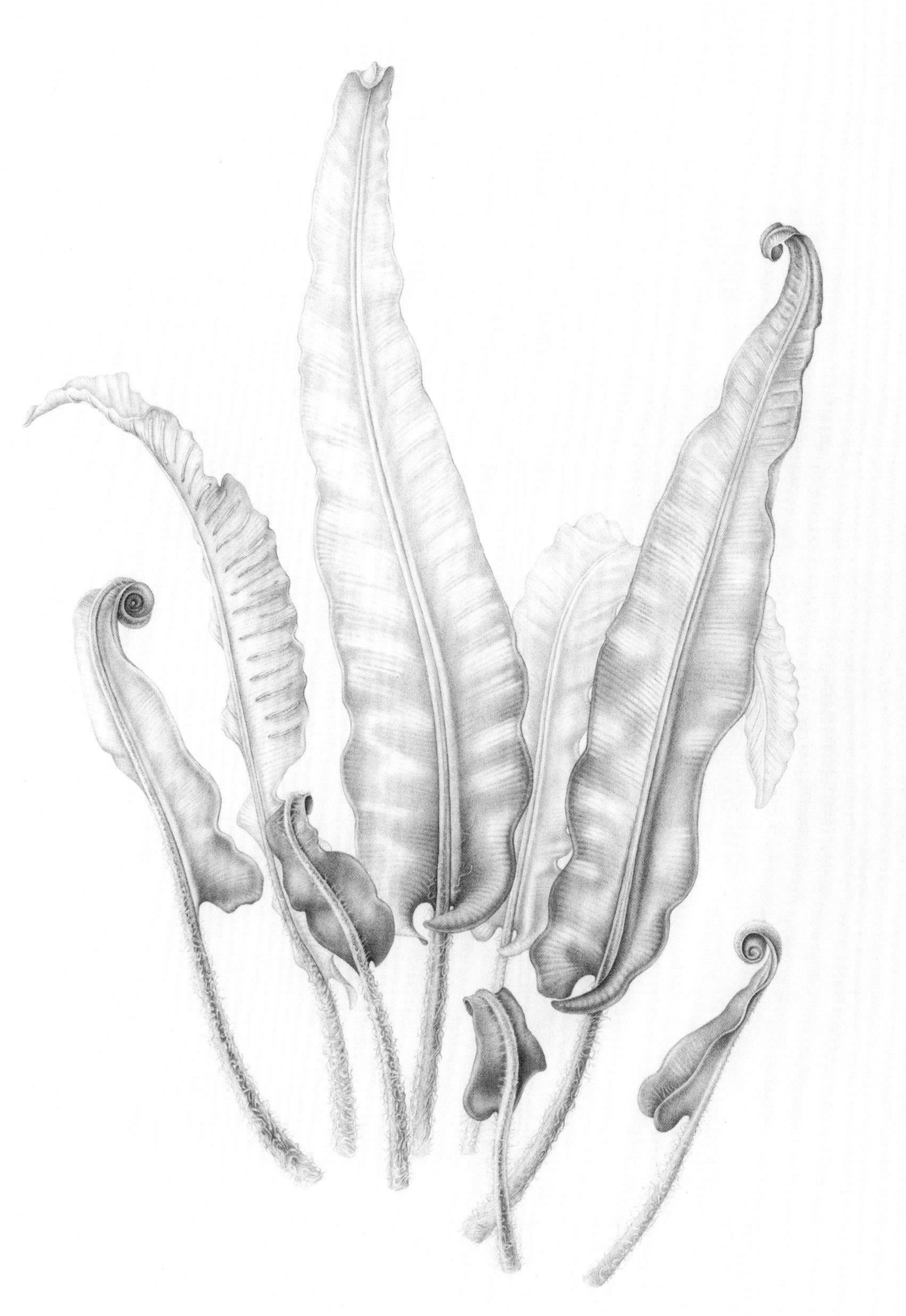

Clare McGhee

RHS medal history

Gold medal: 2010

Clare McGhee exhibited her watercolours of 'Vegetables' with the RHS in 2010, for which she was awarded a Gold medal. McGhee's distinctive, dynamic style confronts the viewer with the shape and texture of her chosen subject.

"The main aim was to show that vegetables that we generally think of as being rather ordinary can possess an extraordinary beauty and fascination when closely studied.

The humble potato is generally ignored and dismissed as anything but 'beautiful', but when examined closely it has an extraordinary depth of form, colour and texture. I wanted to show that the outer 'skins', which we normally dispose of, also have a complexity and intrinsic beauty in themselves.

The cut onion was a fascinating one to paint, although fraught with technical difficulties! I recall having some difficulty trying to paint the inner rings of the onion head and had to be careful not to over-paint this area. It was also a challenge to paint the translucent 'paper' layers of the outer onion head whilst contrasting it with the tangled, withered roots.

The cabbage was an amazing vegetable to study. I love colour and so couldn't resist the wonderful deep blue leaves contrasting against the pink/red veins of this particular variety."

Solanum tuberosum 'Arran Victory' potato peeling, 2011

Watercolour on paper

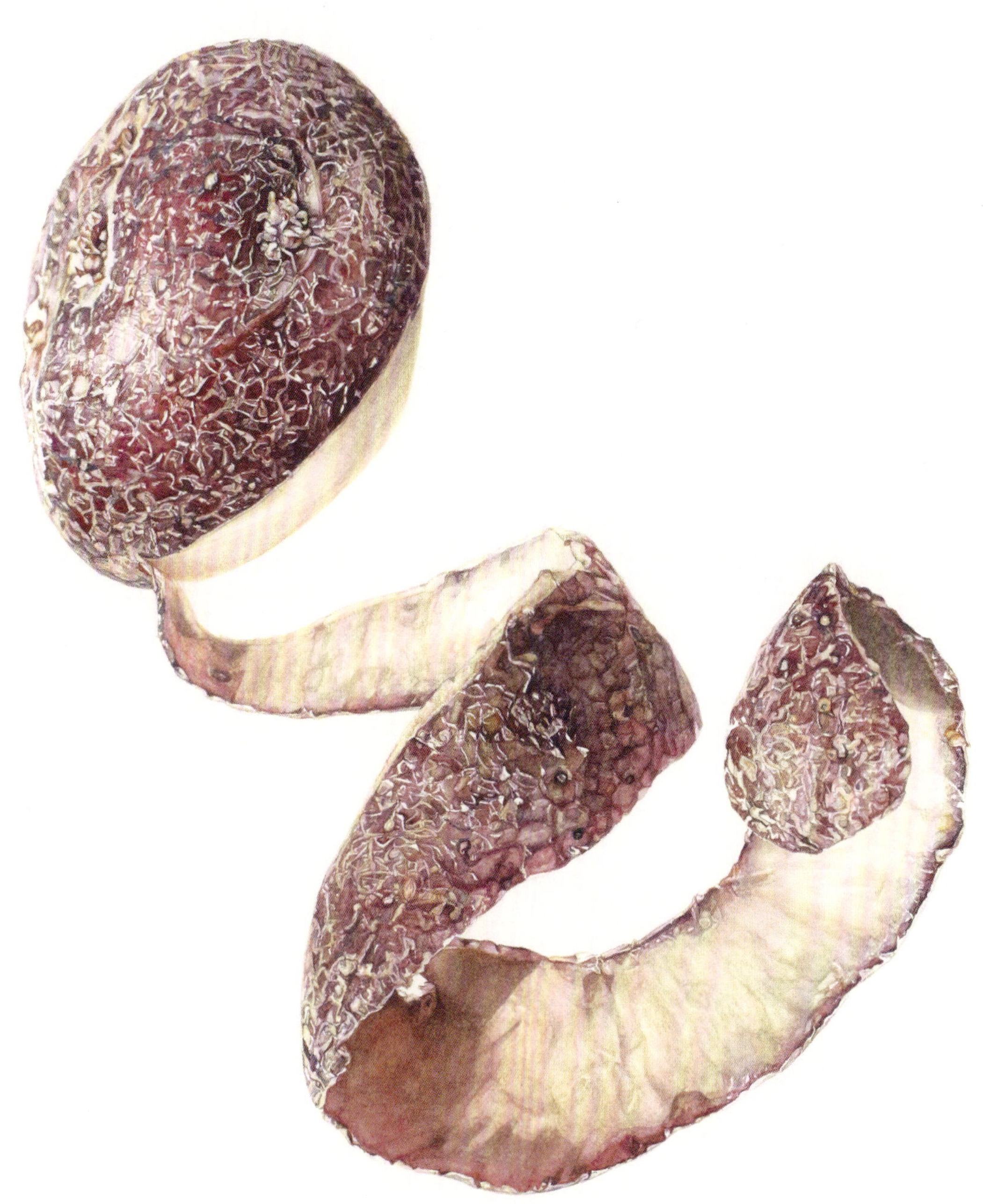

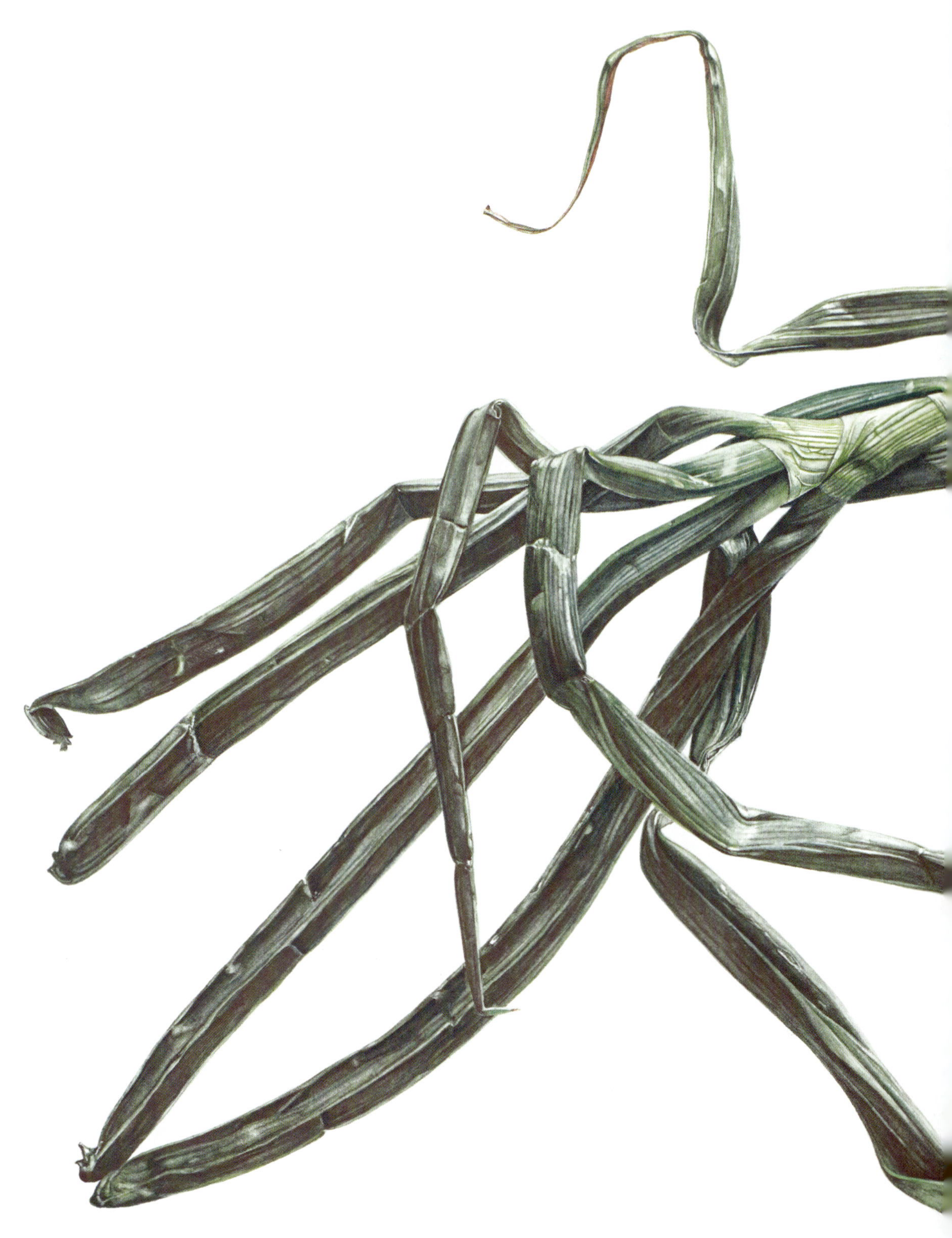

Allium cepa, 2009
Watercolour on paper

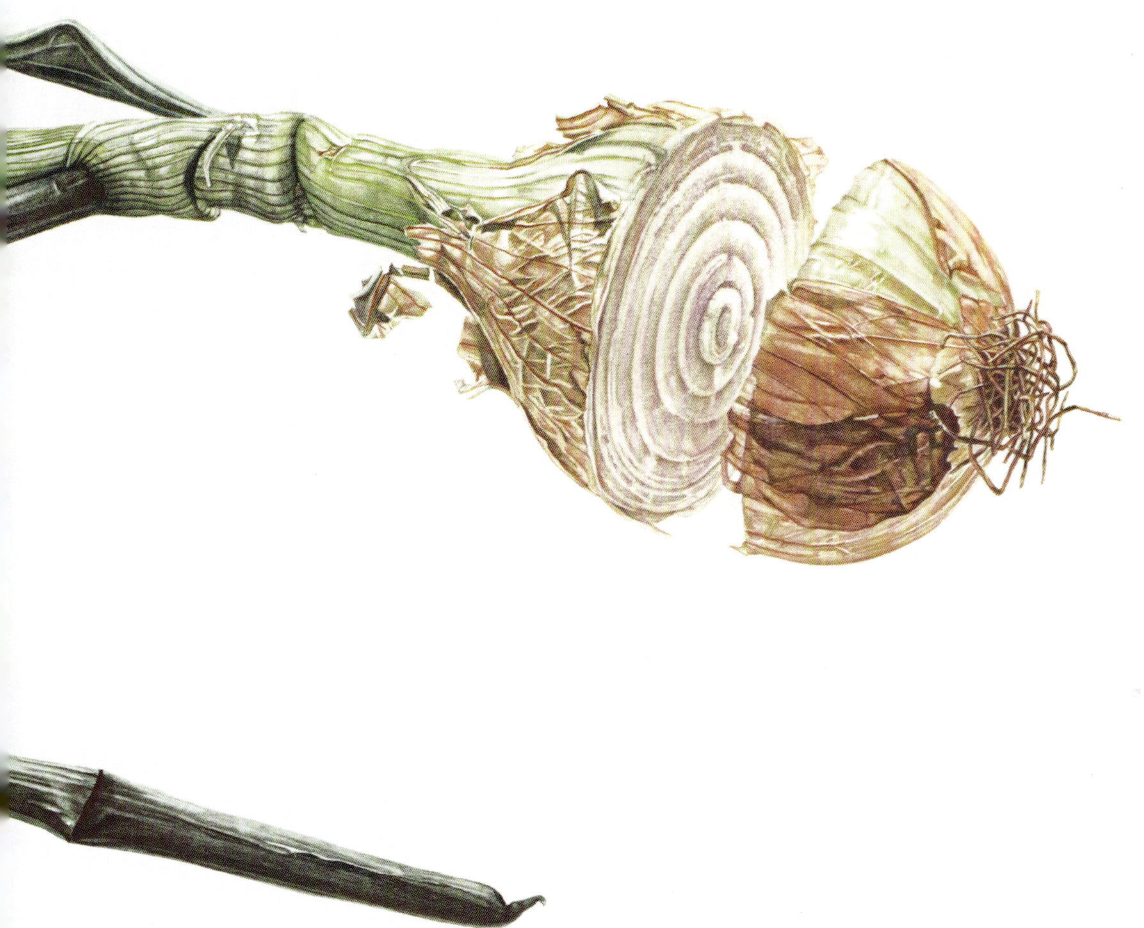

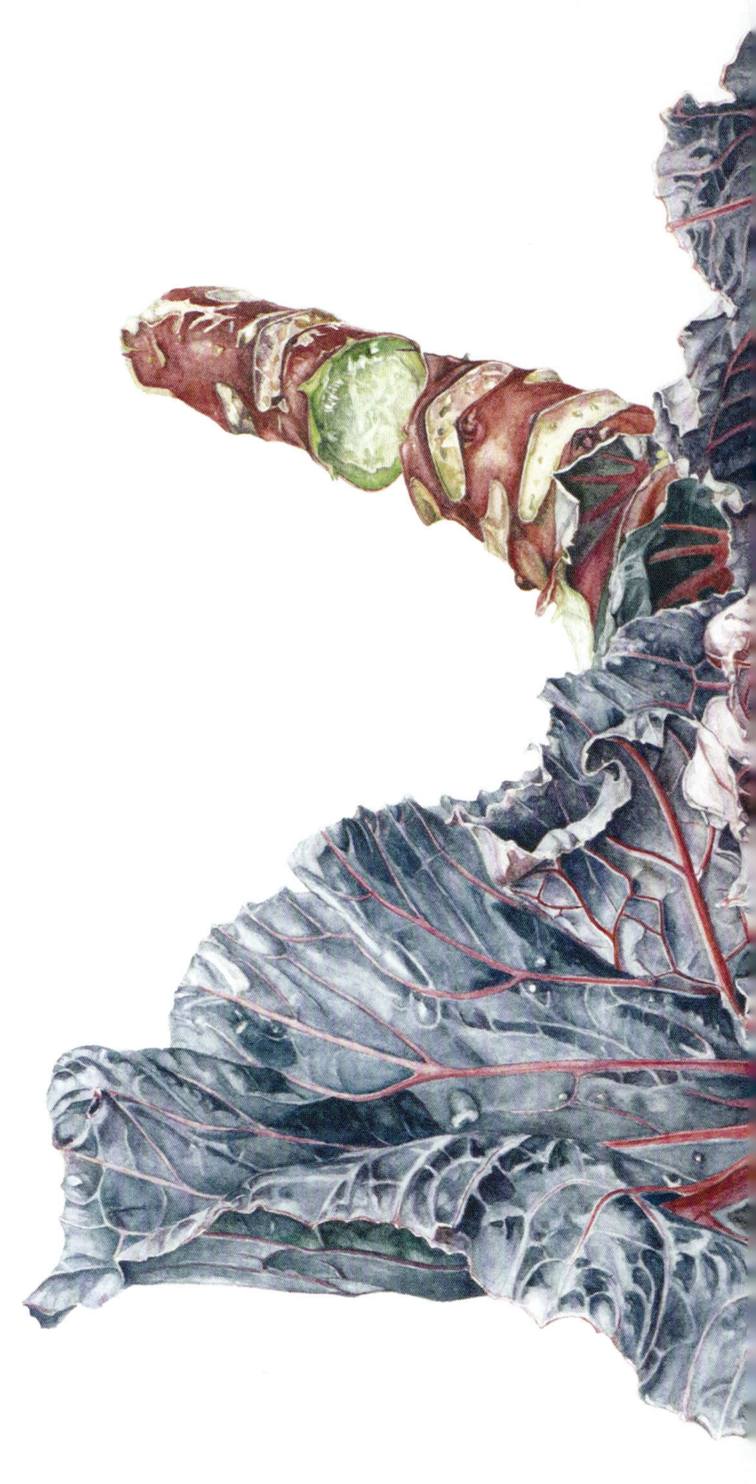

Brassica oleracea (Capitata Group) 'Marner Frührotkohl' (syn: 'Marner Early Red', cabbage), 2010

Watercolour on paper

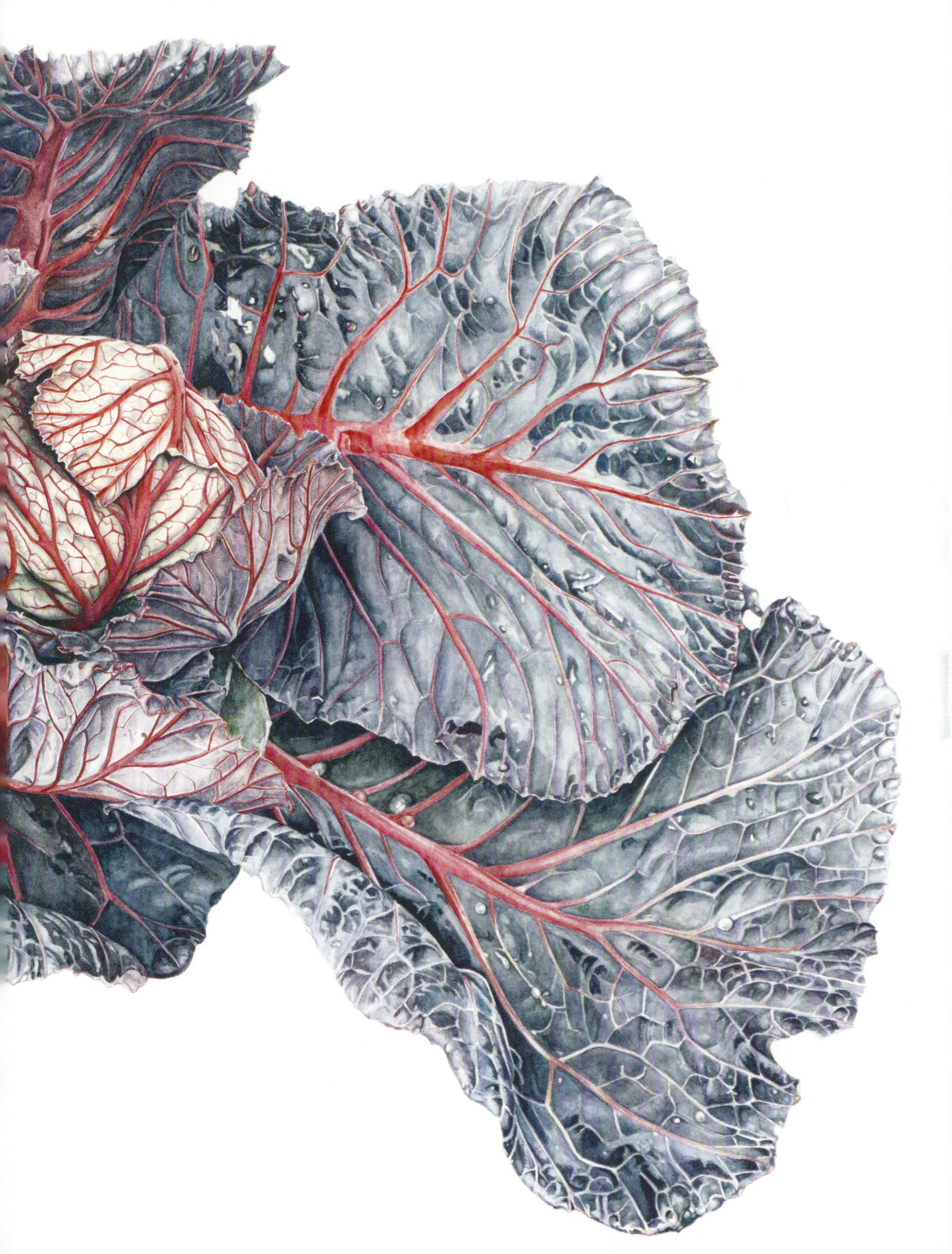

Sheila Mannes-Abbott
(1939-2014)

RHS medal history

Gold medals: 1997, 2000, 2010

Silver-Gilt medals: 1974, 1978, 2012

Sheila Mannes-Abbott was awarded a total of six medals, including three Gold medals, between 1974 and 2012. She was educated at the Ealing School of Art, having been awarded a scholarship at the age of 13 for a portfolio of flowers in watercolour. Following an early role as a Colour Advisor for ICI, Mannes-Abbott was encouraged to take up botanical art by Wilfrid Blunt. She taught and lectured on short courses as well as privately in her studio. She was commissioned to produce designs for use on porcelain, jigsaw-puzzles, stationery and textiles. She provided the illustrations for *Four Seasons: The Life of the English Countryside* (Methuen, 1981) with commentary by Phil Drabble, as well as plates for *Curtis's Botanical Magazine*.

Mannes-Abbott exhibited extensively throughout her career and her work is now held in many private and public collections around the world. In 1986, she became one of the Founder Members of the Society of Botanical Artists and in 2000 she was elected to join the Linnean Society as a Fellow.

In 2010, Mannes-Abbott wrote to the Lindley Library with details of the paintings featured here: *"I've wanted to paint* Digitalis purpurea *again for a very long time. Last year there were so many*

Digitalis purpurea, 2009

Watercolour on paper

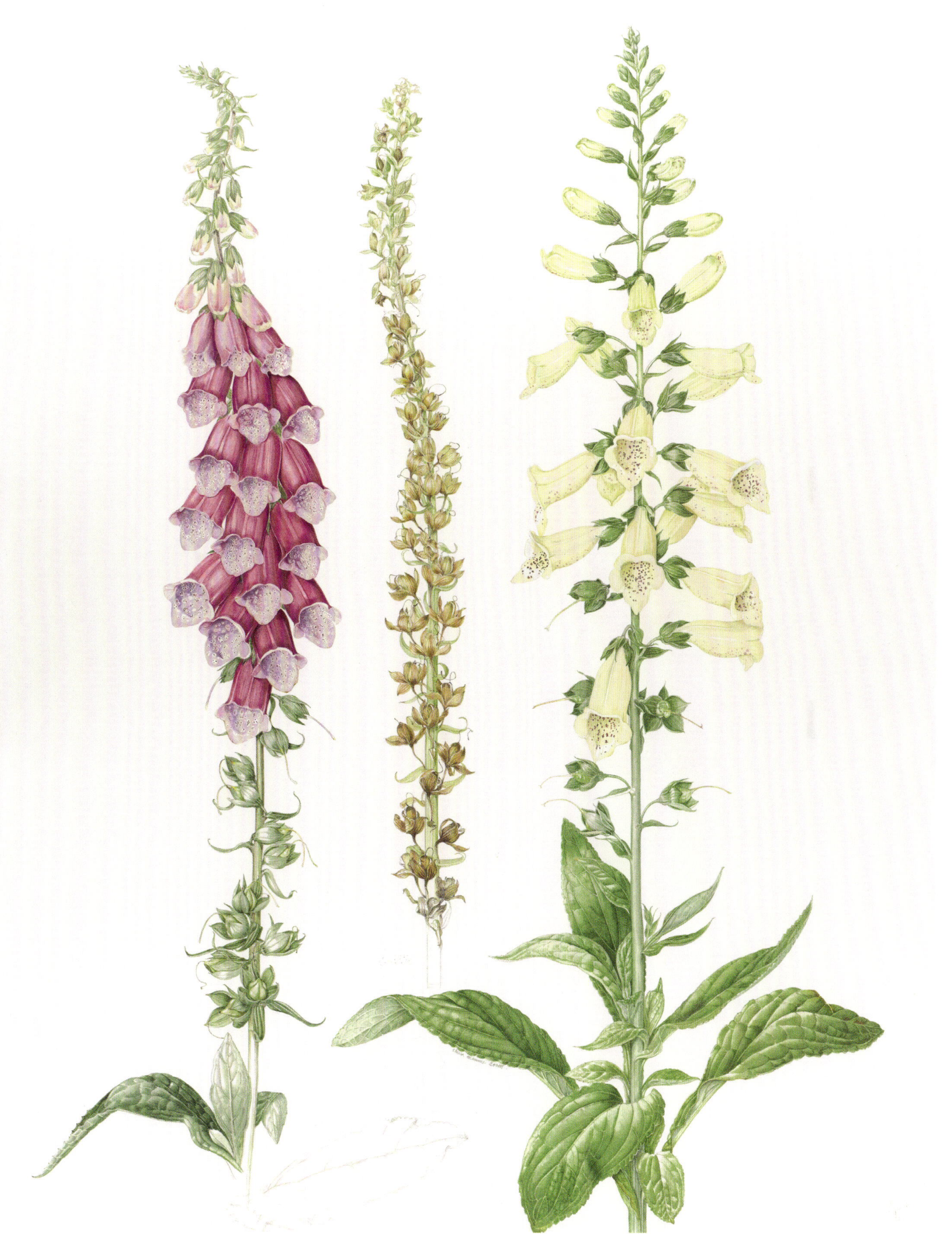

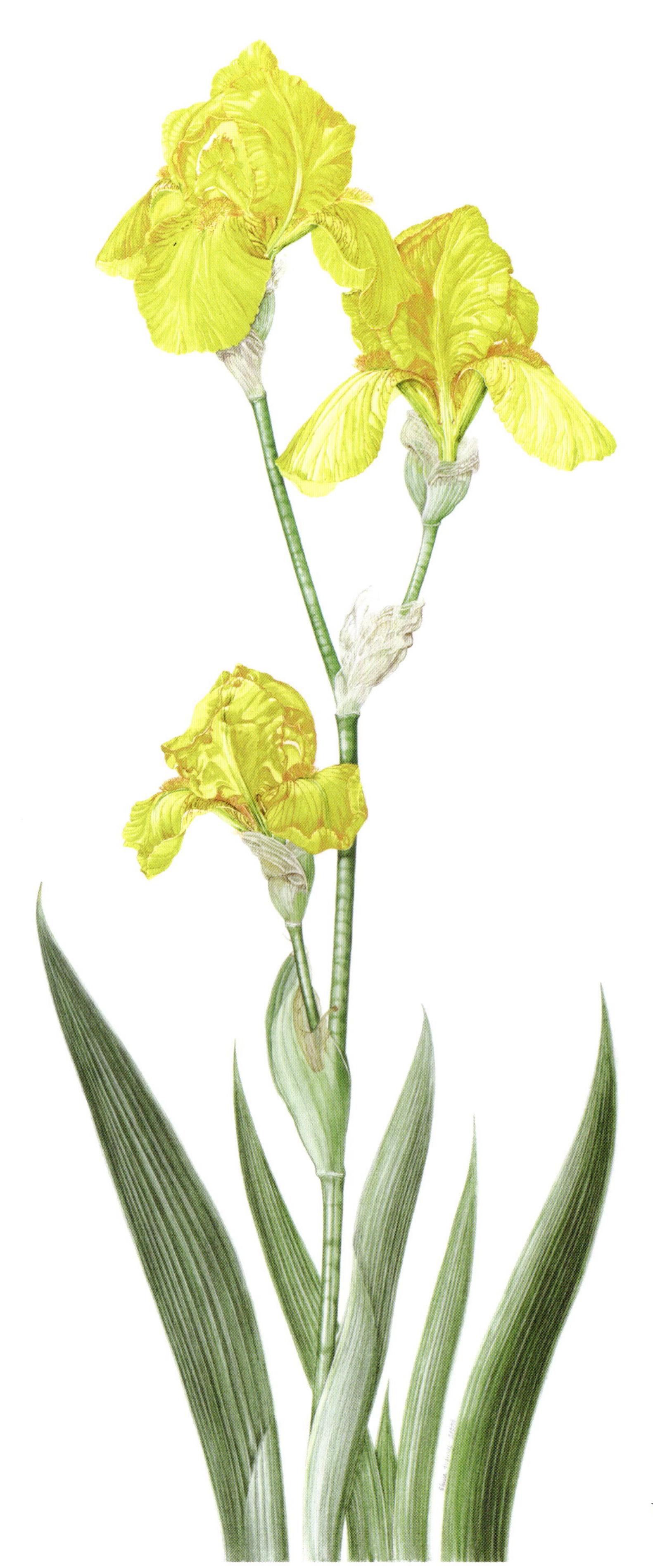

Iris pseudacorus

Watercolour on paper

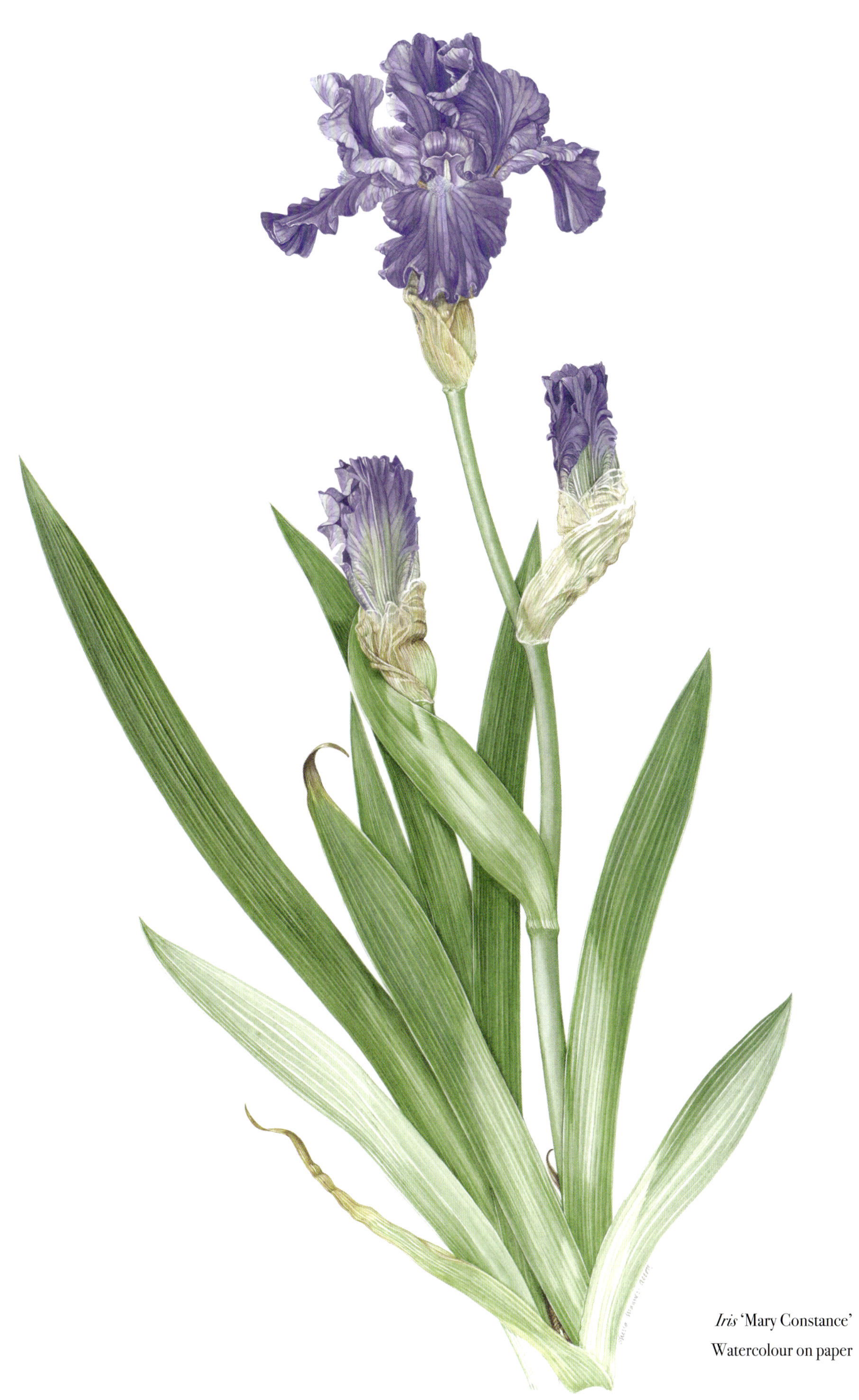

Iris 'Mary Constance'

Watercolour on paper

in the lanes around Exmoor. I couldn't resist them. They grow in our garden as it used to be a steep wild bank. The seed pods are beautiful both before and after they are dry and ripe. The hybrid was rather testing to paint as the cream colour was difficult to mix: neither cream nor white – quite a challenge. I have to say that I much preferred painting the wild Foxglove; I just love the colour. I had previously painted Aconitum *with a hybrid for comparison, together with the dried seed pods from the species. I was fascinated by the comparison of the habit.*

This Iris *'Kent Pride' was a wonderful find in a little nursery, just one flower spike with no leaves and no name. I fell in love with the beautiful purple colour on the flower bud and leaf. All this pleasure and just for the princely sum of £1. I took it home and started work straight away. The flower was such a surprise considering the shading in the green. I had expected a much darker flower, so the lovely terracotta and cream was unexpected. I have since grown it on and the purple still prevails.*

The beautiful Iris, *'Mary Constance', was simply irresistible. I had to paint it to try to capture my feelings for it the first time I saw it. The wavy falls and unusual beard plus delightful scent add up to the perfect garden plant. Cy Bartlett, who bred Iris, lives locally to us and I have enjoyed painting several of his hybrids. This particular flower, he named after his wife – Mary Constance."*

Iris 'Kent Pride'

Watercolour on paper

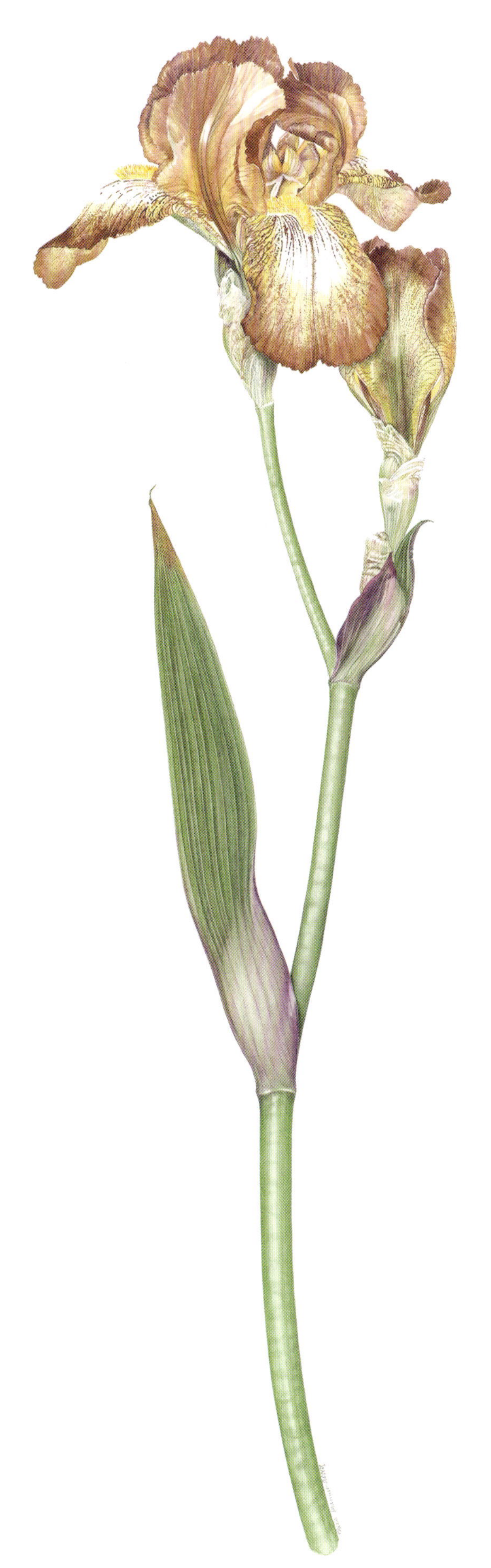

Kimiyo Maruyama

RHS medal history

Gold medals: 2001, 2003, 2005, 2010 (and Best Botanical Art Exhibit), 2015

Silver medals: 2006, 2008

Kimiyo Maruyama has been awarded a total of five Gold medals for her botanical painting. Having been awarded two Gold medals, Maruyama turned her attention to pines and her last three Gold medal-winning exhibits in 2005, 2010 and 2015 have all been entitled 'Trees of Pinaceae in watercolour', revealing her deep passion for this genus, native to Japan. For her 2010 piece she was also awarded the prestigious Best Botanical Art Exhibit, an impressive achievement in a show that saw nine other Gold medal-winning displays of botanical art.

Maruyama's attention to detail and ability to translate the complexity of the pine into watercolour is outstanding. Each of the needles is carefully observed and painted with the finest of brushes, they can each be traced back to a point of connection with the branch. A highly skilled artist, she paints meticulously without making the specimen appear too rigid.

Disa Foam 'San Francisco', *c.*2001

Watercolour on paper

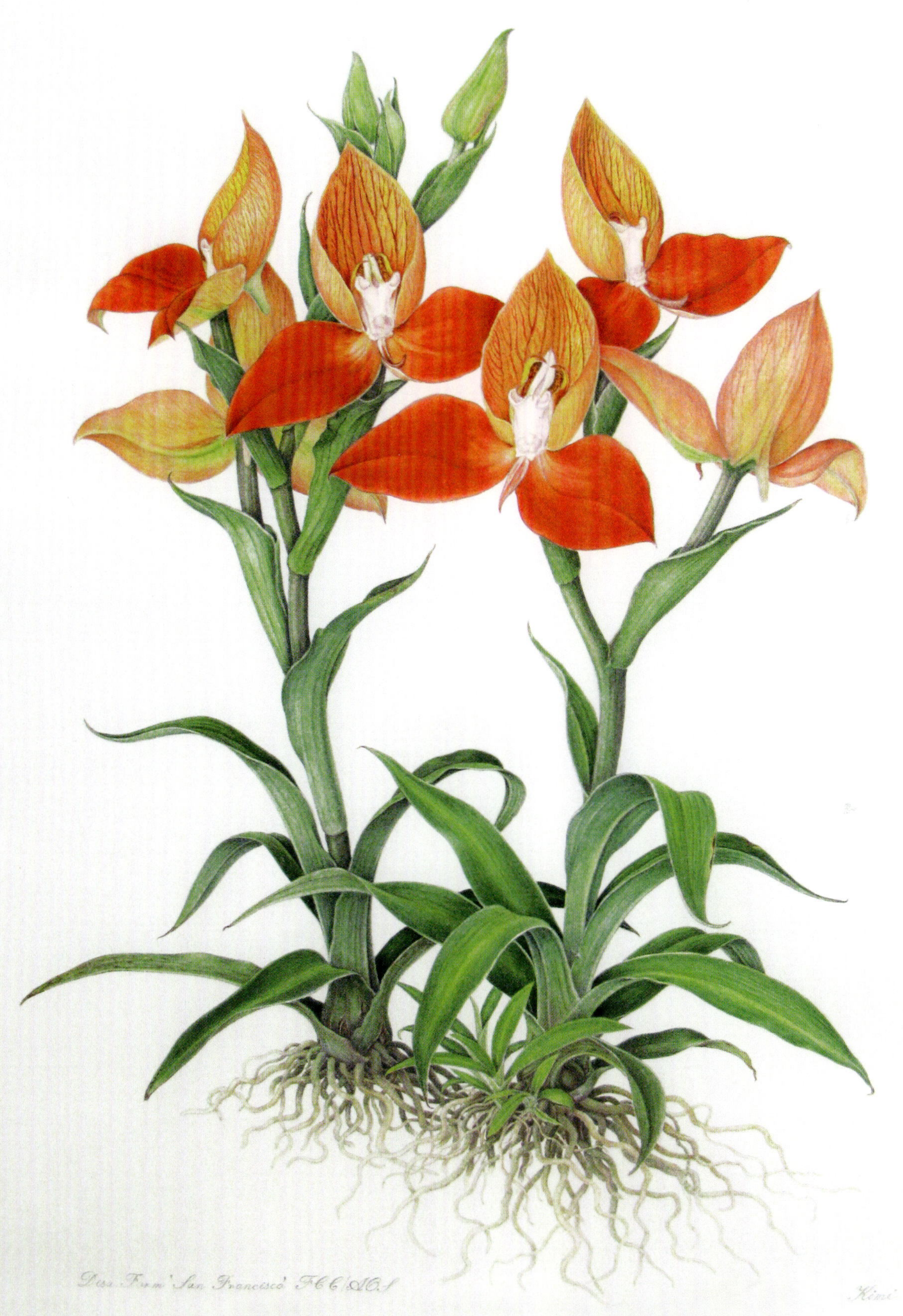
Disa Form 'San Francisco' FCC/AOS
Kimi

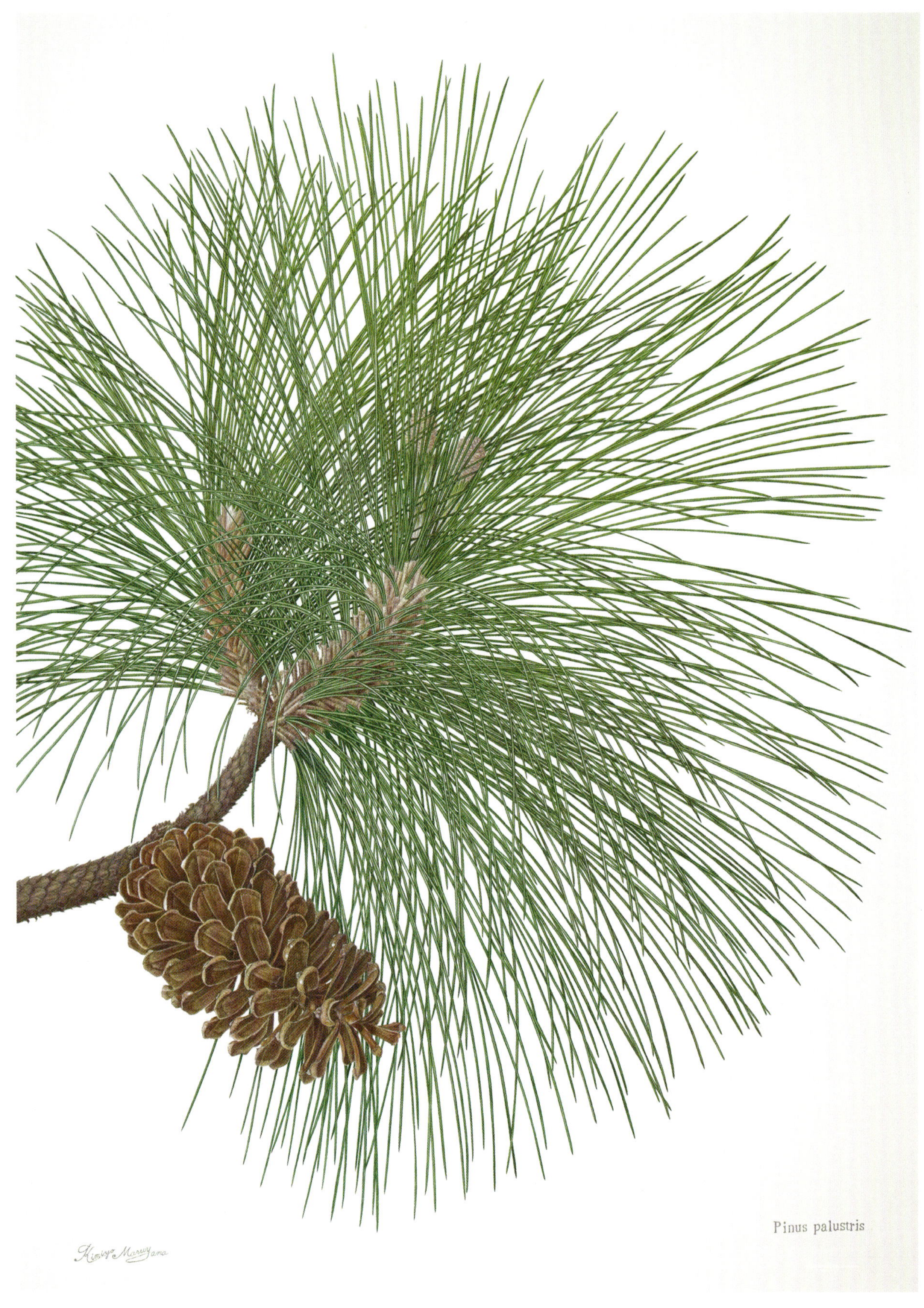

Pinus palustris, 2010

Watercolour on paper

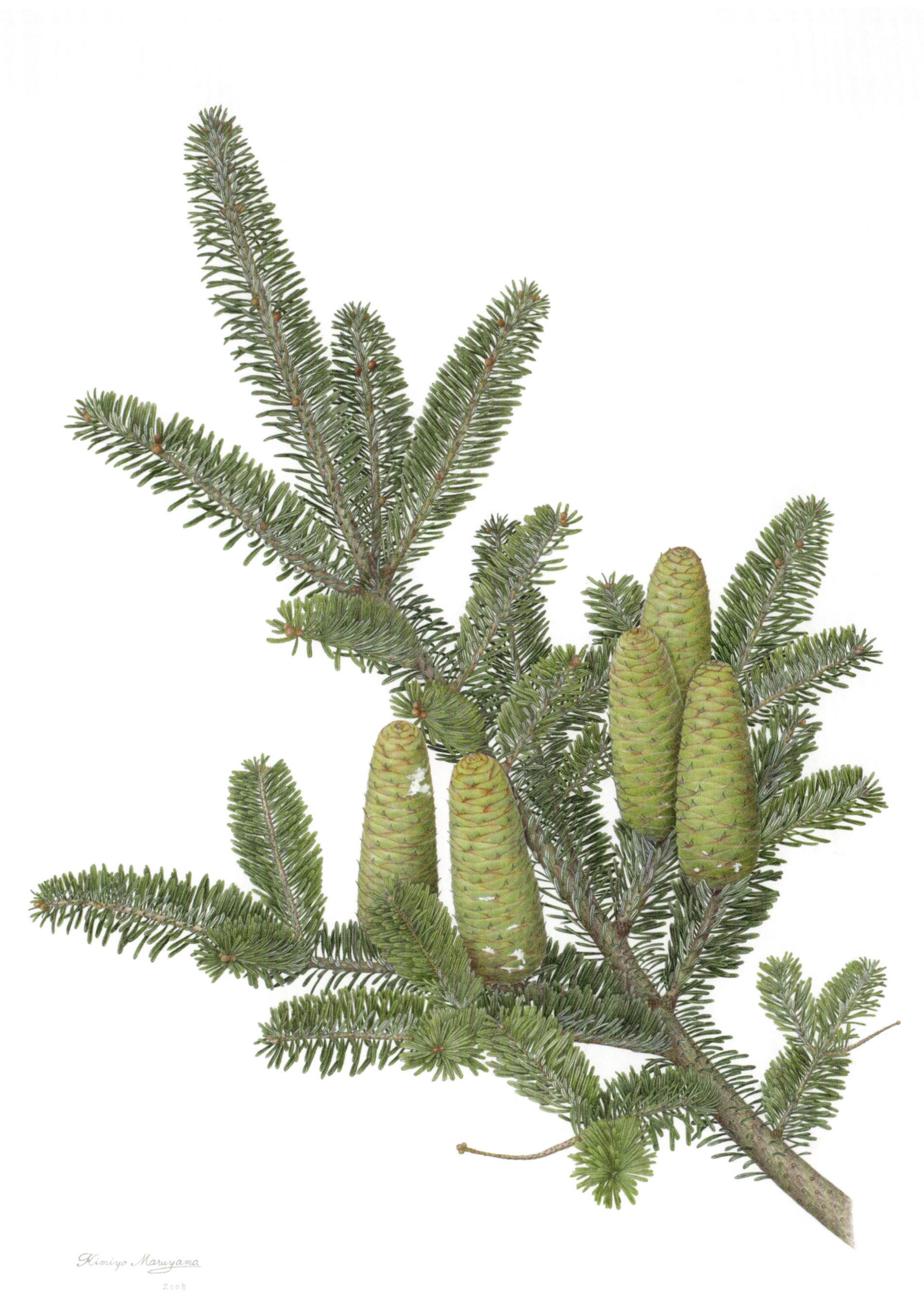

Abies firma, 2008

Watercolour on paper

Anna Mason
(formerly Knights)

RHS medal history

Gold medal: 2007 (and Best Botanical Artist)

Anna Mason gained a Gold medal and was awarded 'Best Botanical Artist' for her series of 20 watercolours of 'James Grieve' apples, exhibited at the BBC's *Gardeners' World* live show at the NEC in Birmingham, in June 2007. Painted throughout the 2006–2007 growing season, from a tree in Mason's garden, each picture captures a different growing stage of the fruit. The scale of endeavour of this project was impressive, as she sought to observe every aspect of the tree and its apples.

Mason is entirely self-taught and now runs a popular online botanical art school. She enjoys creating bold compositions and achieving a realistic and vibrant depth of colour. Mason only began botanical painting in February 2006. The 'James Grieve' series includes some of her first botanical paintings.

By working quickly to capture the changes throughout the development of the fruit, Mason gives a sense of immediacy to her studies. The enlargement of the bud emphasises the emerging blossom, and contrasts in texture with the rest of the branch.

'29th July' (Unripe Fruit of Apple 'James Grieve'), 2006

Watercolour on paper

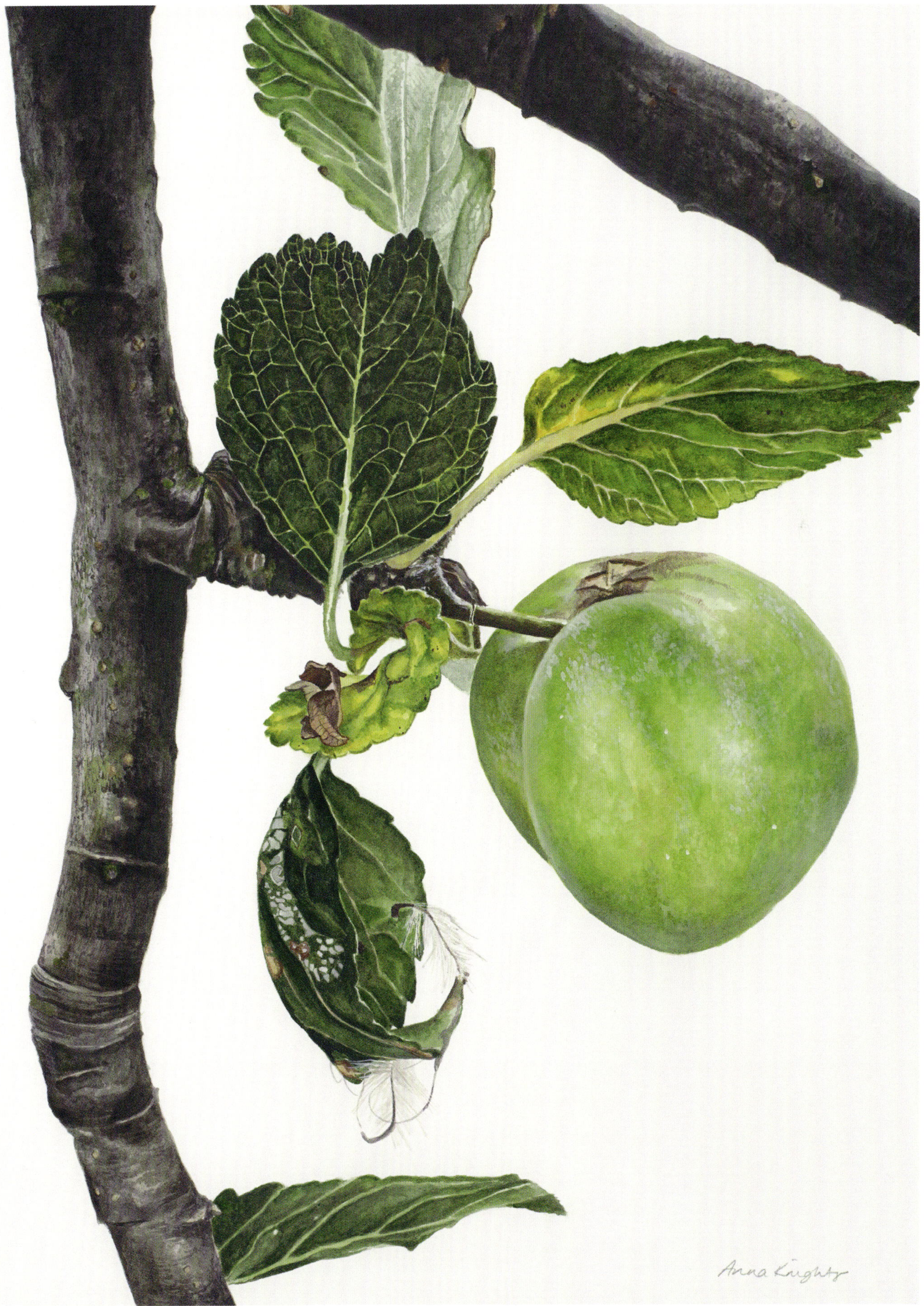

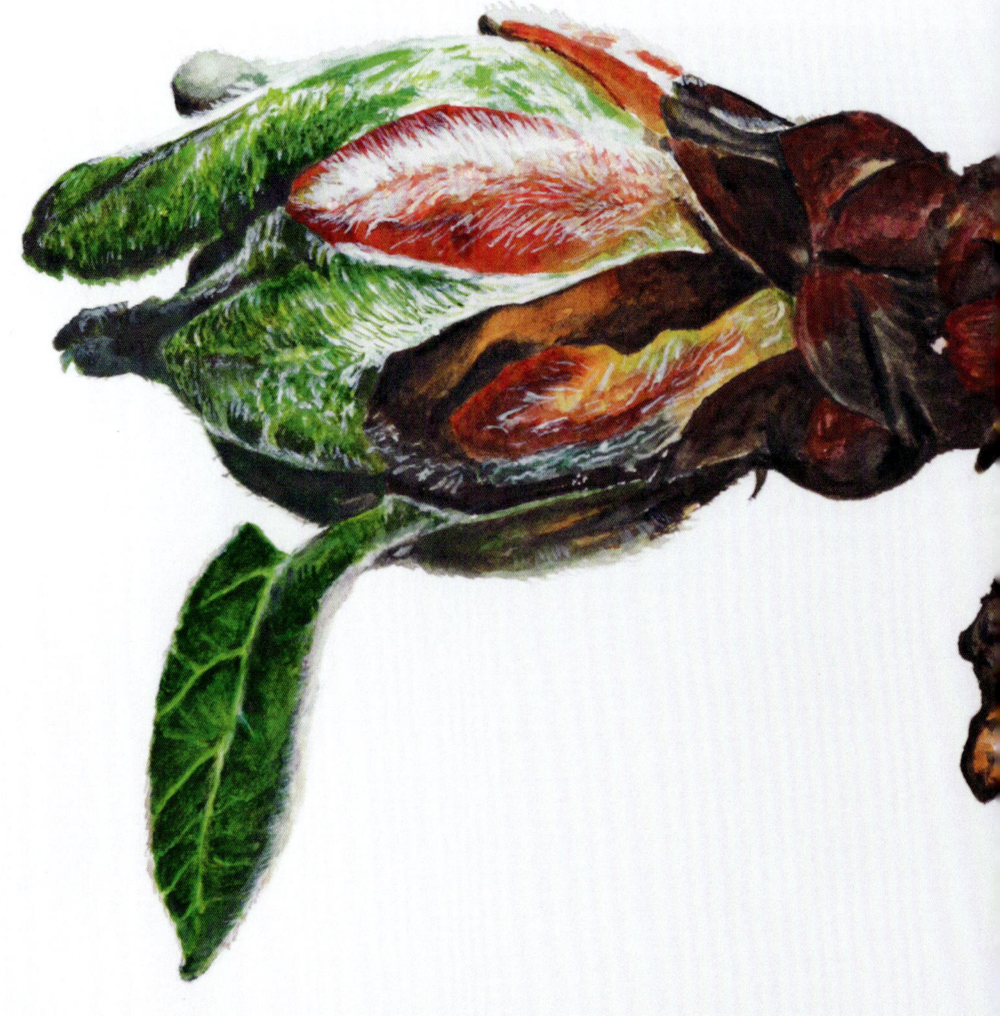

'12th April' (Bud of Apple 'James Grieve'), 2006

Watercolour on paper

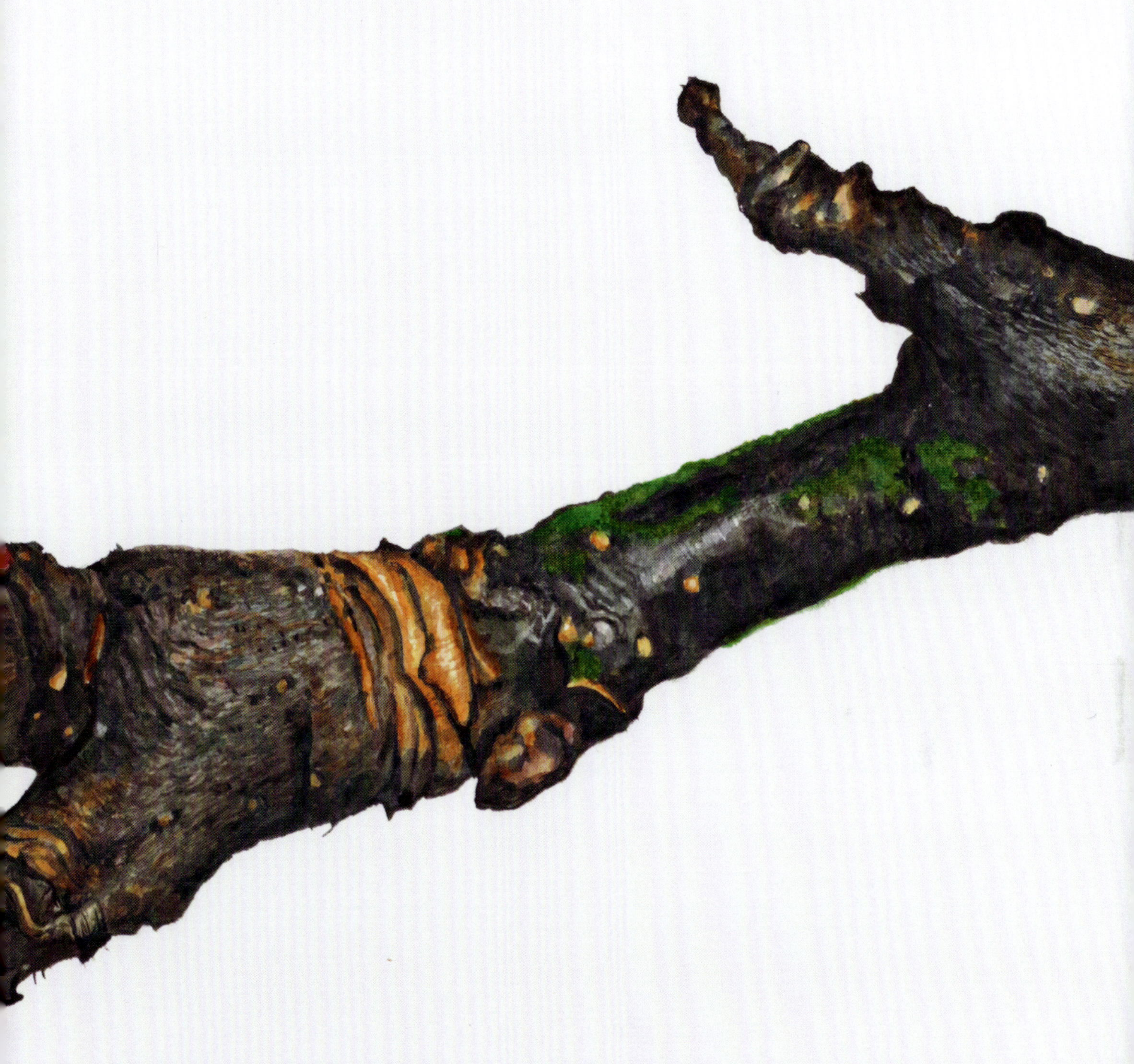
Anna Knights

Nina Mayes

RHS medal history

Gold medal: 2023 (and Best Botanical Art Exhibit)

Nina Mayes studied for a degree in zoology with marine zoology at Bangor University, Wales, followed by a master's degree in wildlife management and conservation at the University of Reading. She attended the Chelsea School of Botanical Art, graduating in 2018. In preparation for her exhibit with the RHS, Mayes brought together her professional expertise and her passion for ecology and conservation, with her series of watercolours titled: 'Macrophytes in the emergent zone of Britain's fresh waters'. Mayes adopted an immersive approach to her study; days out on the water in a small boat enabled her to engage directly with the local environment.

"Macrophytes are freshwater plants. The emergent zone is where macrophytes 'emerge' above the water, their lower parts submerged and rooted in sediment. I aim to produce educational paintings showing the key identification features and habitat of the emergent macrophyte species. After extensive fieldwork and growing macrophytes in my pond, I made life size drawings, colour matched, preserved and pressed them. This informed the compositions. I then applied watercolour, using lots of mini washes, glazes and dry brush layers all with regular burnishing to keep the paper smooth."

Iris pseudacorus (yellow flag or water flag iris), 2021

Watercolour on paper

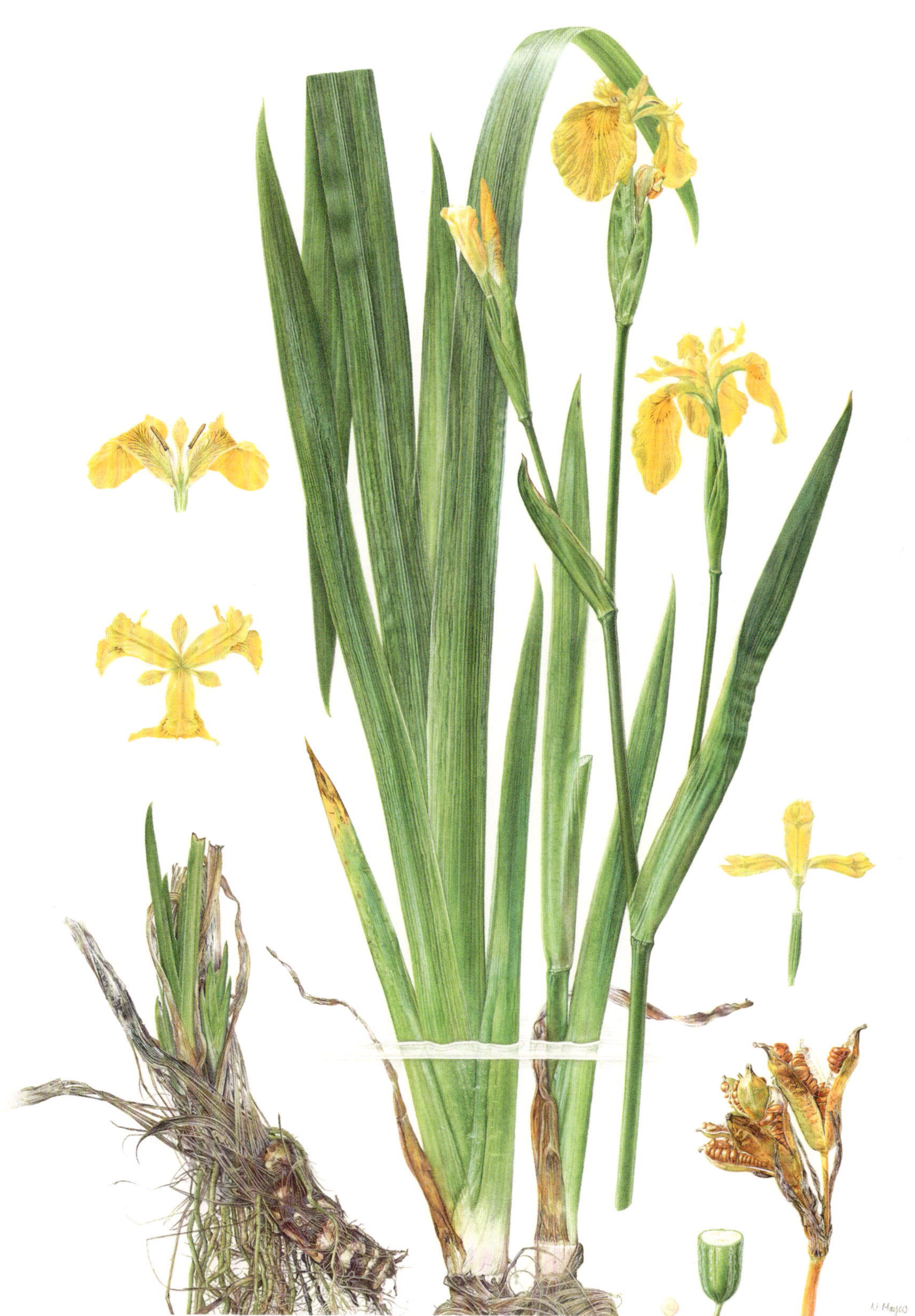

Iris pseudacorus

Angeline de Meester

RHS medal history

Gold medal: 2007

Silver-Gilt medals: 2010, 2013

Silver medal: 2008

Angeline de Meester was awarded four medals by the RHS between 2007 and 2013, including a Gold medal in 2007. The picture featured here of *Ligularia* 'The Rocket' (commonly known as the Leopard plant), was one of a series of eight watercolours exhibited under the title 'Plants with Animal names in their common names', which secured her a Gold medal in 2007.

Born and brought up in the countryside of Surrey, de Meester followed an artistic path from an early age. Her talent was first recognised whilst she was at school, leading her to an Art Foundation Diploma course at Epsom College of Art and Design. She studied jewellery design at Central St Martins College of Art and Design in London and then began a career as a designer, selling collections all over the world.

Upon her return to the UK, de Meester joined the Botanical Painting Diploma Course at the English Gardening School, graduating with a Distinction in 2007. An erstwhile member of the

Ligularia 'The Rocket', 2007

Watercolour on paper

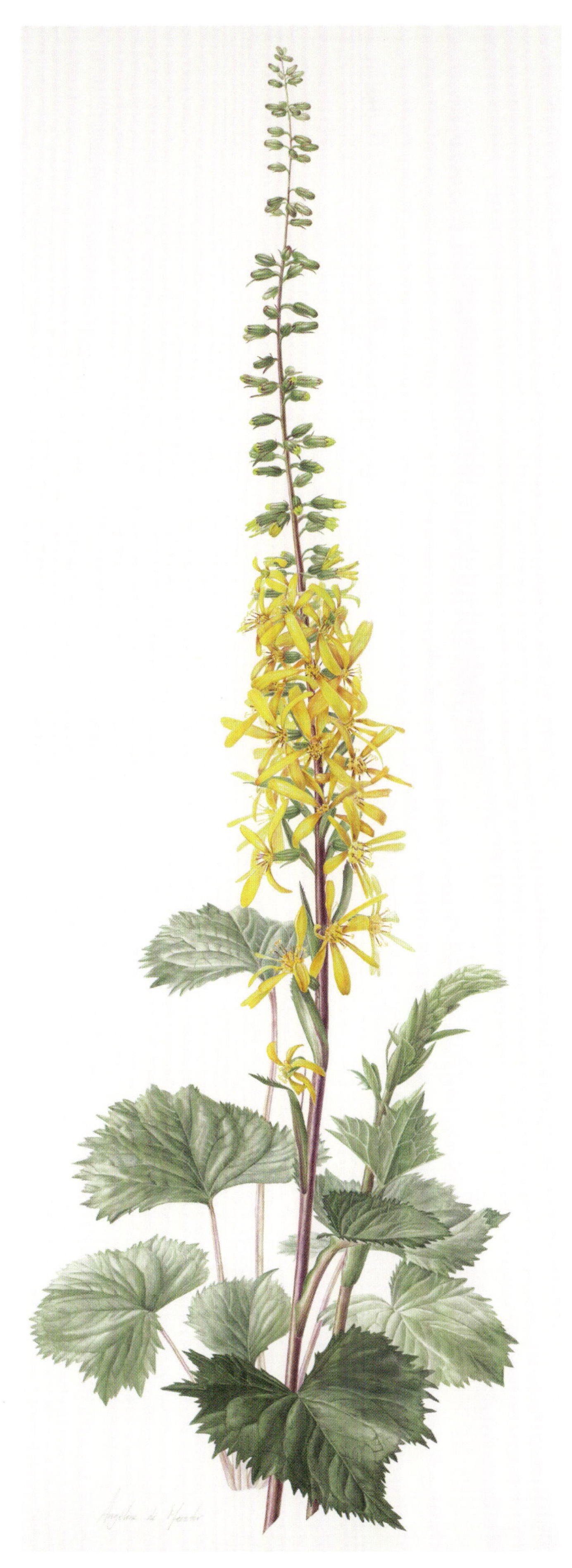

Hampton Court Florilegium Society, she is also a Fellow of the Linnean Society and a full member of the Society of Botanical Artists. De Meester now practices as a freelance botanical artist and teaches workshops for Capel Manor College, London.

"I sourced the Ligularia *specimens for this painting from the RHS Wisley Plant Centre and then planted them in my garden where they still grow happily. I bought three plants to make sure that the growth habit was true and that I could choose the most truly representative flower, bud and leaves. I had chosen the subject of my series already and so was looking for plants that would work within its theme of 'Plants with Animal Names in their Common Names', which meant that I did not have all of the specimens growing in my own garden.*

The painting was planned and painted over a period of six months. I had previously painted six other paintings for the same series over the past 18 months and so knew the composition style I was aiming for, while wanting to show as much information about the plant as I could. I still have my sketches (all on tracing paper as I like to overlay my drawings when planning compositions), photographs and notes for this and all the paintings in the series.

Perhaps one challenge was to paint the yellow colour, which can be one of the more difficult to shade and produce effectively in watercolour. I really loved producing this project and remember being over the moon with its success and the purchase by the RHS."

Kimiko Miyahara

RHS medal history

Gold medal: 2021 (and Best Botanical Art Exhibit)

Kimiko Miyahara lives and works in Tokyo, Japan. Her studies in botanical art began in 1989, under Hiroki Sato, chief tutor of the plant painting course, hosted by the Japan Gardening Society (JGS). As a member of the society, she regularly participates in this exhibition since she first won the Botanical Art Contest for Excellence in 2015.

Over a period of 30 years Miyahara frequently visited Japan's Ogasawara Islands, for a month at a time, to sketch and observe the endemic plants found there. Access to the islands is controlled, taking more than a day by boat from Tokyo. Miyahara's exhibit of 'Endemic plants of Japan's Ogasawara Islands, A UNESCO Natural World Heritage Site', gained an RHS Gold medal and the Best Botanical Art Exhibit award in 2021. Her painting of a palm (*Clinostigma savoryana*) is listed as Vulnerable on the IUCN Red List, Miyahara observed that since the designation of the islands by UNESCO, the number of seedlings of this palm has gradually increased.

"*This evergreen is known as a cabbage palm because its edible young shoots look like cabbage. Around summertime, broom-like inflorescences grow out from just below the base of the crown shaft, blossoming into a riot of tiny, pale yellow flowers. The small, egg-shaped fruit grow in clusters on their stems, ripening from green to yellow to red.*"

Clinostigma savoryana (cabbage palm), 2018

Watercolour on paper

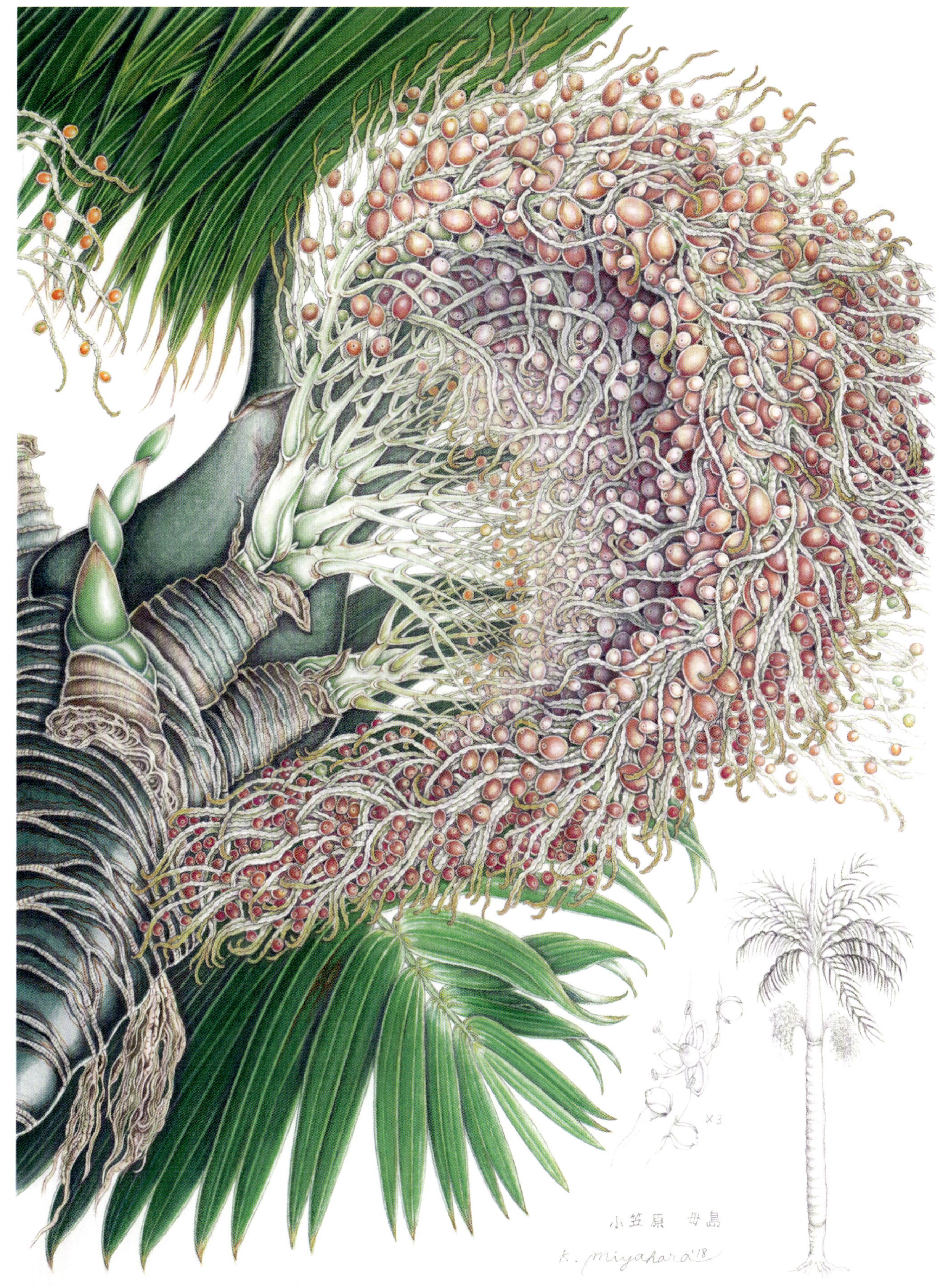
×3
小笠原　母島
K. Miyahara '18

Masako Mori

RHS medal history

Gold medals: 2015, 2019

Masako Mori graduated from Sophia University in Tokyo, with a degree in psychology, in 1976. She undertook botanical art classes with Yoko Kakuta at the Asahi Culture Centre starting in 1999, and in 2003 she gained the first of three awards at the Botanical Art Competition at the National Museum of Nature and Science in Tokyo.

Mori presented her paintings on the theme of 'Edible leguminous plants' for the RHS in 2019, where she was awarded a Gold medal for the second time.

Her rich composition describes the growth of the broad bean throughout the year. She has captured the subtle colour changes as the leaves age; and the full variation in textures, from the silky smooth skin of the bean to the soft fuzz of the pod's interior. These robust plants are favourites with gardeners; Mori grew these in pots in her garden, where they reached between 60cm and 1 metre tall.

Vicia faba (broad bean), 2018

Watercolour on paper

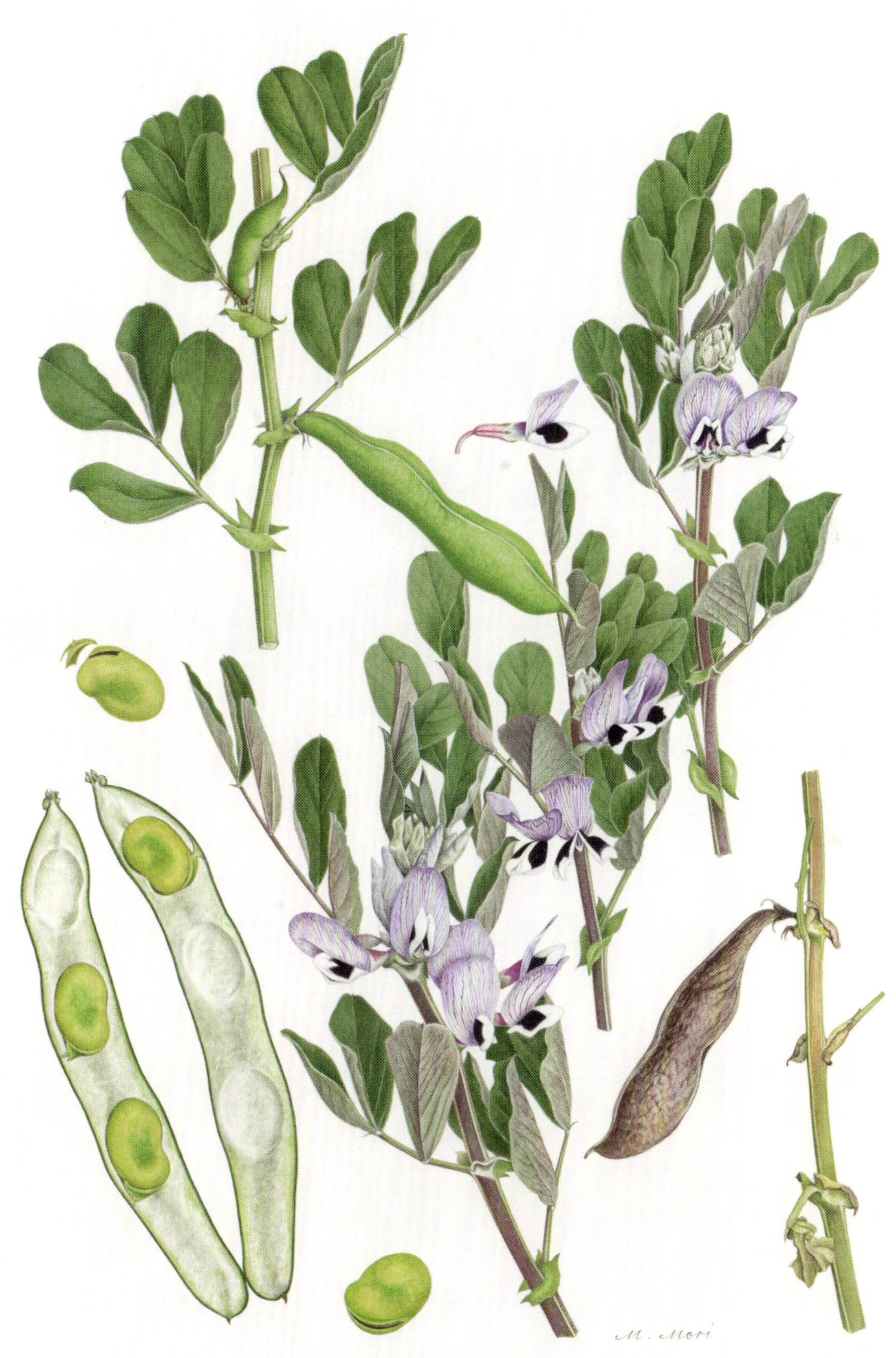
M. Mori

Kate Nessler

RHS medal history

Gold medals: 1990, 1991, 1993

Kate Nessler was awarded three RHS Gold medals for exhibits of botanical art between 1990 and 1993. Her painting of 'White *Phalaenopsis*' was one of a series of paintings of '*Orchidaceae*' exhibited in 1990. The painting was purchased for the library, and for many years it was displayed in the Viewing Room of the Lindley Library in London.

Nessler had a career as a commercial artist in Chicago, before moving to Arkansas. Having always had an interest in painting the natural world, a gift of two skins of vellum from the estate of Rory McEwen, made by the Hunt Institute for Botanical Documentation, encouraged Nessler to continue with botanical subjects. In 2003, she staged a solo exhibition of her works on vellum at Jonathan Cooper's Park Walk Gallery in London, called 'A Singular Focus'. Amongst the paintings featured was 'Hollyhocks #1'. By this time Nessler had transferred to painting almost exclusively on vellum, and started to incorporate the unique colouration and veining found on the surface of untreated vellum into her designs. In the exhibition catalogue, Victoria Matthews observed: *"The flowers in* #1 *are backed by a leaf that has been eaten by insects and converted into lace...the leaves display the sinuous tracts of the dreaded leaf miner, adding interest and authenticity."* The composition also reveals something of the process of creating the work; the degraded form of the leaf leads the eye down to the subtle outline of the lower buds and leaves. Later works by Nessler have continued to balance emerging blooms with dried and decaying elements of a plant.

'Hollyhocks #1', 2003

Watercolour, body colour and graphite on vellum

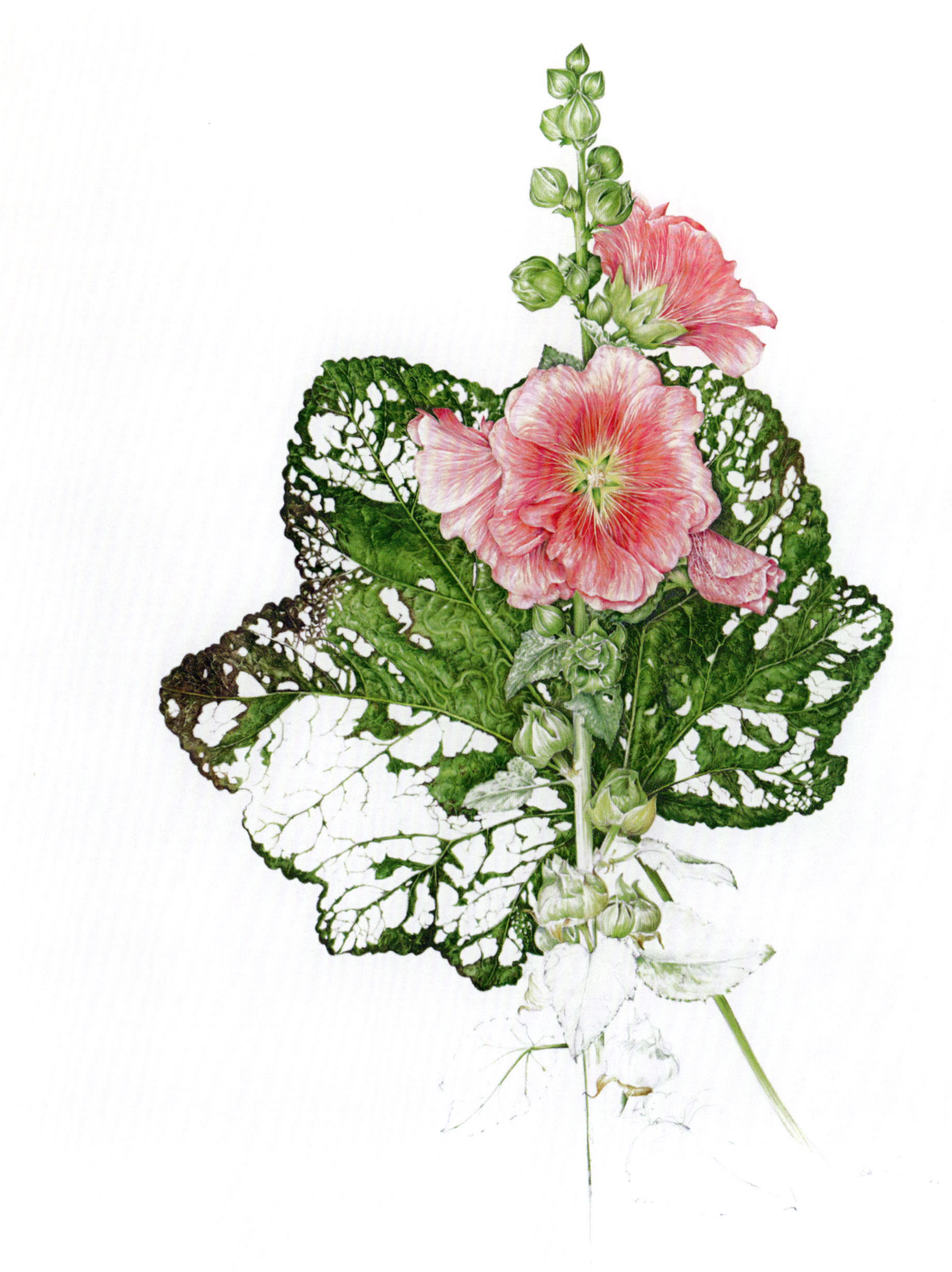

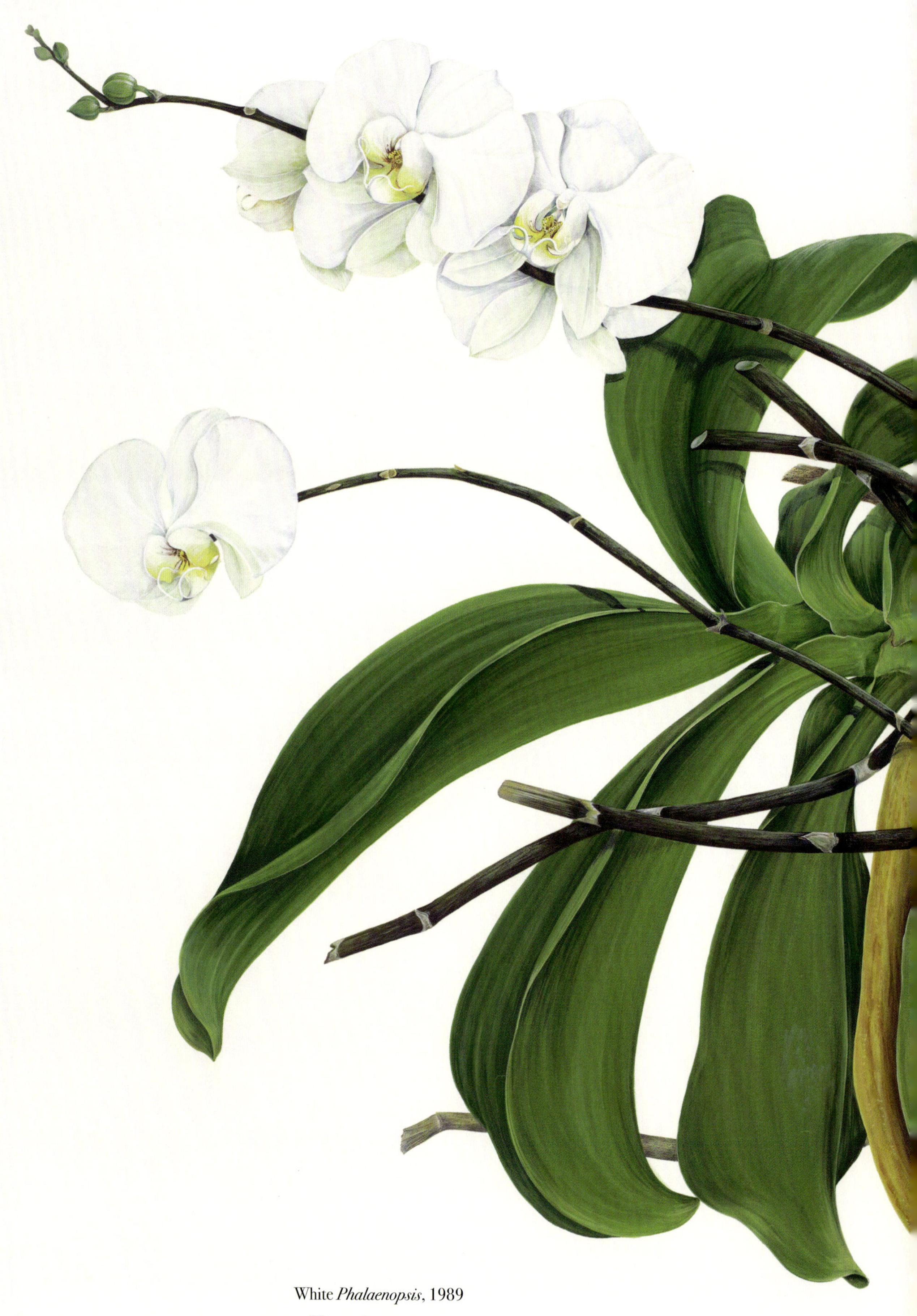

White *Phalaenopsis*, 1989
Watercolour on paper

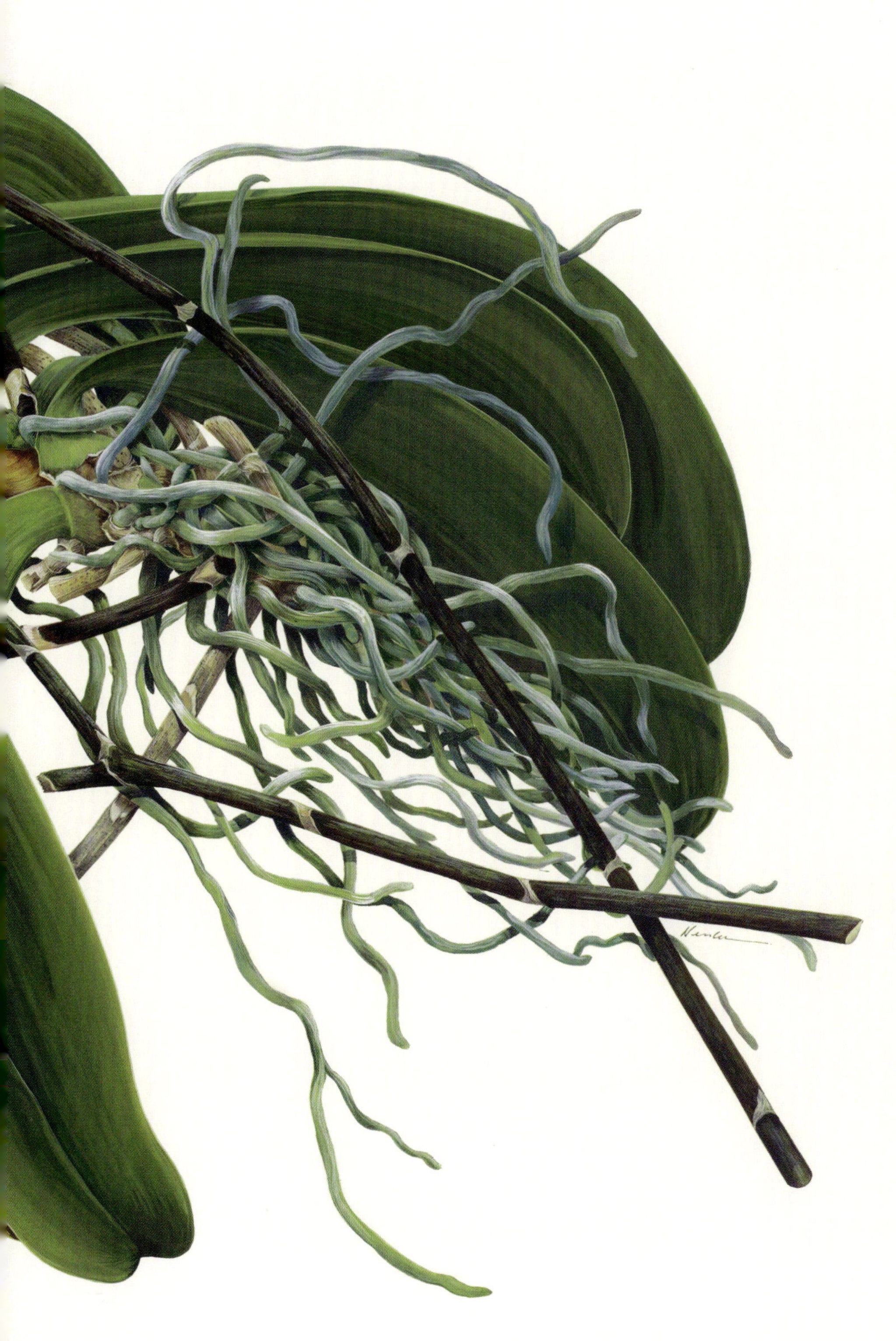

Catharine Nicholson
(1958-2011)

RHS medal history

Gold medals: 2002, 2004, 2006

Silver-Gilt medal: 2000

Silver medal: 2002

Catharine Nicholson first exhibited with the RHS in 2000, for which she was awarded a Silver-Gilt medal. Following this she exhibited a further four times, winning three Gold medals for her meticulous pen and ink studies. The piece featured here of *Picea breweriana,* or Brewer's weeping spruce, was one of a series of 'Pen & ink studies of the conifers of Canford', which saw Nicholson awarded a Gold medal in 2006.

Nicholson studied at the Courtauld Institute of Art and as a student she specialised in Gothic and Romanesque architecture. It was not until she attended classes with Ann Farrer at Kew Gardens, that she discovered her talent for botanical illustration. Her work demonstrates a fascination with texture, form and structure. She pushed the boundaries of botanical illustration, choosing to depict imperfect specimens in minute detail, just as she observed them. Pine cones were a subject Nicholson returned to in the months prior to her death. The final piece she completed of three pine cones, entitled 'Some get more eaten up than others' (2010), shows the degraded form of the cones, drawn as she found them. Enlarged to seven times their actual size, the cones are incredibly powerful as botanical studies, but they also create a poignant impression, as damage and decay is writ large.[1]

Picea breweriana, 2005–2006

Pen and ink on paper

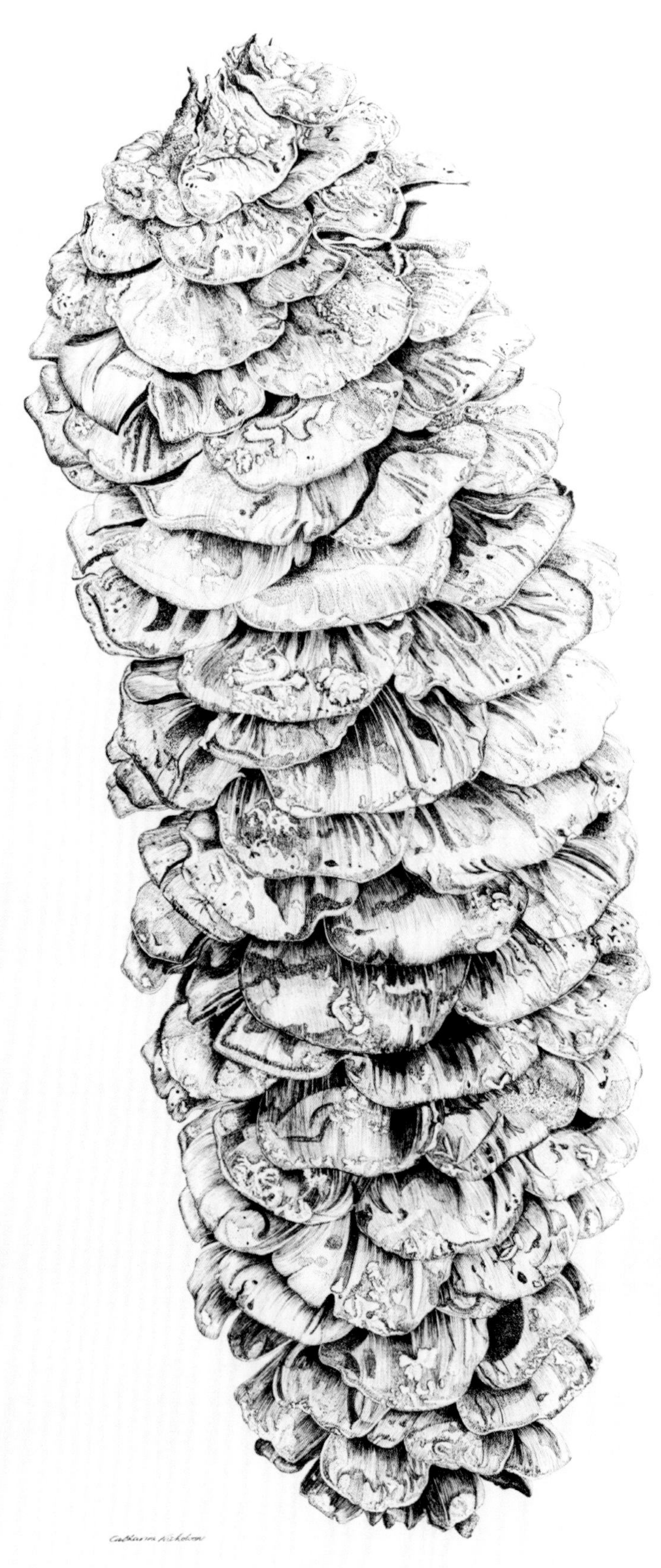

Eunike Nugroho

RHS medal history

Gold medal: 2023 (and Best Botanical Artwork)

Eunike Nugroho graduated with a degree in visual communication design from Sebelas Maret University in Surakarta, Indonesia. After working as an art director in advertising agencies for many years, a pivotal period spent in Sheffield, England, in 2012, sparked her passion for plants and botanical art. Upon returning to Indonesia, she began teaching workshops and eventually brought together individuals who shared the same passion, founding the Indonesian Society of Botanical Artists (IDSBA) in 2017.

Nugroho's works have been exhibited internationally, including in the UK, USA, Australia and Indonesia. Her dedication to native Indonesian plants was showcased in her 2023 RHS exhibit, 'Hoyas of Indonesia', for which she received a Gold Medal and the Best Botanical Artwork award for her watercolour piece, 'Bold under (Sun) Stress (*Hoya latifolia*)'.

"There are around 400 species of Hoya worldwide, with Indonesia estimated to host the highest diversity. I started growing Hoyas in 2018 and was captivated by their unique foliage and fragrant flowers. Through my art, I aim to share the wonder of nature and the beauty of plants."

Hoya spartioides, a leafless, shrub-like species endemic to Borneo, is one of Nugroho's favourites. Thriving in nutrient-poor environments, it relies on modified peduncles for photosynthesis. Her 2022 painting of this fascinating species has been included in the RHS Lindley Library collection.

Hoya spartioides, 'Leafless, NOT Lifeless', 2022

Watercolour on paper

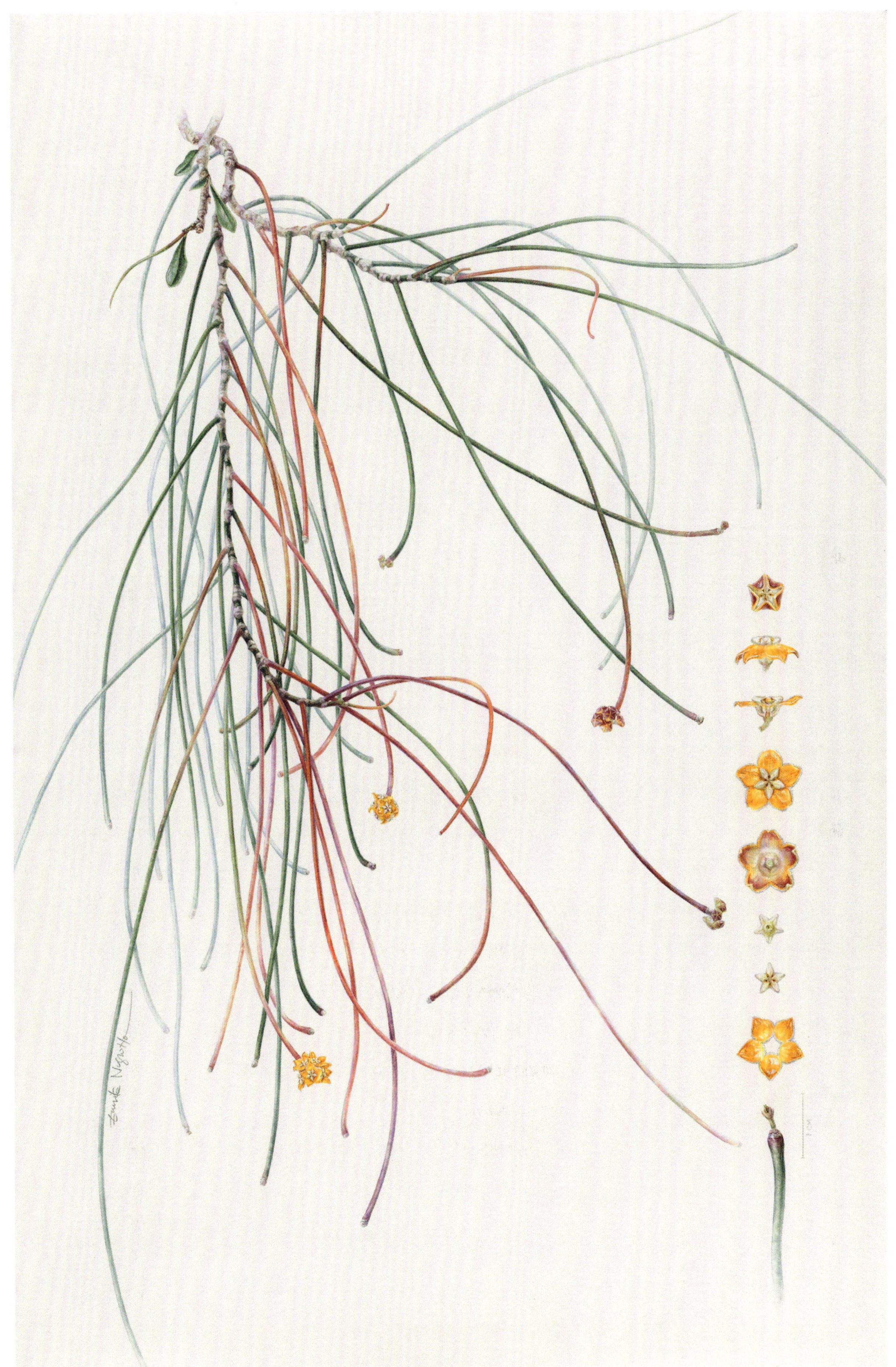

Rachel Pedder-Smith

RHS medal history

Gold medals: 2000, 2001, 2004, 2005

Silver-Gilt medal: 1998

Rachel Pedder-Smith has been awarded five medals by the RHS between 1998 and 2005, four of which were Gold. The piece featured here of a 'Small Gourd' was purchased in 2005, from an exhibition at Jonathan Cooper's Park Walk Gallery, London.

Pedder-Smith is renowned for her technical ability to convey form, colour and pattern. She studied at Leeds Metropolitan University before gaining an MA and PhD in Natural History Illustration from the Royal College of Art. Her PhD project, 'Herbarium Specimen Painting', comprised illustrations of dried, pressed plant specimens from the Herbarium at RBG Kew. Over 5 metres long, it incorporated over 700 images and took more than two years to complete. More recently, Pedder-Smith has also become an art teacher. Combining both aspects of her professional life, she has produced two books in the series *The Watercolour Art Pad*, in conjunction with the RHS, featuring step-by-step tutorials, and her own templates guiding the artist through the watercolour process for botanical painting.

'Small Gourd', 2005

Watercolour on paper

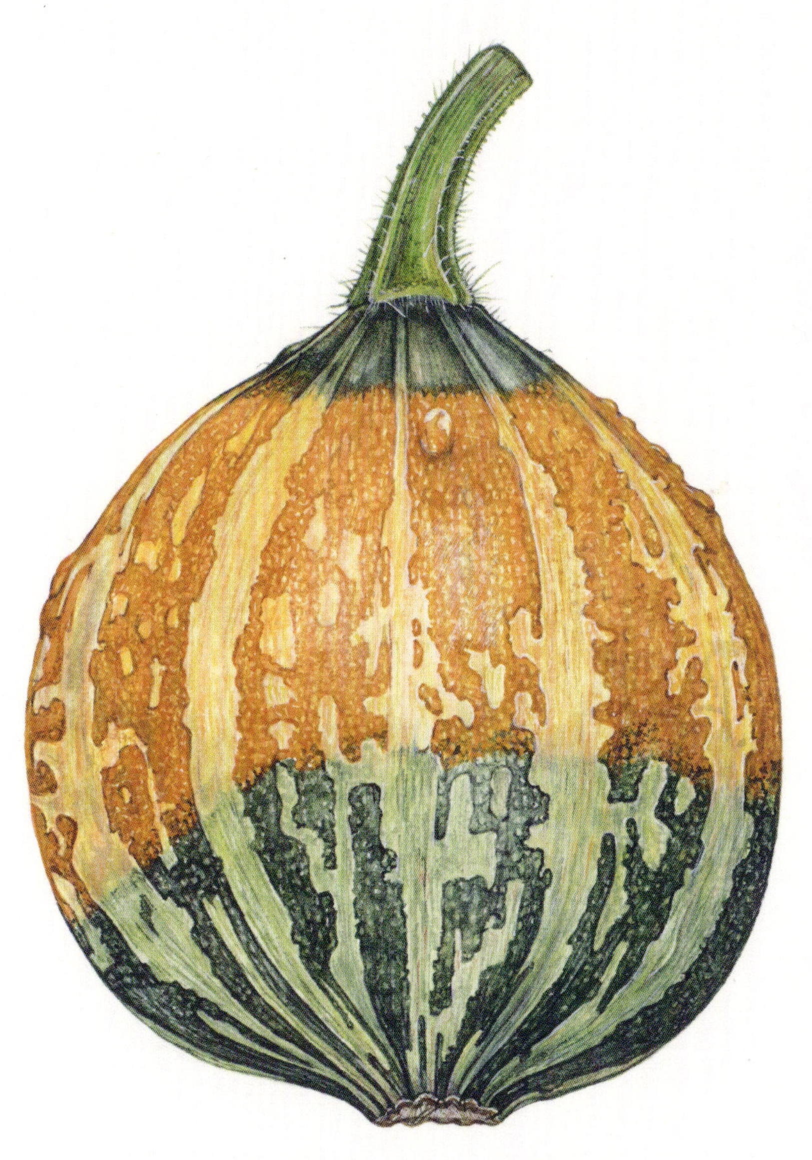

RPS 2005

Jenny Phillips

RHS medal history

Gold medal: 1993

Jenny Phillips won a Gold medal with the RHS in 1993, shortly after having founded the Melbourne School of Botanical Art in Australia (1992).

She began painting studies of flowers in 1971, combining her love of gardening with her skill as an artist. She has been connected with botanical art institutions all over the world, teaching master classes for Shirley Sherwood and exhibiting in the US, Paris, London, Japan and the Netherlands.

Phillips demonstrated her botanical painting technique at an RHS botanical illustration seminar in 2006. This unfinished piece of a globe artichoke was produced as a demonstration piece. She says of the piece: "*my aim with this three-hour sketch was to demonstrate quick drawing technique, with the layering of colours to create form. Unfortunately, there was no time to finish the painting.*"

'Globe artichoke' [unfinished], 2007

Watercolour on paper

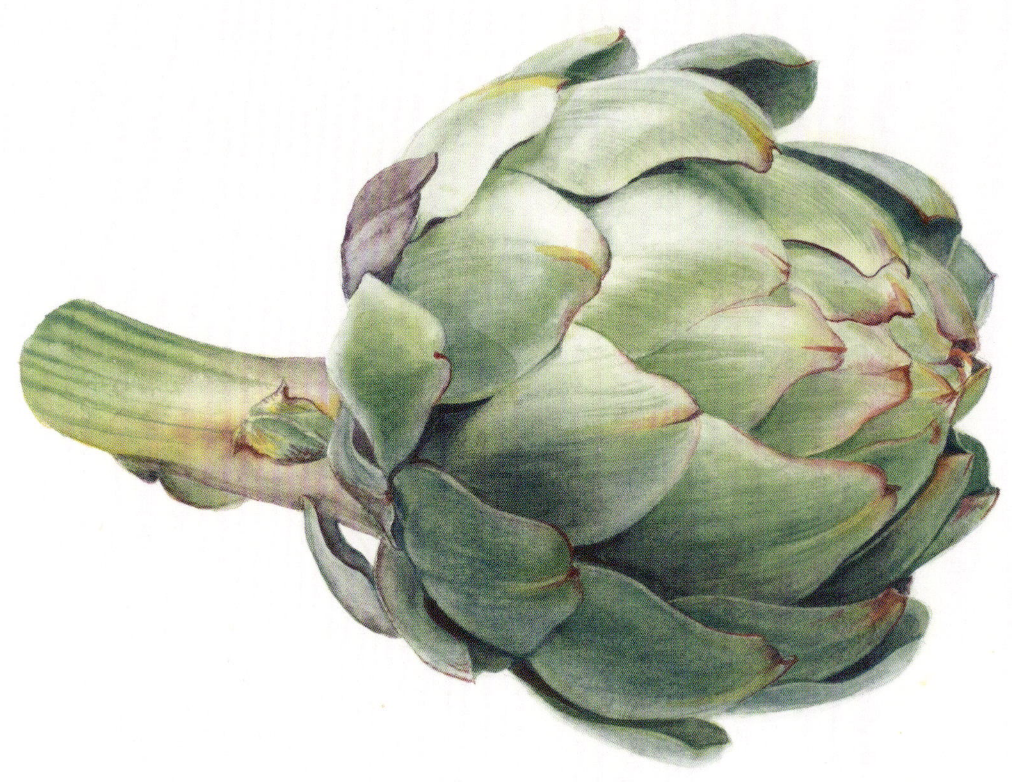
Jenny K. Phillips 2006.
R.H.S. 11/Nov.

Nigel Pickering
(1957-2021)

RHS medal history

Gold medals: 2019, 2022 (and Best Botanical Art Exhibit)

Dr Nigel Pickering studied medicine at Oxford and went on to practise as a GP in Malmesbury, England for 28 years. On retirement he took up botanical art, training under Julia Trickey and joining the Chelsea Physic Garden Florilegium Society and Cirencester Botanical Artists.

Pickering's first exhibit at the RHS in 2019, 'Treasures of the Richtersveld', achieved a Gold medal. He travelled to South Africa to observe plants growing in their natural habitat. The watercolour of *Aloidendron pillansii* (Giant Quiver Tree) features the montane desert environment in the background, drawn in graphite pencil.

"The Giant Quiver Tree is the rarest of the South African tree aloes. It is classified as critically endangered mainly due to its small population size, restricted range and habitat loss. The few remaining populations grow in the barren, mountainous area of the Richtersveld on either side of the Orange River."

Aloidendron pillansii (Giant Quiver tree), 2019

Watercolour on paper

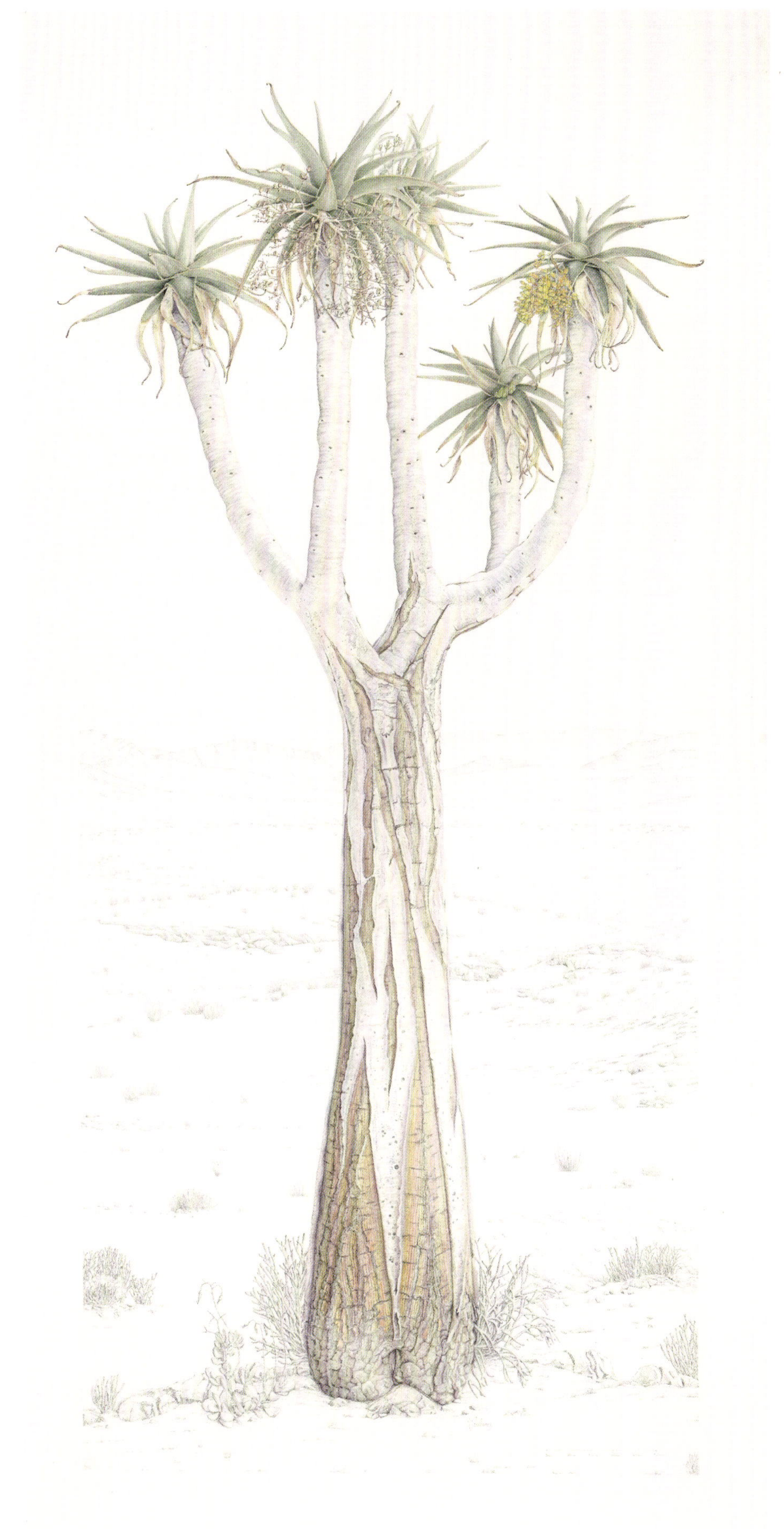

In 2018 Pickering had joined an expedition exploring the foothills of the Andes and Northern Patagonia. The trip inspired his paintings of 'Rosulate Violas of the Patagonia Andes' exhibited in 2022, which gained a further Gold medal and award for Best Botanical Art Exhibit. This South American species has an unusual appearance, with tight rosettes of geometrically spiralled leaves. When not in flower, they can resemble rocks in the landscape.

In September 2019 Pickering was diagnosed with an aggressive brain tumour and lost the ability to read and write. Despite this he continued to paint and found it helped him to cope with the often-gruelling treatment. He was determined to finish these six paintings. Pickering died in January 2021 and in 2022 his family exhibited the paintings on his behalf.

Viola atropurpurea, 17 April 2020

Watercolour on paper

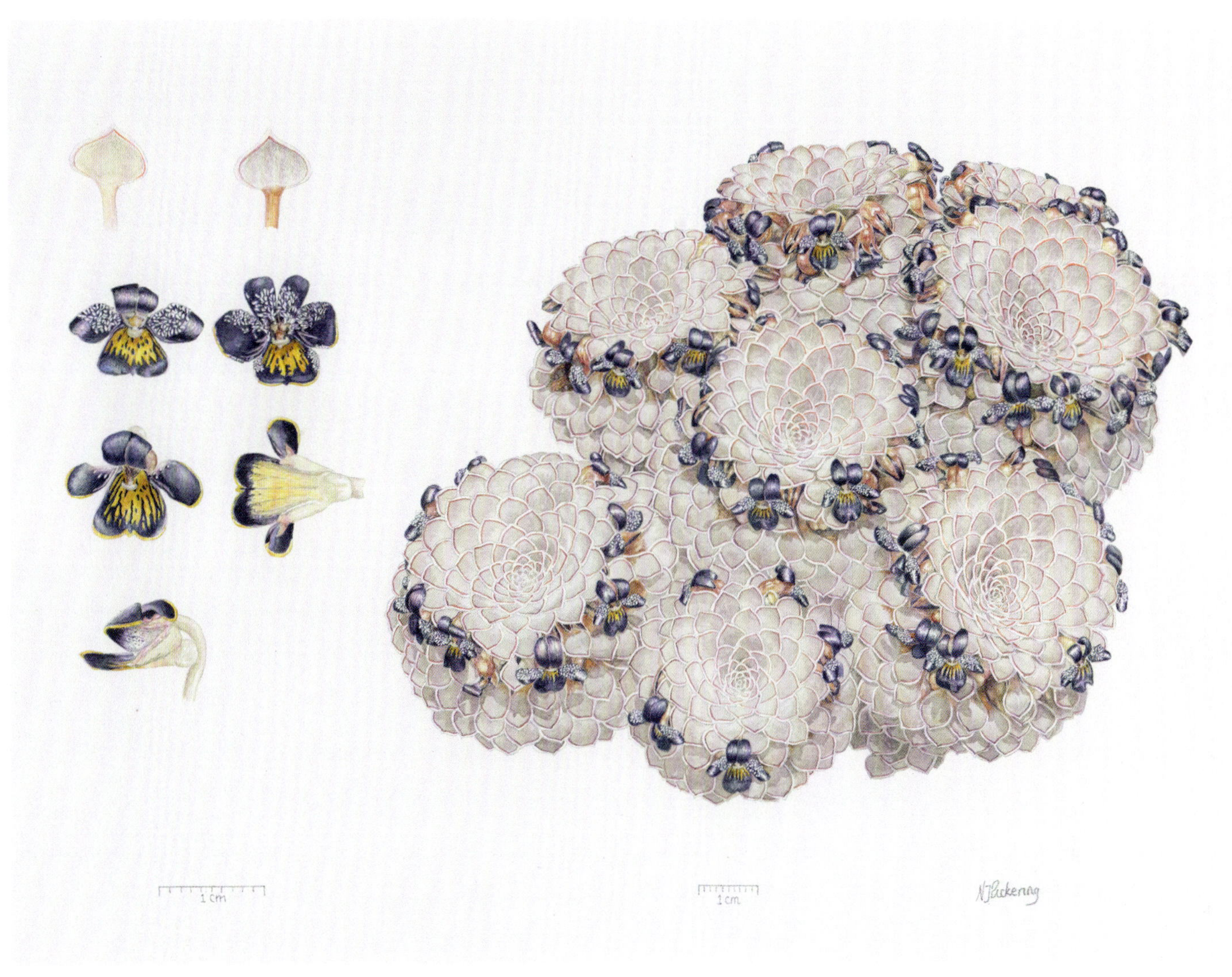
1 cm
1 cm
N J Pickering

Katherine Pickles

RHS medal history

Gold medals: 1991, 1992, 1993, 1994, 1996, 2015, 2017

Since her first Gold medal-winning exhibit in 1991, Katherine Pickles has won a further six Gold medals, the most recent in 2017 for her paintings of 'Clematis'.

Having attended a Foundation Course at Canterbury College of Art, Pickles then studied History of Art at Sussex University. She moved to Orkney, Scotland in the early 1980s, at which point she started painting botanical subjects. In 1996, in recognition of her skill as a botanical artist, Pickles was invited to design the RHS Chelsea Flower Show Plate to celebrate the Golden Wedding Anniversary of HM The Queen and HRH Prince Philip.

Following her Gold medal-winning exhibition of 'Watercolour paintings of Ranunculaceae' in February 1992, the Picture Committee recommended that the Society should seek to acquire examples of her work for the Library Collections; two paintings, 'Fritillaria' and 'Aquilegia', were then purchased.

The paintings of 'Heath Spotted Orchid' *(Dactylorhiza maculata)* and '*Primula veris*', came to the library in 2011 as part of the bequest from the late Joyce Stewart, renowned Orchidologist and former Director of Horticulture for the RHS. Stewart had commissioned the orchid painting

'Heath Spotted Orchid', 1992

Watercolour on paper

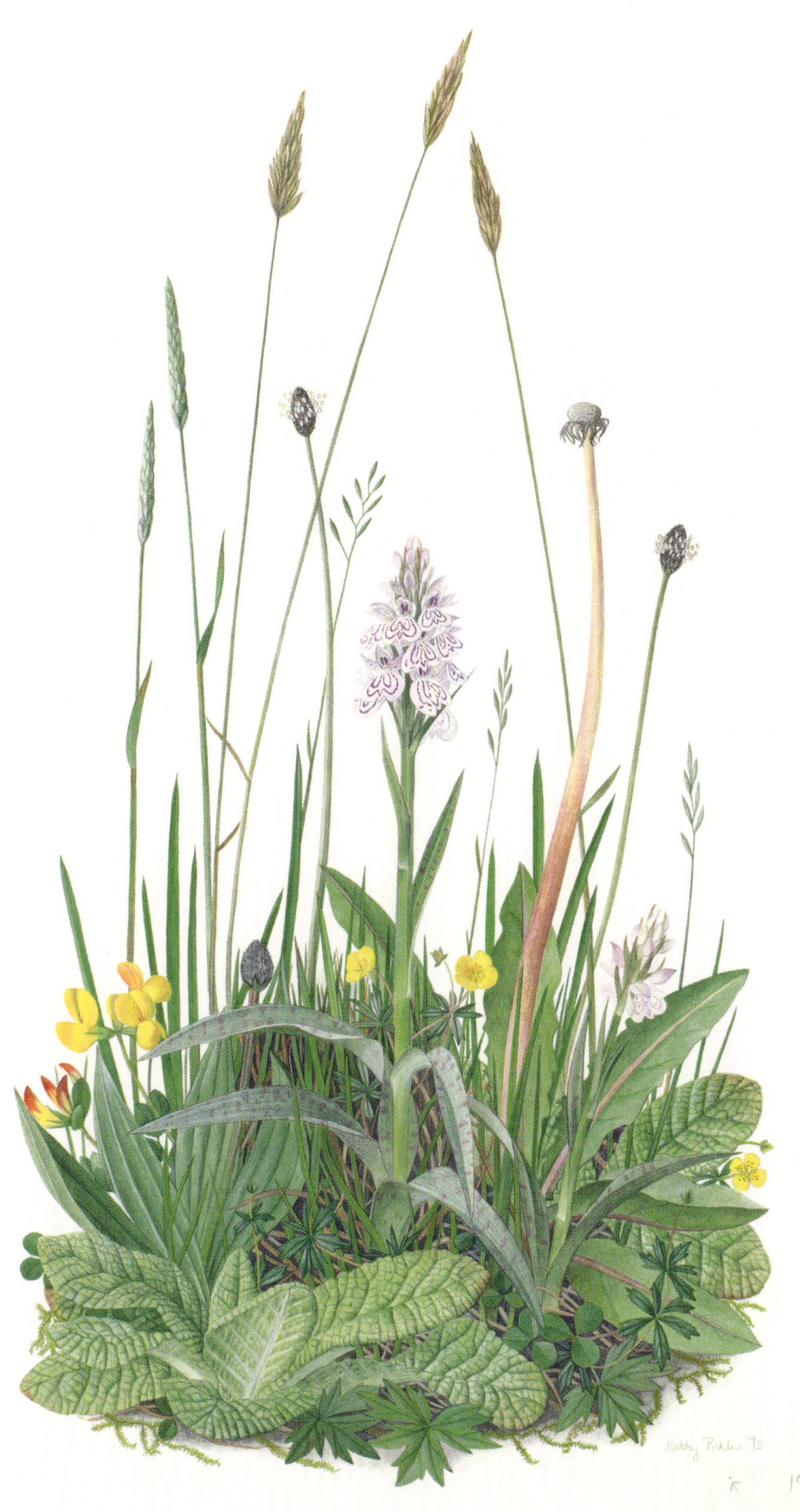
Kathy Pickles '93
19.5 cm x 31 cm
Mounted only
Heath Spotted Orchid

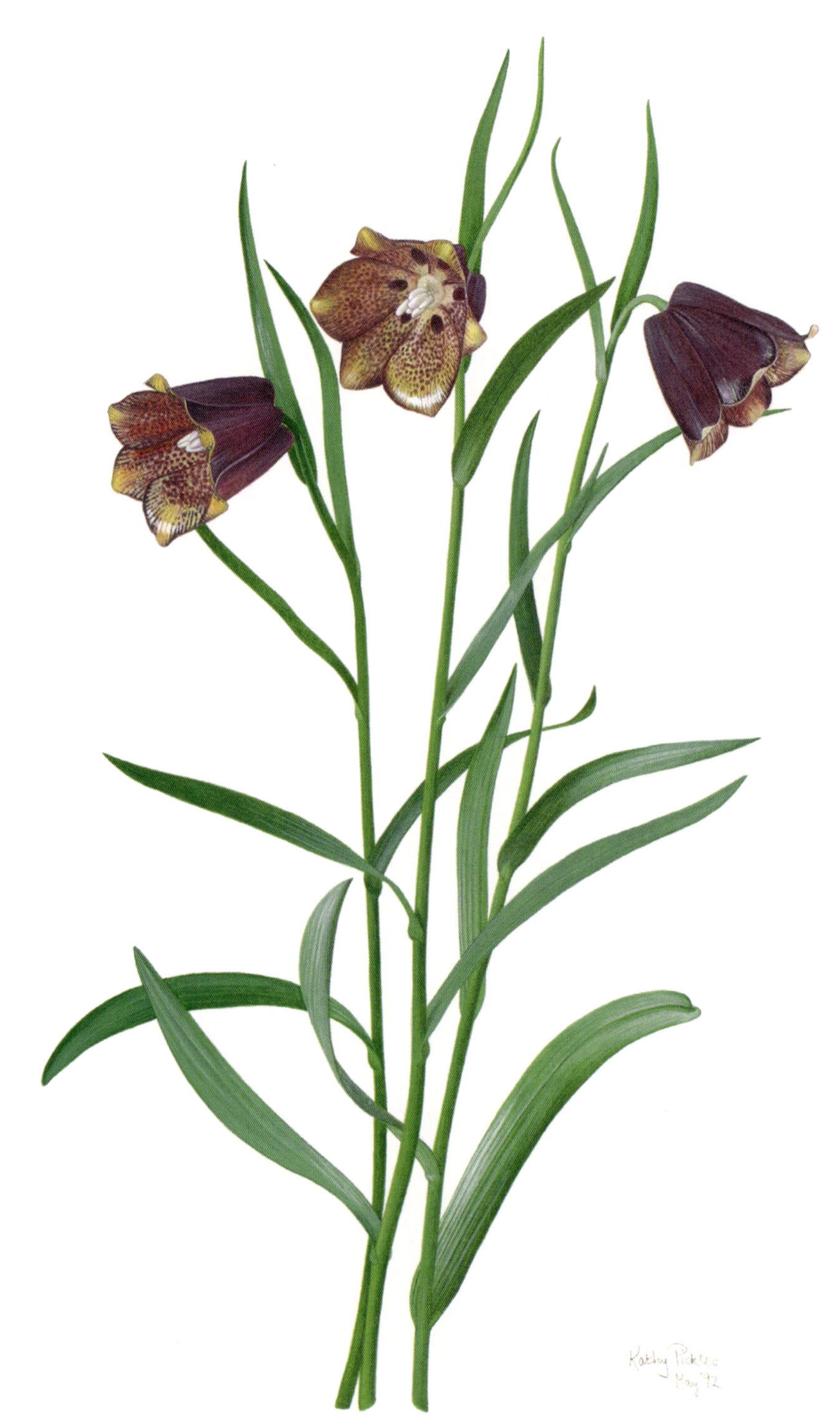

Fritillaria pyrenaica, 1992

Watercolour on paper

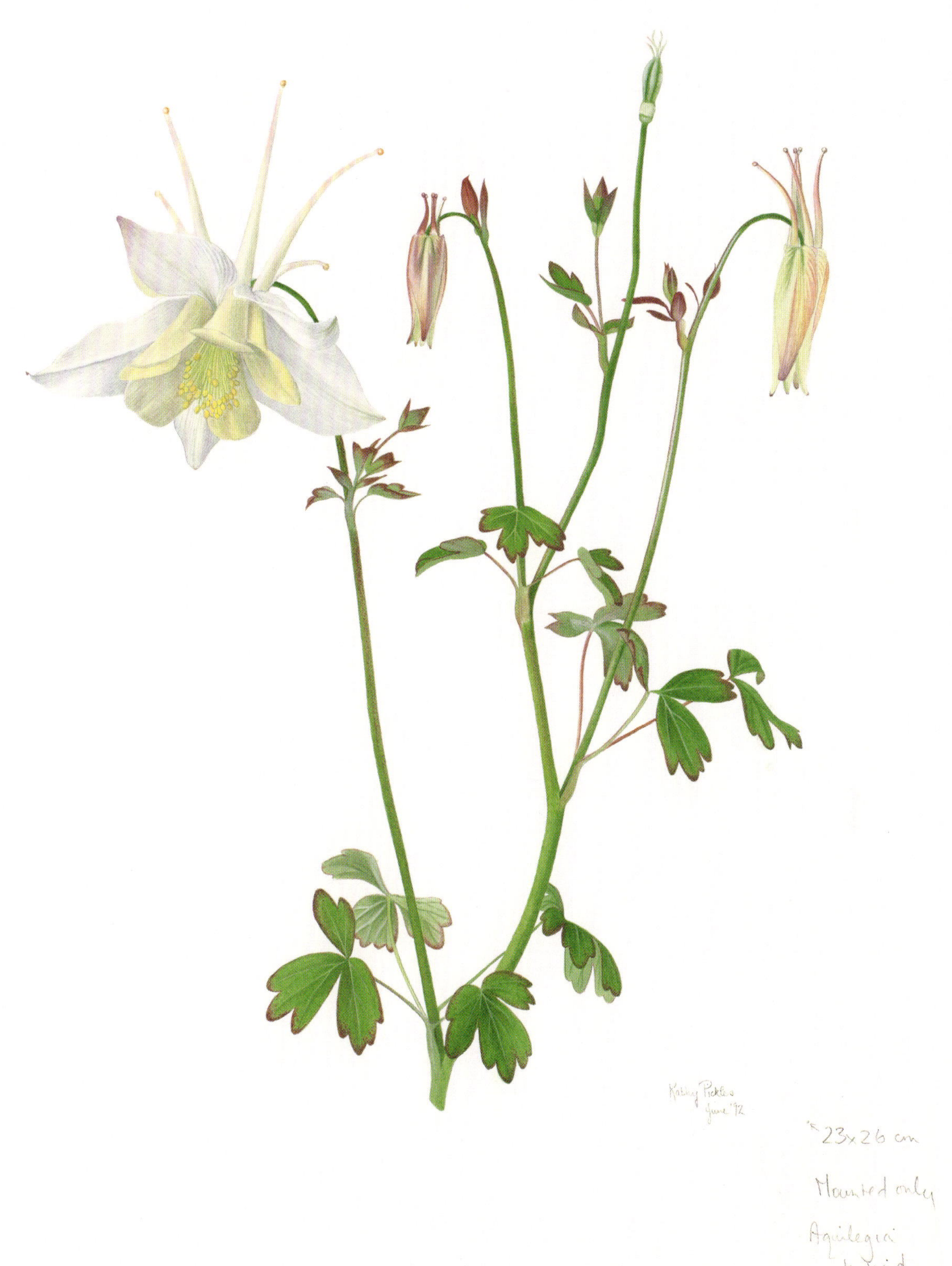

'Aquilegia long-spurred hybrid', 1992

Watercolour on paper

for her personal collection and, as such, it is notably different in composition to the other pieces, including, as it does, the grassland habitat of this wild flower. The watercolour of the *Primula veris* was originally commissioned by Patrick Woods (also an orchid expert) and then made its way to Joyce Stewart, possibly as a gift.

Pickles describes her painting technique as follows:

"*I like to work directly from live specimens, straight onto the stretched watercolour paper, working out the composition as I go along. I use a fine pencil to draw a basic outline of whatever part of the plant is likely to change fastest (usually buds and flowers) and then switch to paints as soon as possible. In this way I try and capture the exact play of light over the specimen in front of me. I very rarely use photographic records or sketches.*

I work at a sloped desk in a small studio, next to a window. I never use artificial light, for the reason given above, which means painting in the depths of winter can be a challenge, especially in Orkney. I don't favour one particular brand of paint, nor do I have a huge range of colours. My paint drawer contains tubes of Winsor & Newton, Daler-Rowney, Daniel Smith and Sennelier.

Specimens can come from the supermarket, garden centre, my garden or, occasionally, the wild (where examples are plentiful, not protected and don't need to be dug up). If I am looking for something in particular, friends locally, or sometimes further afield, can be very generous."

Primula veris, 1992

Watercolour on paper

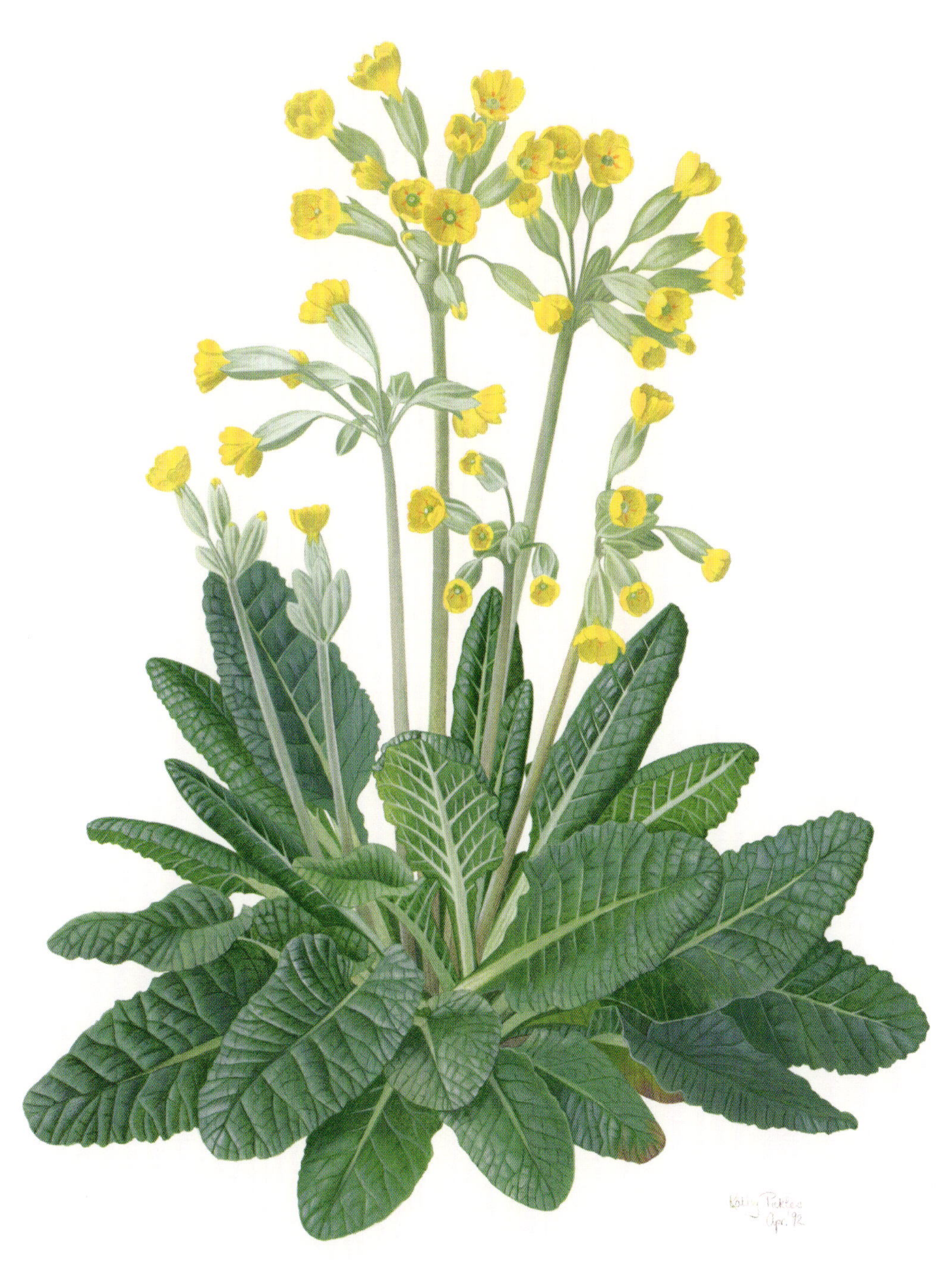

8" x 9½"

Lesley Randall

RHS medal history

Gold medals: 2010, 2017

Silver-Gilt medal: 2012

Lesley Randall has exhibited with the RHS three times between 2010 and 2017, winning two Gold medals and a Silver-Gilt.

Randall first became interested in botanical illustration whilst studying for her undergraduate degree at Cornell University, where she majored in landscape architecture. She started drawing and keeping record sketches of plants to help her learn more about them. Her work has since won a number of international awards for botanical illustration and featured in scientific publications, as well as in exhibitions.

Whilst living in Hawaii, Randall continued to develop her technique. She began to illustrate professionally following a move to California. Favouring pen and ink, she produces highly detailed illustrations. She says, "I find pen and ink to be an elegant art form", although she is skilled in using other media too. One of the challenges of depicting the form and pattern of a specimen in pen and ink, is not to over-complicate the illustration, whilst still successfully conveying enough detail. Randall is skilful in her use of stippling to create the impression of shape and depth in her compositions; her full use of tonal range from the darkest black to the palest stipple is exemplary.

Argyroxiphium sandwicense, 2017

Pen and ink on paper

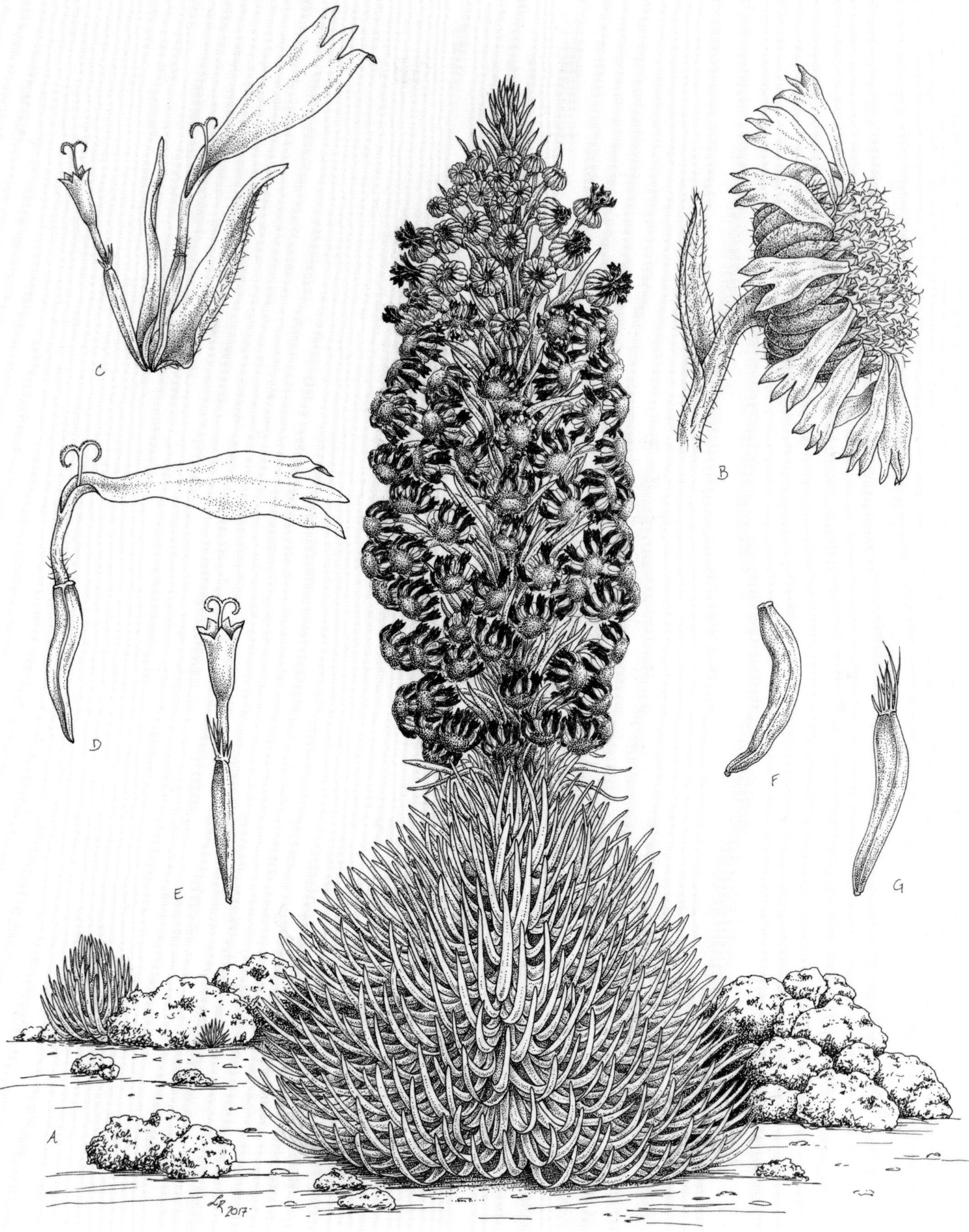
C
B
D
E
F
G
A
LR 2017

Silvana Rava

RHS medal history

Gold medal: 2008

Silver-Gilt medal: 2017

Silvana Rava has exhibited twice with the RHS: first in 2008, when she was awarded a Gold medal and again in 2017, for which she received a Silver-Gilt medal. This painting of *Cyclamen europaeum* was part of Rava's 2008 Gold medal-winning display entitled 'Medical flora of Lake Como'.

"*This drawing was executed for an exhibition held in Salerno, Italy, in collaboration with the botanical garden 'Giardini della Minerva'. I had been asked to draw medical plants, as in Salerno, in the past there was an ancient medical school there. The* Cyclamen europaeum *is a medical plant that grows in my local area, Lake Como.*

The dye extracted from the tubers and administered in drops was used in medicine for headaches, neuralgia and menstrual pains. In the past, the tuber was also used as pig food (it was called 'pig-bread'); only in famine times was it eaten by mankind (the poor man's potato), becoming edible only after being well-dried and cooked. The fresh tuber is poisonous. The roots, which are very poisonous, were given to children against worms for their purging qualities."

Cyclamen europaeum, 2007

Watercolour on paper

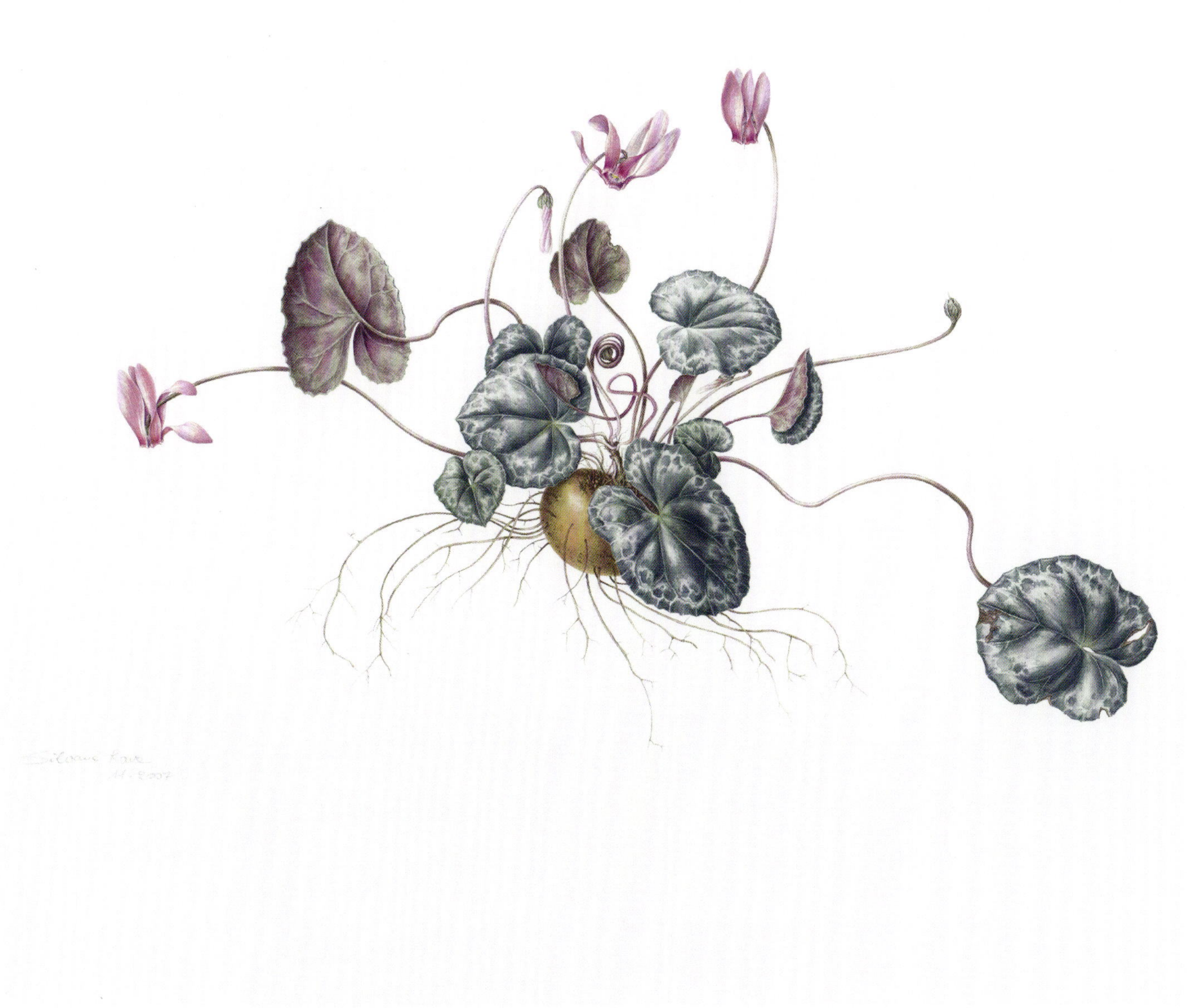

Terrie Reddish

RHS medal history

Gold medal: 2008

Terrie Reddish exhibited with the RHS in 2008 and was awarded a Gold medal for her study of *Phormium tenax*. Her bold composition reveals fine attention to detail. This is one of only a few artworks in the collection that focuses solely on the roots of a plant.

Based in New Zealand, Reddish specialises in drawing native plants, working solely in coloured pencil. She began drawing in 1998 as a hobby and is largely self-taught; she now runs her own private drawing and bookbinding classes. Reddish's work has been exhibited extensively in New Zealand.

'Underground' – *Phormium tenax*, 2008

Coloured pencil on paper

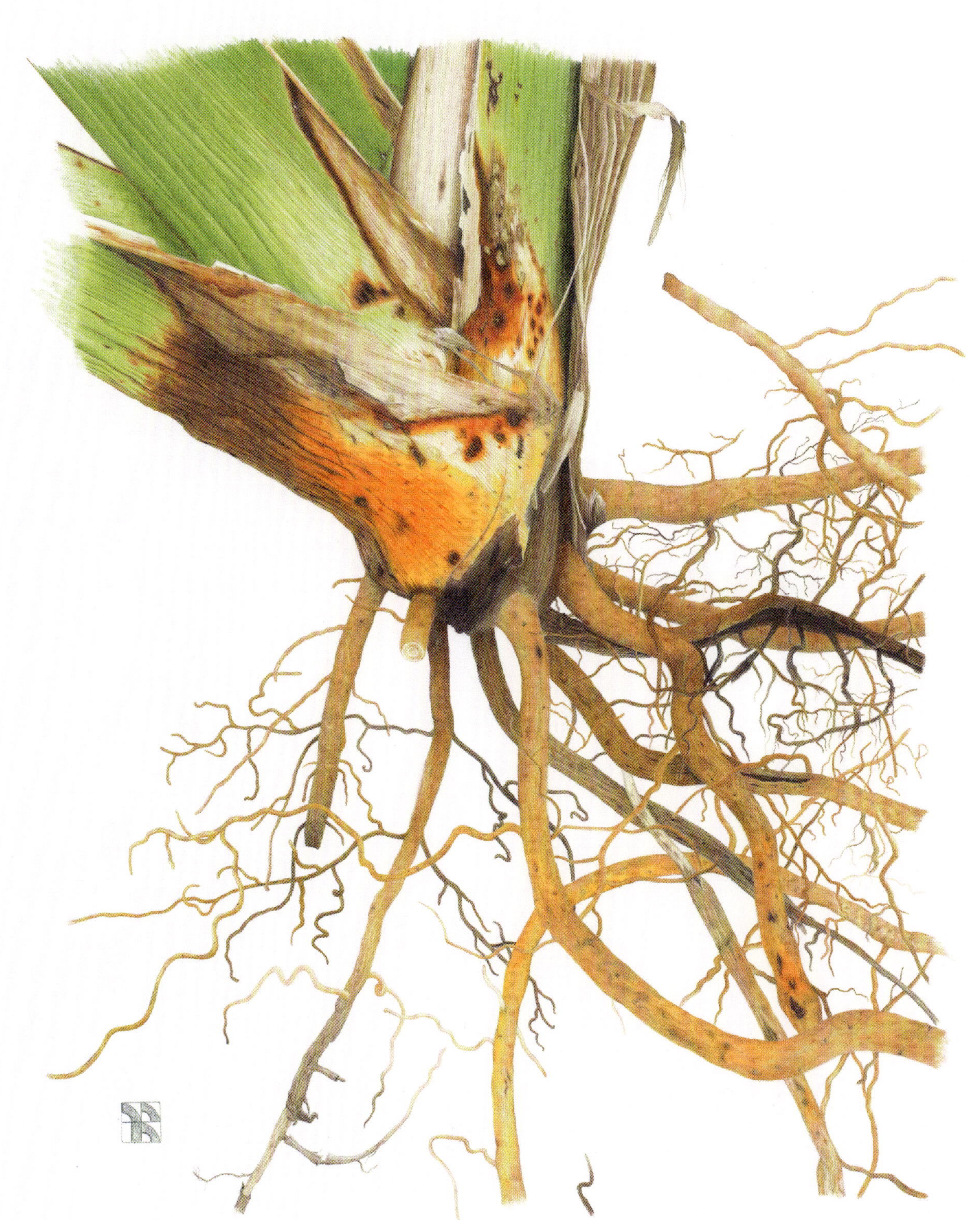

Lizzie Sanders
(1944–2020)

RHS medal history

Gold medals: 2000, 2002, 2004

Lizzie Sanders exhibited on three occasions with the RHS, gaining a Gold medal each time. The watercolour of *Vanilla imperialis* featured here, was from a series exhibited in 2004.

Based in Edinburgh, close to the botanic gardens, Sanders was able to obtain interesting or unusual specimens to paint. The striking compositions she adopted make bold use of the white unpainted space. Offset to give the impression of the climbing branch meandering across the page, the vanilla as it is shown here lays claim to its heritage as a member of the *Orchidaceae* family. Using a dry brush technique to master the surface texture and form of the plant, the focus on the thick fullness of the leaf is balanced against the twisted tendril and pod.

Having studied at Duncan of Jordanstone College of Art in Dundee, Sanders spent the early part of her career working in graphic design and advertising in Italy and New York. On returning to Scotland, she continued her work as a designer in Edinburgh. Having made the transition to botanical illustration 20 years ago, she created works of a consistently high standard. She received accolades from a number of institutions and her work featured in exhibitions and collections of international standing. Until her death in 2020, Sanders was a tutor on the Diploma Course in Botanical Illustration at the Royal Botanic Gardens, Edinburgh.

Vanilla imperialis, 2003

Watercolour on paper

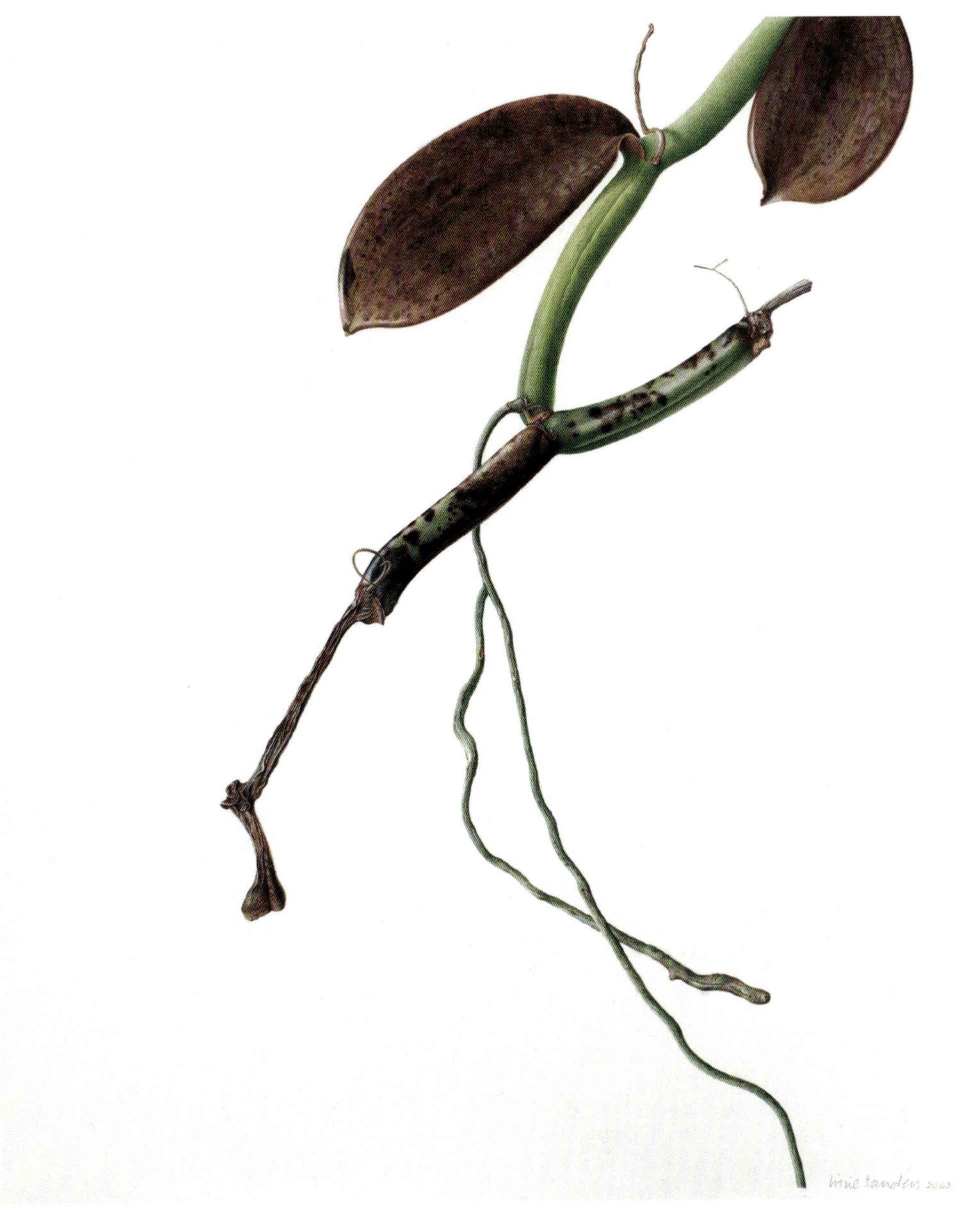

Sandra Sanger

RHS medal history

Gold medals: 2008 (and Best Botanical Artist), 2010 (and Best Botanical Artist), 2013, 2016

Sandra Sanger exhibited twice with the RHS at the NEC in Birmingham (2008 and 2010), being awarded a Gold medal, as well as being the 'Best Botanical Artist' in Show, on both occasions. The illustration featured here is of the illyarrie or red-capped gum (*Eucalyptus erythrocorys)* and was part of her 2010 display of 'Australian Eucalypts'. Sanger's depiction of this native species combines elements of classical botanical illustration, featuring magnifications and cross-sections of the fruit and buds for identification, with a fresh and dynamic composition.

Following a career lecturing in 'Drawing, Art and Design' at the Department of Fashion and Textile Design, RMIT University, Sanger retired and took botanical illustration classes at the RBG Victoria, Melbourne.

"*I enjoy working in a realistic way, and this subject area combines my interest in plant forms, rendering and watercolour. After attending 'Illustrating Plant Dissection' workshops, I developed a special interest in including microscopic details in my botanical studies.*"

Eucalyptus erythrocorys, 2010

Watercolour on paper

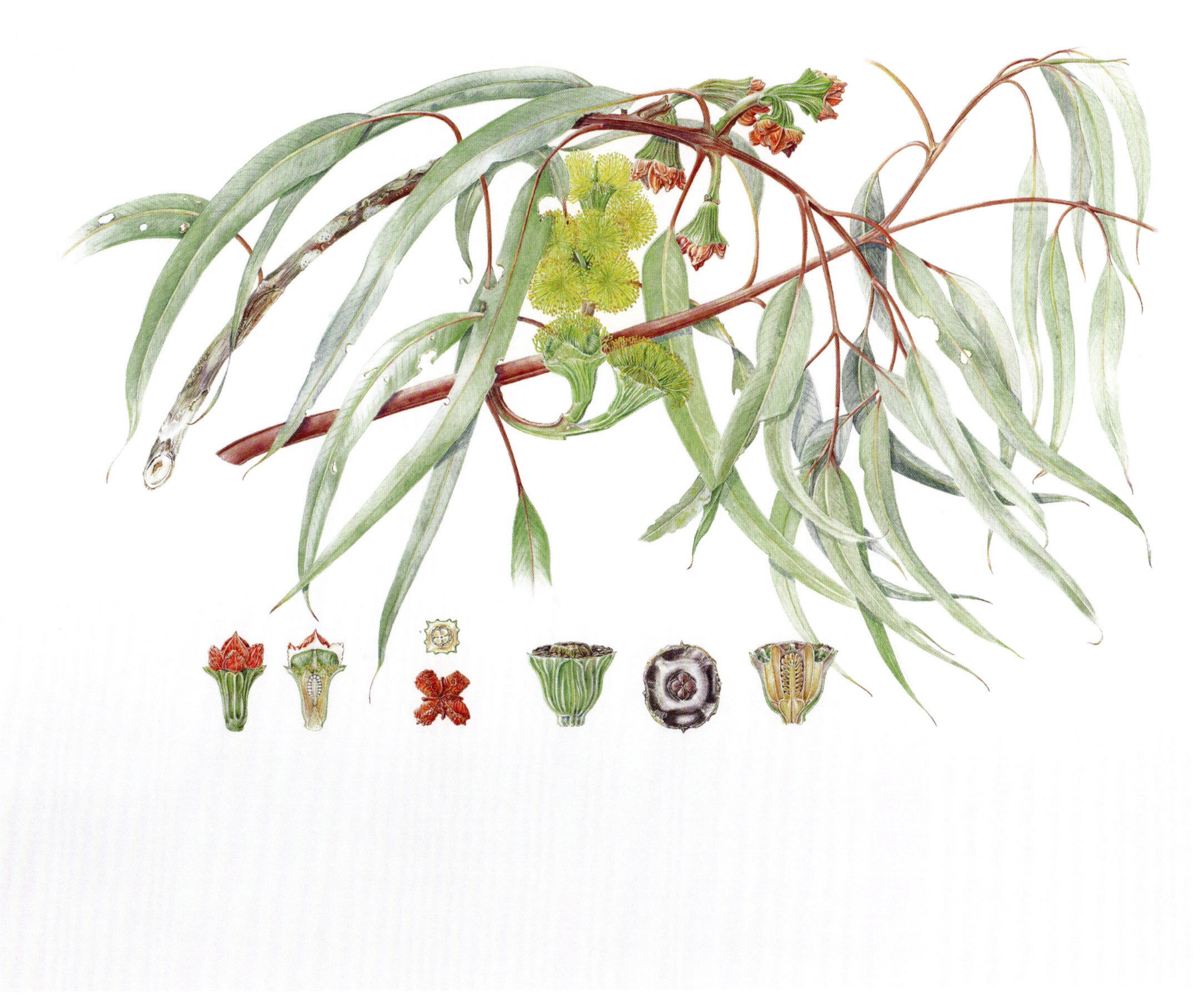

Gael Sellwood

RHS medal history

Gold medal: 2014 (and Best Exhibit)

Silver medal: 2008

Gael Sellwood has more than 25 years' experience as an artist, having studied under Christabel King at RBG Kew. At the RHS Malvern Spring Festival in 2014, she was awarded a Gold medal and Best Exhibit for her set of watercolours of 'Hydrangeas in autumn and winter'.

Sellwood's favourite subjects include dried, curled and care worn specimens that offer the opportunity to study the range of colours that emerge as the plants die back. The specimens of 'Nikko Blue' that were required to complete this study were gathered from the car park at Burncoose Nursery in Cornwall, with help from the staff there. Observed and painted in early autumn, the magenta and violet colours found on the outer edges of the sepals contrast with the deep blue that darkens as the flower heads dry. Sellwood obtained her pigments from a number of places, but was particularly pleased to be able to use a mineral pigment on the petals that has a gentle sparkle when seen tilted in raking light. The unpainted areas of the composition balance the areas of deeply painted shadow at the centre of the inflorescence. This study took somewhere between 70 and 90 hours to complete.

Hydrangea macrophylla 'Nikko Blue', 2013–2014

Watercolour on paper

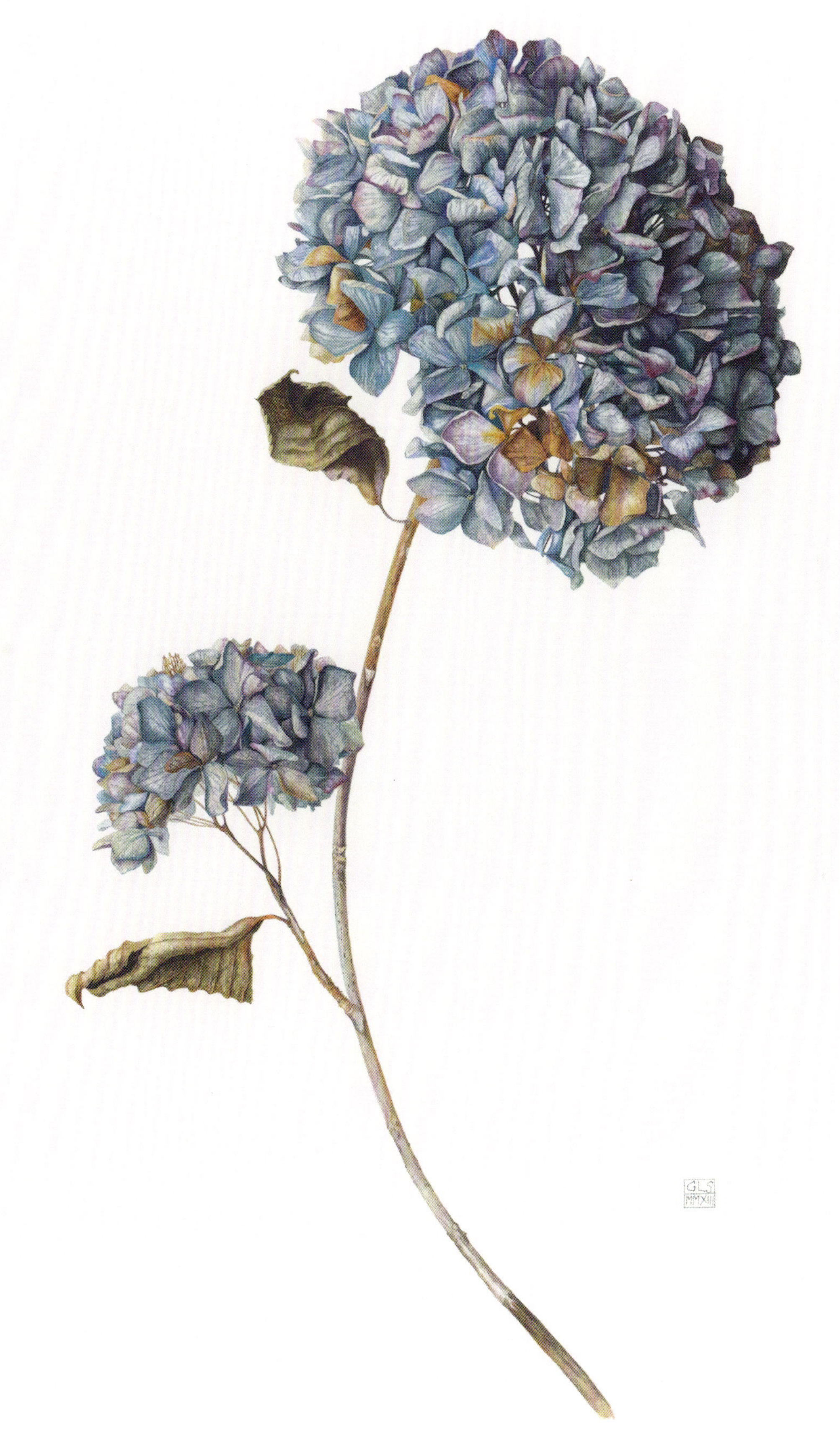
GLS
MMXII

Siriol Sherlock

RHS medal history

Gold medals: 1993, 1994, February 1995, 1999

Silver-Gilt medals: November 1995, 1998

Siriol Sherlock was awarded her first Gold medal in 1993, for her exhibit 'Watercolour paintings of plants from the Sir Harold Hillier Garden and Arboretum'. She exhibited regularly between 1993 and 1999, winning four Gold medals and two Silver-Gilt medals. Sherlock kindly donated two of her paintings to the Lindley Collections in 1995, of *Aeschynanthus speciosus* and *Tibouchina urvilleana.*

Preferring a loose painting style that relies entirely on a layered application of watercolour, Sherlock does not use pencil under-drawing. She works quickly, creating an immediate and vibrant effect.

Her work has featured extensively in exhibitions and publications; she has taught both flower painting and botanical illustration classes at venues around the world, including at RHS Garden Wisley. Sherlock has also produced two highly successful books: *Exploring Flowers in Watercolour* (1998) and *Botanical Illustration: Painting with Watercolours* (2004).

Aeschynanthus speciosus, *c.*1995

Watercolour on paper

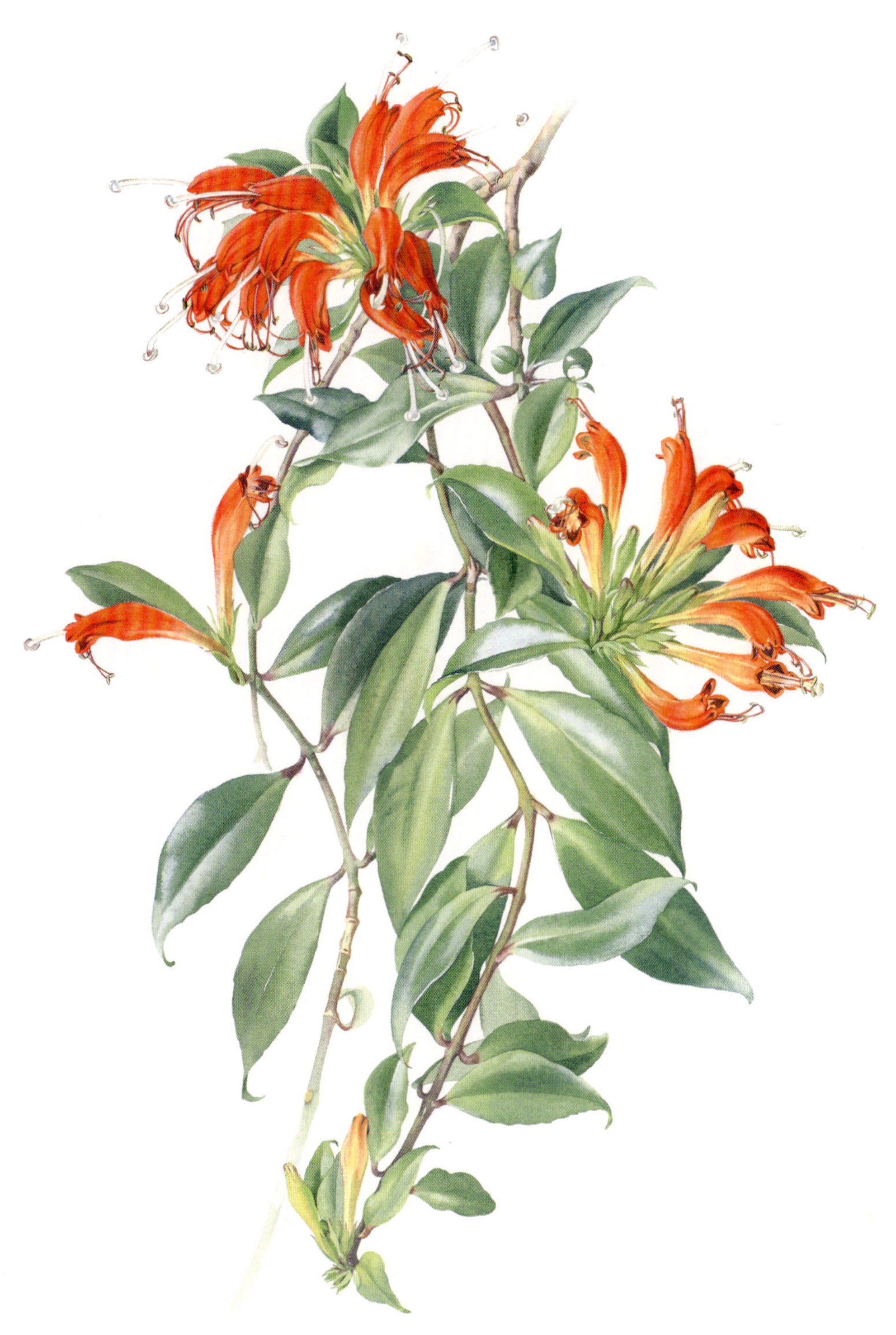

Siriol Sherlock

Aeschyanthus speciosus

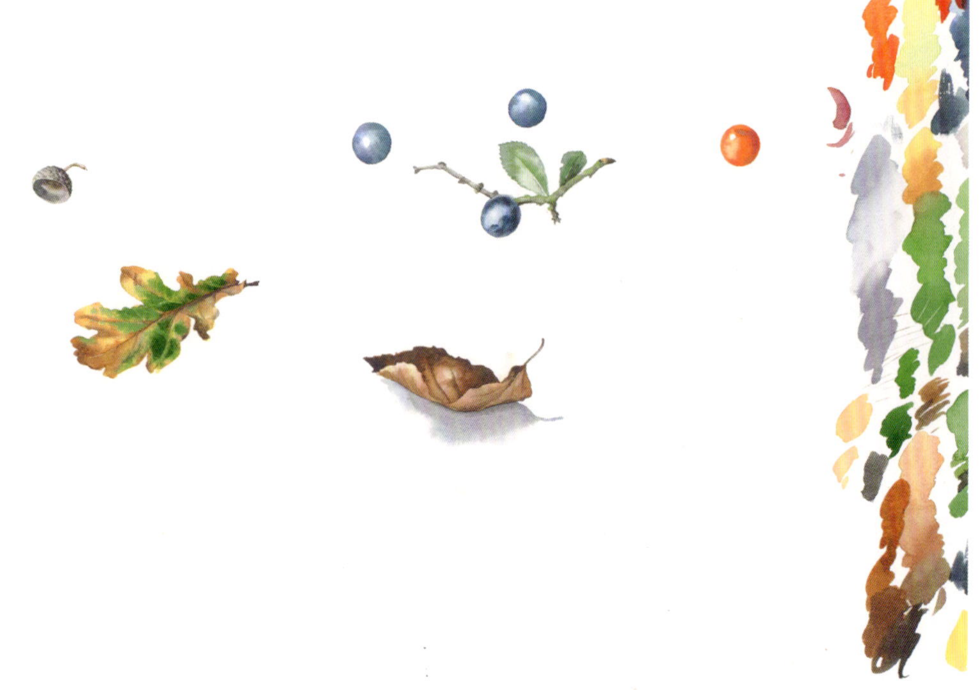

Demonstration sketch, 2006
Watercolour on paper

When not exhibiting her own work, she was a judge with the RHS Picture Committee between 1997 and 2005, and in 2006 participated in the artists' demonstrations as part of the RHS Botanical Illustration seminar day. One of the colour studies featured here was produced during an afternoon of demonstrations and show how she expertly builds layers of pigment.

Having originally studied Textile Design at Winchester School of Art and worked as a freelance designer, Sherlock has recently returned to her early interest in textiles, creating botanically inspired wall hangings in wool and silk felts.

Tibouchina urvilleana (syn: *Tibouchina semidecandra*), *c.*1995
Watercolour on paper

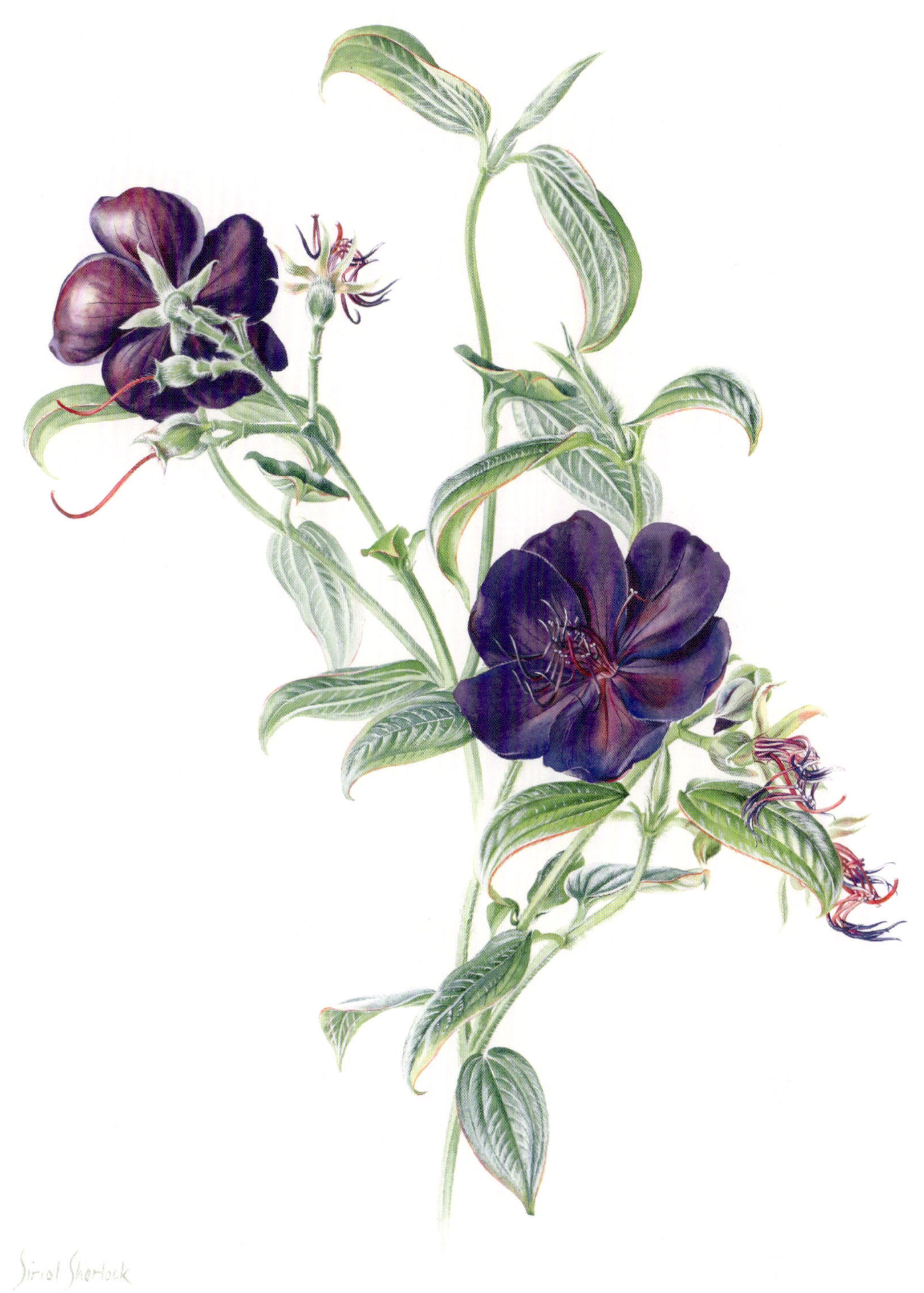

Siriol Sherlock

Tibouchina semidecandria

Hye Woo Shin

RHS medal history

Gold medals: 2013 (and Best Exhibit), 2014 (and Best Exhibit),
2018 (Judges' Special Award), 2022

Hye Woo Shin has exhibited four times with the RHS, in 2013, 2014 and 2018, being awarded a Gold medal on each occasion. Her display of 'Lauraceae in Korea' in 2013 featured her illustration of *Cinnamomum japonicum*, which also won the award for Best Exhibit. In 2018, she gained the Judges' Special Award for her paintings of 'Plants in Dokdo Island'; the compositional complexity of this exhibit was outstanding.

Shin describes herself as a scientific botanical illustrator, although she also undertakes scientific research. She has recently postponed finishing a PhD studying plant DNA, in order to pursue an opportunity as a researcher in the USA, studying the relationship between orchids and fungi.

For the painting featured here, Shin observed specimens in their natural forest habitat of Jeju Island, off the coast of South Korea, where *Cinnamomum japonicum* is found.

Having exhibited extensively in the UK, USA and Korea, Shin has provided the illustrations for a number of scientific publications.

Cinnamomum japonicum, 2012
Watercolour on paper

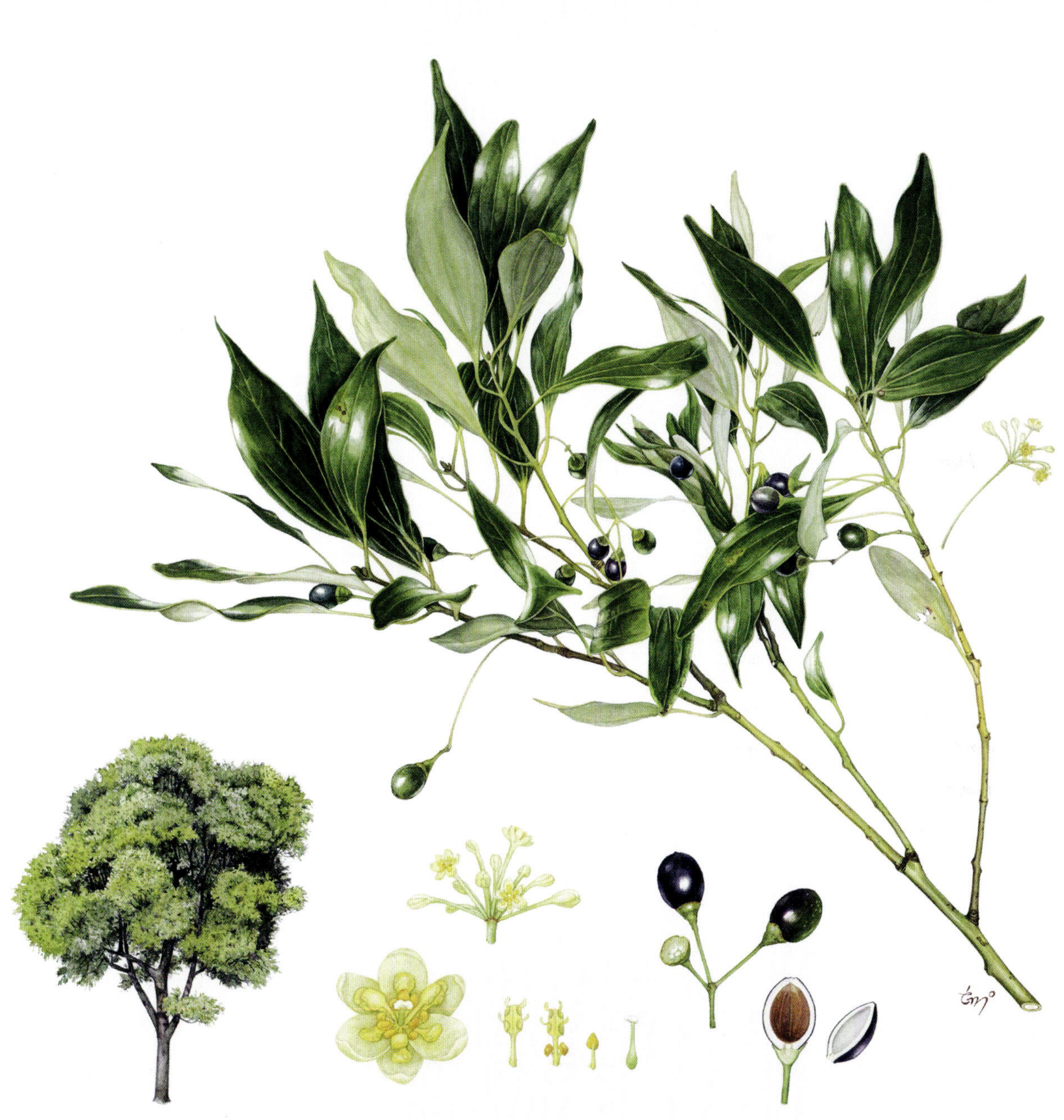

Laura Silburn

RHS medal history

Gold medals: 2013, 2014 (Best Exhibit), 2018 (Best Botanical Art Exhibit)

Laura Silburn had only been painting for three years when she decided on a project to paint for exhibition with the RHS. She chose to focus on 'Hardy Geraniums with an Award of Garden Merit (AGM)' as a means of showcasing some of the best and most varied varieties available in cultivation. Silburn gained a Gold medal for her display in 2013, which was supported by an award from the RHS Dawn Joliffe Botanical Art Bursary.

Silburn set out to capture the botanical attributes of the geranium and to describe its horticultural value. Demonstrating great technical accuracy, Silburn has been able to describe the character of the Geranium as it grows in the garden border, without overcomplicating the composition. One of the greatest challenges Silburn faced when painting *Geranium* 'Patricia' was to match the magenta colour of the petals. She achieved this by trying out numerous combinations of watercolour tests.

With her illustration of *Dryopteris erythrosora,* Silburn won the award for Best Botanical Painting in addition to a Gold medal. Here she again demonstrates her talent for managing colour and texture. The entire series of paintings 'AGM *Dryopteris*: species and cultivars of *Dryopteris* ferns with an Award of Garden Merit', took three years, but the painting itself was completed over the course of six months.

Geranium 'Patricia', 2013

Watercolour on paper

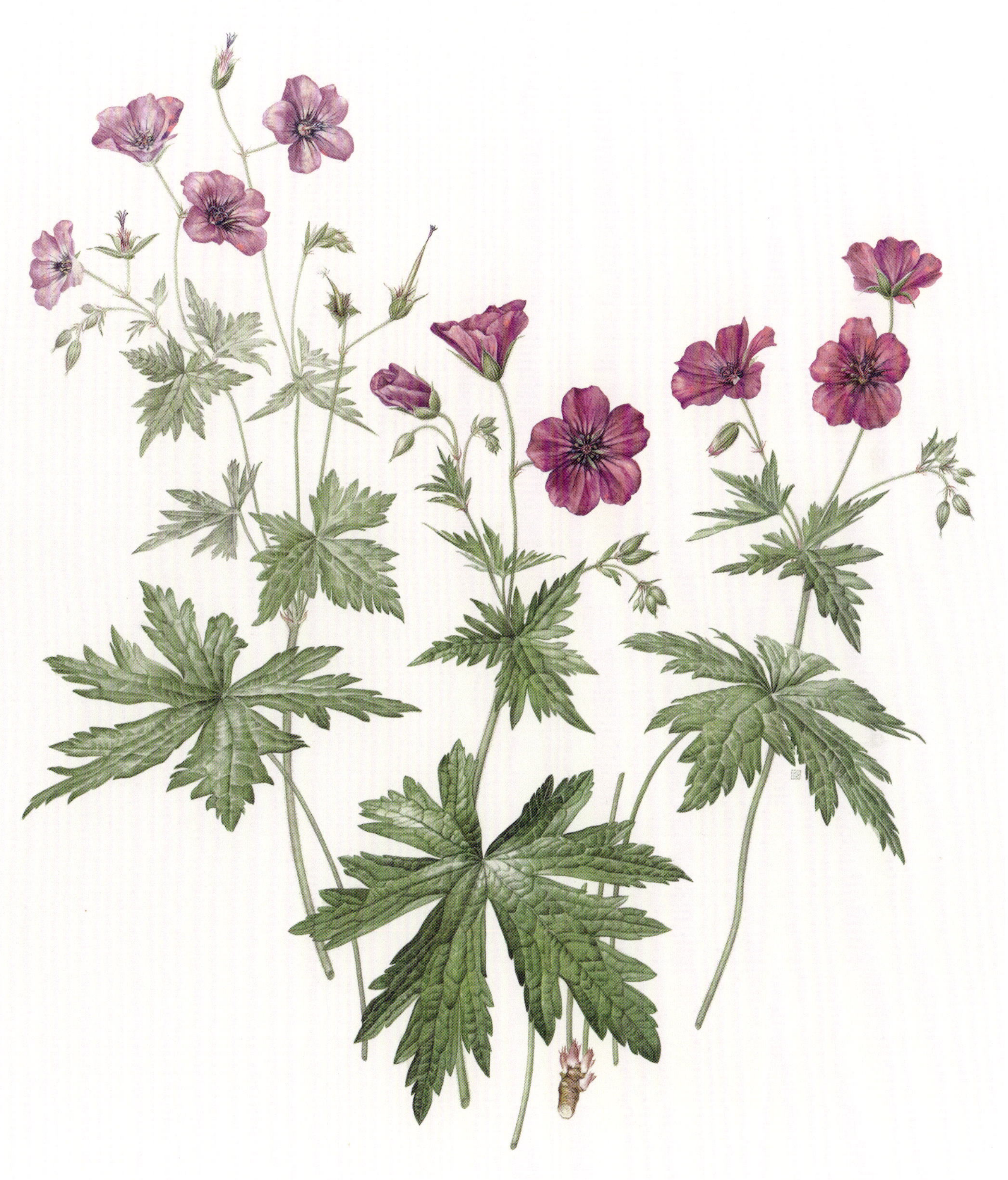

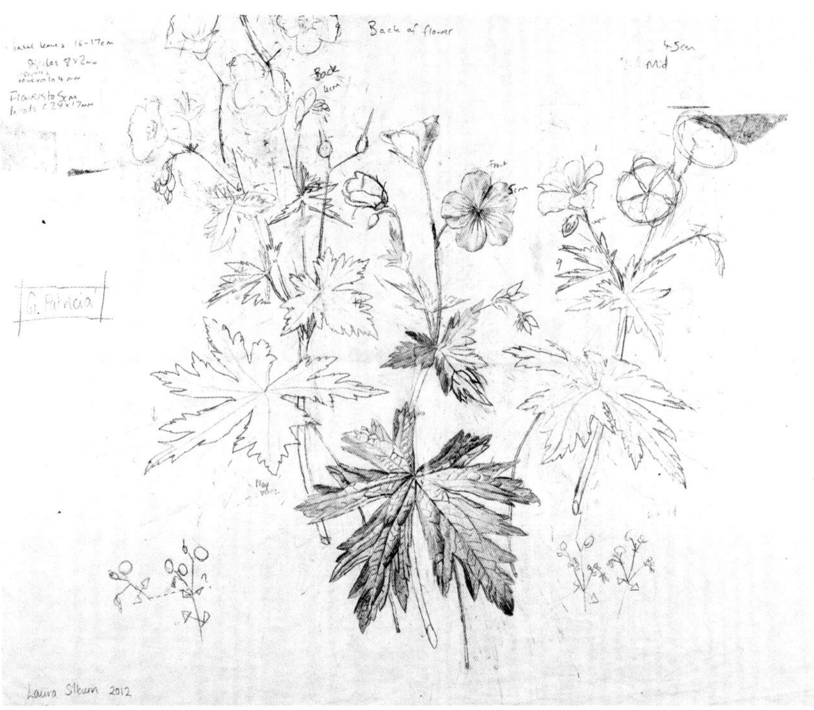

"I researched the plant thoroughly to begin with and visited different gardens that had the plant growing as well as purchasing plants myself. I compared different varieties and looked at how these differed from the typical species plant. I did lots of colour work for this one as it has such a wide variety of leaf colours. I tried to understand which leaves would be coloured and how this changed through the year. This affected the stage I wanted to portray my plant at. The sori colour was tricky with most plants not displaying the red sori it is known for. I was lucky enough to catch one and got the colour work I needed.

I drew, sketched and photographed and then compared my observations to the research I had done. The painting was layered up using drawings on tracing paper, planned carefully in advance to show exactly what I wanted it to. I also planned carefully how it would sit in the exhibit, taking note of the plant next to it: where a frond runs off the edge of a painting, another runs on in the next picture."

Preliminary sketch for *Geranium* 'Patricia'
Graphite on paper

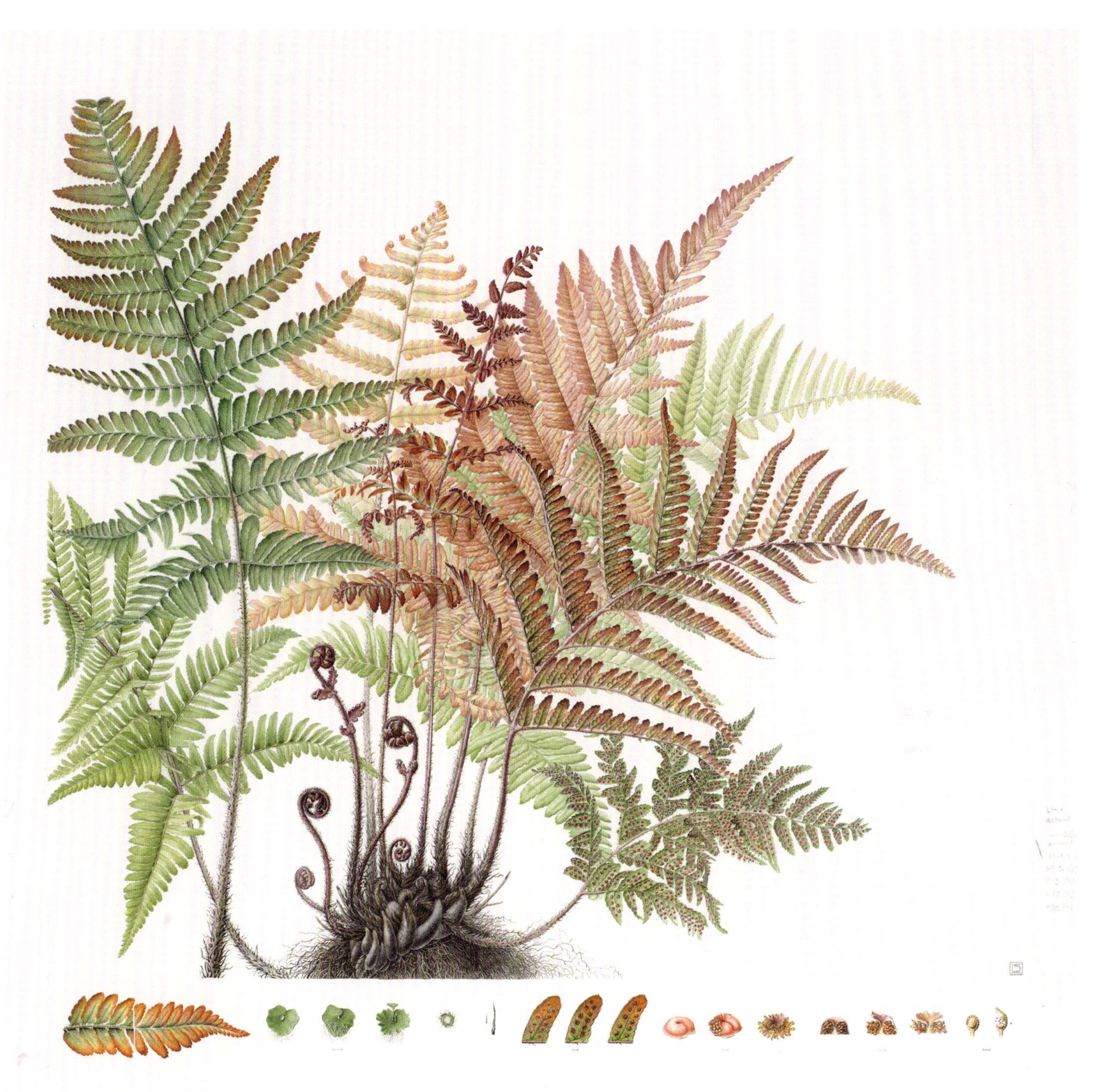

Dryopteris erythrosora (no.6), 2018

Watercolour on paper

Halina Steele

RHS medal history

Gold medal: 2015 (and Best Botanical Art Exhibit)

Silver medal: 2004

Halina Steele has exhibited with the RHS on two occasions; the first was in 2004, when she was awarded a Silver medal. In 2015 she returned to the RHS with a display of six paintings of 'Australian Eucalyptus Mallees' to win a Gold medal, as well as Best Botanical Art Exhibit for her painting of *Eucalyptus recurva,* featured here.

Having taken up ornithological and botanical illustration in 2001 with a focus on rare and endangered species, Steele's work has been extensively exhibited in Australia, the UK and the USA. She has received several awards from the Wildlife and Botanical Artists (Inc), Canberra, Australia.

Eucalyptus recurva is listed as Critically Endangered on the IUCN Red List and with the New South Wales Office of Environment and Heritage. Under the Australian Government Environment Protection and Biodiversity Conservation Act 1999 (EPBC Act) it is listed as Endangered.

Eucalyptus recurva, 2015

Watercolour on paper

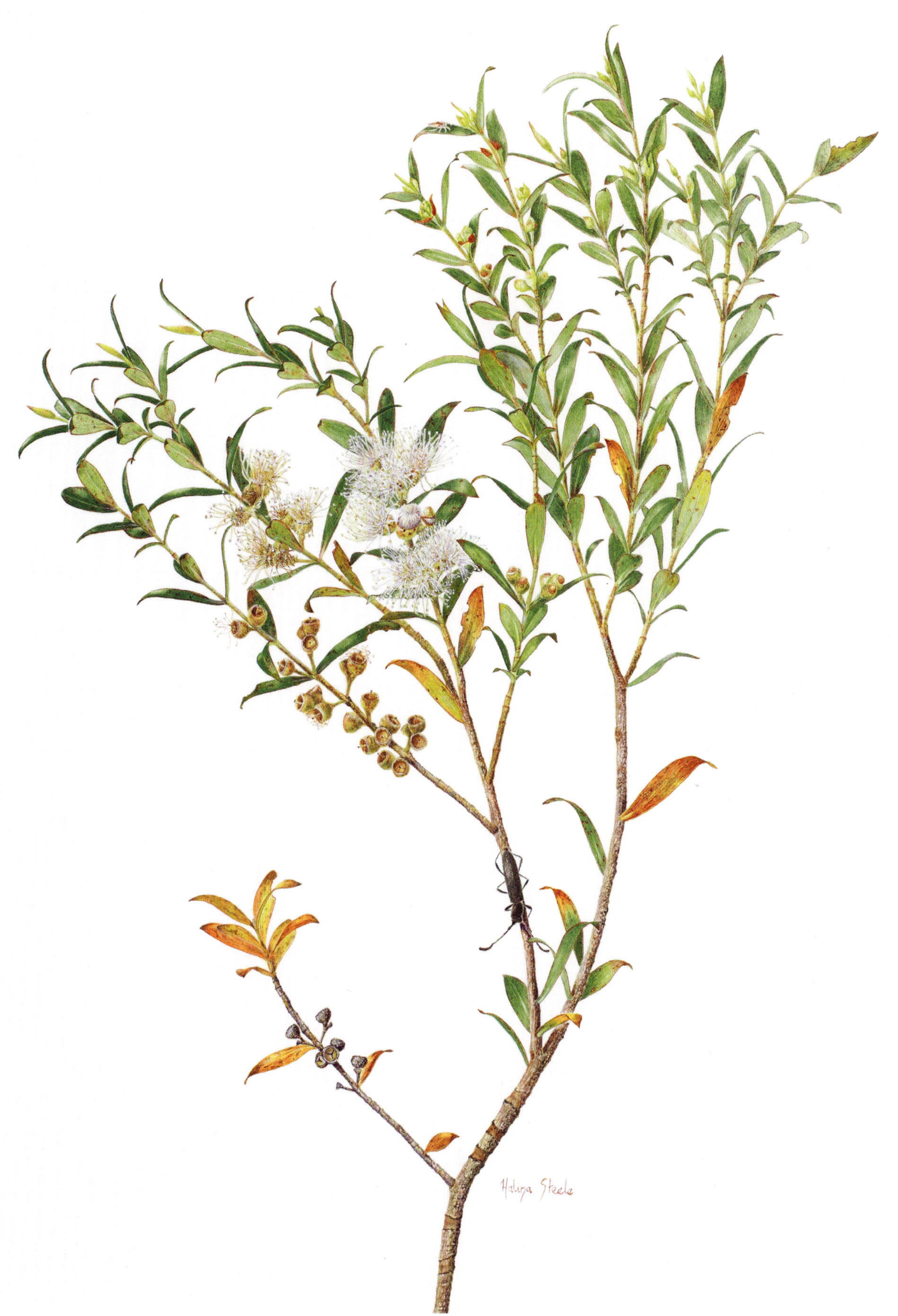

Her passion for conservation led Steele to research her subject meticulously:

"*The Mongarlowe Mallee flowers late December/early January and occurs only on the Southern Tablelands of New South Wales at just four known sites: three near Mongarlowe, which have only a single plant present, and one near Windellama which has two individuals.*

Survival of the species in the wild currently appears dependent on the survival of the existing adults, most of which appear to be already of a great age. It occurs in habitat that has remained largely unaltered since European settlement, with decline possibly being caused by changes in the environment that are unfavourable to this species. The very small number of individuals and their distribution as isolated individuals at few locations makes E. recurva *highly susceptible to stochastic events such as wildfire, damage associated with human access, disease, extreme weather events or severe drought. The extremely narrow genetic base of the existing population also suggests that the species may have limited capacity to adapt to future changes in the environment. The species is therefore projected to undergo a future decline and is facing an extremely high risk of extinction in New South Wales in the immediate future.*

The small Longicorn Beetle (Family CERAMBYCIDAE*) was found on the plant in situ. Most species of* Cerambycidae *are beneficial, playing important roles in woody ecosystems. They act as primary agents for the physical process of breaking down wood tissues and creating access routes through their burrows for saproxylic fungi and other invertebrates involved in the decomposition process. It is thought that flower-visiting Australian* Cerambycidae *may also act as pollinators of some native trees or bushes.*

The painting was undertaken with the assistance of Robert Gourlay, RFD, BAppSc, MAppSc, who very kindly guided me to one of the remaining existing plants; and Wayne West (a former co-worker) who tracked down the plant's location and initiated contact with Robert Gourlay."

Fiona Strickland

RHS medal history

Gold medal: 2008

Fiona Strickland's mantra is 'look, look and then look again'. She believes it is only with very close observation and dedication that an artist can really translate the essence of a plant into a painted work. Finding an unusual angle by which to approach a plant encourages us to look at it differently, but also makes for a technically challenging piece of art.

Strickland won a Gold medal for her series of paintings entitled 'Watercolour decay - an Autumn palette' in 2008; the cost of mounting the exhibition was supported by the RHS Dawn Joliffe Botanical Art Bursary. The painting featured here was part of a set of studies she prepared of *Helianthus* that were growing in her garden in Falkirk, Scotland. A number of these were exhibited with the RHS in 2008, but this picture was not displayed until the following year, at the Society of Botanical Artists' London exhibition.

Strickland studied for her Diploma in Drawing and Painting at Edinburgh College of Art, where she received a travelling scholarship to Italy and France before embarking on a year of Post Graduate study in Edinburgh. She then painted abstract studies while pursuing a teaching career. Strickland has taught observational drawing for 26 years. An interest in botanical subjects began in 1999 with a large drawing of a *Dracaena,* which encouraged Strickland to develop a series of tonal drawings of roots.

'August Sunflower' – *Helianthus*, 2008

Watercolour and gouache on paper

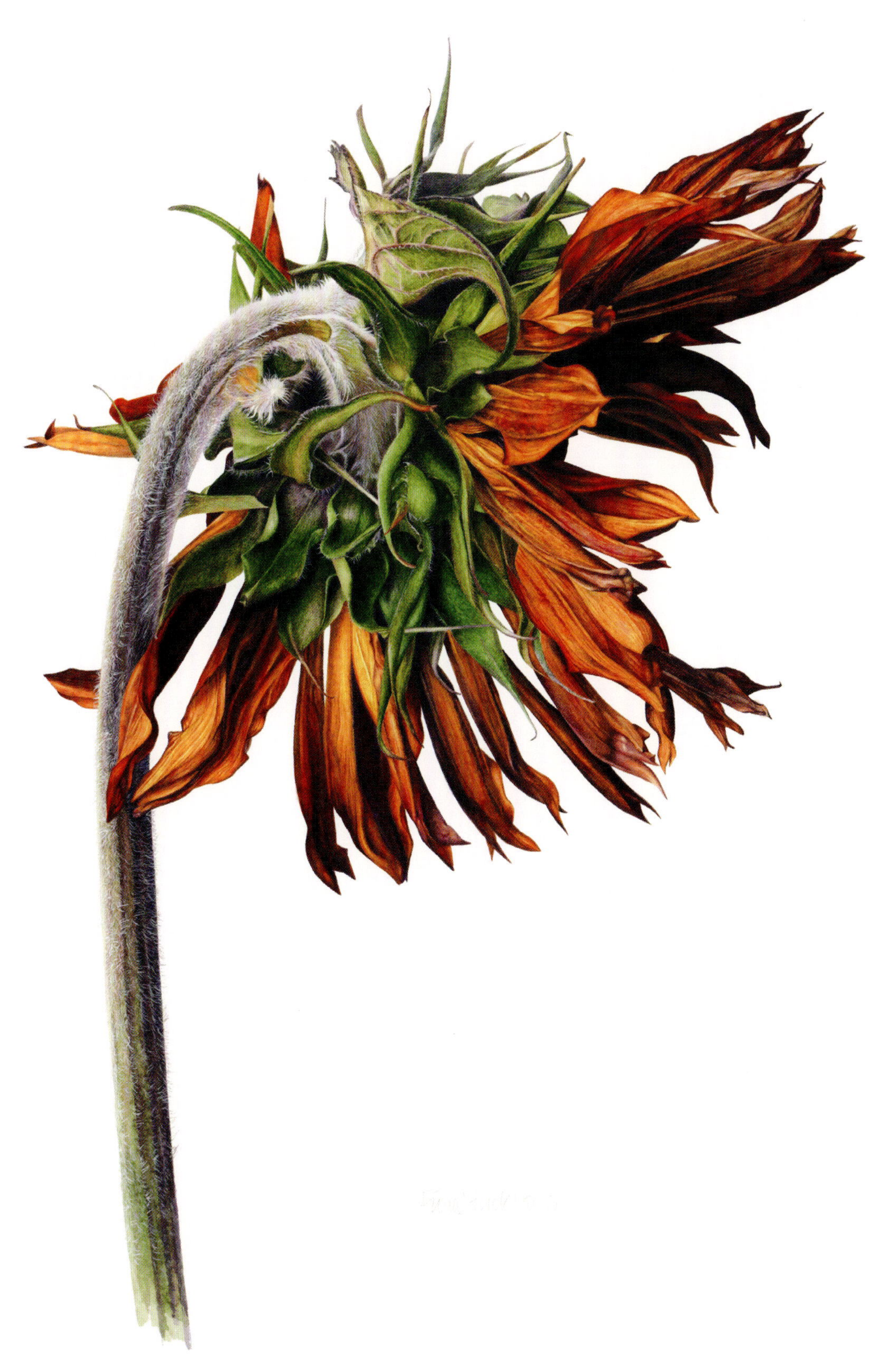

She says she was inspired by an exhibition of Rory McEwen's work and by the flower studies of her tutor, Elizabeth Blackadder. Strickland's approach reflects her interest in the way people 'see' things without really observing them. She begins by aiming to 'discover' an aspect of a plant by surprise, as if seeing it for the first time, from an unusual angle or state of decay. She also likes to enlarge her specimens: a technical challenge that she relishes, the consequence of which is to elevate their significance, encouraging the viewer to look again. Her formal training and love of Dutch still life painters influences a tendency to create a strong three-dimensional form through light and shadow.

The observation and recording of a plant begins with the drawing of the object straight on to the finished surface without preparatory sketches or studies. Strickland currently uses Fabriano Artistico Hot Pressed Smooth 640gsm. watercolour paper in natural white. This paper contains no optical brighteners or chlorine; it is acid free and pH neutral and therefore is highly 'work' and eraser resistant. The internal and surface sizing makes for perfect colour take up.

"I begin by making light marks on the paper, building up the detailed observational analysis required for painting. As I paint, concentration and focus are paramount, and I continually scrutinise the object and the painting, relating one to the other, while observing the play of light on the object and the ways in which it may enhance the form."

Strickland has exhibited at many public and private galleries, including the Royal Scottish Academy, the Royal Scottish Society of Painters in Watercolour, the Royal Glasgow Institute of Fine Arts and the Society of Scottish Artists.

Ann Swan

RHS medal history

Gold medals: 1991, 1993, 1997

Joint Gold medal with Gillian Barlow and Pauline Dean: March 1999

Silver-Gilt medal: 1990

Ann Swan first exhibited with the RHS in 1990, when she was awarded a Silver-Gilt medal. Further exhibitions staged between 1991 and 1999 saw her win four Gold medals. With her most recent display in March 1999, Swan collaborated with Pauline Dean and Gillian Barlow to produce a display of illustrations of *Lycaste* orchids, at the invitation of Dr Oakeley on behalf of the RHS Orchid Committee. Swan served as a judge on the RHS Picture Committee 2009–2013.

Although Swan was awarded her RHS medals for drawings in graphite, she is an early exponent of the use of coloured pencil for botanical illustration. She is well known for her highly detailed drawings and ability to achieve subtle variations in colour. Since she began exhibiting with the RHS in 1990, Swan has also displayed her work at the Hunt Institute, RBG Kew and the Society of Botanical Artists. She published *Botanical Portraits with Coloured Pencils* in 2010, detailing methods for using water-soluble and oil-based pencils.

'Prickly Pear', 2007

Coloured pencil on paper

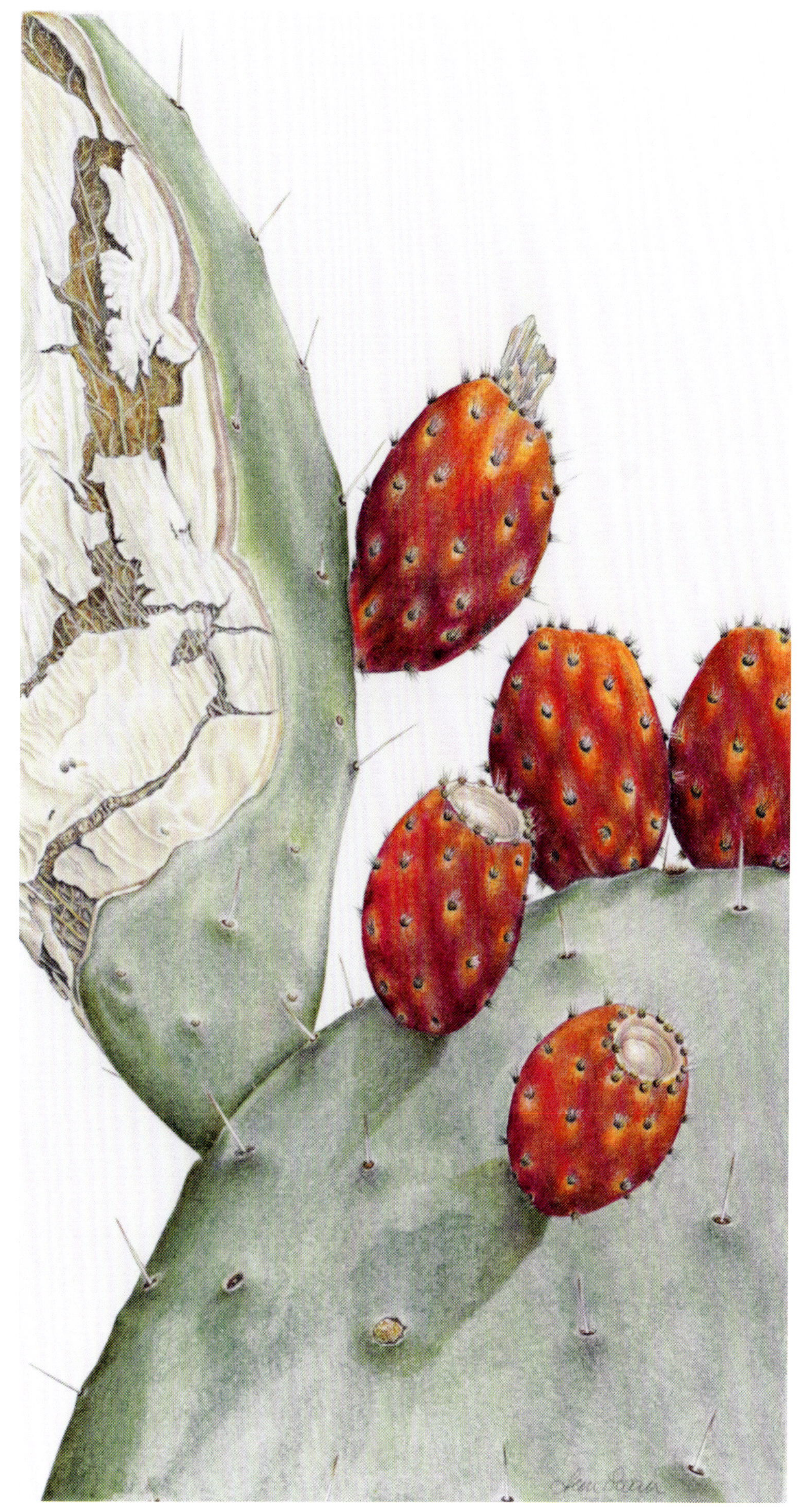

Swan records the process of capturing the 'Parasol Trio' as follows:

"*This drawing was completed in 2005 whilst I was living in Teddington opposite to Bushy Park. I had already drawn some smaller parasols and a couple of Fly Agaric pictures when I came across these very large parasols early one morning whilst walking the dog in the park.*

I chose to draw them depicting three growth stages, as the cap doesn't fully open until the stem has reached nearly full height, and I decided to use graphite pencil over a base of conté pastel and coloured pencil for the stems and cap. This is a favourite technique of mine, which involves laying down a minimal amount of colour using a mix of dry media which I then dissolve using an alcohol based solvent. This melts the colour and takes it immediately into the paper without altering the surface of the paper so when dry (after a few minutes) I am then able to depict all the markings, gills and shading using graphite pencils. So I achieve all the joy of drawing with graphite, plus that tint of colour.

Macrolepiota procera (Parasol mushroom), 2005

Coloured pencil on paper

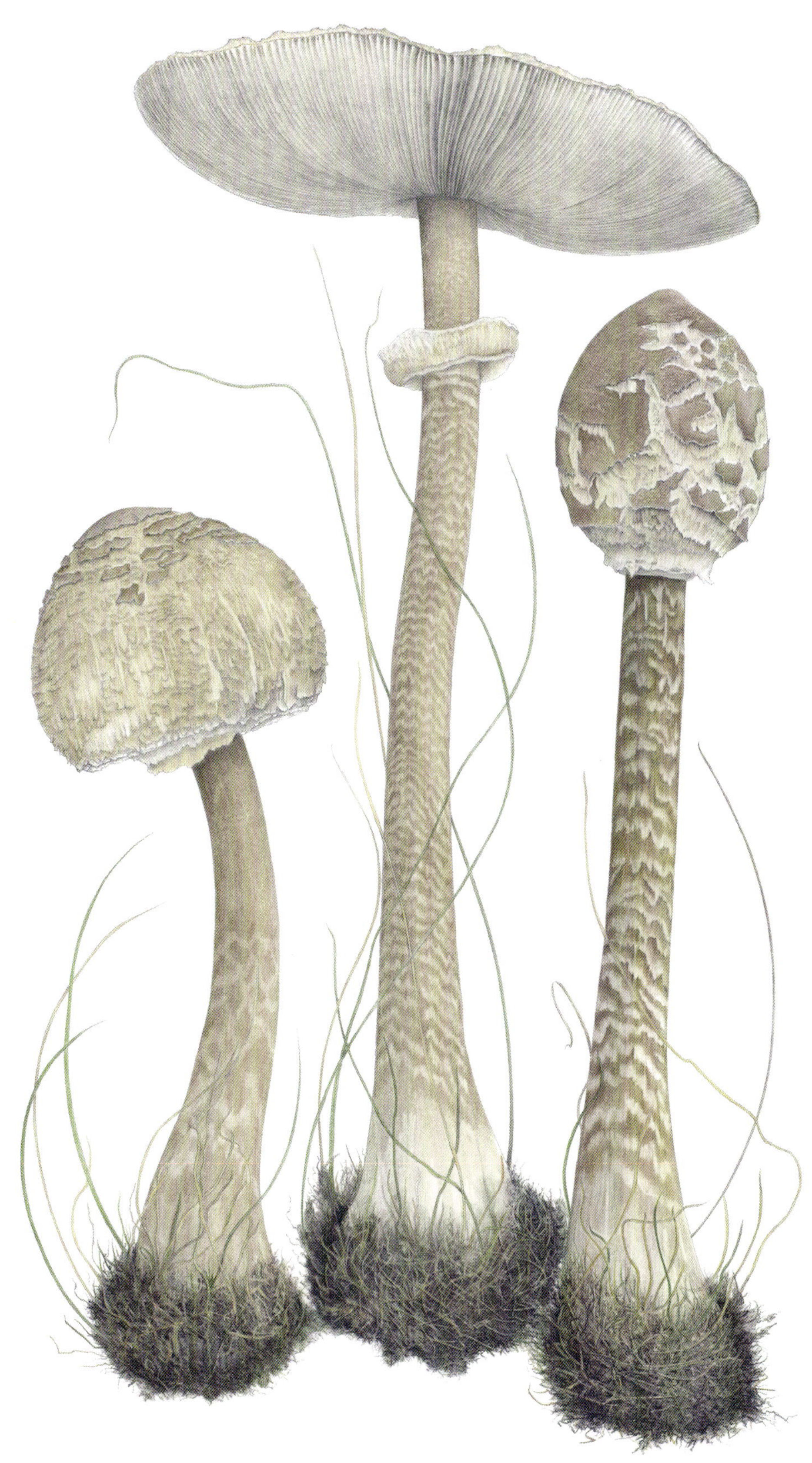

The base of the mushrooms, however, needed some different treatment as I could see so much going on; there was soil, grass and grass roots and other bits and pieces. For this I used a variety of techniques – embossing, wax resist and lighter colours – and then I worked into and over these marks using a selection of much darker colours and more graphite until I felt I had achieved a moderate likeness. I am not a botanist, but my brother, a retired doctor of fungal genetics, on seeing this drawing remarked that I had captured the microscopic tubules of the mycelium well, which I considered praise indeed!"

Zea mays, 2009

Coloured pencil on paper

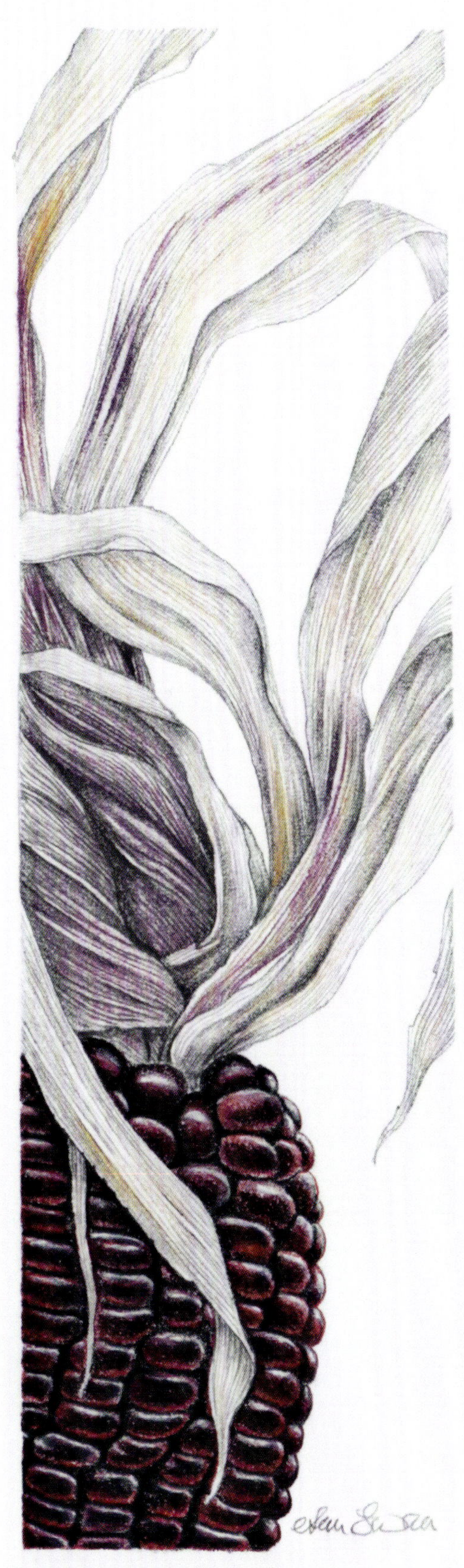

Kumiko Takano

RHS medal history

Gold medals: 2015 (and Best Exhibit), 2019

Kumiko Takano won a Gold medal as well as Best Exhibit with her first show at the RHS in February 2015, for her paintings of 'Climbing plants'.

This picture of *Stauntonia hexaphylla* was amongst those on display and demonstrates Takano's exceptional brushwork skills. The bold composition lends itself perfectly to this vigorous vine.

Painting over a period of approximately two months, Takano began work in the spring of 2014, drawing the flowers of the *Stauntonia* as they emerged. She then returned to the piece six months later, the following autumn, to finalise the composition. At this point she could include the ripened fruit and extended branches with dark green foliage, in contrast to the far brighter green of the young leaves. She was fascinated to observe the process of growth as the climbing plant developed throughout this period.

Living in the countryside in Japan, Takano has access to many different kinds of plants, including roses, fruit trees and vegetables. Much of her inspiration comes from her own garden. Takano took up botanical painting following her retirement; she enjoys classes with Masako Sasaki.

Stauntonia hexaphylla, 2014

Watercolour on paper

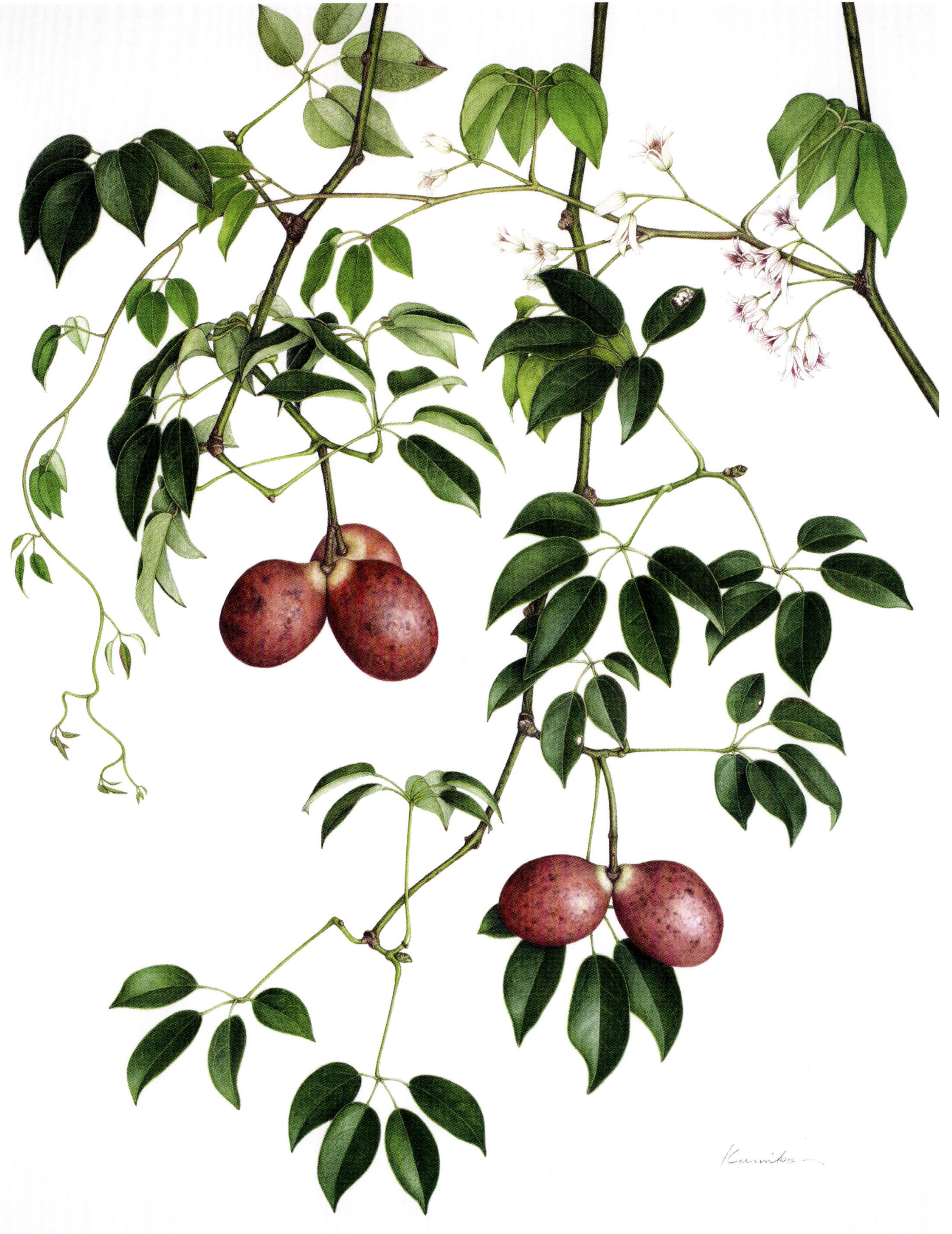

Julia Trickey

RHS medal history

Gold medals: 2006, 2008, 2012, 2013

Silver-Gilt medals: 2001, 2004, 2009, 2014

Julia Trickey started painting botanical subjects in 1998 and three years later produced her first award-winning display at the RHS. Since then, Trickey has exhibited regularly at RHS shows and to date has won a total of four Gold medals. More recently, she has also undertaken demonstrations of her 'wet on wet' watercolour technique for visitors to the RHS botanical art shows. Trickey teaches all over the world, ranging from master classes at the American Society of Botanical Artists' annual international exhibition to online tutorials.

A versatile artist with an interest in textures, Trickey has often favoured decaying subjects that reveal something of the form and structure of the plant. The pictures shown here are from two of her Gold medal-winning displays: 'Leaves – celebrating imperfection' in 2008 and 'Larger than life – fading flowers observed' in 2012.

'Fading anemones' – *Anemone coronaria,* 2011

Watercolour on paper

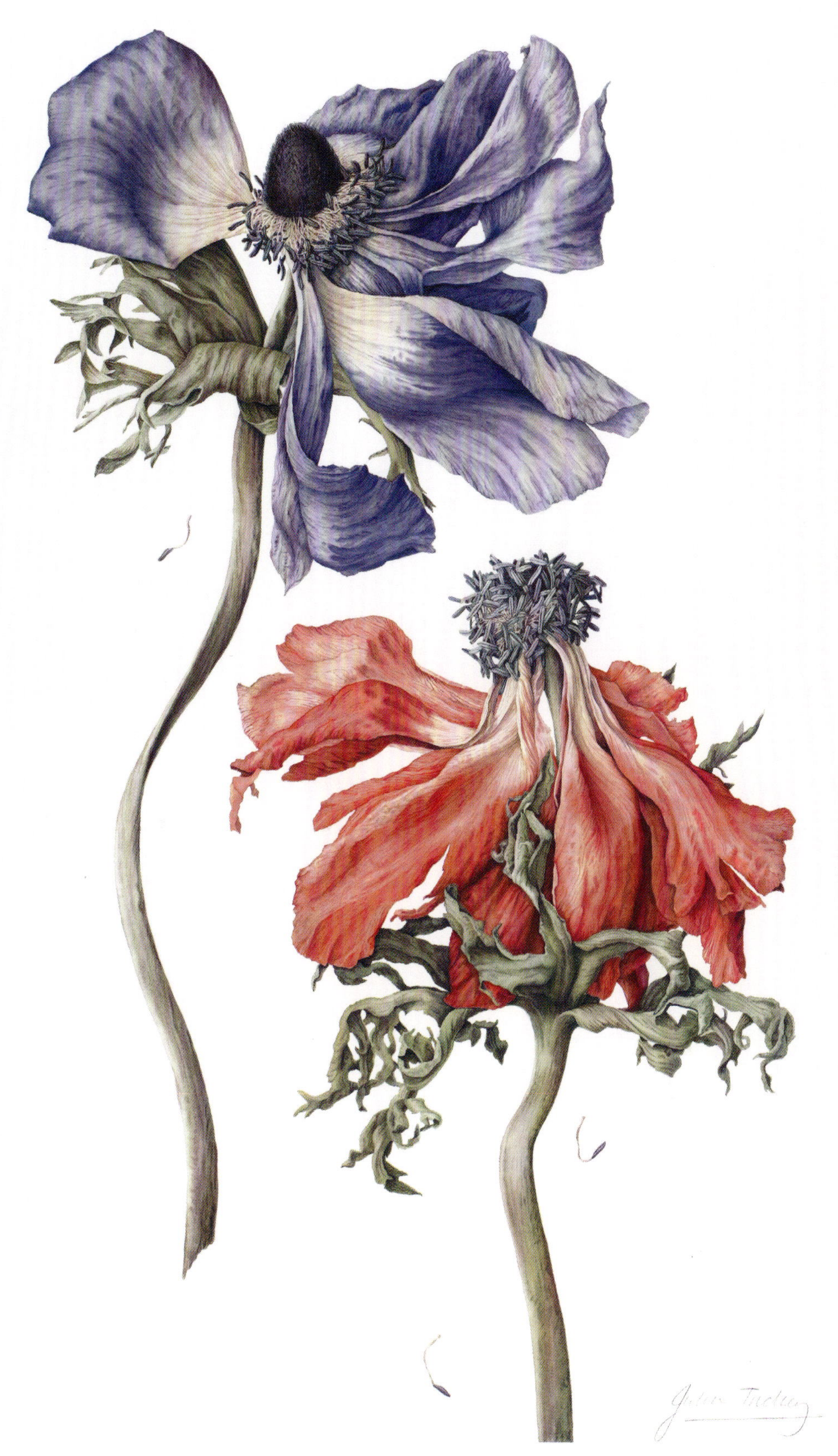

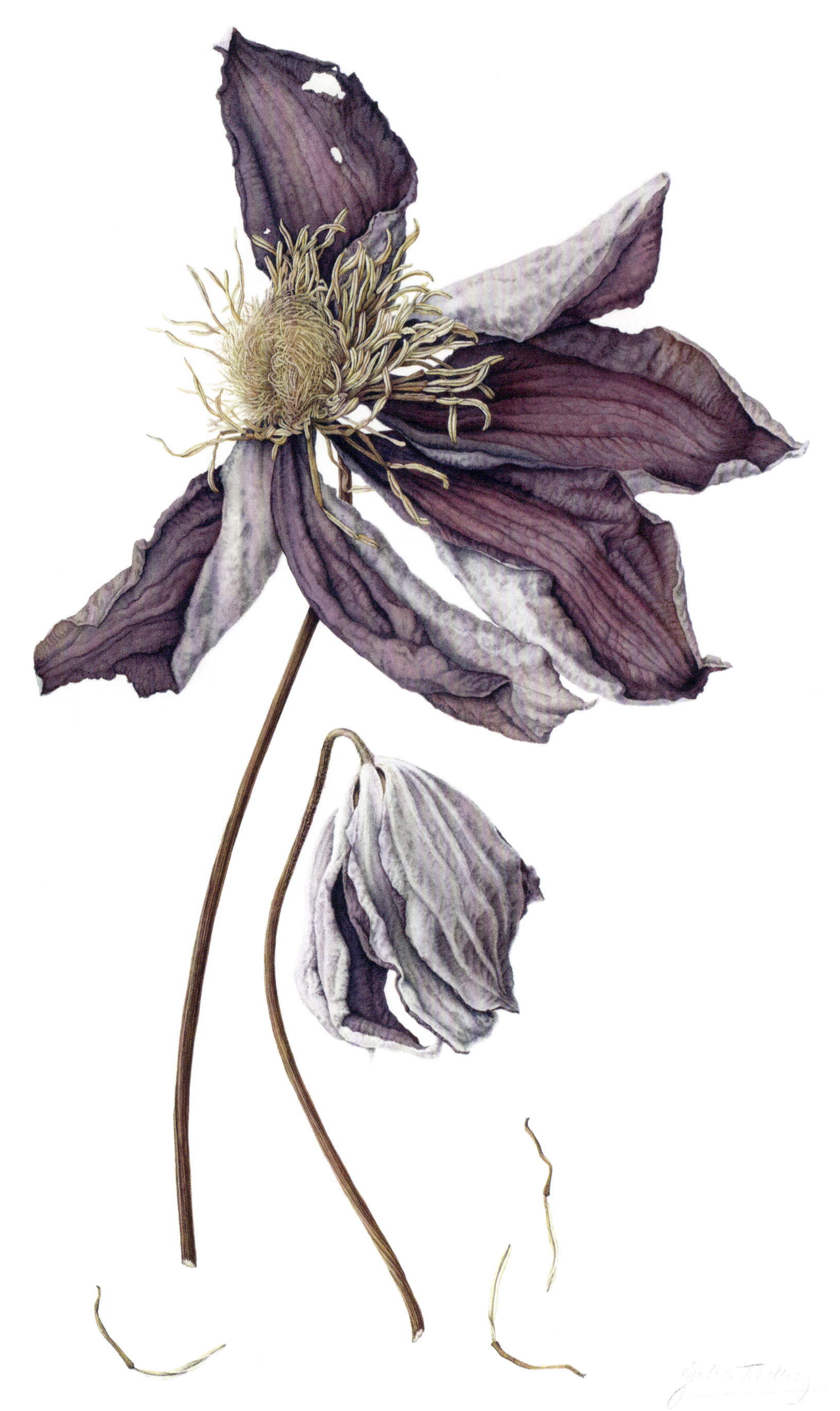

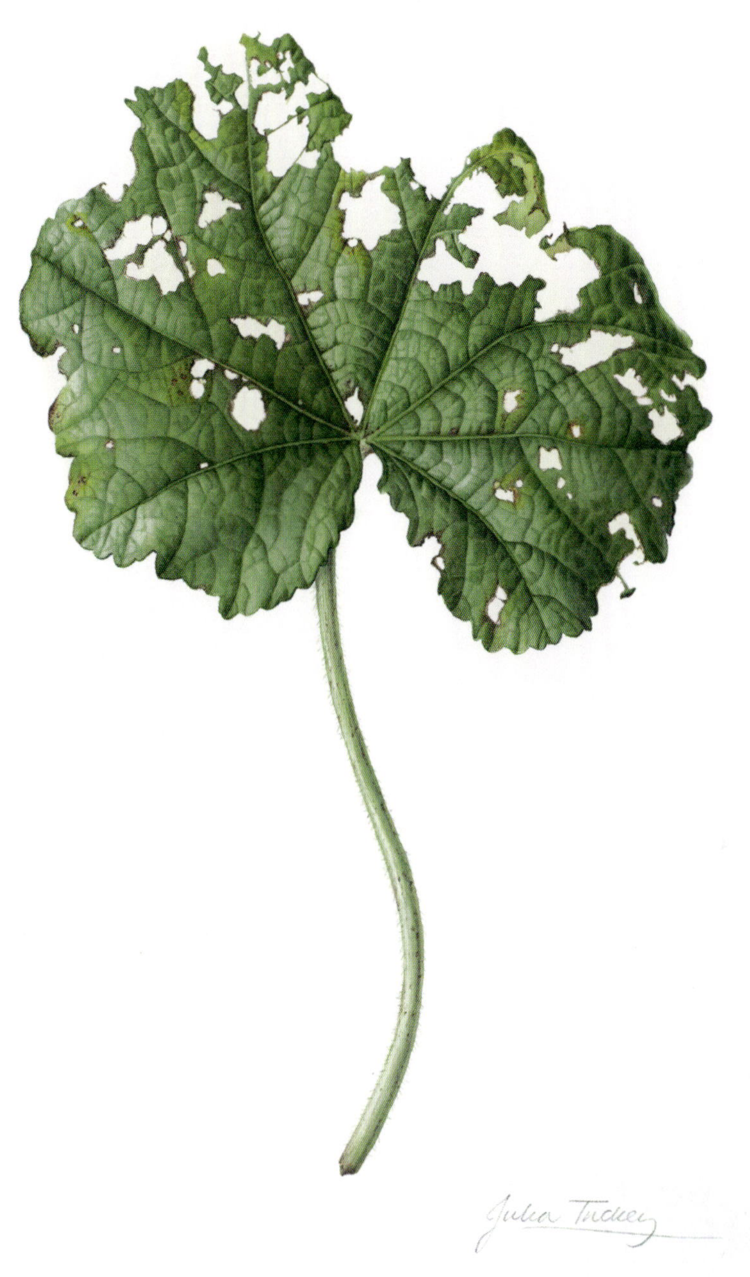

Alcea rosea, 2008
Watercolour on paper

'Dried Clematis' – *Clematis* 'Warszawska Nike', 2011
Watercolour on paper

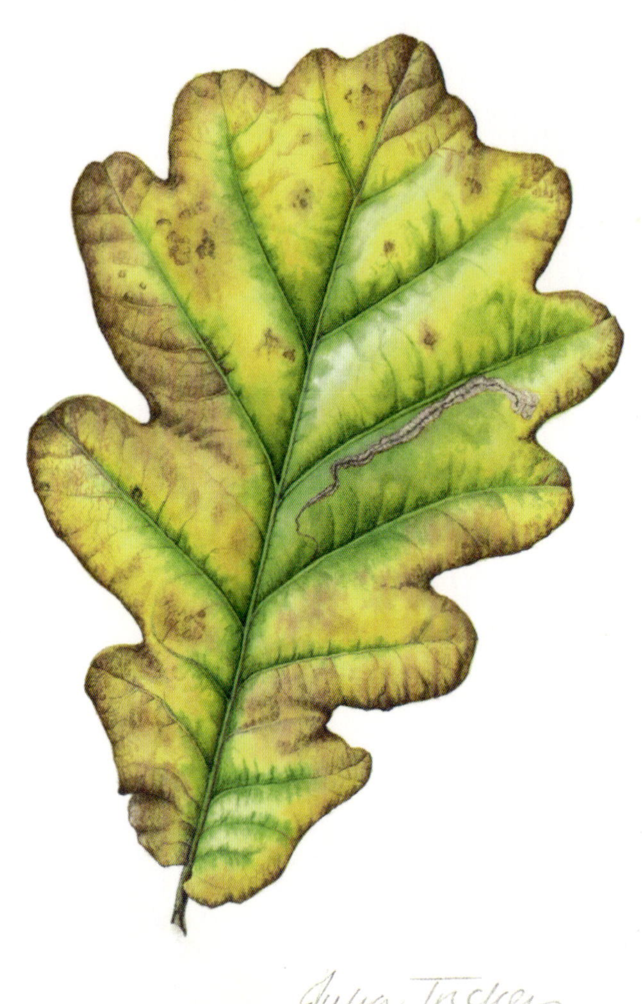

Quercus robur, 2007

Watercolour on paper

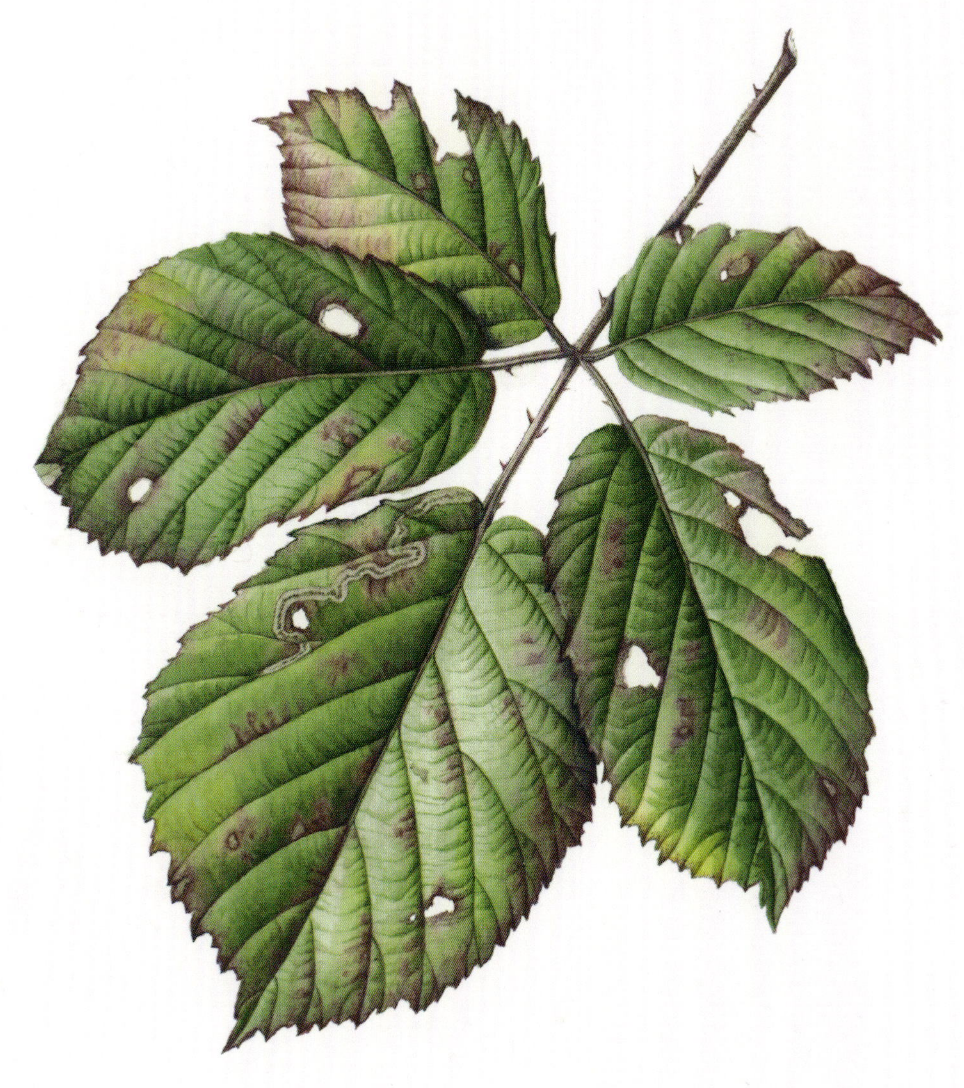

Rubus fruticosus, 2007

Watercolour on paper

Pauleen Trim

RHS medal history

Gold medal: 2021 (and Best Botanical Artwork)

Silver medal: 2018 (SWSBA group exhibit)

Pauleen Trim taught art and design at Bournemouth College for more than 25 years. After retiring she returned to being a student herself when she undertook classes in botanical painting. Her work has been exhibited in the UK, Madrid and Germany. Trim has gained numerous awards for her botanical illustration, notably with the South West Society of Botanical Artists (SWSBA) and the Society of Botanical Artists. She regularly exhibits her work, and has resumed teaching, now with a focus on botanical painting.

Trim's exhibit for the RHS in 2021 was on the theme of 'Native deciduous trees featuring galls', for which she gained a Gold medal and award for Best Botanical Artwork. Working from life, the series took three years to research and complete. All her specimens were observed growing in a Dorset lane, near her home.

"I knew I wanted to research trees for my RHS exhibit, highlighting their importance, beauty and emphasising the need for more trees. While tree watching I discovered many strange abnormalities growing on my subjects and became intrigued with tree galls. To so many people these galls go unseen and unknown, so I wanted to give them an educating place in my painting compositions."

Fraxinus excelsior (Ash tree), April 2020

Watercolour on paper

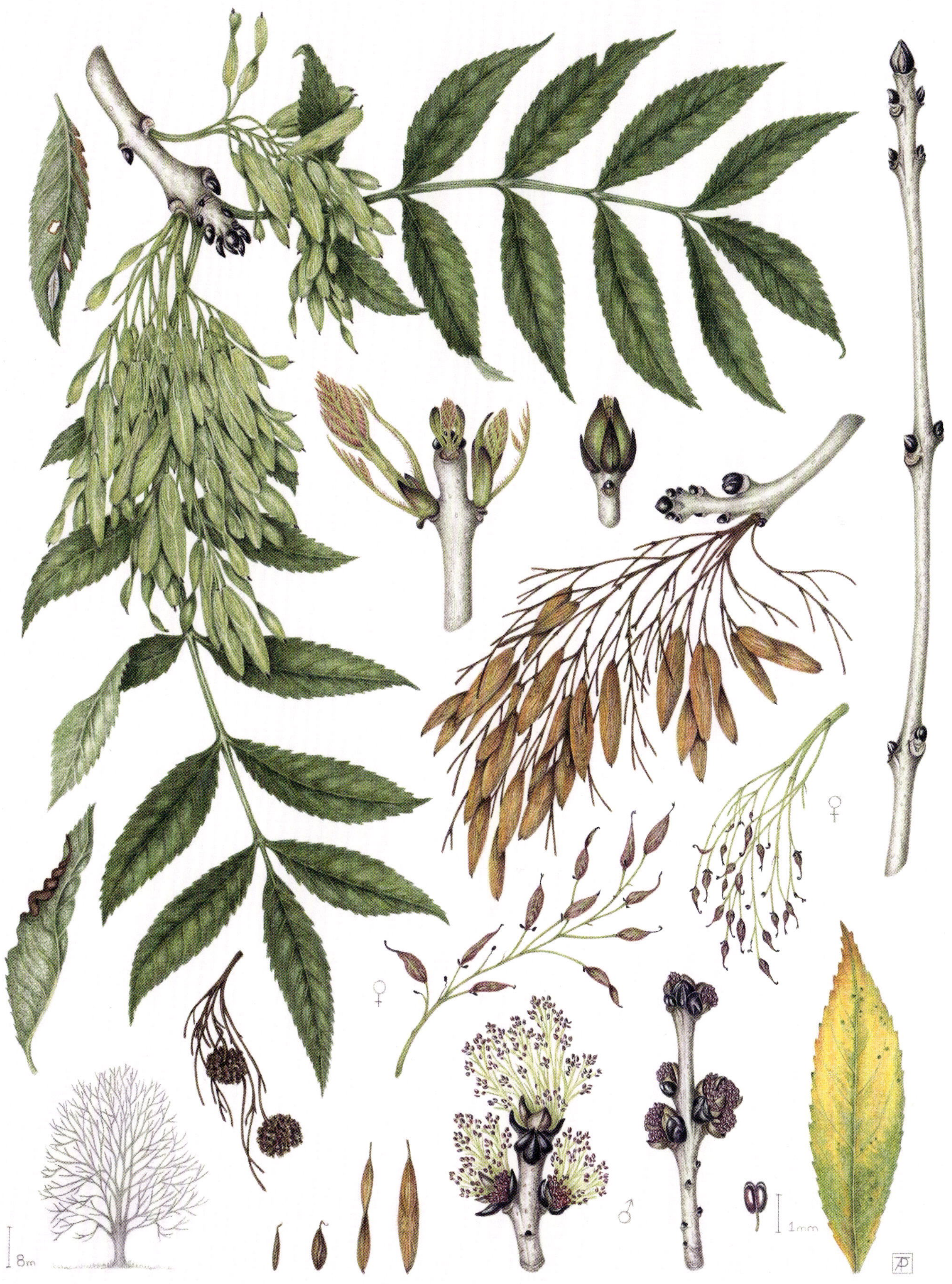
♀
♀
♂
1mm
8m
AP

Lynne Uptin

RHS medal history

Gold medal: 2024 (and Best Botanical Art Exhibit)

Lynne Uptin developed an interest in botanical art as a student at the National Art School, Sydney, Australia. She practised as a leading illustrator before founding two art galleries, a ceramic and a glass art studio. Uptin moved to Tasmania in 1984 and taught at the Tasmanian School of Art before taking a position at Arts Tasmania where she became its director, for almost 20 years. She received the Order of Australia medal in 2010 for services to arts administration.

Uptin was awarded an RHS Gold medal and Best Botanical Art Exhibit for her series of watercolours of The Genus Richea: A relic of Gondwana', presented in 2024. The artworks had been in development since 2020.

"Tasmania has become a refuge for many genera that once thrived on the supercontinent of Gondwana. The genus is endemic to Australia and all but two of its species are found only in Tasmania, being the last region of the major continental plates to split from Antarctica. My research has taken me into the cool temperate rainforests of Tasmania's World Heritage areas where the varied species grow in extreme conditions. My studio overlooks the anchorages of the first French explorers and botanists visiting Tasmania in the late 18th century, which was when the recording of Australian plants began."

Richea alpina (short candleheath), 2023

Watercolour on paper

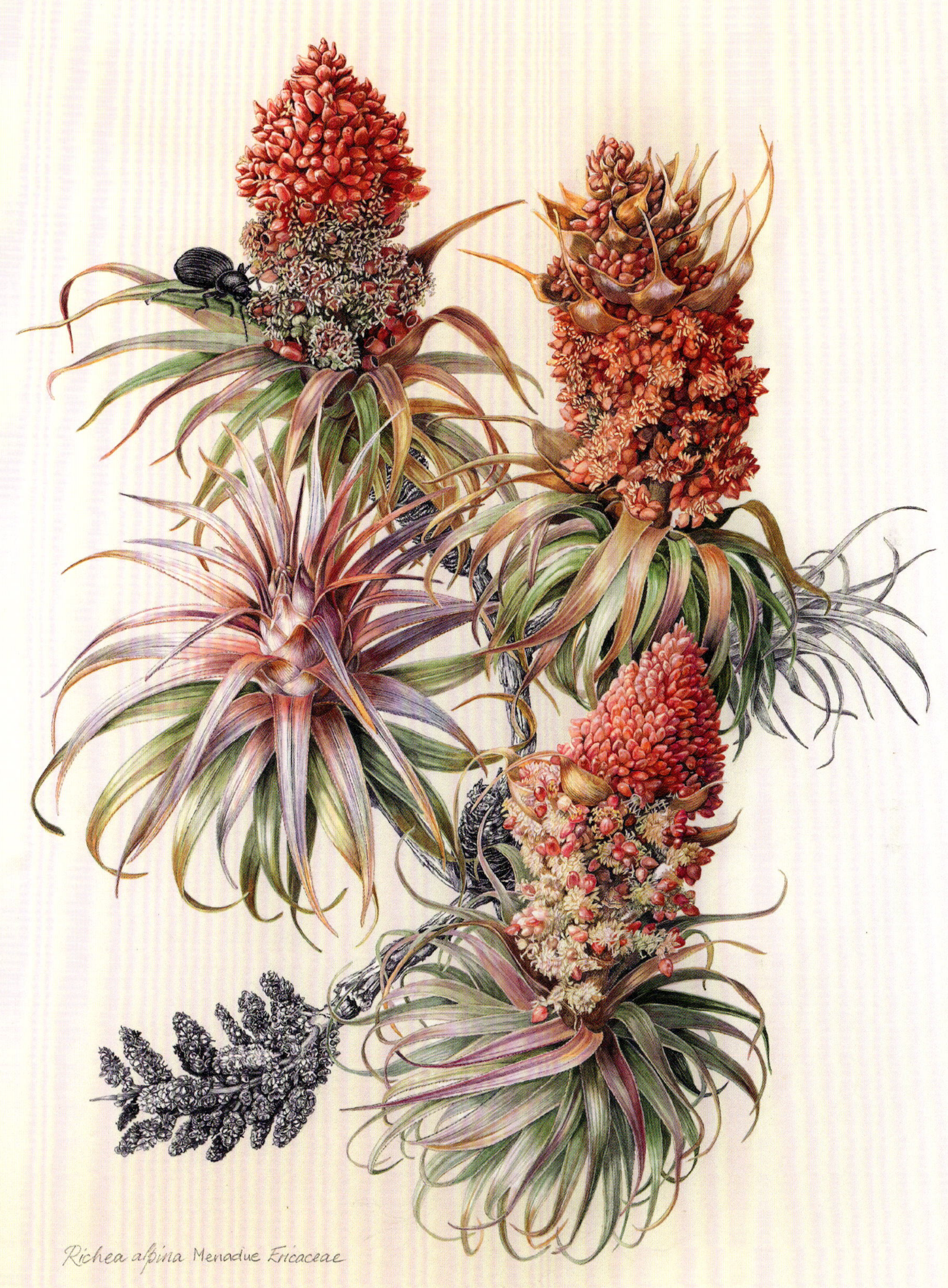
Richea alpina Menadue Ericaceae

Margaret de Villiers

RHS medal history

Gold medals: 2013 (and Best Botanical Painting), 2016

Margaret de Villiers has exhibited twice with the RHS; on both occasions she showed paintings of *Ericas* and was awarded a Gold medal. Her display in 2013 received additional acclaim, with the painting featured here of *Erica bodkinii* judged to be the best painting in Show.

Specimens for this painting of the rare *Erica bodkinii* were a challenge to collect, as they grow high up on the Cape mountains, on old farmland owned by *Erica* expert, Thys de Villiers. These winter-flowering plants are found on very cool, moist slopes, often in inaccessible rocky or marshy areas. When fresh, the flowers have a delicate scent and are white in colour, but this gradually changes from a pale to a deep red and brownish colour, the sepals being the first part to change.

De Villiers first painted *Ericas* in 2009 and explained that this is a difficult and time-consuming genus to paint, as most of the flowers are small and the tiny leaves all have their own set patterns of "climbing" up the stem to the clusters of flowers. Most of her *Erica* paintings take at least a month to complete, so the specimens are kept "fresh" in water, covered in plastic in a designated fridge.

She has been able to make an extensive study of the genus and has completed about 45 paintings of *Ericas* to date.

Erica bodkinii, 2011

Watercolour on paper

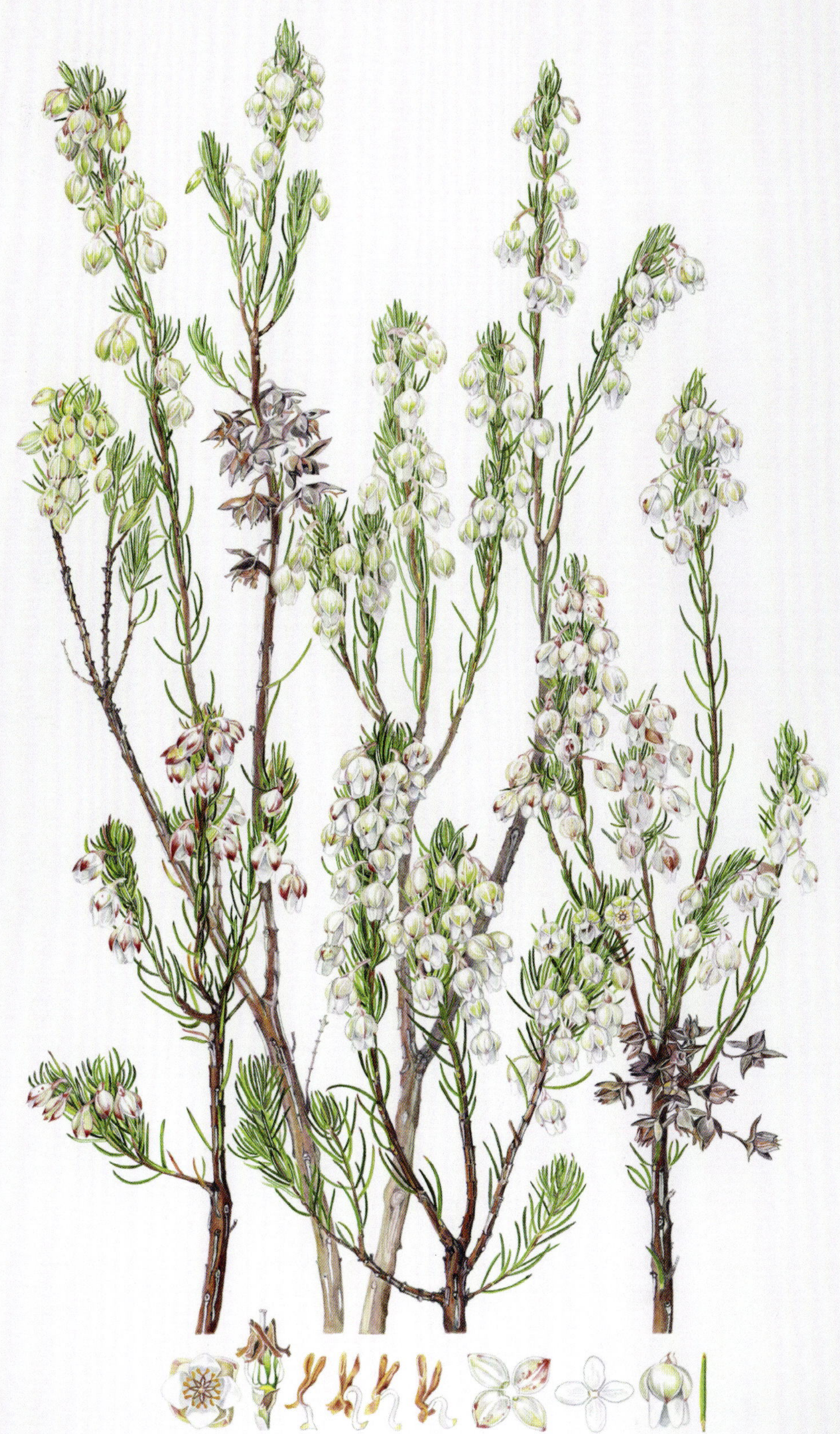
Erica bodkinii
M de Villiers 2011

Noriko Watanabe

RHS medal history

Gold medal: 2006

Silver-Gilt medal: 2013

Noriko Watanabe exhibited a series of paintings of *Hydrangea quercifolia* with the RHS in November 2006, for which she was awarded a Gold medal. The series was produced to demonstrate seasonal change, as this species is renowned for its beautiful flower heads and the striking form it takes as it dries. Although Watanabe had started painting this series in 2005, the two pictures featured here were only just finished prior to the Show, in the following September.

On the recommendation of the Picture Committee, '*Hydrangea quercifolia*, no.7' was purchased for the Lindley Collections. A little while later, Watanabe kindly donated '*Hydrangea quercifolia* no. 8' as a companion piece. The complex arrangement of florets that form the flower panicle of the hydrangea are beautifully modelled, to demonstrate its fragile delicacy. The use of such a limited colour palette means the artist has to achieve the form and shape using a range of tonal shades.

Watanabe originally undertook a B.A. degree in dyework-craft at Osaka University of Arts in Japan, which led her to become a kimono pattern designer. During a period living in Canada, she took botanical art classes with Celia Godkin and Pamela Stagg; on her return to Japan, Watanabe continued her studies with Masako Sasaki.

Hydrangea quercifolia, no.8, 2006

Watercolour on paper

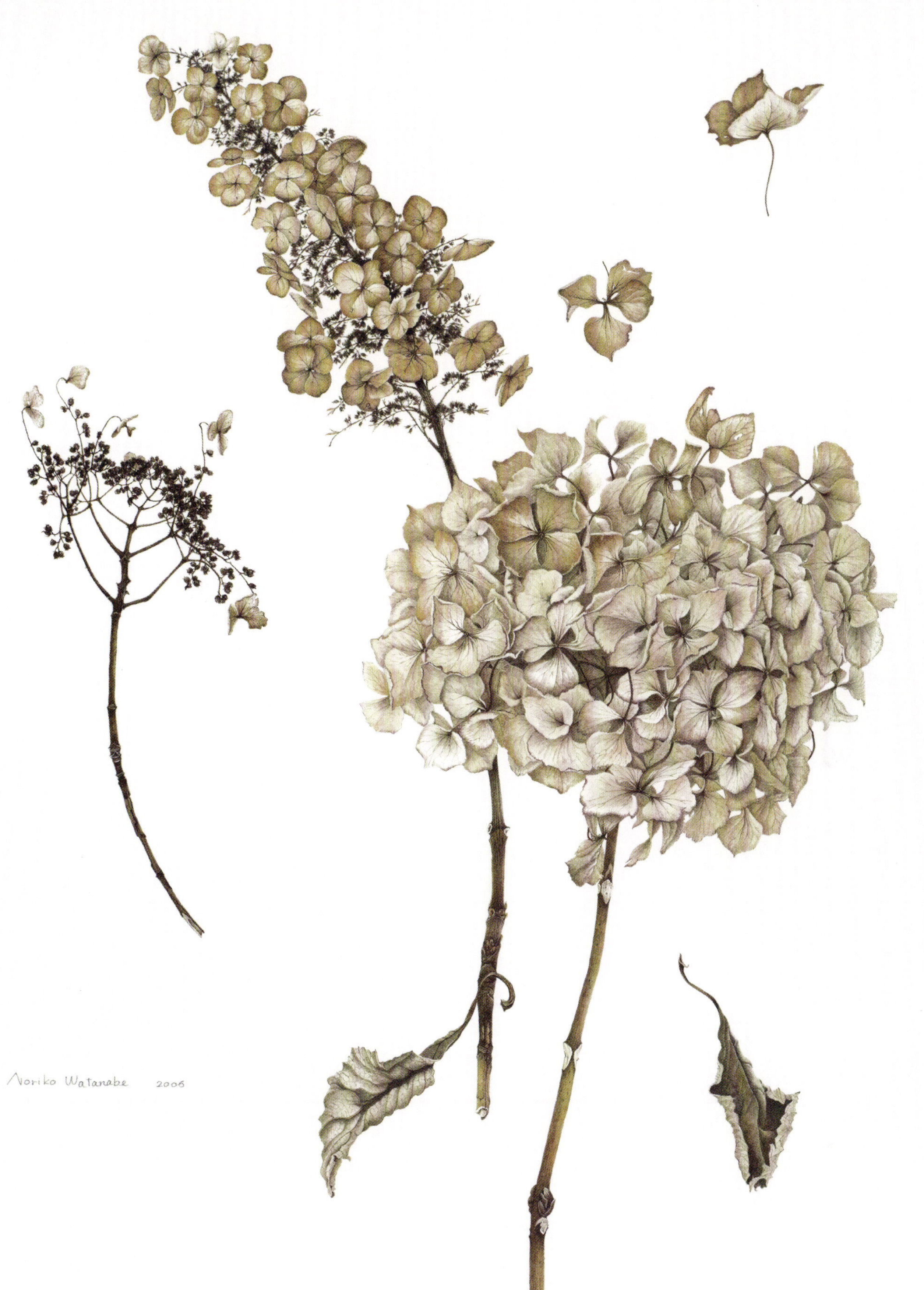
Noriko Watanabe 2006

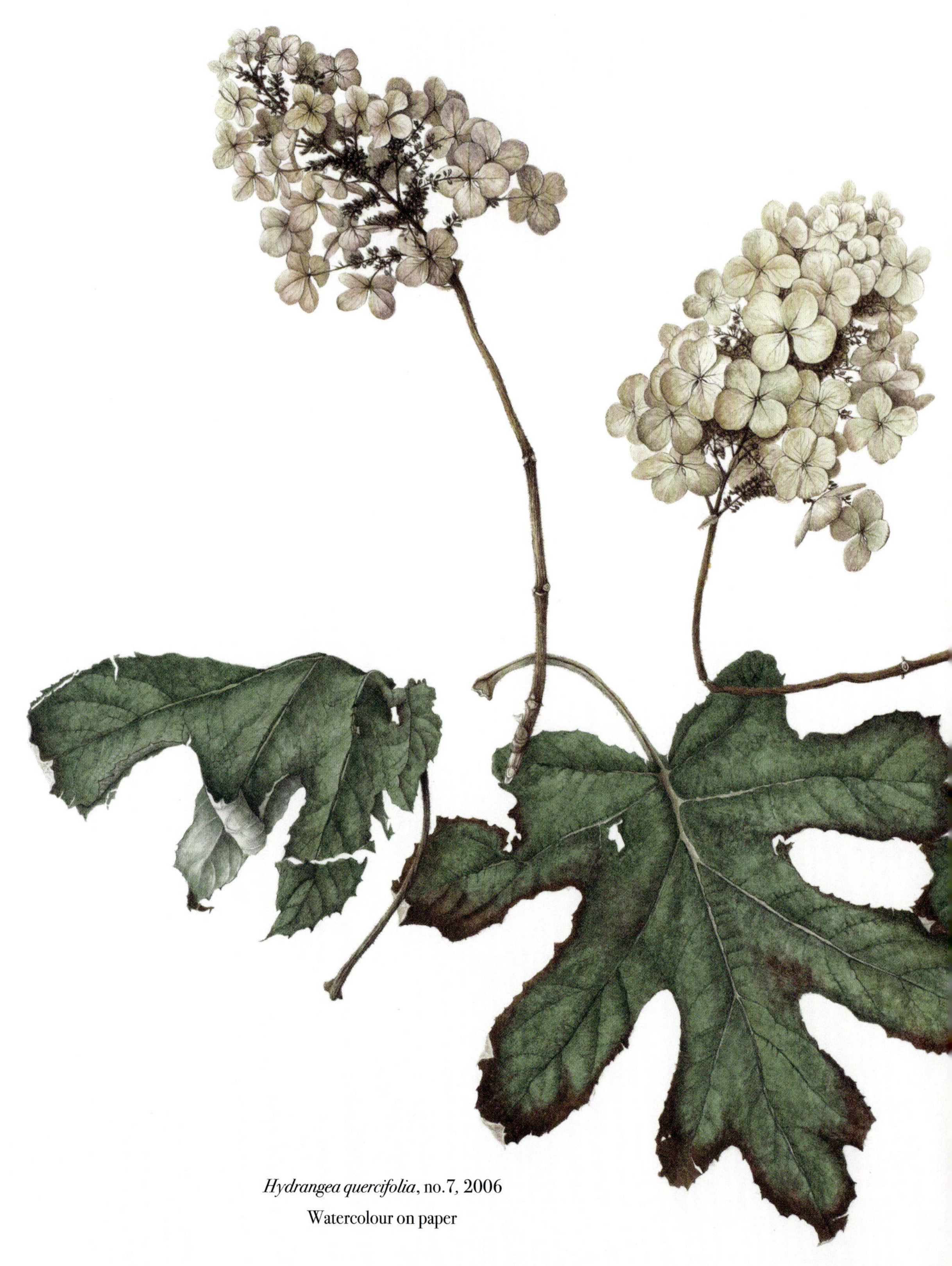

Hydrangea quercifolia, no.7, 2006

Watercolour on paper

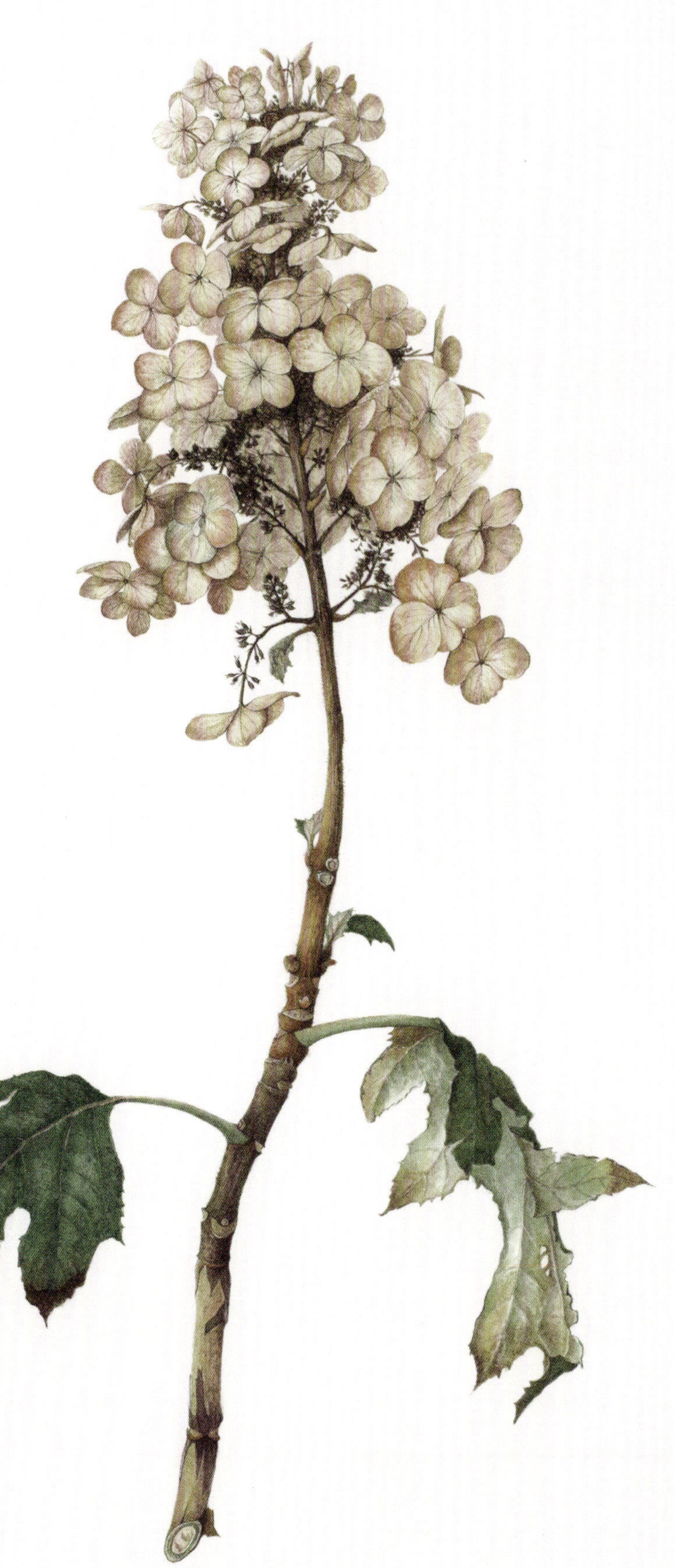
Noriko Watanabe 2006

Hazel West-Sherring

RHS medal history

Gold medal: 2005

Silver-Gilt medal: 2010

Hazel West-Sherring has exhibited twice with the RHS and in 2005 she was awarded a Gold medal. Her exhibition of '*Phlox paniculata* in watercolour', caught the attention of the library staff and West-Sherring was invited to present her work for potential purchase for the Lindley Collections. The three paintings featured here, from a series of *Primula auriculas*, were subsequently purchased.

"*Many years ago I came upon some very old porcelain which featured beautiful striped Show Auriculas in a printed design. These, together with an article on a well-regarded Kent plantswoman named Brenda Hyatt who grew Auriculas, seemed to lodge a clear image of the species in my mind. Whilst researching their history, I discovered that Ash, the very village I live in, was renowned in its day for hosting some of the country's finest Auricula Feasts. Florists Feasts, or Shows, were held in the room above village inns. Visiting the Chelsea Flower Show in 2004, I saw first-hand a traditional display of Show Auriculas.*"

At first overwhelmed by the array of colours and patterns that were available, West-Sherring went on to identify and order the specimens she wanted to paint. She had a few false starts, initially

Primula auricula 'Cockle', 2005

Watercolour on paper

PRIMULA AURICULA (blue show self)
'Cockle'

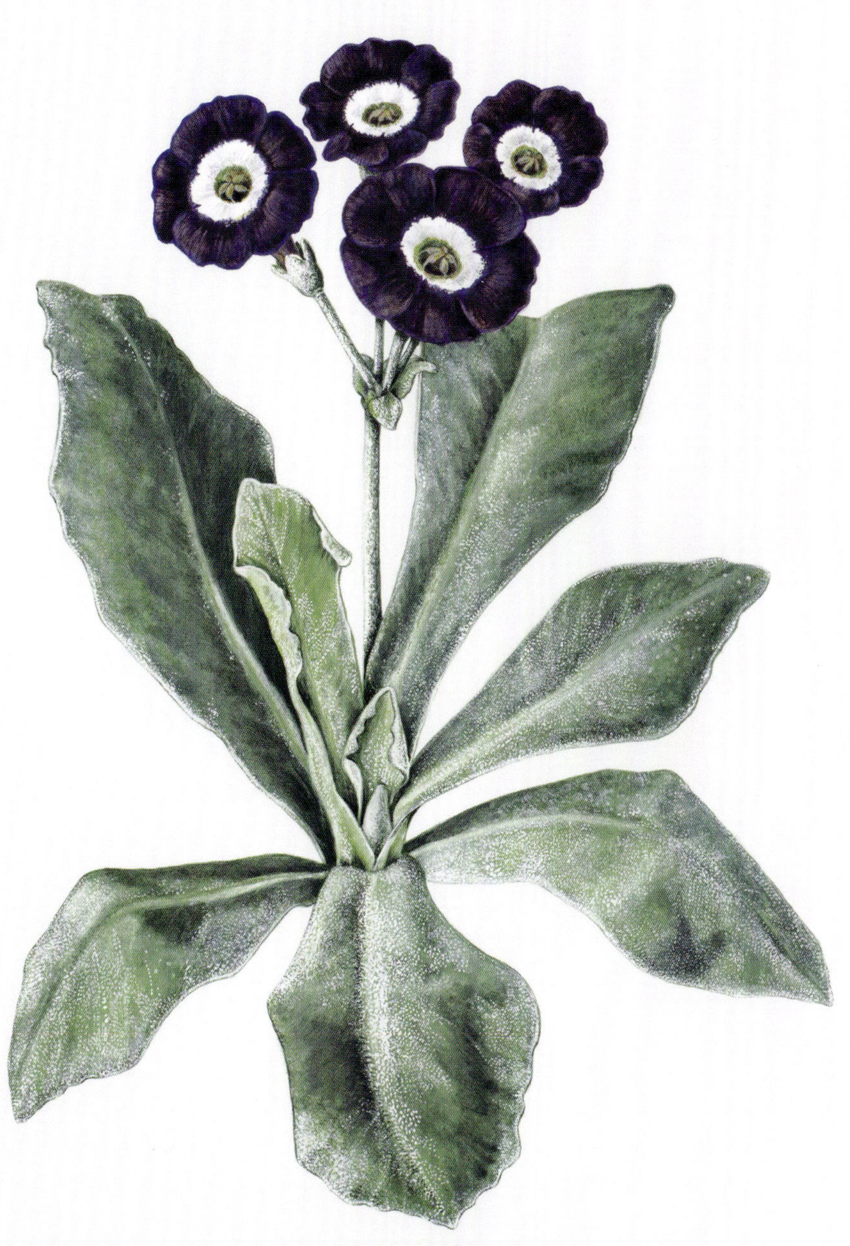

May 2005 HW-S

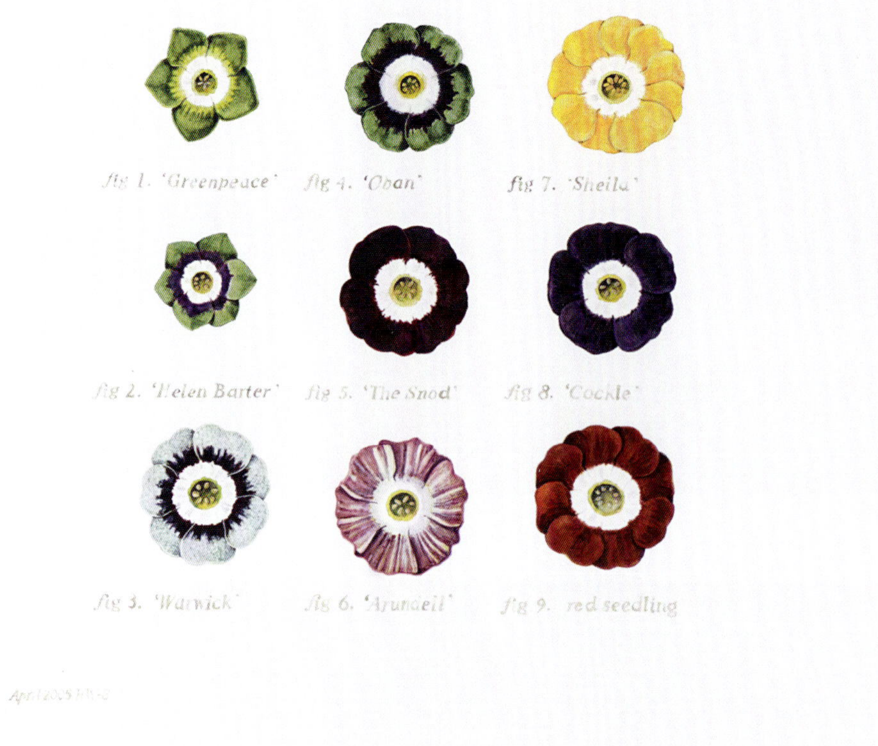

'Grid of Pips', *Primula auricula,* 2005
Watercolour on paper

suffering some poor performers that could not be used. She was then lent some plants by a group of Auricula enthusiasts from Kent, including the 'Cockle', featured here. Auriculas have a very short flowering period, so it is a particular challenge to paint any number of them at a time.

Having undertaken numerous painting projects that focus on native English garden plants, fruits, trees and hedgerows, amongst her most recent work is a Flora of the gardens at Sissinghurst Castle. West-Sherring's work features in public and private collections in the UK and USA.

Primula auricula 'Warwick', 2005
Watercolour on paper

PRIMULA AURICULA (grey edge show)
'Warwick'

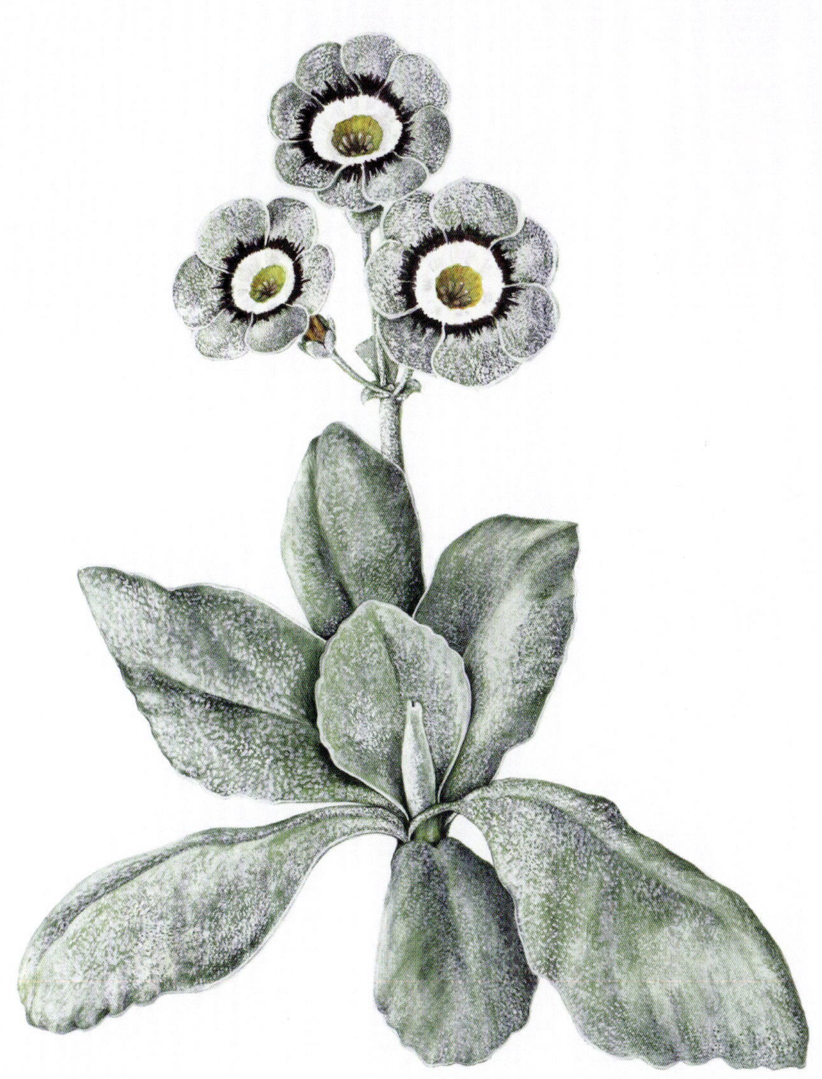

May 2005 HW-S

Lynda de Wet

RHS medal history

Gold medal: 2014

Lynda de Wet exhibited with the RHS for the first time in 2014, winning a Gold medal for her series of 'Parasitic plants'. De Wet's work has been exhibited extensively at the Kirstenbosch Biennale and features in both private and public collections in South Africa, the UK and USA.

She writes of her interest in the Cape region's plants: "*In 1999 I began a five-year project collecting and recording the extraordinary flora of the Sandveld Fynbos on the Cape West Coast, a project that ignited my passion for botanical art and resulted in a collection of over 960 life-size paintings used for identification and housed at Rondeberg Private Nature Reserve. The plants I have painted are holoparasites, completely dependent on their host for water and all their nutrients, having lost the ability to produce chlorophyll and photosynthesize. The parasites are locally host-specific in a certain area, and may be restricted to a particular host, while being exclusive to a different host in another area.*"

The piece featured here is a complex composition of graphite and watercolour. The focus of the study at the centre, in full watercolour, is the parasitic plant *Harveya capensis*, accompanied by its host *Centella asiatica*, which is depicted in graphite covering the wider landscape. This plant was found growing in Kleinmond, South Africa. As shown in the pencil work, it grows on mountain sand slopes, flowering between November and February.

Harveya capensis, 2013

Watercolour and graphite on paper

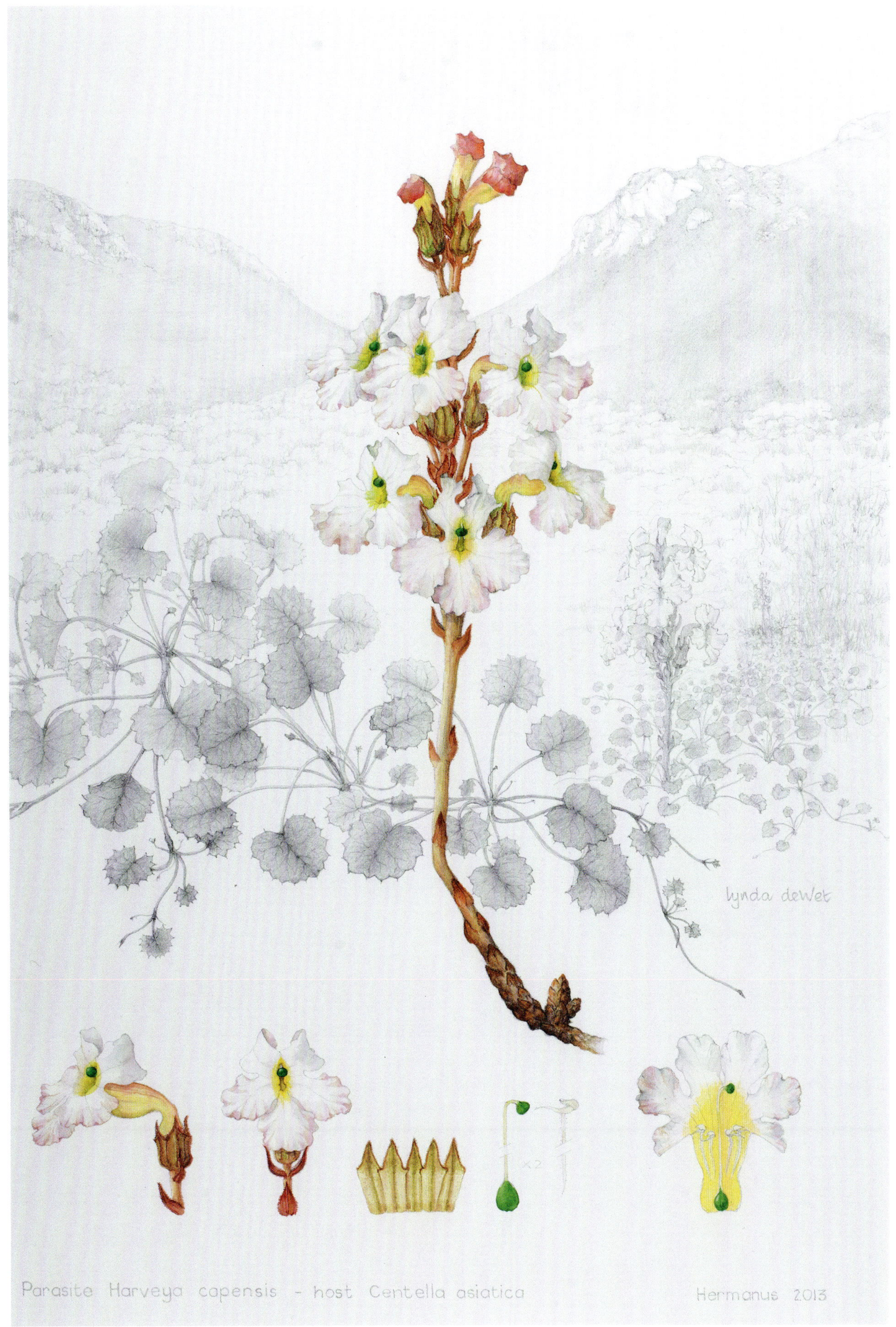
lynda deWet
x2
Parasite Harveya capensis - host Centella asiatica
Hermanus 2013

Sunanda Verma Widel

RHS medal history

Gold medal: 2024 (and Judges' Special Award)

Sunanda Widel's passion for art began in childhood, continuing at school and university. She graduated with a degree in printmaking, which was followed by 20 years in art education at international schools across the world. After finishing her teaching career, she decided to combine a love of plants and painting. Widel gained a Distinction in the Society of Botanical Artists Distance Learning Diploma Course in 2018. She is a founding member of the Botanical Art Society (Singapore). Her work has been exhibited in Singapore, Edinburgh, London and the USA and is held in collections at the Royal Botanic Garden Edinburgh, Singapore Botanic Gardens and the Hunt Institute, Pittsburgh, USA.

Widel's exhibit of 'Ornamental bananas from Southeast Asia', presented for the RHS in 2024, won her a Gold medal and the Judges' Special Award. She is a regular visitor to the Singapore Botanic Gardens.

"Bananas (Musaceae) *are iconic plants found across Southeast Asia. These ornamental species are grown at UNESCO World Heritage Site, Singapore Botanic Gardens, and show the morphological diversity of this fascinating plant group. I was instantly captivated when I first saw them. Their upright habit, variety of flower forms, array of colors and unusual fruits were inspiring. Field studies in the tropical heat of Singapore's climate was challenging. I made detailed drawings, accurate measurements and colour studies over several years to document the life cycle of each species."*

Musa gracilis (slender banana), 2023

Watercolour on paper

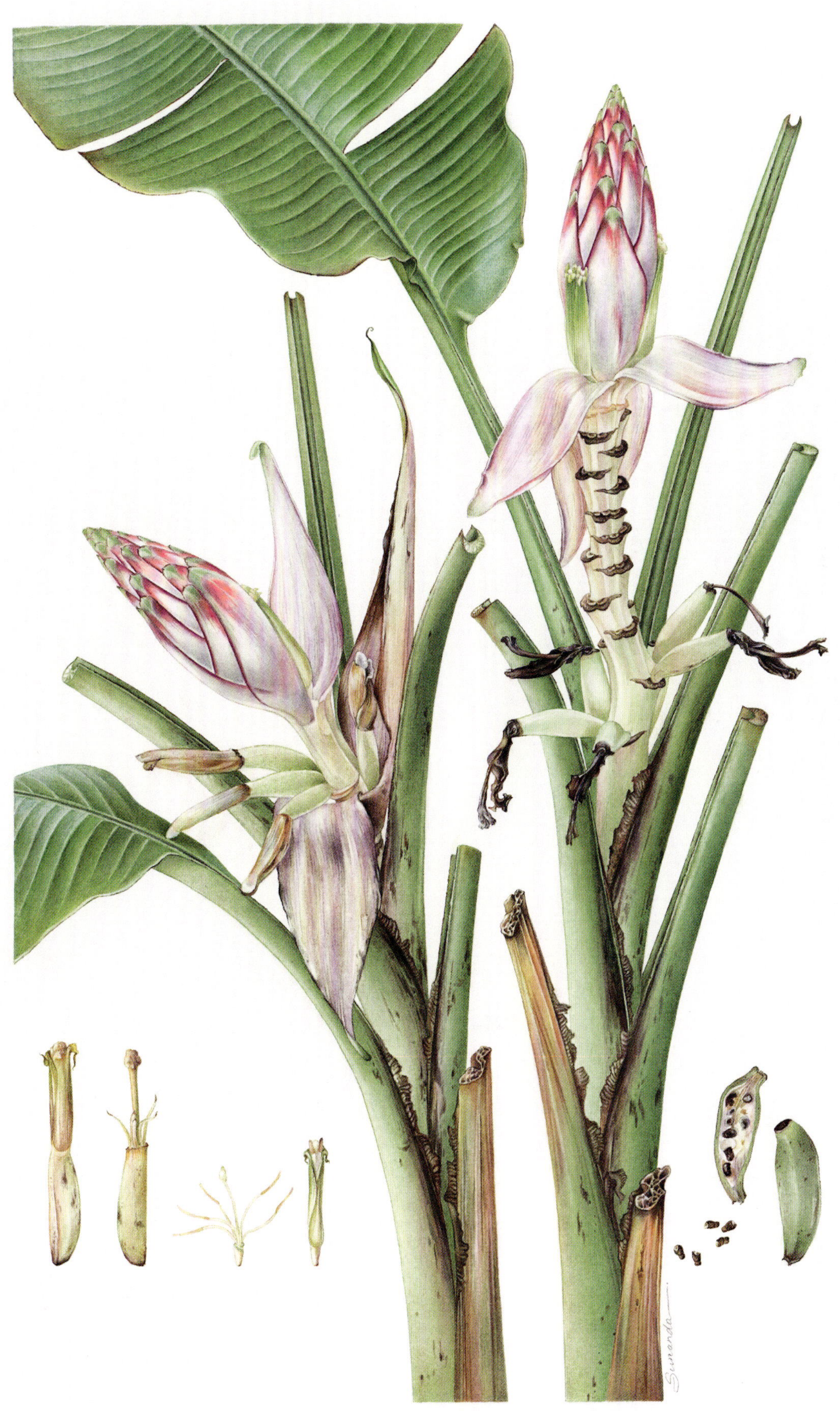

Sue J. Williams

RHS medal history

Gold medal: 2008

Silver-Gilt medal: 2006

Silver medal: 2004

Sue Williams has exhibited with the RHS on three occasions and in 2008 she realised her ambition for a Gold medal with her display of '*Begonias* in watercolour'.

Following her success in 2008, Williams' paintings of *Begonia* 'Red Robin' and *B. masoniana* were purchased for the Lindley Collections. *B.* 'Sal's Moondust' was commissioned and delivered separately, as Williams had to wait for the flowers to bloom before it could be finished. The study of three such different cultivars demonstrates beautifully how varied the colour and pattern can be on these plants. The complex veining and texture of the leaves has been captured perfectly.

Williams originally studied at Oxford University, where she gained an MA (Hons) in Modern Languages, from which she developed a career as a teacher. During periods spent living abroad in Zimbabwe and New Zealand, she undertook to paint native flora, which resulted in a commission to produce botanical stamp designs for the Pitcairn Islands. A member of the Society of Botanical Artists and a Fellow of the Chelsea Physic Garden Florilegium Society, Williams' work features in collections in the UK and the USA.

Begonia masoniana, 2007

Watercolour on paper

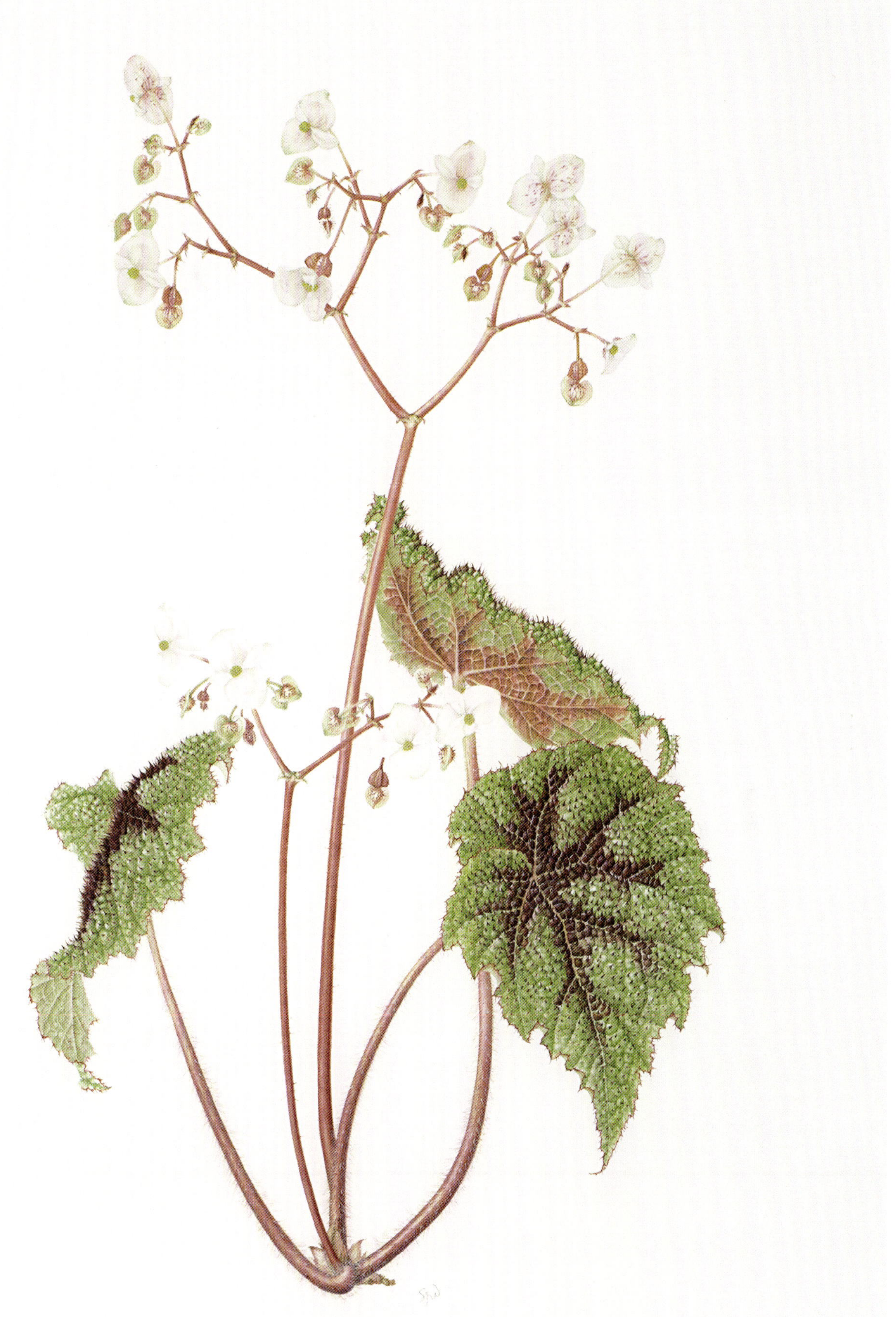

Esmée Winkel

RHS medal history

Gold medals: 2013, 2016, 2018

Esmée Winkel has exhibited at the RHS on three occasions, in 2013, 2016 and 2018; she has been awarded a Gold medal each time.

Growing up in the Caribbean, Winkel developed a keen interest in the natural environment. She studied biology at Leiden University, following which she undertook a traineeship to become a botanical artist at the National Herbarium. More recently, Winkel has also completed a course in Master Scientific Illustration at Maastricht University.

The drawing featured here of *Tadehagi triquetrum* is one of a series of *Leguminosae* by Winkel included in *Flora Malesiana*. This multi-volume Flora describes the vascular plants of the biogeographical region that includes the Malay Peninsula and Malay Archipelago. The artist has employed a range of techniques to describe the form, pattern and shape of the *Tadehagi*.

Following a recommendation from the Picture Committee, the library sought to acquire one of Winkel's drawings as a demonstration of exemplary technical skill using pen and ink. However, as the original picture was commissioned for the *Flora Malesiana* project, it was not available for purchase. Following discussions with the Naturalis Biodiversity Center in Leiden, Winkel kindly undertook to make a copy and the original picture was then donated to the Lindley Collections.

Tadehagi triquetrum, 2012

Pen and ink on paper

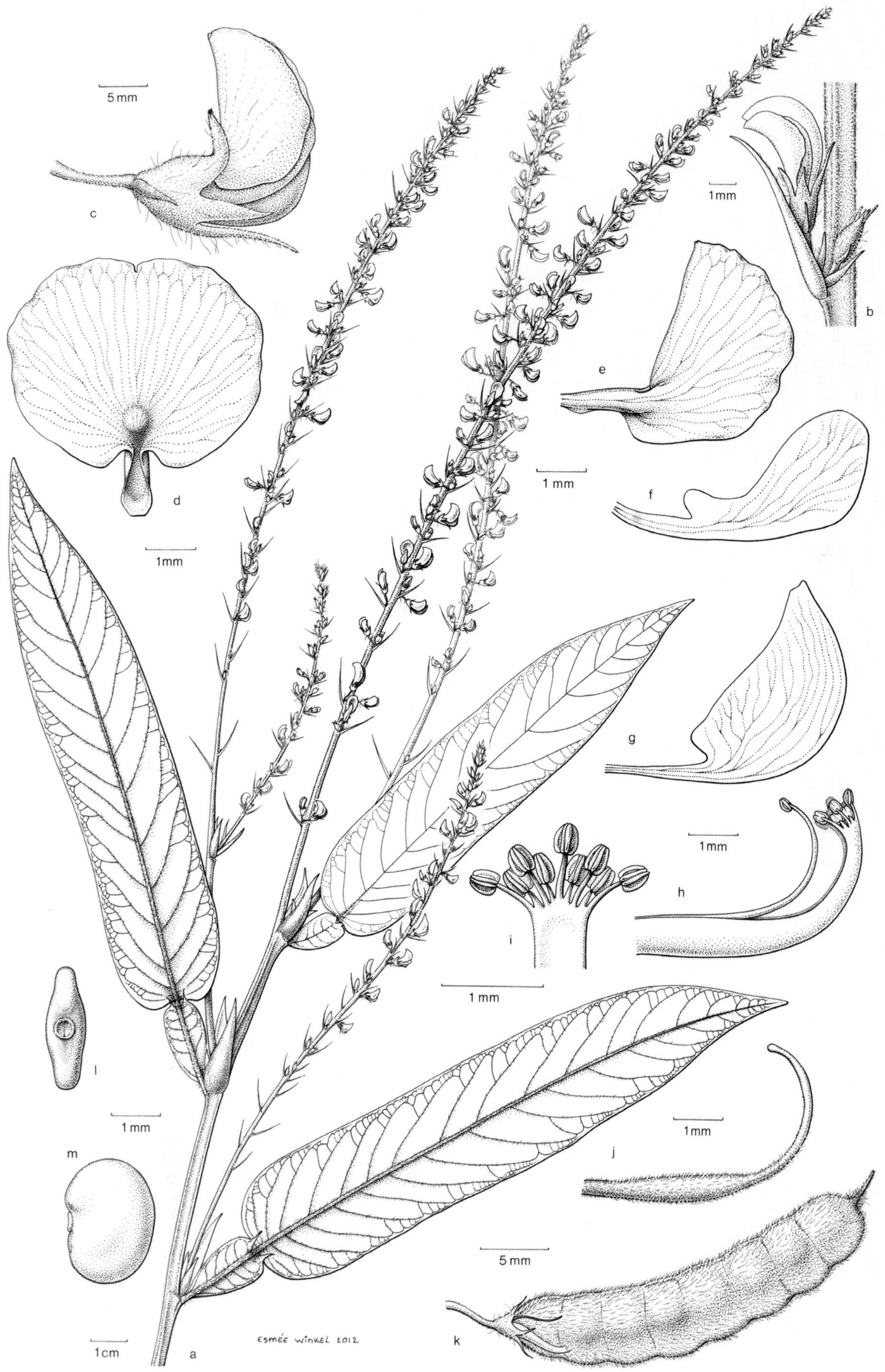

5 mm
c
1mm
b
d
e
1 mm
f
1mm
g
1mm
i
h
1 mm
l
1 mm
1mm
m
j
5 mm
1cm
a
ESMÉE WINKEL 2012
k

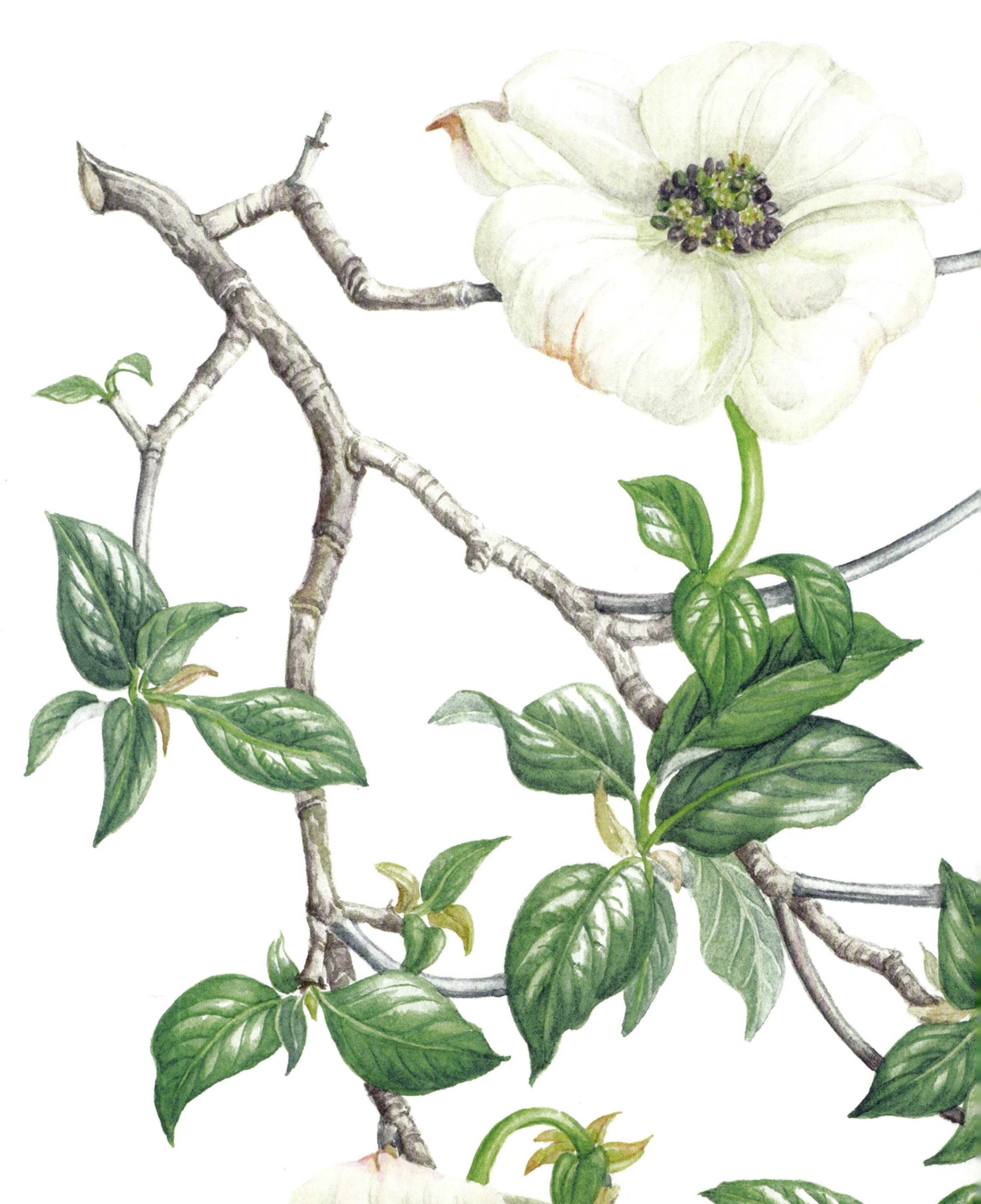

Appendix

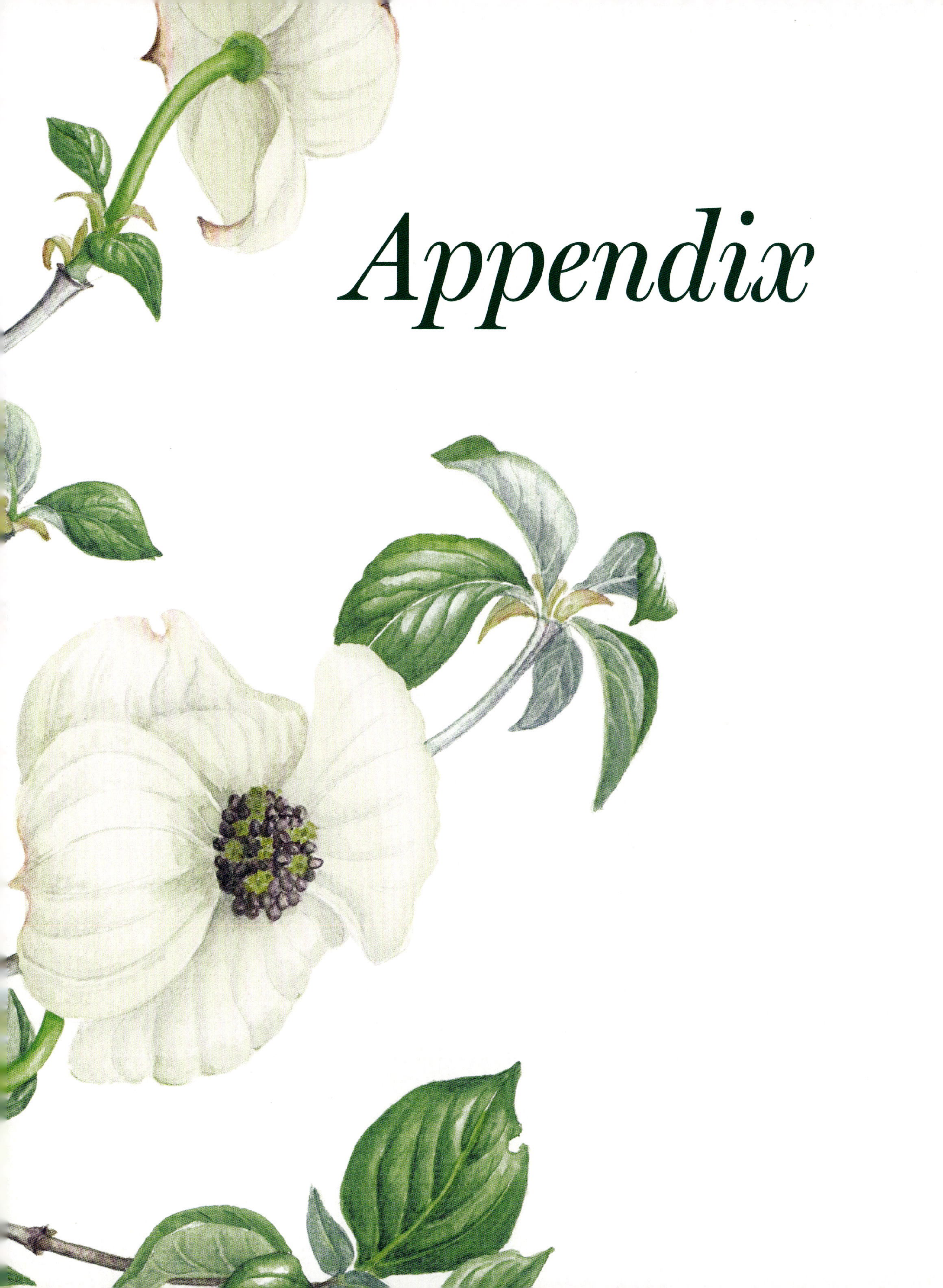

Historical List of RHS Gold Medal Winners

The country listed for each artist indicates the location of the artist at the time of the award and should not be assumed to be the same as their country of origin or nationality.

London, 16 December 1930
Frank Galsworthy, UK

London, 22 November 1932
Frank Galsworthy, UK

London, 5 November 1935
Frank Galsworthy, UK

London, 10 November 1936
M.M. Pycroft, UK

London, 9 November 1937
Frank Galsworthy, UK

London, 5 February 1963
Jeanne Holgate, UK

London, 26 November 1963
J.E. Downward, UK

London, 4 February 1964
John Paul Wellington Furse, UK

London, 10 November 1964
John Paul Wellington Furse, UK

London, 24 November 1964
Jeanne Holgate, UK

London, 23 November 1965
John Paul Wellington Furse, UK
Cynthia Newsome-Taylor, UK

London, 8 November 1966
Mary Grierson, UK

London, 6 February 1968
P.H. Mason, UK
E.G.H. Oliver, UK

London, 19 November 1968
John Paul Wellington Furse, UK

London, 18 November 1969
Mary Grierson, UK

London, 27 October 1970
Barbara Everard, UK

London, 2 February 1971
Barbara Everard, UK

London, 31 October 1972
RBG, Kew (Brian Mathews) UK

London, 21 November 1972
Leslie Greenwood, UK

London, 30 January 1973
Leslie Greenwood, UK

London, 30 October 1973
Mary Grierson, UK

London, 20 November 1973
Sybil C. Emberton, UK

London, 28 October 1974
J.G.Wilkinson, UK

London, 28 January 1975
Felicity Baxter, UK
Suzanne Lucas, UK
Andrew Paterson and Dorothy Bovey, UK

London, 28 October 1975
Barbara Everard, UK
J. Horsley, Jersey

London, 18 November 1975
Dorothy Bovey, UK

London, 17 February 1976
Suzanne Lucas, UK

London, 23 November 1976
Dorothy Bovey, UK

London, 22 February 1977
Suzanne Lucas, UK
C.M. J. Summers, UK
B. Watson, UK

London, 1 November 1977
Barbara Everard, UK
Gwladys Tonge, UK

London, 22 November 1977
Marjorie Blamey, UK
Pandora Sellars, UK

London, 21 February 1978
Mary Grierson, UK
Lady Drewe, UK
Kristin Rosenberg (Jeffery), UK
Graham Stuart Thomas, UK

London, 21 March 1978
Suzanne Lucas, UK

London, 21 November 1978
Jill Coombs, UK
V. Goaman, UK
C.M.J. Summers, UK

London, 20 February 1979
Elizabeth Cameron, UK (Scotland)
Suzanne Lucas, UK
Gwladys Tonge, UK

London, 30 October 1979
Mary Ann Kunkel, Spain
John Morland, UK

London, 20 November 1979
Barbara Everard, UK
Leslie Greenwood, UK
Jeanne Holgate, UK

London, 19 February 1980
Barbara Shaw, UK
Suzanne Lucas, UK

London, 28 October 1980
Dorothy Bovey, UK
Sylvia Boyd Andrews, UK
Barbara Everard, UK

London, 18 November 1980
National Research Institute of Pretoria, South Africa
Wendy F. Walsh, Republic of Ireland

London, 17 February 1981
Kathleen Hindle, UK

London, 3 November 1981
Michelle Emblem, UK

London, 24 November 1981
Joan Bacon, UK
Barbara Everard, UK
Mr and Mrs K. Ross, UK
Rosanne Sanders, UK

London, 16 February 1982
Ann Farrer, UK
Kathleen Hindle, UK
Ivor Coburn, UK (N. Ireland)
Suzanne Lucas, UK
Ann Shelley-Lloyd, UK

London, 16 March 1982
Dorothy Bovey, UK
Elizabeth Cameron, UK (Scotland)
Lys de Bray, UK

London, 2 November 1982
Jenny M. Brasier, UK

London, 8 February 1983
Kathleen Hindle, UK
Patricia Dale, UK
Suzanne Lucas, UK
Stuart Lafford, UK
Ann Shelley-Lloyd, UK

London, 29 November 1983
Benjamin Perkins, UK
J.G. Wilkinson, UK

London, 21 February 1984
Christine Hart-Davies, UK
Suzanne Lucas, UK
National Research Institute of Pretoria, South Africa
Ann Shelley-Lloyd, UK

London, 7 August 1984
Ann Farrer, UK

London, 30 October 1984
Sylvia Boyd Andrews, UK
Coral Guest UK
Rosanne Sanders, UK

London, 19 February 1985
Suzanne Lucas, UK

London, 19 March 1985
Claire Smith, UK

London, 29 October 1985
Jill Coombs, UK

London, 26 November 1985
Ann Farrer, UK
Josephine Hague UK
Rosanne Sanders, UK

London, 28 January 1986
The Botanical Research Institute, South Africa
Elisabeth Dowle, UK
Coral Guest, UK

London, 25 February 1986
Ivor Coburn, UK (N. Ireland)
Suzanne Lucas, UK
Christina Hart-Davies, UK

London, 28 October 1986
Auriol Batten, South Africa
Jeanne Holgate, UK
Susanna Stuart-Smith, UK

London, 25 November 1986
Gillian Griffiths, UK (Wales)
Josephine Hague, UK
Brian Hargreaves, UK
Jillian McDougall, UK (Scotland)

London, 27 January 1987
Pat Harby, UK

London, 24 February 1987
Ann Farrer, UK
Suzanne Lucas, UK

London, 27 October 1987
Sarah Anne Schofield, UK
Lindsay Megarrity, UK

London, 24 November 1987
Brian Hargreaves, UK

London, 26 January 1988
Jill Coombs, UK
Roselinda Foulk, UK
Christina Hart-Davies, UK
Jenny Jowett, UK
Jessica Tcherepnine, USA

London, 23 February 1988
Jenny M. Brasier, UK
Suzanne Lucas, UK
Ann Shelley-Lloyd, UK
Wendy F. Walsh, Republic of Ireland

London, 1 November 1988
Brigid Edwards, UK

London, 29 November 1988
Ann Farrer, UK
Josephine Hague, UK
Rosanne Sanders, UK

London, 21 February 1989
Marjorie Blamey, UK
Ivor Coburn, UK (N. Ireland)
Elisabeth Dowle, UK
Jenny Jowett, UK
Elizabeth Rice, UK

London, 18 July 1989
Jenny Brasier, UK
Elizabeth Cameron, UK (Scotland)

London, 31 October 1989
Elisabeth Dowle, UK
Elizabeth Towner, UK

London, 28 November 1989
Ivor Coburn, UK (N. Ireland)
Pauline M. Dean, UK

London, 31 January 1990
National Botanical Institute, South Africa
Margaret Stevens, UK (Wales)
Jessica Tcherepnine, USA

London, 20 February 1990
Ann Farrer, UK
Mary Grierson, UK
Kate Nessler, USA
Alex Ramsay, UK

London, 29 January 1991
Gillian Scott, Australia
Pamela Stagg, Canada

London, 19 February 1991
Pauline M. Dean, UK
Kate Nessler, USA
Katherine Pickles, UK (Scotland)

London, 26 November 1991
Blackpool & Fylde College, UK
Pauline M. Dean, UK
Marianna Kneller, UK
Sarah Anne Schofield, UK
Ann Swan, UK

London, 18 February 1992
Christina Hart-Davies, UK
National Botanical Institute, South Africa
Katherine Pickles, UK (Scotland)

London, 3 November 1992
Kristin Rosenberg (Jeffery), UK
Sheila Siegerman, Canada

London, 24 November 1992
Dr Andrew Brown, UK
Elisabeth Dowle, UK
Aino Jacevicius, UK (Wales)
Reinhild Raistrick, UK
Rosaleen Wain, UK

London, 26 January 1993
Blackpool & Fylde College, UK
Marjorie Blamey, UK
Susanna Stuart-Smith, UK
Elizabeth Towner, UK

London, 26 February 1993
Christina Hart-Davies, UK
Kate Nessler, USA
Katherine Pickles, UK (Scotland)
Siriol Sherlock, UK
Ann Swan, UK

London, 20 April 1993
J.R. Oddy, UK

London, 2 November 1993
Cherry-Anne Lavrih, UK
Jenny Phillips Goode, Australia

London, 23 November 1993
Pauline M. Dean, UK
National Botanical Institute, South Africa

London, 25 January 1994
Janet Bolton, UK
Brigid Edwards, UK

London, 22 February 1994
Jenny M. Brasier, UK
Andrew P. Brown, UK
Katherine Pickles, UK (Scotland)
Siriol Sherlock, UK
Wendy F. Walsh, Republic of Ireland

London, 1 November 1994
Elisabeth Dowle, UK
Cherry-Anne Lavrih, UK
Masako Sasaki, UK

London, 22 November 1994
Gillian Barlow, UK
Ivor Coburn, UK (N. Ireland)
Christine Grey-Wilson, UK
Reinhild Raistrick, UK

London, 24 January 1995
Martin J. Allen, UK
Francesca Anderson, USA
Celia Hegedüs, UK
Lorna Minton, UK

London, 21 February 1995
Claire Dalby, UK
Pauline M Dean, UK
Lindsay Megaritty, UK
Siriol Sherlock, UK
Annika Silander-Hokerberg, Sweden

London, 31 October 1995
Cherry-Anne Lavrih, UK
Camilla Speight, UK

London, 21 November 1995
Martha G. Kemp, USA
Mary Kenyon-Slaney, UK
Carol Woodin, USA

London, 23 January 1996
Jenny Jowett, UK

London, 20 February 1996
Celia Hegedüs, UK
Kay Rees-Davies, UK (Wales)

London, 5 November 1996
Patricia Davies, UK
Cherry-Anne Lavrih, UK
Benjamin Perkins, UK
Katherine Pickles, UK (Scotland)
J. Wilkinson, UK

London, 26 November 1996
Mary E. Byatt, UK (Scotland)
Mariko Imai, Japan
Reinhild Raistrick, UK

London, 21 January 1997
Evelyn Binns, UK
Elisabeth Dowle, UK
Josephine Newman, UK
Susan Ogilvy, UK
Camilla Speight, UK
Christine Stephenson, UK

London, 18 February 1997
Andrew P. Brown, UK
Sally Keir, UK
Romilly Swann, UK
Martin J. Allen, UK

London, 8 March 1997
Camilla Speight, UK
Ann Swan, UK

London, 4 November 1997
Gillian Barlow, UK
Linda Francis, UK
Martha Kemp, USA
Cherry-Anne Lavrih, UK
Sheila Mannes-Abbott, UK
Camilla Speight, UK
Amanda Jayne Willoughby, UK

London, 25 November 1997
National Botanical Institute, South Africa
Sylvia Sutton, UK

London, 20 January 1998
Brigitte Daniel, UK
Celia Hegedüs, UK

London, 17 February 1998
Evelyn Binns, UK
Vicky Cox, UK
Patricia R. K. Davies, UK
Pierino Delvo, Italy
Elisabeth Dowle, UK
Kay Rees-Davies, UK (Wales)
Annika Silander-Hokerberg, Sweden
Niki Simpson, UK

London, 3 November 1998
Anne Chambers, UK (Scotland)
Catherine Hollman, UK
Cherry-Anne Lavrih, UK

London, 24 November 1998
Jacqueline Dawson, UK

London, 19 January 1999
Francesca Anderson, USA
Evelyn Binns UK
Chelsea Physic Garden Florilegium Society, UK
Brigitte Daniel, UK
Regine Hagedorn, France

London, 16 February 1999
Marta Chirino-Argenta, Spain
Deborah Lambkin, Republic of Ireland

London, 20 March 1999
Gillian Barlow, Ann Swan and Pauline Dean, UK
Mr O. Whalley, RBG Kew, UK

London, 2 November 1999
Andrew P. Brown, UK
Susan Christopher-Coulson, UK
E. Esparza, Mexico
Linda Francis, UK
Cherry-Anne Lavrih, UK
National Botanical Institute, South Africa
Siriol Sherlock, UK

London, 14 December 1999
Pauline M. Dean, Guildford, UK
Yvonne Hammond, UK
Leicestershire Society of Botanical Illustrators, UK

London, 25 January 2000
Jenny Brasier, UK
Celia Hegedus, UK
Susan Sex, Republic of Ireland
Julie Small, UK
L.S. Koon, Switzerland

London, 13 February 2000
Brenda Watts, UK

London, 15 February 2000
R. Cooney, UK
Regine Hagedorn, France
Reinhild Raistrick, UK
Lizzie Sanders, UK (Scotland)
Y. Uchijo, Japan

London, 18 March 2000
Patrick Garton, UK

London, 31 October 2000
Elizabeth Beatrice (Elbe) Joubert, South Africa
Cherry-Anne Lavrih, UK
Sheila Mannes-Abbott, UK
Anne O'Connor, Australia
Rachel Pedder-Smith, UK
Marina Virdis, Italy
Hedvig Wright Østern, Norway

London, 12 December 2000
Rachel Britton, UK
Lesley Catchpole, UK
Moya Davern, UK
Yvonne Hammond, UK
Hemlata Pradhan, India
Sylvia Sutton, UK

London, 16 January 2001
Blackpool and the Design School of Art and Design, UK
Brigitte Daniel, UK
Celia Hegedüs, UK
Susan Sex, Republic of Ireland
Keiko Tokunaga, Japan

London, 13 February 2001
Evelyn Binns, UK
J. Luis Castillo, Spain
Masako Sasaki, UK
Yoko Uchijo, Japan
Brenda Watts, UK

London, 9 October 2001
Blackpool and the Fylde College, UK

London, 20 November 2001
Susan Christopher-Coulson, UK
Sally Crosthwaite, UK
Pauline M. Dean, UK
Martina Grey, UK
Kimiyo Maruyama, Japan
Mali Moir, Australia
Rachel Pedder-Smith, UK
Jean Ricketts, UK
Lucy Smith, UK

London, 22 January 2002
Evelyn Binns, UK
Marjorie Holmes, Greece
Elizabeth Beatrice (Elbe) Joubert, South Africa
Barbara Oozeerally, UK
Rita Parkinson, Australia
Susan Sex, Republic of Ireland
Amanda Jayne Willoughby, UK

London, 19 February 2002
Moya Davern, UK (Wales)
Pauline M. Dean, UK
Junko Iwata, UK
Martha G. Kemp, USA
Catharine Nicholson, UK
Lizzie Sanders, UK (Scotland)

BBC GWL (Birmingham), June 2002
Gillian Griffiths, UK (Wales)
Lucy Smith, UK

London, 1 November 2002
Helen Fitzgerald, Australia
Bridget Gillespie, UK

London, 21 January 2003
Christina Brodie, UK
Brigitte Daniel, UK
Keiko Yoshida, Japan
Elaine Musgrave, Australia

London, 18 February 2003
Kay Rees-Davies, UK (Wales)
Rosie Sanders, UK
Jane Wright, UK

London, 25 November 2003
Rachel Britton, UK
Jill Hallett, UK
Kimiyo Maruyama, Japan
Anna Paoletto, Italy
Ruth C. Walter, Australia

London, 20 January 2004
Sarah Adams, UK (Wales)
Celia Hegedüs, UK
Doreen Jones, UK
Rachel Pedder-Smith, UK
Lizzie Sanders, UK (Scotland)
Bronwyn van de Graaff, Australia

London, 17 February 2004
Evelyn Binns, UK
Georita Harriott, Christabel King and Joanna Langhorne (group exhibit), UK
Catharine Nicholson, UK
Barbara Oozeerally, UK

BBC GWL (Birmingham), June 2004
Celia Crampton, UK
Elvia Esparza, Mexico (+ Best Botanical Artist)
Yoko Uchijo, Japan
Anita Walsmit Sachs, Netherlands

London, 18/19 January 2005
Evelyn Binns, UK
Brigitte Daniel, UK
Caroline Holley, UK
John Pastoriza Pinol, Australia
Hazel West-Sherring, UK

London, 15/16 February 2005
Regine Hagedorn, France
Georita Harriott, UK
Martha G. Kemp, USA
Rachel Pedder-Smith, UK

London International Orchid Show, September 2005
Mayumi Hashi, UK

BBC GWL (Birmingham), June 2005
Christina Brodie, UK
Jean Emmons, USA
Anita Walsmit Sachs, Netherlands (+ Best Botanical Artist)

London, 15/16 November 2005
Elizabeth Beatrice (Elbe) Joubert, South Africa
Kimiyo Maruyama, Japan
Hilary Buckley, UK (Wales)

London, 17/18 January 2006
Norma Gregory, UK
Jenny Jowett, UK
Deirdre Bean, Australia
Dick Rauh, USA

London, 14/15 February 2006
Samantha Cook, UK
Catharine Nicholson, UK
Irene Schmidt, Germany
Julia Trickey, UK
Mieko Ishikawa, Japan
Derek Norman, USA
Peta Stockton, Austria

BBC GWL (Birmingham), June 2006
Lucilla Carcano, Italy (+ Best Botanical Artist)

London, 10/11 November 2006
Noriko Watanabe, Japan

London, 16/17 January 2007
Beverly Allen, Australia
Brigitte Daniel, UK
Margaret Walty, UK (Scotland)

London, 13/14 February 2007
Yvonne Arnsdorf, UK
Lara Call Gastinger, USA
Keiko Sasaki, Japan

BBC GWL (Birmingham), 2007
Anna Mason (née Knights), UK (+ Best Botanical Artist)

BBC GWL (Birmingham), 2007
Bryan Poole, UK

London, 9/10 November 2007
Mayumi Hashi, UK
Martha G. Kemp, USA
Tobita Noriko, Japan
Angeline de Meester, UK

London, 15/16 January 2008
David M. Pethers, UK

London, 12/13 February 2008
Norma Gregory, UK
Georita Harriott, UK
Silvana Rava, Italy
Julia Trickey, UK
Sue J. Williams, UK

BBC GWL (Birmingham), June 2008
Beth Phillip, UK
Sandra Sanger, Australia (+ Best Botanical Artist)

London, 16/17 December 2008
Jacqueline Dawson, UK
Bridget Gillespie, UK
Eiko Hamada, Japan
Maki Nishimura, Japan
Michiko Shibata, Japan
Terrie Reddish, New Zealand
Fiona Strickland, UK (Scotland)
Lidia Vanzetti, Italy
Sue Wickison, New Zealand

BBC GWL (Birmingham), June 2009
Janie Thorogood (Pirie), UK (+ Best Botanical Artist)

London Orchid and Botanical Art Show, 20 March 2010
Kay Rees-Davies, UK (Wales)
Margaret Walty, UK (Scotland)
Masumi Yamanaka, UK
Celia Crampton, UK
Brigitte Daniel, UK
Gulnur Eksi, Turkey
Isik Guner, Turkey
Sheila Mannes-Abbott, UK
Kimiyo Maruyama, Japan (+ Best Botanical Art Exhibit)
Clare McGhee, UK (Scotland)

Malvern Spring Gardening Show, May 2010
Ann Fraser, UK (Scotland)
Christine Battle, UK
Lesley Randall, USA

BBC GWL (Birmingham), June 2010
Sandra Sanger, Australia (+ Best Botanical Artist)

London Botanical Art Show, March 2011
Jean Emmons, USA (+ Best Painting)
Norma Gregory, UK
Annie Hughes, Australia
Carolyn Jenkins, UK (+ Best Exhibit)
Kayoko Miyazawa, Japan
Tomoko Ogawa, Japan
Lidia Vanzetti, Italy

London Botanical Art Show, March 2012
Gulnur Eksi, Turkey
Annie Hughes, Australia (+ Best Painting)
Heeyoung Kim, USA
Kumiko Kosuda, Japan
Louise Lane, UK (+ Best Exhibit)
Julia Trickey UK
Christiana Webb, UK

Malvern Spring Festival, May 2012
Bernard F. Carter, UK
Brigitte Daniel, UK (+ Best Botanical Art Exhibit)
Caroline Holley, UK

London Botanical Art Show, April 2013
Gulnur Eksi, Turkey
Annie Hughes, Australia
Sandra Sanger, Australia
Hye Woo Shin, Republic of Korea (+ Best Exhibit)
Laura Silburn, UK
Julia Trickey, UK
Margaret de Villiers, South Africa (+ Best Painting)
Esmée Winkel, Netherlands

Malvern Spring Festival, May 2013
Janet Dyer, UK (Scotland) (+ Best Botanical Painting)

London Botanical Art Show, April 2014
Lynda de Wet, South Africa
Isik Guner, UK (Scotland) (+ Best Painting)
Louise Lane, UK
Nikki Marks, UK
Hye Woo Shin, Republic of Korea (+ Best Exhibit)
London Botanical Art Show April 2014
Sharon Tingey, UK (Scotland)

Malvern Spring Festival, May 2014
Janie Pirie (Thorogood), UK
Dr Julia Craig-McFeely, UK
Gael Sellwood, UK (+ Best Botanical Art Exhibit)
Giuliana Sordi, Italy

London, Shades of Autumn Show, October 2014
Ruth Kirkby, UK
Denise Ramsay, New Zealand
Laura Silburn, UK (+ Best Botanical Art Exhibit)

Malvern Spring Festival, May 2015
Ros Franklin, UK
Karen Musgrave Hill, UK
Giuliana Sordi, Italy
Halina Steele, Australia (+ Best Botanical Art Exhibit)

London Botanical Art Show, February 2015
Gulnur Eksi, Turkey
Hideo Horikoshi, Japan (+ Best Painting)
Kimiyo Maruyama, Japan
Masako Mori, Japan
Katherine Pickles, UK (Scotland)
Kumiko Takano, Japan (+ Best Exhibit)

London Botanical Art Show, February 2016
Mariko Aikawa, Japan (+ Best Exhibit)
Sansanee Deekrajang, Thailand
Akiko Enokido, USA
Sarah Howard, UK
Hiromi Hyogo, Japan
Julie Nettleton, Australia (+ Best Painting)
Simonetta Occhipinti, Italy
Chiyoko Ohmi, Japan
Roger Reynolds, UK
Sandra Sanger, Australia
Lidia Vanzetti, Italy
Margaret de Villiers, South Africa
Esmée Winkel, Netherlands

London Botanical Art Show, February 2017
Denver School of Botanical Art and Illustration, USA
Keiko Fujita, Japan
Bridget Gillespie, UK (+ Best Painting)
Annie Hughes, Australia
Mariko Ikeda, Japan (+ Best Exhibit)
Mayumi Ishii, Japan
Suyeon Kim, Republic of Korea
Katherine Pickles, UK (Scotland)
Shirley Slocock, UK

Malvern Spring Festival, May 2017
Bernard F. Carter, UK (+ Best Botanical Art Exhibit)
Lesley Randall, USA

Malvern Spring Festival, May 2018
Caroline Jackson-Houlston (+ Best Botanical Art Exhibit), UK

London Plant and Art Fair, July 2018
Angela Lober, Australia
Angela Petrini, Italy
Bridget Gillespie, UK
Christina Hart-Davies, UK (Scotland)
Esmée Winkel, Netherlands
Hideo Horikoshi, Japan
Hiroe Sasaki, Japan
Hye Woo Shin, Republic of Korea (+ Judges' Special Award)
Lara Call Gastinger, USA
Laura Silburn, UK (+ Best Botanical Painting)
Mayumi Ishii, Japan
Michie Yamada, Japan (+ Best Botanical Art Exhibit)
Sarah Jame Humphrey, UK
Simon Williams, UK
Yuko Inujima, Japan
Yoshikazu Ohkawara, Japan

London, RHS Botanical Art & Photography Show, July 2019
Kumiko Takano, Japan
Linda Pitkin, UK
Louise Lane, UK
Marianne Hazelwood, UK
Mariko Ikeda, Japan (+ Best Botanical Art Exhibit)
Masako Mori, Japan
Naomi Gumma, Japan (+ Best Botanical Art Exhibit)
Nigel Pickering, UK
Russian Botanical Artists, Russia (Group exhibit)
Shirley Slocock, UK

Saatchi Gallery, London, RHS Botanical Art & Photography Show, Sept 2021
Pauleen Trim, UK (+ Best Botanical Artwork)
Kimiko Miyahara, Japan (+ Best Botanical Art Exhibit)
Francesca Ross, UK
Toni Dade, Portugal
Mariko Aikawa, Japan

Saatchi Gallery, London, RHS Botanical Art & Photography Show, April 2022
Yoko Harada, Japan (+ Best Botanical Artwork)
Jackie Isard, UK
Mitsuko Kurashina, Japan (+ Judges' Special Award)
Nigel Pickering, UK (+ Best Botanical Art Exhibit)
Hye Woo Shin, Republic of Korea
Liz Campbell, UK

Saatchi Gallery, London, RHS Botanical Art & Photography Show, June 2023
Yunjin Park, UK
Eunike Nugroho, Indonesia (+ Best Botanical Artwork)
Youngran Choi, Republic of Korea
Nina Mayes, UK (+ Best Botanical Art Exhibit)
Keahung Lee, Republic of Korea
Asuka Hishiki, Japan
Sarah Jane Humphrey, UK

Saatchi Gallery, London, RHS Botanical Art & Photography Show, June 2024
Anne Hayes, Australia
Besty Rogers-Knox, USA
Daleen Roodt, South Africa (+ Best Botanical Artwork)
Amelia Grass, UK
Hyunjin Cho, USA
Lynne Uptin, Australia (+ Best Botanical Art Exhibit)
Maria Lombardi, Italy
Sandunmali Kulasekara, Qatar
Sunanda Verma Widel, Singapore (+ Judges' Special Award)
Toni Dade, Portugal
Yuko Saito, Japan

Endnotes

Introduction

1. Richard A. Salisbury, *The Paradisus Londinensis: containing plants cultivated in the vicinity of the metropolis* (London: William Hooker, 1806).

2. RHS Drawings Committee Minutes, January 1818, RHS Committee Minutes, RHS Archive.

3. RHS Drawings Committee Minutes, April 1818, RHS Committee Minutes, RHS Archive.

4. Manuscript 'Descriptions of Apples', 1819, RHS History (1818–1835), RHS Archive.

5. Sotheby and Wilkinson Auctioneers, *Sale catalogue: Library of the Horticultural Society*, [2–4 May 1859] London.

6. Joseph Sabine, 'Account and description of five new Chinese chrysanthemum; with some observations on the treatment of all kinds cultivated in England, and on other circumstances relating to the varieties generally'. *The Transactions of the Horticultural Society of London*, Volume 5, 1824, pp.412–428 (p.425).

7. 'Extracts from the proceedings: Report of the Council for the year 1911', *Journal of the Royal Horticultural Society*, Volume 38, 1912–1913, page iv.

8. Charlotte Brooks, *Orchids: A History through Botanical Illustration* (Woodbridge: ACC Art Books, 2022).

9. E.A. Bunyard,'The Hooker and Lindley Drawings', *Journal of the Royal Horticultural Society*, Volume 52, 1927, pp.218–224.

10. Anna Pavord, *The Tulip* (London: Bloomsbury, 1999), p.163.

11. 'Proceedings: Scientific Committee, February 6, 1912'. *Journal of the Royal Horticultural Society*, Volume 38, 1912–1913, page xxxii.

12. 'Proceedings: Section 8 The Chelsea Show 1926', *Journal of the Royal Horticultural Society*, Volume 53, 1928, page v.

13. 'Proceedings', *Journal of the Royal Horticultural Society*, Volume 58, 1934, page clxxiii.

14. 'Exhibitions: General Notes', *Journal of the Royal Horticultural Society*, Volume 60, 1935, pp.34–36.

15. Ibid.

16. Letters from Lady Beatrix Stanley to E.A. Bowles, 1931–1934, E.A. Bowles Archive, RHS Archive.

17. Mea Allan, *E.A. Bowles and his garden at Myddleton House* (London: Faber & Faber, 1973), pp.84, 188.

18. Wilfrid Blunt, 'Botanical illustration', *Journal of the Royal Horticultural Society*, Volume 76, 1951, pp.118–128 (p.127).

19. Patrick Synge, 'Paul Furse', *RHS Lilies*, 1978/9, pp.88-89.

20. Wilfrid Blunt and W.T. Stearn, *The Art of Botanical Illustration* (Woodbridge: Antique Collectors' Club in association with RBG Kew, 1994), p.315.

21. 'Proceedings', *Journal of the Royal Horticultural Society*, Volume 110, 1985, page ix.

22. Mary Newnes, *Picture Committee Report*, 19 December 1990, RHS Picture Committee Minutes, RHS Archive.

23. Letter dated 10 October 1986 from Elizabeth Banks to Chris Brickell, enclosing a copy of a letter written to Lady Loder, RHS Picture Committee Minutes, RHS Archive.

24. RHS Library Committee Minute, 28 November 1989, RHS Committee Minutes, RHS Archive.

25. RHS Picture Committee Minutes, 26 March 1991 and 22 May 1991, RHS Committee Minutes, RHS Archive.

26. Personal correspondence, Gillian Barlow to Charlotte Brooks, May 2018.

Pauline Dean

1. P. Dean, *Portfolio of a Botanical Artist*, (Botanical Publishing, 2014), pp.18–19.

Catharine Nicholson

1. www.catharinenicholson.com and www.theguardian.com/artanddesign/2011/jun/21/catharine-nicholson-obituary

Acknowledgements

There are so many wonderful artists represented in the Lindley Library Collections and I am thrilled to be able to feature the work of many of them here. Where possible I have tried to include the artists' own words to describe their creative practice, but if there are errors, they are mine.

Inevitably, there was not space in this book for everyone, and for that I apologise. If I have even hinted at the creative treasures held in the Lindley Collections, perhaps it will inspire you to visit us to see them for yourself and to experience the delight of exploring these artworks.

I am deeply grateful to Alison South, who has tirelessly researched, cross-referenced and compiled spreadsheets of medal histories. Without her, an overview of the history of medal awards for botanical art would have been nearly impossible to gain. Now, for the first time, these records have been collated from research using several difference sources. Early medal awards were only recorded in RHS committee minutes and publications, and in some cases exhibiting artists and photographers were not distinguished, but just listed under 'Pictures'. A supplementary award for Best Botanical Artist was first recorded in 2004. It was given to Elvia Esparza, who exhibited at the BBC's *Gardeners' World* live show at the NEC in Birmingham. This award was later to become two distinct accolades, one which recognises the best overall botanical art exhibit at the show, and the other, the 'best painting' in show. Brent Elliott was the Society's Librarian and Historian for 40 years and my colleague for nearly 14 of those. His knowledge and patience are near limitless and I thank him for his generosity. My colleagues at the library, in particular Crestina Forcina (image research) and Claire Collins and Georgia Metaxas (photography), and on the Picture Panel have been incredibly supportive and, together, we learn new things every day.

Index of Illustrations

Plants

Royal Signatures

Miscellaneous

About the Author

Charlotte Brooks is the Art Curator at the RHS Lindley Library in London. She has worked with the Society's botanical artworks for over 20 years; caring for, documenting, researching and developing this collection. As the Secretary to the RHS Botanical Art Judging Panel, she supports a lively, international community of practising artists to exhibit their work and to be judged for medal awards at RHS Shows. She has curated the RHS Botanical Art & Photography Show in partnership with Saatchi Gallery, London for five years. She has written various short articles and her second book *RHS Orchids: A History through Botanical Illustration*, in 2022, was published by ACC Art Books. She has a long-held research interest in 19th-century Anglo-Chinese botanical paintings.

The Royal Horticultural Society held its inaugural meeting in 1804 and has been inspiring gardeners across the UK ever since. Now with a membership of over half a million people and an extensive network of community programmes, the RHS reaches gardening enthusiasts at all levels: from the keen novice to the most experienced plantsperson. The Society's libraries are open to all, with books available for lending (members only), reference and research. The libraries at Vincent Square in London, RHS Garden Wisley and Harlow Carr in Yorkshire offer a range of visitor events including exhibitions, study days, tours and talks.

The Lindley Library in London specialises in garden history and design. The library's Heritage Collection comprises early books, photographs and an extensive archive of some of the country's leading practitioners, which complements the unique collection of over 30,000 botanical artworks. Dating back to the c.1630s and still being added to today, the art collection features paintings by some of the most eminent artists from all over the world. A regular programme of curated exhibitions ensures visitors can access these treasured artworks. Plans to digitise the collections and make them available online have been realised with RHS Digital Collections, enabling a far greater reach to both practising artists and those interested in expanding their knowledge further.

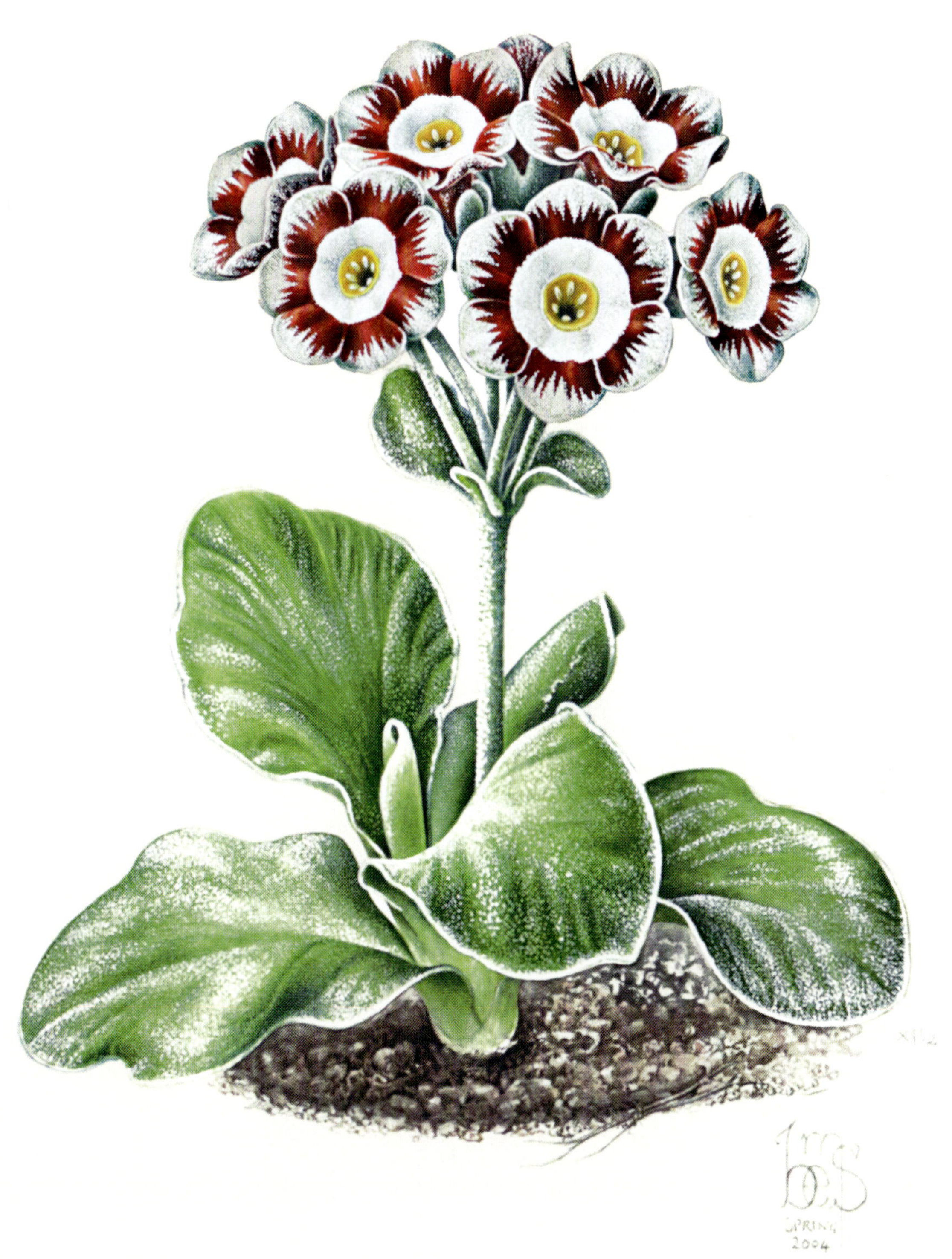

'Queen Bee' © Brigitte E.M Daniel 2004

ISBN: 978 1 78884 338 6

First published in 2019 by ACC Art Books in association with The Royal Horticultural Society
This updated and extended edition published by ACC Art Books in association with The Royal Horticultural Society in 2025

A CIP catalogue record for this book is available from the British Library

The author and publisher gratefully acknowledge the permission granted to reproduce the copyright material in this book. Every effort has been made to trace copyright holders and to obtain their permission for the use of copyright material. The publisher apologises for any errors or omissions in the text and would be grateful if notified of any corrections that should be incorporated in future reprints or editions of this book.

The artworks featured here are all held in the RHS Lindley Library in London. Each of the showcased artists has won at least one Gold medal (in some cases, many more) and the majority of the pictures included here had been part of Gold medal-winning displays. In addition, some of the artworks were acquired from the artists independently of the RHS Shows.

RHS Publisher: Helen Griffin
RHS Head of Editorial: Tom Howard
ACC Art Books Publisher: James Smith

EU GPSR Authorised Representative:
Easy Access System Europe Oü, 16879218
Address: Mustamäetee 50, 10621 Tallinn, Estonia
Email: gpsr@easproject.com Tel:+358 40 500 3575

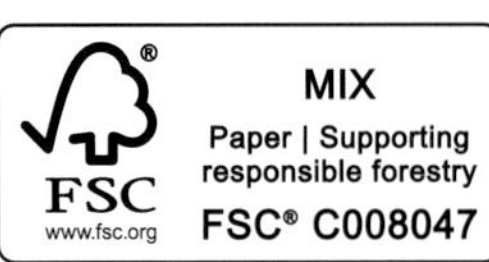

Printed in China by C&C Offset Printing Co., Ltd
for ACC Art Books Ltd, Woodbridge, Suffolk, UK
www.accartbooks.com

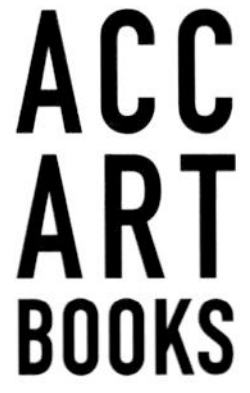

Front cover: *Citrus* no.3 (with lime) by Annie Hughes (see p.125)
Endpapers: *Pinus palustris* (detail from original watercolour) by Kimiyo Maruyama (see p.170)
Page 2: *Iris tectorum* Burma form by Pauline Dean (see p.69)
Page 4: *Hydrangea macrophylla* 'Nikko Blue' (detail) by Gael Sellwood (see p.219)
Page 5: *Dahlia* 'Arabian Night' (detail) by Carolyn Jenkins (see p.141)
Pages 6–7: *Geranium* 'Patricia' (detail) by Laura Silburn (see p.227)
Pages 38–39: *Cyclamen europaeum* by Silvana Rava (see p.211)
Pages 274–275: *Cornus* 'Eddie's White Wonder' (detail) by Jenny Jowett (see p.145)
Page 287: *Primula auricula* 'Queen Bee', by Brigitte Daniel (see p.62)
Back cover: *Iris* 'With This Ring' by Jean Emmons (see p.80)

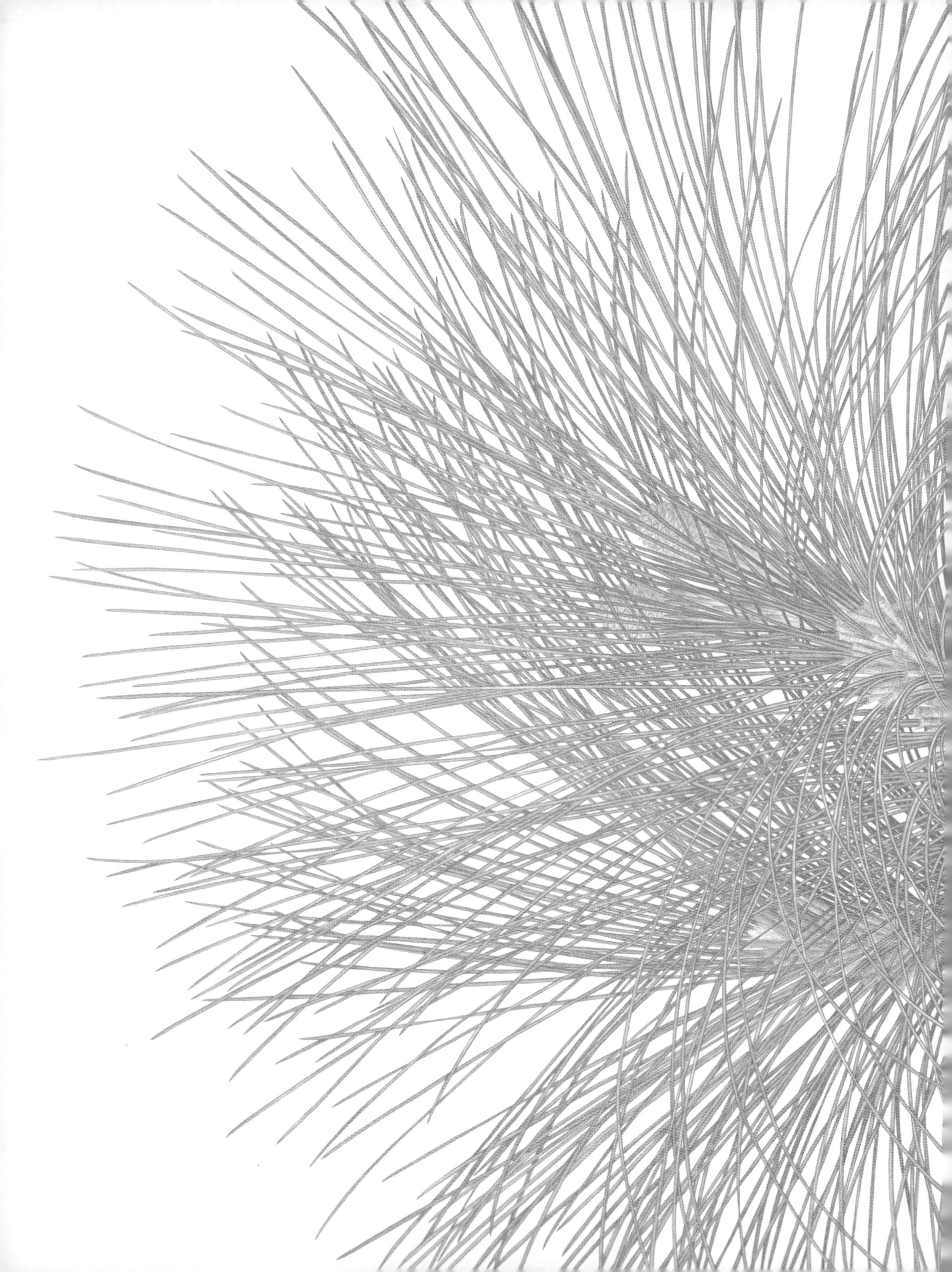